DARE TO DREAM

DARE TO DREAM

Stephen Touthang

GenNext Publication

ISBN : 978-93-8022-242-4

Price : ₹ 490

First Published in 2015

Published by

GenNext Publication
23, Main Ansari Road, Darya Ganj
New Delhi-110002
Ph. : 23282060, 23261060
Fax : 011-23285914
E-mail: gennext@hotmail.com

Laser Typesetting : Rudra Computer Graphics, Delhi
Printed at : G. Print Process, Delhi

Cataloging in Publication Data—DK

Courtesy: D.K. Agencies (P) Ltd.
<docinfo@dkagencies.com>

Touthang, Stephen.

Dare to dream / Stephen Touthang.

p. cm.

Includes bibliographical references and index.

ISBN 9789380222424

1. Goal (Psychology) 2. Self-actualization (Psychology) 3. Success. I. Title.

DDC 158.1 23

Foreword

It is a great pleasure for me to forward the book entitled "Dare to Dream" written by Stephen Touthang.

As the name suggests, this book 'Dare to Dream' is very attractive in its title. There are a number of books written on the theme of dream but in this book the author has treated 'dream' in a lone, unique and distinctive manner. Dream is seen not merely as an imagination but as something that is really real and practically attainable. Dreams are the innermost longings of our minds that give us a sense of direction or purpose in life of which if realized engenders fulfilhnent, satisfaction and meaning.

Dreams can be accomplished only if one DARES. Many people have dreams in life but only few have achieved them. This is because they do not have the courage to work on their dreams. Today, many students in our schools, colleges and universities seem to be without a sense of direction in life — no clarity of vision. There are still many who find themselves at crossroads — confused as to which road to take. Therefore, this book will be a pathfinder for many people especially the student community as it gives practical ways of setting one's goals and achieving them.

This book is truly motivating and challenging for students of the contemporary age. It gives-a sense of guilt for dreamers who are drown in passivity and also gives a sense of inadequacy or 'a want of doing more' for those who are already on the track of realizing their dreams.

I appreciate Stephen Touthang for the great effort he has invested in bringing out such highly commendable book. The book is unique, pragmatic, realistic and proficient in its treatment of the subject. It is so relevant as it deals with the contemporary needs of the student community. The use of real life examples, true stories and pertinent quotes to substantiate the different points make the book very intelligible and meaningful to the reader.

(Prof. H. Nandakumar Sarma)

Contents

Dedication

I fondly dedicate this book to my Mom and Dad.

Preface

I'm convinced that human life has meaning only when it is tied to a worthy goal or dream. Dreams keep hopes simmering. In other words, dreams keep our hope alive. Once a person's life is devoid of a goal, it just sinks into a 'frantic ennui'. Frantic ennui is a state of desperate agility. Here, the person is active but without any aim. His life becomes one of aimless wandering. To have a meaningful life, one must attach oneself to a goal. This is the reason, why I am writing this book "*Dare to Dream*". As I go around interacting with young people, I have come to know that many of them are not sure of what they want to do with their lives. Once I had an interaction with a group of university students and I asked them about their future career and many of them said, "First I will clear my master's degree and after that I will think about it". Once you are not clear of your goal, how will you proceed? It is like groping in the dark. A very minimal few are sure of their life goals and are passionately chasing them. Many young people do have their dreams but lack the passion to chase them. They are just building castles in the air. People who are convinced of their dream can't remain idle. The dream propels them. There is power, force and energy in dreams. You will experience this power, force and energy, if you have a goal you are convinced of. Marcus Aurelius says, "Dare to Dream big dream; only big dreams have the power to move men's souls". If you are no sure of your dream, your energy will begin to dissipate and finally it will give way to lethargy and desperation. Therefore, if one wants to have a meaningful, satisfying and fulfilling life, it is indispensable to have a dream.

Today, many great achievers who bask in the glory of their achievements began their journey with a DREAM. They are the ones who dare to dream. What I would suggest today is that if you are not sure of your dream; stop all your activities; sit quietly and spend time reflecting on yourself. Ask yourself these questions: What I am I doing so far with my life? What do I want to do with my life? Do I have any clear goal to achieve or am I just aimlessly gallivanting? What are that things I must avoid in order to achieve my goal? What are the things I must do in order to make my goal a reality? Also look at your abilities and talents and set your goals accordingly. Once you are convinced, never look back, forward march!

Practice *"back from the future"* thinking. This is a powerful technique practiced continually by high performing men and women. This way of thinking has an amazing effect on your mind and on your behaviour. Here is how it works: project yourself forward five years. Imagine that five years have passed and that your life now is perfect in every respect. What does it look like? What are you doing? Where are you working? How much money are you earning? How much do you have in the bank? What kind of a lifestyle do you have?

Create a vision for yourself for the long-term future. The clearer your vision, the faster you move towards it and the faster it moves toward you. When you create a clear mental picture of where you are going in life and set clear goals, you become more positive, more motivated and more determined to make it a reality. You trigger your natural creativity and come up with idea after idea to help your vision come true. You always tend to move in the direction of your goals, dreams, images and visions. The very act of allowing yourself to dream big dreams actually raises your self-esteem and causes you to like and respect yourself more. It improves your self-concept and increases your level of self-confidence. It increases your personal level of self-respect and happiness. There is something about dreams and visions that is exciting and that stimulates you to do better than you ever have before.

Through my seminars and animation programmes, I have come to realise that there are so many young people who live their lives without any aim. Some of them are not sure of their dreams and goals. Some others wish to achieve some goals but they are not passionate about them. Only a few of them have clear goals and are already on the way to realize them. These are some of the reasons why I have written this book so that those who do not have dreams may gain the insight to construct their dreams; those who have dreams but are lackadaisical about them may feel the need to become passionate about achieving them; and those who are already on the way to realise their goals may become more determined in chasing their dreams.

Stephen Touthang

Acknowledgements

My life is hallowed by a band of rnagnanimous hands that have braced me to complete this book. Without them, it would be impossible for me to transform my thoughts and ideas into a concrete form. I am profoundly grateful to HNK Sarma, Vice Chancellor of Manipur University for having gone through my manuscript and writing the foreword. I would like to recognise the great sacrifice of those who proofread my manuscript. They include: Thangjamang Lhouvum Ph.D, Assistant Professor, MIMS, Manipur University, David K. Zote, Deputy Registrar, Manipur University and Rev. Fr. Victor Arullapan Ph.D. I humbly acknowledge their scholarly corrections and erudite suggestions.

I am grateful to Rev. Fr. Mark Mangkhanpao for his brotherly love, support and encouragement. I would like to express my sincere thanks to my parents, my brother and sister, friends, Sir Joseph Khoibu and family, Mr. John Guite and Mr. Kothel Khaling. I would like to thank all the teachers of St. Joseph's High School, Sugnu and the Sisters of St. Alphonsa Convent, Sugnu.

I am greatly indebted to the team of GenNext Publication for readily accepting my manuscript for publishing it. Last of all, I would like to acknowledge the various authors of many books, magazines and articles which are my primary source of gleaning ideas and information for the birth of this book into a concrete form.

Introduction

Human beings are endowed with life to have meaning. But many people live their lives as if there is no meaning and purpose. One can go through life just skimming superficially or live it with great profundity and intense sagacity. A person can never live a deep and profound life unless he becomes clear of what he wants to do with his life. The *Yoruba* tribe is the largest single ethnic group in West Africa. They have some beautiful vocabularies that describe what life is! They are:

- '*Agbeyewoanu*' – means 'life does everything and with life one can do what one wants'.
- '*Agbexoasi*' –means 'life has value; life is precious'.
- '*Agbenyega*' –means 'life is the greatest thing'.

The *Yoruba* words describe the surpassing value and potential of life. Life is the greatest asset human beings possess. Life is an *élan vital* i.e., vital force or vital impetus with which one can accomplish marvelous things as in the case of Abraham Lincoln, Mahatma Gandhi, Mother Teresa, etc. Antithetically, life also can be used to do the most demeaning acts of depravity as in the case of Hitler, Pol Pot and others. One can do with life what one wants – either one can use it perfunctorily or meaningfully.

We know that life is the greatest asset placed in our hands. This asset is given in a raw or inchoate form and it is the duty of the recipient to refine, improve, polish and perfect it. This process of refining and perfecting is the process of search for meaning in life. The most important thing in life is the discovery of its meaning. The ultimate goal of life is to find a MEANING. Life is meaningful only when it has achieved a worthy goal. To find meaning in life, it must be tied to a goal. This is why 'a sense of direction' must be inculcated in the students *ab initio*. Here comes, the important role of parents, teachers and those who are responsible in forming students to instill and implant in them a strong sense of purpose in life. They should know the WHY of their lives. Once they know and are convinced of the purpose of their lives, they will be able to perform the necessary tasks to accomplish their goals without being told.

Today, many are like a boat adrift from its moorings. Some have lost a sense of direction, some find themselves at an intersection enveloped by confusion and doubt and others have sunk into torpor of laziness and vacuity not willing to congregate their energy for the last try. They need to be toed back. They need a constant motivation and an injection with adrenalin. Due to these, there is an urgent need to waken and galvanise them into action to row their boats in the direction of some destination which will give them satisfaction and meaning. Once they know and are convinced of their destination they will be driven and impassioned to row their boats. Once they start rowing, they need to be constantly motivated keeping the goal alive. This motivation is the most difficult part, as it requires constant fueling and refueling of energy which needs to be performed on a daily basis. Everyone dreams of becoming somebody in life but only a few have made it *ad alta* (to the summit). This is not because they lack purpose but daily motivation. The Hindi word *'Anusandhan'* is a beautiful word that describes a goal-oriented person. It means 'follower of an aim'. In order to achieve a goal or a dream the most important thing is 'FOLLOWING'. The word 'following' is grammatically in a continuous tense. Therefore, 'following one's dream' needs a continuous effort – an effort on a daily basis. This continuous effort will gradually come to fruition.

1

The Indian Situation: Decadence of Values

1.1 Report of the *'Forbes'* Magazine

On March 10, 2010, *Forbes* magazine published the list of richest persons in the world. Mr. Mukesh Ambani, Chairman and Managing Director of Reliance Industries ranked the fourth richest man in the world in 2010 with an estimated net worth of $29 billion. The non-resident Indian Mr. Lakshmi Mittal ranked fifth with an estimated net worth of $26.7 billion. There were eight Indians in the list of 100 wealthiest people in the world. In 2013, according to Forbes' 100 richest people in the world, Mukesh Ambani ranks twenty second and Lakshmi Mittal ranks forty fourth. India is one among the 11 countries which have at least doubled the number of billionaires they had a year ago. India is now a home to 52 billionaires. The combined fortune of India's 100 richest people is $276 billion, one-fourth of the country's Gross Domestic Product (GDP) – the total market value of all officially recognized final goods and services produced in a country in a given year. Indians are shining in the international arena when it comes to reckoning of the world's wealthiest people. But the reality at home is something quite different.

1.2 Incredible India

Incredible India was the name of an international marketing campaign by the Government of India to promote tourism in India in 2002 to the global audience. In what way shall we consider India as truly incredible? Apart from tourism and from the progress of individuals' economic possession, our country is able to spend a huge amount in building nuclear missiles and other defence technologies. We are proud of our technological and scientific achievements, economic advancement and we are able to compete with the first world countries. Another amazing event that shocked the whole country in October 2010 was the releasing of the costliest film *Endhiran* (Robot). Aishwarya Rai Bachchan, a starrer in the film, called it as "a landmark in the history of Indian cinema". The film took two years to make and cost a jaw-dropping Rs. 150 crore – twice the budget of the costliest film to date. Forty per cent of the money was believed to have been spent on special effects alone. Rajnikanth's (the hero of the film) make-up was worth the cost of a small film – Rs. 3 crore – and the set (which the publicity machine emphasises is eco-friendly) was worth Rs. 5 crore. The film has been shot in Vienna, Machu Picchu in Peru, US and Brazil apart from Goa, Kulu-Manali, Pune, Vellore and Chennai ("Endhiran: The costliest film in India." *India Today,* August 2010). Are all these what we eulogise as *Incredible India?*

1.3 The Stark Reality

It is also interesting to look at the other side of Incredible India. *The Times of India* (15 July, 2010) reported that about 645 million people or 55 per cent of India's population is poor. We have 240 million people living Below Poverty Line in 2004-2005. *Indian Currents* magazine reports: a 23 year old woman in West Bengal's Birbhum district exchanged her new born baby for 10 kilos of rice. Another man sold her four year old daughter for Rs. 20 to aid his ailing wife. In 1985, at Kalahandi in Orissa, the sale of 14 year old girl named Benita for Rs. 40 prompted the then Prime Minister Rajiv Gandhi to personally rush to the remote village along with the officials. However, more than two decades after the Prime Minister's visit has not changed the condition of Benita. Today she walks over 8 kms a day to earn a paltry sum of Rs. 260 a month and struggles to support a blind and ailing husband and two kids. At times her family eats and sometimes they sleep on empty stomach.

It is very shameful that India is the world's fourth largest economy in terms of Purchasing Power Parity and boasts of economic growth rate of over eight per cent when 35 per cent of the population lives on less than Rs. 50 a day. While, India boasts of being the second fastest growing economy in the world, it lags behind and millions in the country go hungry. India's slip, two spots down, on Global Hunger Index, 2010 compared to previous year's ranking at 65 has placed her in the list of "very alarming" category of developing countries. The number of poor in 2015 reportedly is likely to be 279 million at all-India level. India continues to be one of the most corrupt nations in the world with many of its public institutions given to rampant misdeeds. Corruption is India's bane and threatens to derail its rapidly growing economy. With 21 per cent of its population undernourished, India accounts for 50 per cent of the world's underweight children under the age of five. India reported trails far behind even Sudan, North Korea, China and Pakistan.

Countries like Uganda (38th); Mauritania (40th); Zimbabwe (58th) and many others have better record than India on hunger and malnutrition (*Indian Currents*, 25-31 October 2010, p. 29).

Many farmers are committing suicide and a quarter of the population does not have access to clean drinking water and proper sanitation. Every year in India, 2.2 million children die without preventive treatment. Fifty-three per cent are malnourished and suffer from chronic sicknesses. Five lakhs people die of TB every year. The exploitation of women is unaccountable. Figures from India's National Crime Records Bureau suggest that a rape is now taking place in India every 22 minutes and every 7 minute a woman is molested. Almost every day newspapers report gang rapes, molestation, abductions and tribal women being paraded naked and the like. Given below are conviction rates in cases of rape in 2010 by National Crime Records Bureau:

State	*Number of Reported Rapes*	*Conviction Rate*
Madhya Pradesh	3,135	28.2
West Bengal	2,311	13.7
Assam	1,721	18.1
Maharashtra	1,599	13.9
Rajasthan	1,571	30.8
Uttar Pradesh	1,563	50.6

Is this Incredible India?

1.4 Who Really Cares about the Poor and the Downtrodden?

Who really cares about the poor and the downtrodden? Care and concern for that poor is only a mere lip service and an empty political magniloquence. Are the politicians, bureaucrats, civil servants and military officers really concern about the plight of the poor and the downtrodden? Of course, few of them are really exceptional. But many of them have demonstrated glaringly their lack of concern by being caught in financial scams and frauds and other unethical and obnoxious acts?

1.5 Indian Black Money

Black money refers to funds earned on the black market, on which income and other taxes have not been paid. Do you know the total amount of black money deposited in foreign banks by Indians? The total amount is unknown but one estimated by R. Vaidyanathan, a professor of Finance at the Indian Institute of Management, Banguluru estimated the total at over Rs. 7,280,000 crores (US $ 1.4 trillion) are stashed in the Swiss Banks.

According to the data provided by Swiss banks, India has more black money than the rest of the world combined. India tops the list with $1500 billion money in Swiss banks, followed by Russia $470 billion, UK $390 billion, Ukraine $ 100 billion and China with $96 billion. This is really ignominious for any country to top the list of black money holders (Nanjappa, Vicky (31 March 2009), "Swiss black money can take India to the top" *Rediff.com* 23 May 2011). The money which belongs to the nation and its citizens is stashed in the illegal personal accounts of nummamorous and lucrepitous politicians, bureaucrats, industrialists, etc. This is an amount which is 13 times larger than the nation's debt. Every year this amount is increasing at a rapid speed but the Indian Government seems to be silent over this matter from a very long time. Jobbery is interspersed everywhere. Silence is a tacit sign of consent and complicity. Today, the BIG question is, "Who will bell the cat?" Will Anna Hazare, the *dux fortissimus,* Arvind Kejriwal, the firebrand crusader of anti-corruption campaign and others succeed in their fight against corruption? Chances are very slim but certainly not an impossibility. Once a teacher asked a student in an English class, "What tense is this sentence? 'India will be free from corruption'. The student answered, "Future Tense". The teacher retorted, "No, it is future impossible tense". The *hoi polloi* are beginning to think that India can't be free from corruption". Our society needs an intense purgation. We need to rid off mammonists, chrematists, philoplutaries and peniaphobes. The purgation process has to begin with our education system which needs an afflux of values into the system.

1.6 The Rift between the Indian Past (Values) and Present (Materialism)

The abovementioned is the condition of our country today. There is disintegration of values in our system. In ancient India, Fahien, the Chinese pilgrim in the fifth century to India during the Gupta age remarked, "*The people were honest, trustworthy and philanthropists. They vied with one another in giving donations and sarais (rest houses) were built on the highways for tired travellers".* This was what Fahein described about the ancient people of India. These ancient values seem to have sunk into obsolescence. This is because the subsequent generations did not want to receive and hand them down to their posterity. We need to relive our ancient values. Another most celebrated Chinese pilgrim to India was Hieun-Tsang. He visited India in the first half of the seventh century. In his book *"Si-Yu-Ki"* (Records of the Western World) he writes about King Harshavardana thus, *"He was indefatigable and forgot sleep and food in his devotion to good works.... The day was too short for him... spent all his time to promote the welfare of his people".* Megasthenes, a Greek historian came to India in the fourth century as an ambassador of Seleukus Nector.

He says about the Mauryan king, *"Chandragupta who takes keen interest in the administration of justice used to sit for the whole day in hearing different cases and giving the decision"*. Harshavardana and Chandragupta were ideal rulers. This is what our present leaders have to learn and emulate from our ancient leaders.

What is happening in our country today has something to do with our Education System. It is through education that our values, knowledge, culture, traditions etc., are passed on from one generation to the next. If our education system is faulty, then our value system will also be adversely affected. Our Education System has stressed intellectual formation (knowledge and competence which are useful instantly) so much so that it has failed to inculcate values. Value-based education emphasises development of character. It is a virtuous living which stresses probity, sincerity, responsibility, love, etc. In the ancient Indian Gurukula system, education was deemed as a means to attain Moksa. Education was not merely earthbound. It had a *meta (beyond-ness)* element. Education affects human life beyond this world. Education therefore was a sacred pursuit. Education was not meant only to impart only good traits of character but it had transcendental element (affecting life beyond death).

Once a *shyshya* was asked, "If you meet your Guru and the deity on the road, whom will you do your obeisance first?" The *shyshya* answered, "My Guru, because without my Guru, I will never know who the deity is!" This sums up the sacredness of education in ancient India. It is based on values and divine principles. Hieun-Tsang gives a beautiful account of the ancient Indian education system. He speaks about the famous ancient University of Nalanda which had 1510 professors and 10,000 students. He says:

> *"Since the establishment of the monastery (university), there was not a single case of breach of its discipline. Those who studied were ideal students. The teachers were esteemed not only for their high learning but for their high character. It had a comprehensive curriculum which included Vedas, Astronomy, Medicine, Science, Logic, Grammar and Philosophy. It is known for the noble character and deep scholarships of its teachers and alumni".*

We need to go back to our past and unlearn the present materialistic proclivities and relearn and relive our ancient values.

2

The Meaning of True Education

"Education is the most powerful weapon which you can use to change the world."

– *Nelson Mandela*

2.1 Introduction

Today is the psychological moment to tarry awhile and give a thought to our contemporary education system. If we turn on the different Television news channels, flick through various magazines and newspapers and surf through the internet, we can find only the cumulative rise in corruption, violence, rape, murder and the list continues. These realities are the manifestations of decadence of values and they are the direct repercussions of an awry education system. For example, most of the people who are charge-sheeted in corruption cases are high profile politicians, bureaucrats, corporate executives, military officers, etc. Are they not the so-called "the educated elite" of our society? Corruption has become a noxious virus that is swallowing up the fabric of our democratic system.

Due to corruption and hoarding in our country, we see a strange economic disparity – the gap between the rich and the poor which seems almost unbridgeable. Rape and murder has become a regular feature. There is lack of mutual trust and reverence for human dignity. The concept of the 'other' as a stranger seems to be taking deep roots in the psyche of the people. Xenophobic waves have caused fragmentation of convivencia. This is because we are not getting the right education that we ought to receive. Therefore, here comes the need to impart value-based education right from the very inception of imparting education to every child. There is a BIG question that lurks in our minds today: "Do we really get *"educated"* in our schools, colleges and universities? If then why so much of corruption, cheating, bribery, hatred, violence, rape, murder, lack of respect and concern for the other? I am not saying schools, colleges and universities are not doing well? Certainly these institutions have produced authentic and good people. At the same time, most of the so-called "educated elites" of our society who have gone through the same institutions have become vehicles of social evils in our society. They have become more of a bane than a boon. Steven Muller, the President of John Hopkins University says, *"Universities are turning out highly skilled barbarians because we don't provide framework of values to young people, who more and more are searching for it"*. The world is full of educated derelicts. So the person who is "educated" is the one who possesses true education.

2.2 What is True Education?

True education is the training of both the head and the heart. *Intellectual Education* influences the head and *Value-based Education* influences the heart. In fact, education that does not train the heart can be very dangerous. Intellectual education emphasises acquisition of knowledge and information, while value-based education stresses the development of fundamental traits of character such as—probity, integrity, rectitude, compassion, reliability and responsibility. It is an engineering of a virtuous life. Our education system today seems to be prioritising intellectual education and as a consequence we have myriads of the so-called "highly skilled barbarians" and this is perilous because they are pernicious to the harmonious growth of the society. We have so many highly qualified intellectuals whose consciences have sunk into passive abdormition. As much as we need intellectual education; we also need value-based education. A person who is morally and ethically educated will be a lot better equipped to move up in life or succeed than a morally bankrupt person, with excellent academic qualifications. Educating the mind without morals creates a menace in society. We don't lack noematical assuagement but values. Our education system is suffering from axiological bankruptcy. It is a high time we permeate values in our education system. Winston Churchill says, *"The first duty of a university is to teach wisdom, not trade; character, not technicalities"*.

2.3 An Educated Person Operates More from the Heart Than from the Mind

While the heart is busy loving and caring, the MIND is busy reasoning and reflecting. When the heart sees a person in need, it at once galvanises into action. But when the mind sees a person in need, it immediately reasons and poses a question, "Is it right to help such a person or does he or she deserve? The Heart simply loves and cares without any condition and cunctation (delay). While, the MIND always operates with a second thought:

"Should I help? Who is he or she? Does he or she deserve? Is it worth helping? Even if I help, how much? The MIND always rationalises, calculates, measures and inquires. It rarely acts. It wants to KNOW only. It is information-oriented. It never passes beyond the boundary of cognition, knowledge and information".

The world of the HEART and the world of the MIND have a vast difference. The world of the HEART is governed by love, care, compassion, sympathy, empathy, peace, joy and understanding; while the world of the MIND is governed by scientific rationality, reflection, calculation and measurement. The language construction of the world of the MIND is so different from that of the world of the HEART. Those who live in the world of the MIND are fond of using words like, why, how, what, where and so on. Unless they used these interrogatives, they don't understand each other. So, the world of the MIND is the world of reflection, calculation, measurement, subtraction and addition. It is the world of mathematics, the world of reason and hectic mental activity. Unless it is rational it will not act or proceed in life. Those who live in this world are very able, acute, astute, brainy, brilliant, clever, canny, intellectual, perceptive, percipient, perspicacious, profound, quick, rational, sagacious, sensible, sharp, shrewd, cunning, smart, witty and trenchant and so on.

Those who live in the world of the HEART don't use any language; the only language they use is the language of love and understanding. Without using words, they understand each other. How nice it would be if we are able to understand each other without using words! i.e., without the person explaining himself or herself, I am able to understand him or her. The people who live in this world are not very clever, not very intelligent or not shrewd but they are very simple, loving, affectionate, ardent, attached, brotherly, caring, closed, concerned, dear, devoted, fond, fatherly, friendly, motherly, sisterly, inseparable, fraternal, protective, tender, warm, genial and amiable.

The need of the hour is the training of the heart. It is a training of a person to live a virtuous life. Our education system needs to be value based. If we train first the heart there will be no corruption, stealing, cheating, violence, selfishness, rape, murder and there won't be any distinction between the rich and the poor. This is what we need to stress in our education system today. But this does not mean I am downplaying the role of intellectual education. We need both to progress and develop but the present ethical kaleidoscope indicates a sharp diminishing of values in our society. Without values our society would be a miserable place to live in.

Civilisation gradually evanesces where there is decadence of values. Theodore Roosevelt says, *"To educate a person in mind and not in morals is to educate a menace to society".*

> The world does not need more 'successful' people. But it does desperately need more peacemakers, healers, restorers, storytellers and lovers of every shape and form. It needs people who live well in their places. It needs people of moral courage willing to join the fight to make the world habitable and humane. And these needs have little to do with success as our present culture has defined it. In other words, the world needs people of values.
>
> – *Dalai Lama*

2.4 Who is Truly an Educated Person?

One of the best delineations on 'who is an educated person' is given by the ancient Greek philosopher Socrates. This is what he says:

> "Whom, then, do I call educated?
>
> First, those who manage well the circumstances which they encounter day by day; and those who can judge situations appropriately as they arise and rarely miss the suitable course of action. Next, those who are honourable in their dealings with all men, bearing easily what is unpleasant or offensive in others and being as reasonable with their associates as is humanly possible. Furthermore, those who hold their pleasures always under control and are not unduly overcome by their misfortunes, bearing up under them bravely and in a manner worthy of our common nature. Most important of all, those who are not spoiled by their successes, who do not desert their true selves, but hold their ground steadfastly as wise and sober-minded men, rejoicing no more in the good things that have come to them through chance in those which through their own nature and intelligence are theirs since birth. Those who have a character which is in accord not with one of these things but with all of them, these are educated–possessed of all the virtues".

2.5 An Educated Person is Rich in Values

An educated person primarily does not refer to a person who has a high IQ. Merely having a high IQ does not determine the value of your education. It constitutes only a fraction of it. True education is an all round development. In the all round development, I think character occupies the most important place, without character all other learning comes to naught. Character is the sum total of positively good values. In other words, character is a manifestation of virtues that are cultivated in a person. Good character is a virtuous manifestation of one's life.

In life, a person's character is known by what kind of dream he pursues. He will pursue his dream according to his value system. If his values are based on love of money and wealth, certainly such person will be dreaming of pursuing a profession that will give him money and wealth. His values will determine his dream or goal in life.

2.6 Values Determine a Person's Dream

An educated person is one who is opulent in positive values. Without values all education is futile. Thus, there is a need to inculcate in the young minds values right from their childhood. Without basic instruction in values, the child's whole education will be preposterous. If the child is given the right values, it will positively affect all the other areas of his life. His value system is the base for forming his attitudes, *weltanschauung* (worldview), relationships, dealings and the like. His dreams and goals also will be based on his value system. His value system affects his future. If a person's character is strongly built on values, he will be able to form the right goals and dreams in his life. Therefore, forming right values at a young age is of phenomenal importance.

A child is supposed to land into the future which is very uncertain; yet he can courageously land without a hitch if such child is firmly based on values. Before the child embarks on to his dream, provide him sufficient values that will be the source of his strength on his journey towards realising his dreams.

3

Building Dreams

"If you don't build your dreams, someone will hire you to build theirs."

– *Tony Gaskins*

3.1 Introduction

If you have nothing to aim at;
If you have nothing to long for;
If you have nothing to strive for;
If you have nothing to fight for;
If you have nothing to dream;
If you have nothing to achieve;
If you have nothing to do;
Then you have no reason for being on earth.

Where do you want to be in five years? In ten years? In twenty years? Many high school or college students don't think much beyond the next weekend. They are focused on what is in front of them today, right now. Know that in life, the direction you take at the intersection could be a road to success or a *cul-de-sac* (dead end). Ask yourself these questions: *Quo vadis?* (Where are you going?) Or Are you dreaming to reach somewhere? If not, start today and someday you will realise that your dream has turn into a reality. Napoleon Hill says,

"The world has the habit of making room for the man whose words and actions show that he knows where he is going".

Do you dream to have a successful career? An artist? A doctor? An engineer? Let the vision take shape in your mind. Determine now what your future could be. Of course, life does not follow a scripted path. It's an improvisation sometimes. But plan anyway. Every successful venture usually begins with a plan – in business, in sports or in the arts. Vision is the deciding factor and the winning factor. You have a great future ahead. Can you see it? Start focusing on your dream! You have miles to go before you sleep. Read and reflect on this poem written by Robert Frost:

Stopping by Woods
on a Snowy Evening

Whose woods these are I think I know.
His house is in the village, though;
He will not see me stopping here
To watch his woods fill up with snow.

My little horse must think it queer
To stop without a farmhouse near
Between the woods and frozen lake
The darkest evening of the year.

He gives his harness bells a shake
To ask if there's some mistake.
The only other sound's the sweep
Of easy wind and downy flake.

The woods are lovely, dark and deep,
But I have promises to keep,
And miles to go before I sleep,
And miles to go before I sleep.

– *Robert Frost*

3.2 The Meaning of Dream

Dream is something that you would *like to be* in the future. Dreams are *aspirations*. It is a DESIRE that directs you to some destination you would like to arrive at. It is purposeful pursuit and gives you a sense of direction. Purpose or a sense of direction in life begins with a dream. Norman Vincent Peale in his book "*Power of the Plus Factor*" defines dream thus:

"*The word 'dream' is not to those shadowy images that flicker through our minds when we are asleep. No, the dreams I'm writing about are the indistinct hopes, the far-off visions, the first faint stirrings of the imagination that come when we are in the earliest stages of planning something worthwhile. And there's a wonderful thing about such dreams. In some uncanny way that no one fully understands, they seem to contain the seeds of their own fulfillment.*

If you dream something long enough and hard enough, a door seems to open and through that door come mighty forces that will guide and support you in your efforts to make the dream come true".

He further says, "*Dreams are not just idle nothings. They are the parents of possibilities. Possibilities are the descendents of dreams. Without the one, there can never be the other. Dream, therefore. Dream big, dream long, dream strong. And remember...*"

3.3 Abdul Kalam's Concept of Dream

"Dream, Dream, Dream.
Dreams transform into thoughts.
Thoughts result in actions."

The repetitive use of the word 'dream' in the above shows that you need to constantly remind yourself of what you want to be in life. This dream should be "transform into thoughts" which means your dream should not be dormant or should not remain as a mere figment of the imagination but must be active in the core of your mind (thought). Constantly thinking about your dream will churn interest within you and then lead to action. Thought is a theoretical aspect which needs to be transformed into action. In short, what you want to be in life must start with a dream and climax in its realisation.

Abdul Kalam here gives one of the most captivating definitions on dream. He says, "*Dream is not that you see in sleep. Dream is which does not let you sleep*". This is one of the best definitions I have come across on dream. There are two sentences in this apophthegm. The first part gives clarity to the meaning of dream. It says that dream is not a chimera or utopian phenomenon. It is something that can be achieved, felt, reached and possessed. It is something that is really real. The second part adds the element of passion in chasing that dream.This element of passion that even takes away one's sleep is clearly demonstrated in the Bible. It is found in The Song of Solomon 3:1-4

"Upon my bed at night
I sought him whom my soul loves;
I sought him but found him not;
I called him but he gave no answer.
I will rise now and go about the city
    in the streets and in the squares;
I will seek him whom my soul loves.
I sought him but found him not.
The sentinels found me
As they went about in the city,

'Have you seen him whom my soul loves?'
Scarcely had I passed them
When I found him whom my soul loves.
I held him and would not let go..."

In this passage of the Bible, we have seen the amorousness of the woman for her loved one. She is so fixated on her lover so much so that she begins to suffer from insomnia. She becomes a noctivagant hunter, a nightwalker, a prowler, a nomad of the midnight streets in order to find her lover. She takes a solivagant perambulation and makes a frantic search in the streets and alleys without any nyctophobia (fear of the night). The intensity of her longing to unite with her lover is beyond reckoning. Finally, after much search, she is able to find him and as soon as she finds him, she holds him tight and would not let go. This is exactly what you must do with your dreams. You need to chase your dreams with passion and courage whatever it may cost you; keep striving till you achieve them. HOLD your dream tight and NEVER LET GO.

Abdul Kalam says, *"Friends, if there are no dreams, there are no revolutionary thoughts; if there are no thoughts, no action will emanate"*. Here, he exhorts students the imperative need to have dreams and realise the dreams they have chosen. He emphasises the active process of materialising one's dream.

"Vita sine proposito languid et vaga est" – Seneca
(Life without pursuit is a vague and languid thing).

3.4 The Need for Having Dreams

No idea without vision
No success without work
No passion without pain
No love without respect
No answer without question
No trust without experience
No future without dreams

A student without a dream is like a ship without a rudder. It turns in any direction as the wind sways. It does not have a sense of direction and it will never reach anywhere. The Bible says, "Where there is no vision, people perish." This saying is proved true in the lives of the people of Israel. Moses was given a clear vision to lead the people of Israel out of the land of Egypt and bring them to the Promised Land. Moses was very clear of his purpose in leading the people. The people too were convinced in the beginning but on the way, their focus began to shift from their destined Promised Land to their present plight – some even longing to go back to Egypt where they were slaves. When they began to concentrate on their problems, they lost sight of their vision. They began to complain against Yahweh, their God. But it was the ability and capability of their leaders that sustained the realisation of their vision.

Where there is no dream or vision, energy dissipates and life is being dragged around by ennui and lethargy. In such state, how can one runs after one's dream? People, who have vision, live their lives with great interest and effervescence and are full of hope because they are clear of their destination. It gives them joy in their purpose-oriented-struggle. This same principle can be applied to students. Students who do not find a purpose in their study will never exert their effort to study. Study becomes a perfunctory performance of a daily routine. Many students today, find study as 'a big impedimenta' to carry along. This is because they are not made to realise the purpose. In other words, vision is not set before them. So, giving them a sense of purpose or direction in their studies will make their burden light and interesting. What is important is 'purposeful learning'. If students know the 'WHY' of studying Mathematics, Science or English; this will somehow ignite the fire of interest in them. If they know clearly that studying Mathematics or Science can lead them to become engineers or professors, surely they would work hard to realise such dreams. Knowing the 'WHY' gives a sense of direction and purpose. The greatest tragedy in life is not death but life without purpose. If there is no dream, there is no hope and if there is no hope, there is no life. Every single action that you perform must have a purpose.

> "The trouble with not having a goal is that you can spend your life running up and down the field and never scoring."
>
> —*Bill Copeland*

Norman Vincent Peale relates this incident in his book *The Power of Positive Thinking*:

• A young man of twenty-six consulted me because he was dissatisfied with his job. He was ambitious to fill a bigger niche in life and wanted to know how to improve his circumstances. His motive seemed unselfish and entirely worthwhile.

"Well, where do you want to go?" I asked.

"I just don't know exactly," he said hesitantly. "I have never given it any thought. I only know I want to go somewhere other than where I am."

"What can you do best?" I then asked. "What are your strong points?"

"I don't know," he responded. "I never thought that over either."

"But what would you like to do if you had your choice? What do you really want to do?" I insisted.

"I just can't say," he replied dully. "I don't really know what I would like to do. I never thought it over. Guess I ought to figure that one out too."

"Now, look here," I said, "you want to go somewhere from where you are, but you don't know where you want to go. You don't know what you can do or what you would like to do. You will have to get your ideas organised before you can expect to start getting anywhere." This is the failure point with many people. They never get anywhere because they have only a hazy idea where they want to go, what they want to do. No objectives leads to no end.

You need to be sure of where you are going. To live a meaningful life, you need to have a 'propriate striving'.

Allport, an eminent psychologist uses the word "propriate striving" which means the 'self' has a sense of direction or purpose. The culmination of 'propriate striving' according to Allport is the ability to say that 'I'm the proprietor of my life, i.e., owner and the operator.

3.5 Knowing Your Dream Engenders 'Meaning' to Your Life

Every human being is created to have a meaning. This is why there is a frantic search for meaning in life. There are many people trying dubious methods like astrology or psychics to discover the meaning of their lives. When life has a meaning you can bear almost everything and without it nothing is bearable. A teenager once wrote,

"I feel like a failure because I'm struggling to become something and I don't even know what it is. All I know how to do is to get by. Someday, if I discover my purpose, I'll feel I'm beginning to live."

Let us analyse what the teenager has said, "I feel like a failure...becoming something and I don't even know..." This teenager feels that he is a failure because he is ignorant of his purpose in life. But if you look at the last sentence of what he said, "If I discover my purpose, I'll feel I'm beginning to live." This shows that the discovery of purpose will give meaning to his life. The meaningfulness of life begins with a purpose.

Without purpose, life has no meaning. Without meaning, life has no significance or hope. Without significance or hope, life is futile.

3.6 Knowing Your Dream or Purpose Defines What You should Do and What You should not Do

Your purpose is the standard you use for evaluating which activities are essential and which are not. You ask yourself, "Does this activity help me to fulfill my chosen dream?" and you avoid the things that will distract you or take your focus away from your dream. Without clear purpose or dream you have no foundation on which you base decisions, allocate your time and use your resources. You will only tend to make choices based on circumstances, pressures and your mood at that moment. People who do not know their purpose try to do too much and that causes stress, fatigue and conflict within themselves.

It is impossible to do everything people want you to do. You just have enough time to do things that will take you closer to your dream. Doing too many things is equal to doing nothing. Do what is the most important that will take you to your dream as Eddie A. Rios does:

> "I cheated on my fears, broke up with my doubts, got engaged to my faith and now I'm marrying my Dreams. Soon I will be holding hands with Destiny!"

3.7 Knowing Your Dream Helps You Focus in Your Life

> "If you chase two rabbits, both will escape".
>
> – Unknown

Life is like a camera. Just focus on what is important and capture it. Your dream or purpose is your FOCUS. Focus means 'clarity of vision'. If you watch television channels like *Discovery* or *Animal Planet*, you will find the eccentric behaviour of every animal. For example, when a lion is famished, it looks for its prey. Once it finds its prey say, a herd of deer, it begins to stalk and keeps focusing on one, just one. Then as it gets closer, the lion begins to chase only the one on which it focuses. As the deer scarper in fear and some of them begin to run in close propinquity to the lion but the lion does not attend to them except the one on which it focuses. This is because the lion wants to catch the deer by all means. Focusing on one alone, gives a concentrated attention and energy and the lion knows this is the surest way to catch its prey. But if the lion chases more than one, its attention would be divided and can miss its prey. In a similar way, the kingfisher bird too keeps focusing on a shoal of fish playing in the stream. It focuses on one and then dives straight into the water and picks up the one it focuses upon. If a shooter instead of focusing on the bull's eye started focusing on the bow string or the arrow itself, will he get the target? Not possible.

When you are laser focused, the brain has an amazing power to pick up information and decipher opportunities. For example, you must have noticed yourself when you want to buy a new car; you begin to see different models, shapes, colour etc. In other words, you become very focused and selective. This process of being selective is what gives you clarity of vision. You are able to see what you really want. This is not a coincidence as many neuroscientists will agree. When we're totally focused on what we want, amazing things happen. We become hypersensitive to opportunities, strategies, people and ideas that can help you meet your goals.

3.8 Knowing Your Dream Makes You to Keep that Dream

If you hold on to your dream, no one can take it away. And you are so convinced of it that you will never let go, come what may. It becomes the treasure in your life.

> Monty Roberts who owns a horse ranch in San Isidro was letting his house used by a friend Jack for fund-raising events for youth at risk programme. Monty Roberts shared the following to the gathered youth group saying "I want to tell you why I let Jack use my horse ranch. It all goes back to a story about a young man who was the son of an itinerant horse trainer who would go from stable to stable, raise track to race track, farm to farm and ranch to ranch, training horses. As a result, the boy's high school career was continually interrupted. When he was a senior, he was asked to write a paper about what he wanted to be and do when he grew up by his teacher. That night he wrote a seven-pages paper describing his goal of someday owning a horse ranch. He wrote about his dream in great detail and he even drew a diagram of a 200-acre ranch, showing the location of all the buildings, the stables and the track. Then, he drew a detailed floor plan for a 4,000-square-foot house that would sit on a 200-acre dream ranch. He put a great deal of his heart into the project and the next day he handed it in to his teacher. Two days later he received his paper back. On the front page was a large red F with a note that read, 'See me after class.' The boy with the dream went to see the teacher after class and asked, 'Why did I receive an F?' The teacher said, 'This is an unrealistic dream for a young boy like you. You have no money. You come from an itinerant family. You have no resources. Owning a horse ranch requires a lot of money. You have to buy the land. You have to pay for the original breeding stock and later you'll have to pay large stud fees. There's no way you could ever do it.' The teacher added, 'If you will rewrite this paper with a more realistic goal, I will reconsider your grade.' The boy went home and thought about it long and hard. He asked his father what he should do. His father said, 'Look, son, you have to make up your own mind on this. However, I think it is a very important decision for you.' Finally, after sitting with it for a week, the boy turned in the same paper making no changes at all. He stated, 'You can keep the F and I'll keep my dream.'

> Monty then turned to the assembled group and said, 'I tell you this story because you are sitting in my 4,000-square-foot house in the middle of my 200-acre horse ranch. I still have that school paper framed over the fireplace.' He added, 'The best part of the story is that two summers ago that same school teacher brought 30 kids to camp out on my ranch for a week.' When the teacher was leaving, he said, 'Look, Monty, I can tell you this now. When I was your teacher, I was something of a dream stealer. During those years, I stole a lot of kids' dreams. Fortunately, you had enough gumption not to give up on yours.'

Do not let anyone steal your dream. Follow your heart, no matter what. No dream is too big or too small when one works hard to realise it. Have the courage to pursue the dream that you have in spite of the challenges. There will be many people including your own teachers who can discourage you to give up your dream due to your family background or low grade in the school.

3.9 Knowing Your Dream Makes You Direct Your Effort and Energy to What is Most Important

You become effective by being SELECTIVE. The element of selectivity is an essential ingredient in achieving your purpose. Selectivity is the process of eliminating all other issues and activities and choosing what is the most important in achieving your dream. It is human nature to get dissipated by minor issues. We play trivial pursuits with our lives. Many people today live, lives of aimless distraction. They are like gyroscopes spinning around at a frantic pace but never going anywhere.

> "Without a clear purpose, you will keep changing directions, jobs, relationships...or other externals – hoping each change will settle the confusion or fill the emptiness in your heart. You think, may be this time it will be different, but it doesn't solve your real problem – a lack of focus and purpose."
>
> *—Rick Warren in "The Purpose Driven Life"*

STOP doing everything except what matters the MOST. Don't live carelessly and unthinkingly. Make sure you understand what is most important in your life. Stop gallivanting. Stop trying to do many things. Do less. PRUNE away even good activities and do ONLY WHAT MATTERS THE MOST. One can be busy without a purpose. This will not pay any dividend. There is nothing as portent as a focused life, one lived on purpose. The people who made the greatest difference in history were the most focused people. The power of focusing can be seen in light. Diffused light has little impact but you can concentrate its energy by focusing it. With magnifying glass, the rays of the sun can be focused to set grass or paper on fire. When light is focused even more as a laser beam, it can cut through steel. Clarity of focus is important.

3.10 Clarity of Purpose can be a Source of Motivation

There is a beautiful French phrase "*raison d'être*" which means purpose or reason for living. If you have found your *raison d'être*, you will never sit idle; it will drive you. The discovery of your purpose or the reason for your existence will act as a strong source of motivation. Purpose always produces passion. Passion is the engine that propels you in a given direction. Without engine the vehicle will never move and as a result it will never reach its destination. A clear purpose is a great energiser. Clarity of purpose gives birth to passion. Both purpose and passion are two sides of the same coin. They support and complement one another. Without purpose, passion dissipates and without passion, purpose is a dead thing. For a student going to school or college without a purpose is a very meaningless act that wears him down, saps his strength and robs his hope. George Bernard Shaw says, "*This is the true joy of life: the being used up for a purpose recognised by yourself as a mighty one...*"

> When the entire concentration of all your force – physical, emotional and spiritual – is brought to bear, the consolidation of these powers properly employed is quite irresistible. Expecting the best means that you put your whole heart (i.e., the central essence of your personality) into what you want to accomplish. People are defeated in life not because of lack of ability, but for lack of wholeheartedness. They do not wholeheartedly expect to succeed. Their heart isn't in it, which is to say they themselves are not fully given. Results do not yield themselves to the person who refuses to give himself to the desired results. A major key to success is this life, to attaining that which you deeply desire is to be completely released and throw all there is of yourself into your job or any project in which you are engaged. In other words, whatever you are doing, give it all you've got. Give every bit of yourself. Hold nothing back. Life cannot deny itself to the person who gives life his all. But most people, unfortunately, don't do that. In fact, very few people do and this is the tragic cause of failure or if not failure, it is the reason we only half attain.
>
> —*Norman Vincent Peale, The Power of Positive Thinking.*

The key to creating a powerful vision for your life is going deep, not just skimming the surface. Your vision or dream should make you feel excited and motivated when you read it; you want to really feel achievement. To do that you have to focus on all aspects of your dream, including how it impacts your life and the people around you.

3.11 Dream must be beyond the Conditions of the Outside World

Your dreams are more real than the conditions of the outside world. Therefore, you need to take care and nurture them. Many of the young students are hypnotised by the world and their family belief system that there is the "real world" and this is just the plain old "fantasy." Their dream is just the "real world". The dream needs to be beyond the "real world". The "real world" looks something like this: 'you make a lot of money; live a comfortable life with modern amenities.' This is only security not beyond. As a result, the outside world has more power over you than you do and things are done the way you do them because that is how it has always been. This is how many people understand dreams. Dream is supposed to lead us beyond all these conditions of the world; take you to a realm where you feel satisfied, fulfilled and happy after doing something that you really like doing it. John C. Maxwell, an internationally acclaimed leadership expert, speaker, coach and author who has sold over 19 million books narrates this story in his book "*The 21 Indispensable Qualities of a Leader*":

> "In 1947, Lester Wunderman was arbitrarily fired from his advertising job in New York. But the young man knew he could learn a lot from the head of the agency, Max Sackheim. The next morning, Wunderman went back to his office and worked just as he had before – but without pay. Sackheim ignored him for a month, but finally walked up to Wunderman and said, "Okay, you win. I never saw a man who wanted a job more than he wanted money." Wunderman went on to become one of the most successful advertising men of the century. He is known as 'the father of direct marketing.' He is an example of a person who dreamt beyond the conditions of the world.

4

Goal Setting

"In the absence of clearly defined goals, we become strangely loyal to performing daily acts of trivia".

—*Anonymous*

Eileen A. Klemm says, "*We want students to be able to live their dreams. We want them to live intentional lives with those dreams in mind. However, it will be extremely difficult for students to live their dreams if they're at high risk, if they don't identify their dreams. For students and adults alike, the possibility of living one's dreams begins with setting goals for the here-and-now. Goal setting helps students think about their future; they set short-and long-term goals with their future intentions in mind*". When describing goal setting with students in their influential book "*Learning and Leading with Habits of Mind*". Kosta and Kallick state, "It is important to encourage students to think big and then act small – one chunk at a time". While we need to encourage students to envision their dreams and set long-term goals, we also need to help them take small steps towards these goals. When they experience small successes, they receive a boost in self-efficacy, which can lead to greater expectations for success in the future. Their future dreams and goals may expand as they engage in learning and see themselves making educational progress.

Your dreams or visions for your future can be powerful motivators. Setting goals based on your dreams will give you the strength and energy you will need to face challenges and make changes in your life and career. For example, you'll know why you are struggling with high school Mathematics because, you will see how upgrading will help you move towards your dream. Making your dreams a reality starts when you set attainable goals and create a plan to reach them.

4.1 The Many Small Steps

The Chinese philosopher *Lao Tzu* said, "*The journey of a thousand miles begins with a single step.*" When you understand this, you can set goals and not feel overwhelmed by how far you have to go to reach them. Here is how it works: when your goals arise from your dreams, they are the right goals for you. They are connected to what you need and desire. Setting goals based on your dreams will give you the strength and energy you will need to face challenges and move towards change in your life.

- For example, your *long-term goal* is your dream or vision —the general direction you want to move in. Your *short-term goals* describe the smaller steps you take to get from where you are to where you want to be.
- To move towards your dream, you divide the distance between you and your long-term goal into many smaller short-term goals.
- You take steps to reach each of those smaller goals one by one over a period of time.
- By reaching each short-term goal, you eventually reach your long-term goal.

Let us explicate this with an example,

John's dream is to become a journalist.

Long-term goal: To be a *Journalist*.

Short-term goals: They are the small steps that John takes in order to realise his dream of becoming a journalist. They are like,

- To complete his graduation (Bachelor of Journalism) and master's degree in Journalism or Mass Communication, John must *study daily* and pass his semester examinations.
- Another is to master communication skills (mastering the language).
- Spend one hour to practice elocution every day–improving pronunciation, diction, vocabulary, etc., if he is going to be a news anchor or reporter.
- Watching the performance of journalists on the Television daily.

The small steps John takes are the short-term goals that have to be practiced on a daily basis in order to reach his long-term goal of becoming a journalist.

4.2 Effective Goals must be S.M.A.R.T.E.R

If you ask most of the people today what is their ultimate goal in life? They would probably give you vague answers such as, 'I want to be successful', 'I want to be happy' or 'I want to make a good living' and that is it. These answers are all mere wishes or desires and none of them are clear goals or specific goals. They lack clarity and specificity. Goals must be SMARTER. SMART/SMARTER is a mnemonic to guide people when they set objectives, often called *key performance indicators* (KPIs). The letters broadly conform to the words specific, measurable, attainable, realistic or relevant and time-sensitive with the addition of the words evaluate and re-evaluate used in more recent times. Paul J. Meyer in his book *"Attitude is Everything"* (2003) also describes the characteristics of S.M.A.R.T goals. Let us analyse this SMARTER goal:

S – Specific. A goal must be specific. A goal like "I want to be happy" or "I want to be successful" is too general to be useful. A goal like "I want to be a medical doctor" is specific and gives you something to aim at. You can be still more specific and pursue deeper by asking yourself a question "what kind of doctor? A gynaecologist, cardiologist or neurologist etc.?" This term stresses the need for a specific goal over and against a more general one. This means the goal is clear and unambiguous; without vagaries and platitudes. A specific goal will usually answer the five "W" questions:

- What: What do I want to accomplish?
- Why: Specific reasons, purpose or benefits of accomplishing the goal.
- Who: Who is involved?
- Where: Identify a location.
- Which: Identify requirements and constraints.

M – Measurable. A goal must be measurable. A goal like "I will do well in my examination" does not give you a way to assess your progress. A goal like "I will get at least 80 per cent in my examination this time" is a measurable one. It indicates your progress. Your goal is quantifiable. This term stresses the need for concrete criteria for measuring progress towards the attainment of the goal. The thought behind this is that if a goal is not measurable, it is not possible to know whether a person is making progress towards his goal. Measuring progress is supposed to help a person stay on track, reach its target dates and experience the exhilaration of achievement that spurs it on to continued effort required to reach the ultimate goal. A measurable goal will usually answer questions such as:

- How much?
- How many?
- How will I know when it is accomplished?

A – Achievable. A goal must be achievable. "I will win a lottery" is not an effective goal because you have no control over whether or not you will achieve it. "I will start my own business by the time I'm 30" is an effective goal because you can take steps to achieve it. This term stresses the importance of goals that are realistic and attainable. While an attainable goal may stretch a person in order to achieve it, the goal is not extreme. That is, the goals are neither out of reach nor below standard performance, as these may be considered meaningless. When you identify goals that are most important to you, you begin to figure out ways you can make them come true. You develop the attitudes, abilities, skills and financial capacity to reach them. The theory states that an attainable goal may cause the goal-setter to identify previously overlooked opportunities to bring himself or herself closer to the achievement of the goal. An attainable goal will usually answer the question:

- How: How can the goal be accomplished?

R–Realistic or relevant. A goal must be realistic. If your goal is to walk 30 miles in five minutes, you are not being realistic. Calculate that you must walk every mile in 15-20 minutes. This is being realistic. This term stresses the importance of choosing goals that matter. A bank manager's goal to "make 50 peanut butter and jelly sandwiches by 2:00 pm" may be specific, measurable, attainable and time-bound but lacks relevance. Many times you will need support to accomplish a goal: resources, a champion voice, someone to knock down obstacles. Relevant goals drive a person forward. A goal that supports or is in alignment with other goals would be considered a relevant goal. A relevant goal can answer yes to these questions:

- Does this seem worthwhile?
- Is this the right time?
- Does this match your other efforts or needs?
- Are you the right person?
- Is this acceptable for correction?

T–Time-bound. A goal must be time-bound. You must set a starting date and a finishing date to reach your goal. This term emphasises the importance of grounding goals within a time frame, giving them a target date. A commitment to a deadline helps a person focus his or her efforts on completion of the goal on or before the due date. This part of the SMART goal criteria is intended to prevent goals from being overtaken by the day-to-day crises that invariably arise in a person. A time-bound goal is intended to establish a sense of urgency. A time-bound goal will usually answer the question:

- When?
- What can I do in six months from now?
- What can I do in six weeks from now?
- What can I do today?

E–Evaluate. A goal must be evaluated and assessed from time to time. Review your overall progress towards your goals. Make sure you're making progress. If you are not making progress or feel stymied, consult some motivation gurus, tap into the support of loved ones, analyse why the goal is not being met. Don't allow the goal to just fade away. Figure out what you need to do to accomplish it. No matter how positively you are thinking, you need to assess your lack of progress. Adopt a bit of a pessimist's viewpoint to get better result. Anticipate that something will and probably go wrong but not that you are going to fail, NO! Take a look at all of the factors that are keeping you from accomplishing your goal and develop a plan to overcome them.

R–Re-evaluate. Goals must be re-evaluated and reassessed. This will give a deeper insight into the various parameters of progress and failures committed on the way to achieving your goal. Through this exercise you will be able to know where you have gone wrong, the reasons for your stagnation and what steps can be taken to overcome them and continue to make progress towards your goal. You will also realise the speed at which you are making a progress and if your speed is slow, you can take steps to progress better than before.

Goals can be:

- *Short-term:* up to one year.
- *Mid-term:* up to three years.
- *Long-term:* up to five years or above.

Goals which take more than five years become purpose of life. And having a purpose and achieving it brings fulfillment and meaning to one's life.

4.3 Evaluation of One's Goals

In the pursuit of goals, winners see objectives and losers see obstacles. Goals must be challenging enough to avoid discouragement. Any activity that we perform either takes us closer to our goal or further away. According to Shiv Khera, every goal must be evaluated in the light of the following:

- Is it the truth?
- Is it fair to all concerned?
- Will it get me health, wealth and peace of mind?
- Is it consistent with my other goals?
- Can I commit myself to it?

The following examples fail the test:

(a) If one of a person's goals is to be the embodiment of good health with no money, it is quite obvious that it will be hard to survive. That means it is not consistent with their other goals.

(b) A person could make all the money in the world, yet if he loses his family and health; it is not worth it, is it?

(c) A person could make a million dollars by selling drugs but then for the rest of his life, he would be running from the law. This kind of behaviour would be socially reprehensible, illegal and take away peace of mind and good will.

You need to evaluate your goals by putting it to the question test above, and make sure all your goals are in congruence. Goals without action are empty dreams. Actions turn dreams into goals. Even if a person misses his goals, it does not make him a failure. Delay does not mean defeat. It only means you have to revise your plan to reach your target. Your goal should be consistent with your values.

4.4 In Short Setting Goal Looks Like This

- Write out your long-term goal. Make it SMARTER and make sure it is your dream or vision for your future, not anyone else's.
- Identify your assets—the people and things that will help you reach your goal for example, determination, a supportive family, friends, skills, experience.
- Look at the barriers—the things that stand between you and your goal, for example, lack of money, need for day care, transportation problem, lack of skills and not enough experience.
- Brainstorm around the barrier. Be creative and be responsible. Come up around the barriers between you and your goal. Write the ideas down.
- Map out your short-term goals—the small steps you'll take to reach your long-term goal:
  - On the left side of a piece of paper, mark an X and label it 'I'm here'. On the right side, write out your long-term goal.
  - Divide the distance between you and your goal into smaller goals. Write each one out. Make sure each one is a SMARTER goal.
  - Under each short-term goal, write out the steps you will take to reach that goal.
  - Share your thoughts and plans with the supportive people in your life. Ask for help in reaching your goals.

4.5 Goals can Change

As you continue to create positive change in your life, your dreams and goals may change too. New experiences, skills and relationships may lead you in new directions. And that's okay. Keep checking back on your dreams and goals every few months or so to see how you feel about them and make adjustment as you go. Working towards goals that are based on your dreams can be nurturing, strengthening process. You will feel a sense of direction in your life as if you are finally becoming the person you were meant to be. This can be a very satisfying experience.

The Three Golden Rules to Live By—

- If you do not go after what you want, you will never have it.
- If you don't ask a question, you will never get the answer.
- If you do not step forward, you will always remain in the same place.

5

The Accoutrements for Achieving One's Dream

"The heights great men reached and kept were not attained by sudden flight, but they, while their companions slept, were toiling upward in the night."

—*Henry Wadsworth Longfellow*

If you aim for the sky, you may reach the stars. If you aim for the stars, you may reach the clouds. If you aim for the clouds, you may reach the tree tops and if you aim for the tree tops, you may not reach even the branch. Therefore, there is a need to aim high and ascend the fastigium so that when you look down, you may be able to help those who begin to climb the same height. There are certain things to be kept in mind while trying to ascend your goal.

5.1 Make Your Dream as Your Priority

Make your dream as the *dominating thought* in your life and never exchange it with anything cheap. Make your goal more important than anything else. Take care of your dream and *protect it.* In spite of difficulties and problems tell yourself, "Come what may, I will never let go my dream". Do not get hypnotised by the world outside. The outside forces will try to dissuade you from your dream and try to satisfy you with the mediocrity so that you don't climb higher than them. Priority is something that you consider the most important in your life and without it you find so difficult to go on in life. It dominates your thoughts, actions and your belief system. It is identifying the most important action to be taken in order to achieve your dream or goal. Prioritising is also the process of eliminating all the unimportant and the not so important things which may not be required in pursuing your dream. Learn to prioritise your life.

> "I'm unpredictable, I never know where I'm going until I get there, I'm so random, I'm always growing, learning, changing, I'm never the same person twice. But *one thing you can be sure about me is I will always do exactly what I want to do.*"
>
> —*C. JoyBell C.*

Doing exactly what you want to do is what is most important in your life. If you are sure of what you want to do in life and work at that you will soon reach where you want to reach. Priority refers to doing what is the most important for you i.e., what you want to do. You will surely do, if it is very important for you.

Exegesis of the above saying of C. JoyBell C

- "One thing you can be sure about me" refers to the certainty of the knowledge of oneself – strength and weakness.
- "I will always do" points to one's willingness and constancy in doing what one wants to do or achieve. "I will" is different from 'I may or I might'. "Always" means 'continuously without resting'.
- "Exactly what I want to do" – "exactly" refers to being accurate in one's intention and action. It means being accurate in doing what one wants to do or achieve in life.

5.2 Keep Your Dream Alive

You keep your dreams alive by constantly thinking or imagining about it. This is known as "dreams transform into thoughts". Your dream must occupy a central place within your thought and imagination. You keep reminding yourself of your chosen dream by telling yourself "Hey, John, you are going to be a doctor!" Repeat this many times as possible during the day – when you walk, before you study, before you go to school, after your school, before you play etc. Constant reminder will keep the amber of your dream alive.

Another powerful way of keeping your dream alive is through visualisation and imagery. This is possible through your mental eyes. With your mental eyes you can see what you want to be in your life. One of the powerful ways to put your dream in motion is to spend some times each day visualising it. Top athletes, including Tiger Woods, Mia Hamm and Andy Roddick use imagery or visualisation to power their performances. In fact, most athletes use mental imagery instinctively and spontaneously on and off the field.

> As a boy Tiger Woods famously had a poster of Nicklaus in his room. It served as a reminder of his goal in his golf career. To top Nicklaus' record of 18 major championship wins, Woods finished the US Open in a tie for 32nd but still ahead of legend's winning pace.

Doing the following exercise daily will help you to keep your dream alive:

Keep Visualising Your Dream

Write it down in a paper and carry in your pocket
So that whenever you put your hand into your pocket,
You will be reminded of your dream.
And also write it and paste it in your room
Where you can see it easily.
Look yourself in your mirror and call your own name
And tell yourself of your dream.
Everyday wake up with your dream
That YOU CAN achieve it.
Get up with your dream
Remind yourself of your dream.
Remind yourself
As many times as possible during the day.
And the ember of your dream will never be put out,
Instead will turn into conflagration.

5.3 Believe in Yourself that You can Achieve Your Dream

Believe in yourself that you *can* become what you dream of and tell yourself, "I will work for my dream till I become my dream". Make "I BELIEVE ME" as your personal CREED to ascend your set goal. "I believe that I can do or make it" is the fulcrum of my personal CREED. This is a CAN DO attitude. I CAN is 100 times more important than IQ. Most people fail in life not because they lack knowledge and skills but they don't believe that they can do it. Most of the people who succeed in life are usually not the cleverest people but people who *believe* in themselves. Napoleon Hill says, "Faith is the 'eternal elixir' which gives life, power and action to the impulse of thought!"

In life, we believe other people more easily than we believe in ourselves. Believing yourself is the best way of empowering yourself. If you believe that you can, you'll see what you can accomplish in life. On the other hand, not believing in yourself also will make you see what you cannot accomplish in life. You become what you believe. People are easily swayed by those who believe strongly in themselves.

David Hume, the famous philosopher was a confirmed agnostic, but he used to go and hear the famous preacher and minister, John Brown. When criticised for his inconsistency, Hume answered: "I don't believe all that he says but he does. And once a week I like to hear a man who believes what he says."

In life, everything collapses when you stop believing. Have faith in yourself. Faith is the mental anticipatory knowledge coupled with certainty that you will become what you want to be before actually reaching the goal. Those who climb great heights in life are those who have the strongest faith in themselves. The Bible says, "Where there is great faith, great things happen." The Bible also says, "Faith can move mountains." If you are convinced of your goal and you are determined to achieve it, it will happen, no matter even if there is a mountain to block you. Your faith is greater than the mountain. All the armies of Europe felt that it was impossible to cross the snowy Alps but Napoleon Bonaparte and his army crossed it. Napoleon believed that what others could not, HE COULD. When you are filled with faith, you become fearless in pursuing your goal. Your faith, gives you the strength and confidence to walk through all the odds. Start believing in yourself. Tell yourself, "If others can, why can't I?" Louis Fischer writes about Gandhi thus:

> "Gandhi was not born great. He was a blundering boy, a mediocre student, a poor lawyer, an ordinary individual until he remade himself. He was a self-remade man. He had FAITH in himself".

If You Think You Can, You Can!

You can be a total winner even if you're a beginner,
If you think you can, you can,
If you think you can, you can,
You can wear the gold medallion,
You can ride your own black stallion,
If You Think You Can, You Can,
If You Think You Can, You Can,
It's not your talent or the gift at birth,
It's not your bank book that determines worth,
And it isn't in the colour of your skin,
It's your attitude that lets you win,
You can upset Connors or Austin,
Or win the marathon at Boston,
If You Think You Can, You Can,
If You Think You Can, You Can,
You can profit through inflation,
You can redirect this nation,
If You Think You Can, You Can,
If You Think You Can, You Can,
It doesn't matter if you've won before,
It makes no difference what's the half time score,

It's never over until the final gun,
So keep on trying and you'll find you've won,
You grab your dream and then believe it,
Go out and work and you'll achieve it,
If you think you can, you can,
If You Think You Can, You Can!

—*Denis Waitley*

5.4 Learn to Forgo Pleasure

A person who is not able to forgo pleasure usually doesn't go far in life. Pleasure can benumb you from being sensitive to your dream. It is the most difficult thing to forgo in life. A person who loves pleasure cannot sacrifice anything and will seldom be willing to experience struggle and pain. It reduces the degree of your mental toughness. Without sacrifice, struggle and pain nothing great is ever achieved in life. Pleasure is a very highly pleasant feeling that a person can experience either by himself or with some other entities. Because of its pleasurability, many get addicted to it. Once a person tastes pleasure, he will seldom be willing to go through pain. Pain is just the antithesis of pleasure. They are two different entities and the twine shall never meet. If a person first experiences pain and struggle, he can experience pleasure later. But the vice versa is something that seldom happens. Kahlil Gibran in *The Prophet* wrote, "The lust for comfort murders the passion of the soul". Comfort is one of the pleasures that human beings seek but has the power to mactate (kill) the passion of one's soul.

> When Ulysses was passing through the Island of the Sirens (sea nymphs) in his ship, he filled the ears of his seamen with wax so that they would not hear the mellifluous and illecebrous music of the mermaids and had himself bound to the mast so that he would not be tempted to yield to their attractions. Letting go pleasure is a great indication that you are serious about realising your dream. Pleasure is addictive and it reduces and kills the capacity to suffer and endure pain and struggle in life.

5.6 The Contravallation Strategy

Contravallation is a fortification set up to protect a besieging force from attack by the defenders. The word originated from French word *'contravallation'* which in turn is derived from three Latin words namely, *'contra'* which means counter, *'vallatio'* which means entrenchment and *'vallum'* which means wall. The word therefore means a wall or an entrenchment made as a defense mechanism against (counter) an outside attack (besieging force).

A person who wants to attain his definite goal must apply the Contravallation Strategy. You have to build a defence or a fortification against the outside enemy that is trying to snatch away your priced goal. The external enemy will try harm or dissipate your focus. The outside enemy or the besieging force is nothing but your own ENVIRONMENT. Every human being is affected both positively and negatively by the environment. According to Napoleon Hill, the term "'Environment' covers a very broad field. It consists of the books we read, the people with whom we associate, the community in which we live, the nature of the work in which we are engaged, the country in which we reside, the clothes we wear, the songs we sing and most important of all, the religious and intellectual training we receive prior to the age of fourteen years." Environment also includes media, friends, family situation, cellular phone, films, etc.

The mind feeds upon that which you supply or that which is forced upon through your environment. Therefore, you select your environment as far as possible with the object of supplying your mind with suitable material out of which to carry on its work of attaining your dream. You need to screen your environment. Sometimes, it can be potentially dangerous in achieving your fixed dream. It can alter your mind to things other than your dream. Therefore, build a strong fortification around yourself so that nothing outside or foreign destroys your dream. Insulate and protect your dream from all the harmful influence around you.

5.7 Never Give Up on Your Dream

"Go all the way with it. Do not back off.
For once, go all the goddamn way with what matters."

-- Ernest Hemingway, *The Complete Short Stories*

Do not expect success at least without a 'temporary failure'. When failure comes accept it as a signal that your plans are sound, rebuild those plans and set sail once more towards your coveted dream. If you give up before your goal has been reached, you are a "quitter". Napoleon Hill says, "A Quitter Never Wins–and–A Winner Never Quits". He continues "Live this sentence out, write it on a piece of paper in letters an inch high and place it where you will see it every night before you go to sleep and every morning before you begin your day". No man is ever whipped until he QUITS – in his own mind. Be consistently insistent in persistence in chasing your dream. A stream is able to hollow the rock not because of its strength but its persistence.

• Demosthenes, the Greek orator demonstrated that the power of oration was greater than the power of the king. He was the most famous and powerful political orator of antiquity. Demosthenes was a congenital stammerer. Growing up as a weakling, often falling ill, he was subjected to the ridicule and pity of his fellow pupils. After hearing a famous Greek orator speaking, Demosthenes developed a keen desire to achieve something remarkable: to become an orotund orator. To achieve this dream, he had to encounter unlimited obstacles. The moment he opened his mouth to speak, the stammering choked him. He had no ability to speak a long sentence at a stretch. To improve his elocution, Demosthenes talked with pebbles in his mouth and recited verses while running along the seashore over the roar of the waves. He practiced going up to high hills and coming down steep slopes, took deep breaths and tried to speak very long sentences without interruption. After extensive and incessant practice he surmounted his difficulty of speech. Gradually, he was transformed into one of the most powerful orators of antiquity. His oratorical skill was cogent, persuasive and invincible so much so that Philip, the Greek King said, "You may conquer the whole world, but you cannot defeat Demosthenes in speech".

• Hawking was precocious as a child, but he was not the brightest in his competitive A stream class. Many of his classmates did not believe he could do well. Shortly after his 21st birthday, Hawking was diagnosed with the motor neuron disease, an illness that is incurable and that can eventually kill him. When he knew there wasn't much time for him to live, he suddenly realised that there were plenty of worthwhile things he could indulge in! Hawking is fully confined to a wheelchair that is fitted with a speech synthesiser and a portable computer. Through this system, he continued his research on theoretical Physics and gave public lectures around the world. So far he has been awarded 12 honourary degrees. Hawking has said that he never wants to be treated differently, just because he is physically challenged. That is the spirit that makes him different from others. "It matters if you just don't give up," said Hawking. Professor Stephen Hawking, one of the greatest geniuses alive today is the quintessence of a person who never gives up.

• Dr. APJ Abdul Kalam, the fifth amongst seven siblings of a poor father used to sell newspaper as a small boy to earn his living. He was neither educated abroad nor was his family financially strong to support his academic pursuits. His neighbours remember him as an introvert interested in reading. Kalam was not exceptionally smart at school but was fascinated by religion and rockets. He went for an interview conducted by the Indian Air Force but was not selected. The first rocket he built crashed. A missile that he built crashed multiple times and he was made a butt of ridicule. But he never let himself be carried away by the waves of disappointment.

Kalam is by no means a miracle man. His life and mission is a vindication of what a determined person can achieve against extraordinary odds. Even at 71, this former President of India is indefatigable and has dreams to make India a technological superpower.

• In the beginning of his career, the legendary Bollywood Mogul Amitabh Bachchan had to struggle a lot because of his unconventional looks and his height. At 6 feet 3 inches, he was considered far too tall by the filmmakers. Surprisingly, despite having a rich baritone, he failed in an audition at the All India Radio and even played a mute in one of his early films. He was also told that with his obnoxiously long name, he would never be famous. The first eleven films of Bachchan were unequivocal flops. Many would have given up and sought other means of employment, but he persevered. Later in his career, he was seriously injured during the filming of '*Coolie*', but he continued to act. Bachchan's own production company, ABCL for film distribution fell on bad days and he was buried neck deep in debt. The company's cup of woe spilled over when his films flopped miserably at the Box-office. And he was once again 'written off' by the industry. This time too Bachchan bounced back in style through his performance on the small screen.

Today, Bachchan is a name profusely used in popular parlance and he is able to curve out a niche for himself in the film industry and finds himself 'locked' in the hearts of millions of film lovers. The 'Big B' is an icon who has survived three decades of competition and even trends.

• "Drill for oil? You mean drill into the ground to try and find oil? You're crazy!" This was what prospectors said to Edwin L. Drake, the father of oil drilling, when he tried to enlist them in his oil drilling project in 1859.

• "Try any other profession, not this," John Murray Anderson, Anderson School of Drama instructor said to the young Lucille Ball, renowned American comedienne of the "I love Lucy" TV serial fame.

• Let us recapitulate the story of Abraham Lincoln. Lincoln's story is one of the most evergreen and ever inspiring saga of a man whose odyssey had been fraught with unfortunate concatenation of mishaps and failures but finally saw a light at the end of the tunnel. Born in a very poor family, Lincoln had no means to have formal education. He earned his meagre living, wandering from place to place. At last he thought of improving his lot. There being no steamers or other means of transport in those days, he voyaged through the big rivers on a country raft made of wooden planks and visited the various towns in America. At one place he got the job of a shop assistant. While working there, he bought a few books and began to study them by himself. While standing once in a slave market, his soul rose in rebellion against slavery and his silent resolution has revolutionised history. Lincoln had a very strong desire to make a difference, so he entered politics. Then, he began to face defeat after defeat but never gave up. He lost eight elections, twice failed in business and suffered a nervous breakdown. He could have quit many times – but he didn't and since he didn't quit, he became one of the greatest presidents in the history of the United States. Let us see how he traversed the road littered with struggles and failures till he became the President of the United States:

- In 1816, his family was forced out of their home. He had to work to support them.
- In 1818, his mother died.
- In 1831, he failed in business.
- In 1832 he ran for state legislature but lost it. In the same year he also lost his job. So, he wanted to go to law school but couldn't get through.
- In 1833, he borrowed some money from a friend to begin business and by the end of the year he was bankrupt. He spent the next 17 years of his life paying off this debt.
- In 1834, he ran for state legislature again – won.
- In 1835, he was engaged to be married, sweetheart died and his heart was broken.
- 1836, he had a total nervous breakdown and was bedridden for six months.
- 1838, he sought to become speaker of the state legislature but defeated.
- In 1840, he sought to become elector – defeated.
- In 1843, he ran for Congress – lost.
- In 1846, he ran for Congress again – this time he won – went to Washington and did a good job.
- In 1849, he ran for re-election to Congress – lost.
- In 1849, he sought the job of land officer in his home state – rejected.
- In 1854, he ran for Senate of the United States – lost.
- In 1856, he sought the Vice-President nomination at his party's national convention – get less than 100 votes.
- In 1860, he was elected as the President of the United States.

This is the man who never gave up his dream. Those who don't quit always win. Paul Guildea in his book "*The Pepple*" writes:

"If you can hear the bell for the next round,
Then you are still in the fight!
Get off your stool and start swinging...
Never give up and never quit
On your dream!"

Don't Ever Give Up

Don't ever give up
Failure and Success is in everyone's cup.

Rain becomes more enjoyable if it follows a sunny day
Food becomes more relishing if for days Hungry you stay

So, don't ever give up
Failure and Success is in everyone's cup.

Pebble becomes smooth by constant rolling
Pencil becomes usable by sharpening

So, don't ever give up
Failure and Success is in everyone's cup.

—*Kavitha Krishnamurthy*

5.8 If You Want to Realise Your Dream, Never Depend on LUCK

Diligent hard work casts away luck dependence. "Only crackpots depend on jackpots", says Shiv Khera. Luck has an element of fatalism. A student who does not prepare himself well for his examination will greatly depend on luck. He studies only few answers and if those few answers that he has studied come in the exam, he concludes that he is lucky. But another student works very hard and studies everything and he is able to answer all the questions in the examination. To this student luck does not matter. Luck dependence is completely futile in the case of the second student. If you work hard you don't need luck. Luck is for sluggards and those who do things by halves. Samuel Goldwyn says, "The harder I work, the luckier I get". Luck is for unprepared people.

- Ray Kroc was the first businessman to apply the principles of mass production in a service industry. He is famous for making the fast food franchise, *McDonalds*, one of the largest and most popular chains of fast food restaurants around the world. Kroc was a school dropout. Young Ray Kroc believed that opportunity only knocked once and took his chances as they came. When he was 15 years old, he lied about his age and got himself the job of an ambulance driver for Red Cross. After that he tried his hand at myriad things, finally settling down to be a salesman. He initially sold paper cups. In 1954, Kroc, the 52-year-old milkshake machine salesman, saw a hamburger stand in California and envisioned a massive new industry – fast food. Kroc opened his first *McDonalds*. Though the concept caught on quickly and sold several franchises, he ran into some financial problems that nearly bankrupted him early on. It was the time when Kroc was suffering from diabetes and arthritis. His gall bladder and thyroid gland had already been surgically removed. But the desire to succeed burned in him. From his early days of starting *McDonalds* to even after the chain was a well-established concern globally, Kroc experienced a fair share of failures. However, he was immune to disappointment. "*Luck is a dividend of sweat,*" said Kroc, "*the more you sweat, the luckier you get*".

• "Weak-minded people fall easy prey to fortune-tellers, horoscopes and self-proclaimed God-men who are sometimes conmen. They become superstitious and ritualistic. If you want to fail believe in LUCK. If you want to succeed believe in hard work".

—*Shiv Khera*

Some people think they are just unlucky. This breeds a fatalistic attitude. People who get involved half-heartedly say things like:

- I will give it a try
- I will see if it works
- I will give it a shot
- I have nothing to lose
- I have not put much into it anyway

If you think this way, you will surely fail because you do not possess dedication and determination. This type of happy-go-lucky attitude lacks courage, commitment and confidence. Attempting half-heartedly is like expecting failure and achieving it.

> "That at certain point in our lives, we lose control of what's happening to us and our lives become controlled by fate. That's the world's greatest lie."
>
> —Paulo Coelho, '*The Alchemist*'

5.9 Choose Your Friends Wisely

As a student I would recommend not to have too many friends. Too many friends will engender too many appointments and obligations. You will not be able to say 'no' to these unimportant peer appointments and obligations. King Solomon, the wisest man in the world had as many as 700 wives from different pagan tribes. These wives led him to their own gods and finally he forgot the commitment he made to Yahweh (the God of Israel).

5.10 Apply Self-confidence Formula

Napoleon Hill in his book "*Think and Grow Rich*" gives a very scintillating self-confidence formula.

• First, I know that I have the ability to achieve the object of my Definite Purpose in life, therefore, I DEMAND of myself persistent, continuous action toward its attainment and I here and now promise to render such action.

• Second, I realise the dominating thoughts of my mind will eventually reproduce themselves in outward, physical reality and gradually transform themselves into physical reality; therefore, I will concentrate my thoughts for thirty minutes daily, upon the task of thinking of the clear mental picture of that person.

• Thirdly, I know through the principle of auto-suggestion, any desire that I persistently hold in my mind will eventually seek expression through some practical means of attaining the object back of it; therefore, I will devote ten minutes daily to demanding of myself the development of SELF-CONFIDENCE.

• Fourth, I have clearly written down a description of my DEFINITE CHIEF AIM in life, and I will never stop trying, until I shall have developed sufficient self-confidence for its attainment.

• Fifth, I fully realise that no wealth or position can long endure, unless built upon truth and justice, therefore, I will engage in no transaction which does not benefit all whom it affects. I will succeed by attracting to myself the forces I wish to use and the cooperation of my willingness to serve others. I will eliminate hatred, envy, jealousy, selfishness and cynicism by developing love for all humanity because I know that a negative attitude toward others can never bring me success. I will cause others to believe in me because I will believe in them and in myself.

I will sign my name to this formula, commit it to memory and repeat it aloud once a day, with full FAITH that it will gradually influence my THOUGHTS and ACTIONS so that I will become a self-reliant and successful person.

Back of this formula is a Law of Nature which no man has yet been able to explain. It has baffled the scientists of all ages. The psychologists have named this law "Auto-Suggestion". The name by which one calls this law is of little importance. The important fact about it is – it WORKS for the glory and success of mankind, IF it is used constructively. On the other hand, if used destructively, it will destroy just as readily. In this statement may be found a very significant truth, namely; that those who go down in defeat and end their lives in poverty, misery and distress do so because of negative application of the principle of auto-suggestion. The cause may be found in the fact that *all impulses of thought have a tendency to clothe themselves in their physical equivalent*.

The subconscious mind (the chemical laboratory in which all thought impulses are combined and made ready for translation into physical reality), makes no distinction between constructive and destructive thought impulses. It works with the material we feed it, through our thought impulses. The subconscious mind will translate into reality a thought driven by fear just as readily as it will translate into reality a thought driven by COURAGE or FAITH. If your mind is filled with FEAR, doubt and unbelief in your ability, the law of auto-suggestion will take this spirit of unbelief and use it as a pattern by which your subconscious mind will translate it into its physical equivalent. Like the wind which carries one ship East and another West, the law of auto-suggestion will lift you up or pull you down according to the way you set your sails of THOUGHT. The law of auto-suggestion, through which any person may rise to altitudes of achievement which stagger the imagination is well described in the following verse:

"If you think you are beaten, you are,
If you think you dare not, you don't
If you like to win, but you think you can't,
It is almost certain you won't

If you think you'll lose, you're lost
For out of the world we find,
Success begins with a fellow's will –
It's all in the state of mind.

If you think you are outclassed, you are,
You've got to think high to rise,
You've got to be sure of yourself before
You can ever win a prize.

Life's battles don't always go
To the stronger or faster man,
But soon or late the man who wins
Is the man WHO THINKS HE CAN!"

5.11 Build Your Self-confidence

To achieve one's dream, a high degree of self-confidence is required. Confidence is a self-empowering energy that gives you the courage to face any challenges. Therefore, you need to build your self-confidence by yourself. This is the poem that I have composed. Reading it again and again leads me to believe and appreciate my 'SELF'. In other words, it builds self-confidence. A person who appreciates himself will be affluent in self-confidence.

The Self-Confidence Formula

I am me, so beautiful

Even if I cross the farthest seas and planets
I will not find one, who will be exactly like me
I am singular and unique
Made special and beautiful
I am the masterpiece of a perfect Artist
I am no accident, no happenstance
I was in my Creator's eternal plan
Whose action I believe, doesn't happen by chance
Therefore, I love me
There is no vanity in this, for it is not ostentation
But APPRECIATION.

I have potentials and powers within me
With this, I can make myself what I want to be
I also know that there are myriads of false goodness within me
However, I accept them as part of me
And I shall tame them with the power bestowed upon me
I shall take an INWARD JOURNEY and explore
The MYSTERY within me
And THERE, I shall change and eliminate the false goodness
And whatever I cannot I shall accept
This is a noble task and when I complete,
I shall become more beautiful
And I shall leave my footprint
On the planet, I walk upon, to know that
This singular "I" has walked upon this earth.

5.12 Take Care of the Means as You are Fixed on Your Dream

The means is as important as the end (goal). Swami Vivekananda in his speech at Los Angeles in 1900 says:

> "One of the greatest lessons I have leant in my life is to pay as much attention to the means of work as to its end. Our great defect in life is that we are so much drawn to the ideal, the goal which is so much enchanting, so much alluring and so much bigger in our mental horizon that we lose sight of the details all together. But whenever failure comes, if we analyse it critically in ninety-nine per cent of cases we shall find that it was because we did not pay attention to the means. Proper attention to the finishing, strengthening of the means is what we need. With the means all right, the end must come. We forget that it is the cause that produces the effect; the effect cannot come by itself; and unless the causes are exact, proper and powerful, the effect will not be produced."

Once you have chosen the goal and the means determined, you must make sure that the means you employ are perfect i.e., attention must be given to details of the means for achieving the goal. Focusing on the means therefore is the great secret of success in life. You can be so obsessed with the goal that you can be lackadaisical about the means. This can be detrimental to the realisation of the goal.

5.13 Play in Order to Win Your Dream

> "Life is like the Olympic games; a few men strain their muscles to carry off a prize, others sell trinkets to the crowd for a profit; some just came to look and see how everything is done."
>
> —*Pythagoras*

The world in which we live and move is like a mighty stadium. In this stadium, there are three kinds of people performing different roles. They are:

- The players
- The spectators
- The chatters

The first group of people comes to the Stadium to PLAY and to WIN. They come with this singular aim. Nothing can distract them. They work very hard and prepare themselves in order to play and win. They strive till their goal is achieved. They are ever active, enthusiastic, effervescent, cheerful and ready to face any challenge in the competition. They are the cynosure in the stadium.

The second group of people comes to the stadium not to play but to SEE. They see and enjoy the game of the players from a distance. The aim of these people is just *to see* and not to play. In real life if you ask this type of people, to perform any task or help, their answer will be nothing but "*let me see*". For anything and everything, their answer remains the same. They are viewers of life and have only time for seeing and not playing. They fear action and prefer to live in a utopian paradise.

The third group of people comes to the stadium just to barter their time in pastime. They come to the stadium to socialise. They chat with one another and squander their precious time. They take delight in current events, high sounding philosophies and so on. They are neither interested in the players nor seeing them. They are interested in their own petty affairs and take delight in blarney. These people neither understand life nor value life. They are contented with peripheral existence. They passed this beautiful stadium without leaving a footprint on it. Life is not to be seen from a distance or to be squandered or wasted. It must be played and won. Otherwise it is only a futile existence. Live and lead your life towards where you want to ascend.

A Brief Analysis of the Above

The players are those who are clear of their goals and they work hard in order to win. The second group of people has only wishes. They don't want to be players but just wish to enjoy the players. In real life when they are asked, "You can also try". Their common answer would be, "Let me see". Seeing does not lead to action and where there is no action, nothing happens. The last group of people is not interested in what is going on in the stadium. They just come to while away their time. For them, it is only a pastime. They are the ones who do not know the meaning and purpose of life. They just merely exist and nothing more!

5.14 Keep Working on Your Talents

The Dodo (Raphus cucullatus) was a *ratitae* bird that lived on the island of Mauritius. Related to pigeons and doves, it stood about a meter tall (three feet), lived on fruits and nested on the ground. According to ornithologists, the Dodo bird had all food available and enjoyed the climate of the island. As a result, the Dodo had no need to migrate to other lands for food and climate. Gradually, it lost its ability to use its wings. Colonisers came to the island and brought with them hunting dogs. The colonisers with their dogs preyed on them and finally the bird came to be extinct. The extinction took place in the mid-to-late 17th century.

Today, this bird is used as the archetype of an extinct species because its extinction occurred during recorded human history and was directly attributable to human activity. The adjectival phrase *"as dead as a dodo"* means undoubtedly and unquestionably dead. The verb phrase *"to go the way of the dodo"* means to become extinct or obsolete, to fall out of common usage or practice or to become a thing of the past.

This story of the Dodo is a moving story. If the dodo were to use its wings constantly it would surely escape death and it would have lived to this day.

• When you don't use your talents and abilities, they will be *as dead as the dodo*.

The Oyster

There once was an oyster whose story I tell,
Who found that some sand had got into his shell.
It was only a grain but it gave him great pain,
For oysters have feelings although they're so plain.

Now, did he berate the harsh workings of fate
That had brought him to such a deplorable state?

Did he curse at the government, cry for election,
And claim that the sea should have given him protection?

No–He said to himself as he lay in the shell,
Since I cannot remove it, I shall try to improve it.
Now the years have rolled around,
As the years always do,
And he came to his ultimate destiny – stew

And the small grain of sand that had bothered him so
Was a beautiful pearl all richly aglow,
Now the tale has a moral;
For isn't it grand what an oyster can do
With a morsel of sand?

What couldn't we do if we'd only begin
With some of the things that get under our skin.

—*Anonymous*

5.15 On Your Mark, Set Set, GO!

Sajith Cyriac, the Editor of *Inspirational Quote* writes thus:

Do not live your life on the mountain of 'someday'. Unfortunately, you may never come down from that 'someday'. Have you ever wondered why your dreams don't come true? For many of you the problem does not lie in accomplishing the task at hand, but in getting started in the first place. You have countless excuses, such as, the time isn't right, you aren't prepared enough and the list goes on. Unless you move beyond the daydreaming stage and get started, you will never become successful in realising your dreams. As Zig Ziglar once said, "You don't have to be great to start, but you have to start to be great!" you never know what you can achieve until you try. Thus, all you can do is to begin with small steps. As you move further and further, you will realise how far and in what direction you ought to go. Life is a bold adventure and only enterprising people can get the maximum out of it. Too much thinking about your dream may prevent the unnecessary action." So, on your mark, get set, GO!

6

Condiciones Sine Quibus Non for Achieving Your Dream

"Whatever the mind of man can conceive and believe, the mind can achieve."

– *Napoleon Hill*

Earl Nightingale, the father of modern personal development defines "Success" as *"the progressive realisation of a worthy ideal"*. In other words, your repeated progress towards something noble or worthy is what makes you successful. By this definition success is not the end destination but instead it is something to be achieved on a daily basis. Therefore, there are many daily tasks that need to be performed regularly in order to arrive at your dream. That is why habits are incredibly powerful because they determine your level of success towards your dream. Ideally, you will make daily progress towards goals you have pre-determined to be worthy in your life. There are certain conditions that are indispensable in order to maximise your productivity, effectiveness and overall success. They are called '*condiciones sine quibus non* (literally means 'conditions without which it could not be') for achieving your dream'. These conditions are:

6.1 A Flaming Desire

"Without desire, one is a walking cadaver."

– *Karldon Okruta* in 'Kaz'

You need to deeply desire your goal if you really want to succeed. A desire is the starting point and a burning desire spontaneously compels and expedites the ascension into the realm of success. Apply the principle "*ex scintilla incendium*" (from a spark, a conflagration). The first step you must take if you want to realise your dream is to fan the spark of your desire into flame and the flame into conflagration. Conflagration then will engulf you, i.e., your dream controls you. This conflagration can be described in a more appropriate word called *aeipathy* which means an enduring and consuming passion. Once you have an *aeipathy* for your goal, you are sure to achieve it.

Continuous fanning of your small desire will metamorphose into a burning desire. Napoleon Hill in his landmark book "*Think and Grow Rich*" had it right, "The starting point of all achievement is DESIRE. Keep this constantly in mind. Weak desires bring weak results, just as a small amount of fire produces small amount of heat." So, if you really want to realise your dream you need to deeply desire. Without a burning zeal or desire nothing great can be achieved in life.

A young man asked the wise Socrates the secret to success. Socrates told the young man to meet him near the river the next morning. They met. Socrates asked the young man to walk with him towards the river. When the water got up to their necks, Socrates took the young man by surprise and dunked him under the water. The boy struggled to get out but Socrates was strong and held him down. When the boy started turning blue, Socrates raised the boy's head out of the water. The first thing the young man did was to gasp and take a deep breath of air. Socrates asked, "What did you needed most when you were under the water?" The boy replied, "Air". Socrates said, "That is the secret to success. When you want success as intensely as you wanted air under water, then you will have it". There is no other secret.

An ardent desire is a driving force that takes you to success. In his book *Cosmic Ordering Guide*, Stephen Richards writes, "*Always has an air of expectancy.*" You need to be expectant in the process of moving towards your goal. Desire must be transformed into curiosity. Curiosity is a PERSISTENT DESIRE to know things by oneself. Curiosity will try to find its way to see and know things for itself. A desire can evanesce but curiosity persists on till the hidden things are unfolded.

> "Curiosity is the single most important attribute with which humans are born. More than a simple desire to discover or know things, curiosity is a powerful tool, like a scalpel or a searchlight. Curiosity changes us. It is also a way to effect change, perhaps even on a global level."
>
> —Loren Rhoads in "*Morbid Curiosity*"

6.2 Be Determined

"*Justum et tenacem propositi virum*" is a Latin phrase which means *a man upright and tenacious of purpose.* You need to be made of such a sterner stuff if you really want to realise your goal. A person who is upright and tenacious of purpose will certainly achieve his goal. In other words, it means being determined is the key to success. In trying to perfect the revolutionary piece of technology, the incandescent electric bulb, inventor Thomas Edison conducted more than a thousand experiments. Nearly all of them failed. At this, a reporter asked Edison what he had learned from one thousand failed experiments. He said, "I've learned one thousand ways not to invent the light bulb." We live in a brighter world because Edison conducted experiment one thousand and one times. It is Edison's determination that keeps us out of darkness today. If Edison had given up after the third experiment, it is possible that electric bulb could not have been known to this day.

Never give up. Your life is worth too much to leave it half done. Do not play the role of a *finifugalist*. Finifugalist is one who hates endings. He tries to avoid or prolong the final moments of a story, relationship or some other journeys. Such person will never do things to the finish and as a result he will never arrive at his dreams. Such an attitude will not take you to where you want to be. If you begin a higher education degree, finish it and do not delay like the finifugalist. You will be glad you did it. If you start a job, see it through the end. You will always regret what you leave half done or undone. If you begin working on a personal discipline, stick to it. With a determined effort, you can do it. Finish what you have started. "Determination may start with a 'D' says Stan Toler, "but it will give you an 'A' on your finals." Whenever you feel like giving up, ask yourself: "*why you started it?*"

- Pele *aka* the king of football who is known for his beautiful skills, astonishing speed and ball control will be perennially in the minds of sports-lovers around the world. His life is a manifestation of what a determined person can achieved. Pele was born in a poor family and due to poverty he had to drop out of school at the age of 10 while studying in the fourth class. The family situation became even harder when his father, a fairly good football player had to quit playing it professionally due to a knee injury. His father had started training him in football as soon as he started walking. Pele used to play barefooted in the streets of Bauru where he grew up, not with a ball but with a sock filled with rags. Later he took up odd jobs for his living. At the age of 11 Pele drew the attention of Waldemir de Britto, the renowned coach who trained him for four years and taught him all the techniques and tricks of the game. Pele worked all the harder to master the game. That paved the way for his promising future. Pele scored two goals in the world cup final at the age of 17, an achievement that is unlikely to be matched ever in world cup history. As he was a Negro with dark skin, Pele earned the name 'Black Pearl' of football. It has been more than a quarter of a century since his last competitive game and yet Pele cannot visit a country without crowds flocking to meet him.

• The legendary mountaineer Edmund Hilary on May 29, 1953 became the first man to set foot on the summit of Mount Everest. In 1952, he attempted to climb Mount Everest but failed. A few weeks later a group from England asked him to address its members. Hillary walked on stage considering himself as a failure. He made a fist and pointed at a picture of the mountain. He said in a loud voice, "Mount Everest, you beat me the first time, but I'll beat you the next time because you've grown all you are going to grow... but I'm still growing!" After continued efforts, finally Edmund Hillary reached the top of Mount Everest. He explains his experience in his autobiography, "As I rested a little, a disturbing voice from inside me started to take control of me. 'Congratulations, Eddie! You have just reached the highest level any human being has ever reached. Now plant your flag firmly and go back and enjoy the fruits and fame of your labour!" "I was puzzled. I looked up. The top of the mountain was good 10 to 20 metres above. I hadn't reached the top yet. The voice became shriller and started to beg, abuse, cajole and persuade me to stop and return and even started creating pictures in my mind as to what would happen if I slipped or suffered frost bite or my gas mask developed a leak." "I somehow managed to shut out this incessant negative voice and millimeter by millimeter covered the last few metres, which almost felt like eternity until with a fierce sense of exultation, I realised that I was on top of Mount Everest and there I reverently planted my flag. I did not overcome that mountain. I overcame myself." Determination and undaunting courage took Edmund Hillary to the formidable summit of Mount Everest.

• Jack Canfield was a motivational speaker who conducted workshops for 30 years by narrating stories across the United States. It just occurred to him one day to write all those stories down. He shared his idea with Mark Victor Hansen and they decided to pool their resources and compile a book. They eventually grouped their contributions according to topic and chose a catchy title. When they approached the publishers to publish the same, in the first month alone, thirty-three of New York's biggest publishing houses turned them down. The enthusiastic authors were told, "Anthologies don't sell." "We don't think there is a market for this book." "The book is too positive." "It's not topical enough." In all, they were rejected by 140 publishers. To top it off, their agent said, "I can't sell this book; I'm giving it back to you guys". But nothing could deter Canfield and Hansen from their ambitions. Finally in 1993, a small publishing house in Florida agreed to publish the book. The rest is history. The first book sold over 2 million copies and launched the series, popularly known as *Chicken Soup Series*. Canfield and Hansen succeeded in producing more than 100 titles in this series, each directed at a specific group of people. There are now over 100 million copies in print and in 54 languages world-wide.

• Winston Churchill is one of the most scintillating leaders the world has known. In his high school, he failed the sixth grade. He took three years to get through the eighth grade because he had trouble learning English. However, that never stopped him from working harder! Doesn't it sound ironic that years later, Oxford University asked him to address its commencement exercises? Churchill was subsequently defeated in every election for public office until he became the Prime Minister of the United Kingdom at the age of 62 during the Second World War. His greatest contributions came when he was a senior citizen. He later wrote, "Never give in – in nothing, great or small, large or petty – Never, Never, Never, Never give up". In a poll conducted by the BBC in 2002 to identify the 100 Greatest Britons, participants voted Churchill as the greatest of all. This master statesman stood against fascism and renewed the world's faith in the superiority of democracy.

• Powdered coffee, shaving cream, plastics, paper, shampoo, milk, cream, synthetic rubber, beverages, mental polishes... all these products and hundreds more can be extracted from the peanut and the man responsible for all these is George Washington Carver. Carver's parents were slaves. His father died right before George was born, then while he was still a baby, slave traders kidnapped him and his mother. He taught himself to read. His family was so poor that he couldn't afford to buy a pencil; so he made a holder and used a pencil that was only one-fourth inch long. When he was 12 years old, Carver left home to attend a black school. While other children played at recess, he would study. Carver was denied admission to Highland University because of his race. He did many things to earn money to pay for his expenses; sometimes he ironed the clothes for his classmates. He found an old stove at the city dump and brought it home to cook meals for his friends. He used old wrapping paper for notebooks. Rising from slavery to become one of the world's most respected and honoured scientists, Carver had this to say, "99 per cent of the failures happen to people who have the habit of making excuses".

• When Julius Caesar sailed across the Channel from Gaul and landed with his legions in what is now England, he issued a challenge to his soldiers. He lined them up along the chalk cliffs of Dover and boldly announced that they had no option but to fight for victory or face death. There was no returning back. Looking down the waves 200 feet below, the soldiers could see every one of the ships that had carried them across the Channel – completely ablaze. They were stranded in the enemy's country and their last means of retreat was going up in smoke. So, they have no option but to fight with every ounce of their strength and gained victory.

• CN Janaki was the first ever differently abled person who swam the English Channel in 1992 in a relay team; she was afflicted with the disease of polio when she was only two years old. She suffered from polio on both of her legs. She with her might and grit proved to the world that you do not need to have legs to swim. Though she suffered from polio on both her legs, she successfully swam the English Channel and made her relay team proud. She is famously known for this feat, which was previously believed to be impossible. "My fight" said Janaki "in the course of the swim was against nature. The Channel waters were so cold that I needed much more energy than usual to keep my arms moving. Then I had the problem of my legs moving to the left or to the right, whichever way the waves were moving. So I really needed a lot of energy. The water was very salty and when it entered my mouth I felt sick. And then there were the seaweeds and jelly fish. These fish kept sticking to my body and I felt very uncomfortable". This is the story of real grit and determination.

Invictus

Out of the night that covers me,
Black as the pit from pole to pole,
I thank whatever gods may be,
For my unconquerable soul.

In the fell clutch of circumstance,
I have winced but not cried aloud.
Under the bludgeoning of chance,
My head is bloodied but unbowed.

Beyond this place of wrath and tears,
Looms but the horror of the shade.
And yet the menace of the years,
Finds, and shall find me, unafraid.

It matters not how straight the gate,
How charged with punishments the scroll,
I am the aster of my fate,
I am the captain of my soul.

—William Earnest Henley

6.3 Be Mad after Your Dream

There is a popular adage that says, "Excess of everything is bad". Excess in everything may be bad but "Excess in some positive things is good". Instead of the word 'excess' I would like to use the word *'obsess'*. The word 'obsess' may sound negative for many but to my mind it sounds very positive. Obsession with a positive goal leads to perfection and obsession with a negative goal leads to perfect destruction. I know a friend of mine who was so obsessed with playing the guitar. His interest was pulled to the extremes. He could play the whole day and half the night and forgets all other things. He would doze off and yet his fingers were still active on the truss rod and today he plays perfectly. The world has advanced in different fields because of *obsessive people*. Thomas Edison was obsessed with his scientific research, Einstein was also obsessed with the study of the universe, and Mother Teresa was obsessed with the poor. When people are able to remark that "you are mad with dance", blessed are you, for you are on the path to perfection. The word "MAD" shows your passion. Passion is not a mere interest but the summit of enthusiasm. Passion does not lead you but DRIVES or IMPELS you. So, we need to be MAD after our dreams. Your dream is the *idée fixe*, an idea that dominates the mind or that which you are obsessed with. Chase your dream *tout de suite* with a certain amount of madness and you will see miracles taking place. Be fearless in the race.

The word *Meraki* is often used by modern Greeks to describe doing something with soul, creativity or love. It means you put something of yourself into what you are doing whatever it may be. There is an English word that has the same semantic connotation with *meraki*, which is *Linchpin*. *Meraki* would be the act of doing something you love and *Linchpin* would be the person who is doing the thing one loves. The word *Linchpin* is used by Seth Godin in his book *"Linchpin"*. The word *Meraki* must be supported by another word of Greek origin *Palinoia* which means the obsessive repetition of an act until it is perfected or mastered. This is what you need to do if you want to realise your dream.

> M.S. Oberoi is undoubtedly the father of Indian hotel industry. As a young man, he dreamed of starting a five star hotel that would be counted among the best in the world. But it was a dream far removed from reality because he had only just a few coins in his pocket. As the immediate question before him was that of survival, he decided to find a job. When he saw the Sezil Hotel just in front of him, he got in to meet the General Manager. Oberoi directly went to the Manager's cabin and told him that he was interested in working at the hotel. But he knew only typing and shorthand. Unfortunately, there was no vacancy for that post in the office. But he was not ready to give up. He said, "I'll do anything you tell me. I can go to the market to buy groceries. I can..." After a thought, Oberoi was given a job in the hotel. His

presence changed the hotel within a few days. He succeeded in cutting down the expenses. He made the service better. And soon he was given a promotion. Later he was appointed the Assistant General Manager of the Carlton Hotel in Shimla. Earnest Clark was the owner of this hotel. When Clark left for England, Oberoi became the manager as well as the business partner of Clark. Soon he became the sole owner of Carlton Hotel and later he became the owner of a chain of hotels in India and abroad all through his own sheer efforts. Mr. Oberoi is the recipient of many prestigious national and international awards and accolades. He is a man who was in a way crazy after his dream and he worked on it and realised it.

Everything is easy, when you are CRAZY about it.
And nothing is easy, when you are LAZY about it.

6.4 Be Committed

Success is the result of thought and decision. Once you have decided, stick to it, come what may! This is called commitment. Commitment is being true to what you say, promise and decide. It is telling yourself, "I have decided and I will not change and I am willing to face the consequences of my decision and I will be faithful to it till the end." Commitment is being faithful in spite of difficulties and problems on the way to achieving your goal. Here is the story of the great automobile emperor Soichiro Honda, the founder of the famous Honda Company:

Soichiro Honda is a Japanese industrialist who made history in the automobile world. He is the eldest son of a blacksmith who repaired bicycles. The young Honda had only an elementary school education when, in his teens, he left home to seek his fortune in Tokyo. An auto repair company hired him but for a year he was forced to serve as a baby-sitter for the auto shop's owner and his wife. He was also a failure in his career as a car racer. Honda was turned down by Toyota Motor Corporation during a job interview. He continued to be jobless until his neighbours started buying his 'home-made scooters'. Subsequently, he set out to start his own company '*Honda*' by building motorised bicycles with small, war-surplus engines. Over the years the company has grown to become the world's leading manufacturer of motorcycles and today one of the leading automakers. Honda created a motor vehicle industry when it was considered impossible. The time was the turn of the century, when Ford, Peugeot and Daimler were created. Japan had its own established giants and they wanted no new competitors. By mid-century, one man could no longer create such a manufacturing empire but Honda somehow made himself their equal. He learned to regard failures as necessary steps towards understanding. "Success represents the one per cent of your work that results from the 99 per cent that is called failure", are the words of Honda. His life is a true example of true commitment in spite of umpteen failures.

Interest and Commitment

There is a chasm between interest and commitment. When you're interested in doing something, you do it as long as that interest is alive and once that interest dies you stop doing it. But when you're committed to something, you do it whether you have interest or not. You no longer depend on interest or mood. You do it because you have to do it. In other words, you are committed to it. Your commitment does not allow you to obey the promptings of ennui, boredom, disinterest, lethargy etc. No mood dependency.

I will win
Not immediately
But DEFINITELY

6.5 Be Responsible

Taking responsibility means "I am responsible for my present stage of life. I have to make myself what I want to be. I don't blame anyone for the present state of my life. Some people who don't want to take responsibility often say, "If my family were rich, my life could have been different or if my Dad were clever, I would have been better". They follow the *theory of disability* or *situation transfer*. This is transfer of one's disability to someone else or some situations in the past. Blaming or projecting one's failure to someone or some situations will not help you to improve your life. It is just shirking one's responsibility.

Tell yourself *"I am 100 per cent responsible for my life"*. In your life do not blame anyone for your troubles because that does not solve anything. Sure, at first it might seem reasonable to expect your problems to be solved by those who helped create them but stop and think about it. Do you want to give the people who created past problems for you any additional control over your future? You must move your life forward, be willing to take full responsibility for it. That means moving past what is easy and accepting that you are going to have to do things for yourself. Perhaps life has given you a burden you don't deserve. Instead of seeing this as an excuse to give up, see it as an opportunity to take charge and give it all you have got. You are stronger and more capable than you think you are.

Responsibility is a character quality that needs to be developed if you plan to succeed in life. It is not an inborn trait. Nearly, everyone has a natural tendency to skip the hard parts in life. It is easier to let someone else do it than it is to roll up our sleeves and do it ourselves. Every successful venture begins with someone who says, "That's my work, I'm responsible." This person accepts responsibility for their own actions and for the actions of others too.

Do you have interest in medicine, engineering, computer, politics or sports? Start small. Do your homework. Do your job sincerely, study your subjects and so on. The habits you form today will be stepping stones of success and reward tomorrow. Take responsibility for your life and your dream. Tell yourself that you are sorely responsible for the realisation of your dream. Others can act only as facilitators and ultimately you have to weave your own destiny.

6.6 Be Courageous and Take Risk

> *"Whatever you can do, or dream you can do, begin it. Boldness has genius, power and magic."*
>
> *—Johan Von Goethe*

True courage is pursuing your dream even when everyone says 'it is impossible for you to reach'. The more that you are able to let all of your inhibitions go and the more that you are able to say goodbye to fear and greet risk and courage with a passionate hug, the more you will be able to do throughout your life as a whole. Getting to your dream is a daily practice. Not everyone is strong enough to work hard towards one's goals on a daily habitual basis and not everyone will. Only those who dare and are willing to keep dreaming and only those who are willing to keep climbing towards their dreams will be the ones who are able to do. Remember the Latin aphorism: *fortis cadere, cedere non potest* (the brave man may fall, he cannot yield). This is why dreamers, real dreamers can do more because they dare. You must not only keep dreaming; you must also constantly keep working towards your dream. Here is the story of Dhirubhai Ambani, the business tycoon who dares to build a Reliance empire in the business world beginning with nothing.

> Dhirubhai Ambani rose from the lowest rungs of the society in Gujarat, who rewrote India's industrial destiny in a manner no man has done in any democracy. Born as the son of a school teacher in rural Gujarat, Dhirubhai Ambani failed to pass his school exams in the first attempt and earned his first money as a child selling snacks to pilgrims over weekends. His early years were relatively unremarkable. A job with an Indian trading company took him to Aden and he moved on from there to work for Shell, as a petrol pump attendant. Later Ambani took the form of a small-

trader in the Mulji-Jetha Textile Market, Mumbai. Slowly his business expanded to other places but life was tough. Kokilaben, his wife writes: "*During all those years, I had never seen him in a miserable or a desperate state of mind. That does not mean he never faced difficulties. But when engulfed by difficulty, he used to resolve it with courage and imagination*". "*Pursue your goals even in the face of difficulties and convert adversities into opportunities*", says the undergraduate business genius. Ambani's great achievement is a demonstration of what an Indian can achieve in the international arena. With no Oxford or Yale degree and with no family capital, he built an ultramodern, profitable and global enterprise in the international forum. Today, he can be called as *the Asian Tiger*.

Courage is not something that you see only in Bruce Willis movies. It's a down-to-earth virtue that you need in order to excel in life. If you believe in something, sooner or later that belief will be challenged. That is where you exhibit courage. A dream chaser needs courage because one has to traverse through the rugged terrain and sail through the rough waves. If you don't stand courageously for something, you will fall for anything. This holds true in life. Be a person who has strong values and then stick to those values.

"Take risks in your life.
If you win, you can lead.
If you lose, you can guide."

—*Swami Vivekananda*

Courage is not something that is loaned from others. It comes from a person's inner strength. It springs from the conviction that a person adheres to. It is the strength to say "no" when it does not tally with your convictions. Courage is the ability and inner stamina to face any risk on the way to realising your dream.

"*Ergo primam tollo, nominor quoniam leo;*
Secundam, quia sum fortis, tribuetis mihi;
Tum, quia plus valeo, me sequetur tertia;
Malo afficietur, si quis quartam tetigerit."

(I take the first share because I am called lion;
The second share you will give me because I am brave.
The third will come to me because I am more powerful.
If anyone touches the fourth he will suffer for it!
This is the lion's argument in robbing his
three partners of their share of booty).

In the same way, to achieve your dream you need to recognise the lion in you. You need to be BRAVE and be MORE POWERFUL than others. Once you recognise these essential elements you are bound to get what you want in life.

- When David Livingstone was working in Africa, a group of friends wrote to him: "We would like to send other men to you. Have you found a good road into your area yet?" Dr. Livingstone sent this message in reply: *"If you have men who will only come if they know there is a good road, I don't want them. I want men who will come if there is no road at all"*. A lot of courage is required in order to take the road that is not trodden because it involves risks. Without taking risks nothing great is ever achieved in life. Great achievements and discoveries are the result of great risks taken by courageous people. You don't need courage to take the road that has already been trodden.

- Steven Spielberg is one of the most successful film directors of our times. His films have been so popular and so consistently entertaining that people rush to see anything tagged as 'A Steven Spielberg Production', or even the movies he merely financed. Growing up as an awkward and lonely child, Spielberg took solace in movies. During his childhood, he dropped out of junior high school. He was persuaded to come back and was placed in a learning-disabled class. He only lasted a month and then dropped out of school forever. Unlike many of his contemporaries, Spielberg did not attend a major university film programme and was thus, largely self-taught. Spielberg applied to U.S.C. film school but was rejected at three different times. At 16, Spielberg fashioned his first film '*Firelight*' – a two-hour science fiction movie that a local movie house consented to run for one evening. That was his humble beginning against the numerous odd he was confronted with. Who can forget the spellbinding first glimpse of the living dinosaurs in Jurassic Park by Spielberg? If not for anything else his films were landmarks in special effects, both in their visual and aural aspects and they additionally possessed an uncanny knack for eliciting the response of the audience. Spielberg has bagged three Oscars and he ranks as one of the world's top motion picture directors. He is a man who has the courage to pursue his dream in spite of his personal academic inadequacies.

- William Somerset Maugham was an English playwright, a novelist and short story writer. He was one of the most popular authors of his era and reputed the highest paid in his profession during the 1930s. At the age of 10, Maugham was orphaned. His boyhood was blighted by insecurities including a stammer that forced him to withdraw from most social interaction– this was the undercurrent motivating force for Maugham to become an observer of life and an author. What strikes is the manner in which Maugham eked out fame and fortune from his stammer. At the age of 86, still speaking rather stammering, he says, "What has influenced my life more than any other single thing has been my stammer. Had I not stammered I would probably have gone to Cambridge as my brothers did, perhaps have become a don and every now and then published a dreary book about French literature." Maugham had a tremendous courage to transform a crippling adversity into a creative advantage. This world-renowned literary giant has more than twenty books, thirty plays and scores of short stories and essays to his credit. Many of his novels, short stories and plays have been adapted into movies.

- Sir Ernest Shackelton's expedition to the South Pole in 1915 is a story of a daring adventure. A voyage of such magnitude, uncertainty and risk required a special crew of tough and sterner stuff. To recruit his men, Shackelton placed a tiny advertisement in the *London Times*: "*Wanted: Persons for dangerous journey. Small wages, bitter cold, long months of complete darkness, constant danger, safe return doubtful, honour and recognition if successful*". There was an overwhelming response. Sir Ernest had to select twenty-eight out of over five thousand applicants. They sailed in his ship called *Endurance*, facing innumerable hardships but eventually returning heroes.

6.7 Take the Offensive

As you pursue your dream you need to be made of a sterner stuff. You need to chase your dream aggressively and offensively. This will clear your way to realise your treasured dream. Here is a true incident narrated by Robert H. Schuller, author of the international best-seller " *Tough Times Never Last, But Tough People Do!*" He says,

> When I was visiting Gautemala, I was escorted by a brilliant young man in his early thirties who holds a dual passport to Gautemala and the United States. He shared with me his concern for the country. He said, 'Dr. Schuller, Christianity is losing the battle in Gautemala because they're fighting defensively. All of the missionaries have fled. They are afraid of being kidnapped and held for ransom by the Communists or of being shot down by terrorists. There is no way we can win the fight without changing our tactics from defensive to offensive. He continued, 'Did you know that I served in Vietnam?'
>
> I answered, 'No. I was not aware of that.'
>
> Then he shared with me this fascinating story. He was an officer in Vietnam, assigned to keeping one area clear of the enemy. Every day he and his men would have to go into the jungle. Every day he saw a casualty or two, even though he approached all battles cautiously.

One day his commanding officer, a colonel visited. He said, 'Lieutenant, how are you doing? Are you keeping the area clear of the enemy?'

My young friend replied, 'I think I'm doing quite well, sir.'

The Colonel took a look at the lieutenant's casualty count. He shook his head and said, 'There are some losses here.' Then he looked at the lieutenant and said, 'Do you know what you're doing wrong?'

'No, Sir.'

He said, 'You're trying to hold and clear the territory, but you're trying to avoid all contact with the enemy.'

'That's correct, Sir. I don't want to lose my men. Every life is very valuable, Sir.'

The Colonel said, 'Don't tell me that. I know that! Look, you are trying to hold the territory; you're not trying to conquer the territory. You're fighting defensively. I'm giving you a command now to go out there and contact the enemy at any time and any point you can.'

My young friend looked at his commander and said, 'Sir, with all due respect, may God help my men. I don't know how many lives I'd lose.'

But the Colonel only looked firmly at the young man and said, 'That's a command! With that he got into his helicopter. The blades whirled slowly, then faster and faster. As he took off, the lieutenant looked at his staff sergeant who had heard the whole conversation. He said, 'Sergeant, did you hear that? That colonel must be a crazy man. "Go out there and contact the enemy!" How many bodies will I have to count tomorrow night?'

The sergeant said, 'Sir, may I say something? With all due respect, I think the colonel is right. Look at how many casualties we've had this past month.'

The lieutenant said, 'Well, if you think he's right and if the colonel is commanding me, I guess I have no choice but to change my strategy.'

The next morning they went on the offensive. There were several casualties. The second day they plunged deeper and took more casualties than they usually had in an average week. But on the fourth day there were no casualties. The fifth day they went deeper into the jungle. Again there were no casualties. The sixth day they penetrated as far as they could and still there were no casualties. On the seventh and eighth days they couldn't even find the enemy. The lieutenant said to the sergeant, 'What happened to the enemy?'

The sergeant replied, 'Sir, I think the enemy has gone off to fight somebody who's fighting on the defensive.'

In chasing your dream you need to take the offensive.

6.8 Be Prepared

"*The future belongs to those who prepare for it today.*"

—*Malcolm X*

Scouting has been a great creation but greater still was the mind that created it. His full name was Sir Robert Stevenson Smith Baden Powell. He is known to the world affectionately as BP. The very motto of the Scouts "BE PREPARED" is in fact the expansion of BP's own initials. It means under any circumstances peace or war, life or death, "*Be Prepared.*"

The two words of the Scout's motto are invaluably down to earth practical words which you can execute in the process of chasing after your dream or goal. Preparation is a condition *sine qua non* for successful and fruitful living. A student who does not prepare for his examination is bound to fail. So is the person who does not prepare for his life examination is bound to fail in life. It is a hard and painstaking process. Only a prepared person will be ready. Many people from the high pinnacle of joy sink into abysmal dejection because they have failed to learn the art of preparing themselves. A prepared person is a ready person. Such a person is ready to face anything that comes on his way. The hardest realities of life can be faced boldly and without fear and even happily with satisfaction if one is prepared to meet them.

Another word for preparation is planning. To reach our goal we need to PLAN AHEAD. If you want to go to your friend's house, you just don't go out the front door and stand to take you there. You make some preparations. You think about the meeting time, transportation, what you're going to wear, and the route you're going to take. You plan ahead. Stan Toler has given us the PLAN AHEAD formula:

P – Pray. Ask God for wisdom and direction.

L – List the things that need to be accomplished.

A – Acquire the information and resources you need to do the job.

N – Notice what others have done in similar situations.

A – Ask advice from some experts.

H – Heed your inner voice. Use caution if you feel uneasy.

E – Expect adversity and plan to overcome it.

A – Act decisively. Once you make your decision, stick to it and go for it.

D – Do your best and leave the rest to God.

With little preparation, you can work smarter and more effectively and worry less about what needs to be done. Preparation gives birth to inspiration and inspiration in turn leads to aspiration and aspiration couple with perspiration arrives at a destination.

> ***"One important key to success is self-confidence. An important*** *key to self-confidence is preparation."*
>
> — *Arthur Ashe*

Fear is the result of not being prepared for a task. A student who does not prepare for his or her exam will certainly be stricken with fear. But fear is a positive thing. It is a warning bell that rings within you and alerting you to get ready in at once, to face an event or circumstance. If there is no fear that acts as an alarm bell, many people would have been unprepared in life. Fear points to something worth that you can achieve if you pay heed in advance. C. Joy Bell C says:

> *"I tell people not to be afraid of their fears; because their fears are not there to scare them, they're there to let them know that something is worth it. Yet I am often afraid. I guess that means in my life, lots of things have been worth it!"*

Remember the Latin phrases: *Semper paratus* (always ready) and *nunquam non paratus* (never be unprepared).

6.9 Be a Person with a Plus Factor

Norman Vincent Peale in his famous book *"Power of the Plus Factor"* speaks about people with the Plus Factor. He says that the Plus Factor is:

- The quality of *extra*-ness that we see in certain people.
- People who live with more eagerness, more energy, more enthusiasm than others.
- Who set higher goals and achieve them more often.
- Who keep going despite adversity and hardship.
- Who shrug off misfortune and give out warmth and caring and encouragement wherever they go.
- People, in short, who have, in themselves, a marvelous Plus Factor at work.

The Plus Factor is a potential but it is not self-activating. It is latent in human beings and will remain latent until it is activated. As a student, you need to cultivate and tap the Power of the Plus Factor in order to achieve your dream. Activate the Plus Factor and this will be an immense source of strength and energy that will take you to the summit you want to ascend.

6.10 The Mother Teresa Principle

Mother Teresa once said, "*We are not called to be successful but to be faithful*". This saying holds true in life too. Mother Teresa is not against success. What she wants to tell us is that we should not crave or work for the sake of success. One must be detached from the motive and concentrate on the present task. Mother Teresa is in fact showing us a sure way to success, i.e., FAITHFULNESS. If we work faithfully, someday we will surely succeed. If we want to be successful tomorrow, we need to work hard *faithfully* today. If we want to achieve our goal, we need to perform faithfully our daily tasks that will eventually lead to the attainment of our goal. Being faithful to the task will determine your success. Without being faithful, you can't succeed.

6.11 Diligent Hard Work

Hard work devoid of diligence is a wasted energy. Hard work needs to be qualified by the adjective 'diligent'. According to Oxford Advanced Learner's Dictionary the word 'diligent' means showing care and effort in one's work. The word 'diligent' therefore means *careful*. What is important here is the word 'careful'. If you are not careful you can waste a lot of your energy. A person can be very hard working but fruitless. What is important is not the quantity of hard work but the amount of DELIGENCE that you put in your work that will decide the size of your success. For example, a student who studies with diligence and a student who studies without diligence will produce different results. The first one knows what to study, how to study, and when to study etc. The second student without knowing what, how and when to study may labour blindly on one particular subject all the time which he likes. Certainly the latter is hard working but lacks diligence. Now you can guess the result! Hard work alone will not produce the expected or desired result. It has to be qualified by the adjective 'diligent'. As a student you may not be the best in your class. Your IQ (Intelligence Quotient) may be lower than the first rank holder but you can compete him in EFFORT and DELIGENT HARDWORK. You can even outdo him in effort. The output of two persons who have the same IQ will be different. The one who puts more effort and diligence in their work will still do better.

- Charles Darwin, the man who propounded the *Theory of Evolution* by Natural Selection was sent to study medicine but seeing the brutality of surgery, he neglected his studies. Eventually he gave up his medical career and was told by his father, "You care for nothing but shooting dogs and rat catching". In his autobiography, Darwin wrote, "I was considered by all my masters and by my father, to be a very ordinary boy, rather below the common standard of intellect". Later, his revolutionary ideas on evolution sparked controversy and shed light on many unanswered questions that the scientific community had about the subject during the nineteenh century. Darwin was vehemently attacked by the

Church because his theory was opposed to creationism, a theory held by the Church. However, being a strong man, Darwin stood by his ideas. Today, the world has accepted his position and acknowledged it as one of the greatest discoveries.

• He was short and sharp, the brightest boy in his class. He came from a poor but educated family. Like all the boys in his class, he was trying to get admission into some engineering college. There was an entrance test for IIT. This boy, along with his friends applied to appear for the test. He did not have any special books or coaching to prepare himself. He was then only sixteen years old. The IIT entrance results came. He had passed with flying colours and the highest rank. He went to his father who was reading a newspaper, "Anna, I have passed the exam. I want to join IIT." His father stopped reading the paper. He lifted his head, looked at the boy and said with a heavy voice, "You know our financial position; I cannot afford your expenses at IIT. You can stay in Mysore (Karnataka) and learn as much as you want." His heart bled but he did not get angry with anyone. Later he said to himself, "All students from the IITs study well and do big things in life. But it is not the institution; ultimately it is you and you alone who can change your life by hard work." And he began his journey with determination despite many hardships on his way. This son of a school teacher became a pioneer of India's software industry. He is none other than N R Narayana Murthy, an Indian industrialist, software engineer and the founder of *Infosys Technologies*, a global IT services company which employs more than 70,000 people worldwide. In November 2006, the *Time* magazine featured him in its list of 'Asian Heroes'. Mr Murthy's motto is: 'Powered by intellect, Driven by Values'.

• Mahatma Gandhi says, "I claim to be an average man of less than average ability. I have not the shadow of a doubt that any man or woman can achieve what I have, if he or she would make the same effort and cultivate the same hope and faith".

• Michaelangelo says, "If people knew how hard I had to work to gain my mastery, it wouldn't seem wonderful at all". Napoleon Bonaparte had the capacity for incessant hard work to the extent of 18 hours a day. His brain was never idle. He had an unbounded faith in his abilities. He once said, "Impossible is not a French word." John Milton, the famous Victorian poet described his life at school and says: "My father destined me from a child to the pursuits of literature and my appetite for knowledge was so voracious that from 12 years of age, I hardly ever left my studies or went to bed before midnight."

• This was how Theodor Lenek discovered stethoscope: One day a woman with a heart complain was brought to the hospital where Theodor Lenek was working. In those days doctors were checking the heart beat of a patient by keeping their ear close to the chest of patients. When Lenek tried to check the woman this way, she demurred. Lenek therefore, took a sheet of paper, rolled it into a pipe and kept one end close to the chest of the patient, the other end he kept close to his ear and did the checking. This gave Lenek the idea of stethoscope. Behind every discovery there is often a story of hardships and sacrifices.

• Premchand's wife scolded him for working hard in spite of his failing health. The famous Hindi author replied: "The duty of the lamp is to spread light. Whether this benefits or harms others is no concern of the lamp. So long as there is oil and a wick in it, it will go on doing its duty. And when the oil runs out, it will go out." Premchand died the following year, leaving his last novel unfinished. There is no surrogacy for hard work.

• Between 1902 and 1907, Rabindranath Tagore lost his wife Mrinalini, his father Debendranath, his daughter Renuka and his youngest son, Samindranath. The experience of sadness, solitude and reflection gave birth to his famous *Gitanjali* which was published in 1910.

• "The average person puts only 25 per cent of his energy and ability into his work. The world takes off its hat to those who put in more than 50 per cent of their capacity and stands on its head for those few and far between souls who devote 100 per cent".

— *Andrew Carnegie*

• Difficult does not mean impossible; it simply means you have to try harder.

• A famous athlete said, "I can't sleep when I see my competitor practicing, I can't even sleep when he is sleeping, because that is the only time to practice and move ahead!"

Never hide from struggle because through struggle you come to know that you are living a real life. Remember the words of Friedrich Nietzsche, "One must still have chaos within oneself to give birth to a dancing star."

6.12 A Positive Attitude towards Failure

Whenever you fail, remember that you are not the first one to fail. There are thousands of people who have failed before you but there are some who defied against their failure and left their footprints in the sands of time. They never gave up. If you give up, you are a coward!

There is a guaranteed prognostication that holds true in life: "You will fail and everyone fails". But failure is not the end. It is the beginning of a new strategy. Remember, if you FAIL, it means 'First Attempt in Learning' and not the end of everything. END means Effort Never Dies. Therefore, First Attempt can never be the END. It is only the first attempt and you need to put more effort. And if you get NO as an answer. Then, remember NO is "Next Opportunity". Alphabet "O" stands for "Opportunity" which is absent in "Yesterday". Available only Once in "Today" and Thrice in "Tomorrow". Always put an effort. Never give up!

Failure has an element of inevitability and forms part of human existential factuality. The worst response to failure is to become discouraged or even worse, to quit. Be courageous and never allow *atychiphobia* to grip you. Atychiphobia is the abnormal, unwarranted and persistent fear of failure. As with many phobias, atychiphobia often leads to a constricted lifestyle and is particularly devastating for its effects on a person's willingness to attempt certain activities. A person afflicted with atychiphobia considers the possibility of failure so intense that they choose not to take the risk.

Some of your failures will be small. You fail to be in time for class and you are being upbraided by your teacher. Such experience will teach you to manage your time well. Some other failures can be painful. You fail to keep a promise to someone you care about. That situation will hurt but you will discover the value of faithfulness and gain a life lesson. This is a positive way of looking at failure. Each failure is an opportunity to grow. Don't plan to fail but plan to learn from your mistakes. In her book *"Gateway to Hope"*, M. Boulding writes, "Learning to deal with failure is part of life; a necessary part for those who aspire to be human".

There is a Difference between the Person Who Fails and Failure

When you fail in an examination, you do not become a failure. You only have failed in that particular examination and you are not a failure. Remember, you have not failed in other areas of your life. Failing in one examination occupies only one small area. It is only a fractional failure. Many people tend to equate their fractional failure with failure in all other areas of their lives. Failing in one examination does not mean you have failed in all the examinations. It will be illogical and preposterous to accept fractional failure as a comprehensive failure. The worst attitude is to consider fractional failure as a comprehensive failure. Once this attitude grips you, there is no room for trying again. The upshot will be: you will begin to sink into despondency which will never allow you to get up again.

The Tree

The tree that never had to fight –
For sun and air and light
That stood out in the open plain
And always got its share of rain
Never became a forest king
But lived and died a scrubby things
The man who never had to toil
Who never had to win his share
Of sun and sky and light and air
Never became a manly man
But lived and died as he began

—Douglas Mallock

Remember, you are not the first one to fail. There are so many people who failed before you but they never gave up. Let us see some of them:

- George Bernard Shaw is one of the extraordinaire dramatists, literary critics and socialist spokespersons of the 20th century theatre. Shaw's childhood was marked by turbulence. His drunkard father took no care of his studies. In his regular schooling which ended when he was fifteen, Shaw was generally near the bottom of the class. At a young age, he was forced to take up the job of an office boy to run ordinary errands. Life did not seem promising to Shaw. He wrote novels and faced utter failures. He then took to art, music, critical reviews, etc., and nothing offered him a reason to smile. "When I was young I observed that nine out of every ten things I did were failures, so I did ten times more work," says spirited Shaw. His first novel *Immaturity* was turn down by eleven publishers. Finally, Shaw tried drama and that clicked. As a dramatist, Bernard Shaw could climb the zenith and obtain the highest award, the Nobel Prize. "The people who get on in this world are the people who get up and look for the circumstances they want and if they can't find them, make them," Shaw said this and proved it in his life.
- A phenomenal athlete with a unique combination of grace, speed, power, artistry, improvisational ability and an unquenchable competitive spirit, Michael Jordan single-handedly redefined the NBA superstardom. Basketball might have been in his genes but Jordan had to work very hard to grow to his full potential. He was cut from his high school basketball team and was told that he was too small and not good enough. After that Michael Jordan went home, locked himself in his room and wept bitterly. But later he

became one of the most successful basketball players in the world. This is what he said later in his life, "I have missed more than 9000 shots in my career. I've lost almost 300 games. 26 times, I've been trusted to take the game winning shot and missed. I've failed over and over and over again in my life. And that is why I succeed". The number of records that Jordan holds will boggle the minds of even the most seasoned mathematics wizard. His ability to rise above his peers and competitors is captured by his statement, "Body could stand the crutches but my mind couldn't stand the sideline".

• Robert J. Sternberg is one of the greatest American psychologists. Sternberg has proposed a *Triarchic Theory of Intelligence* and a *Triangular Theory of Love* which are very popular. Sternberg's interest in studying intelligence first peaked in the sixth grade after suffering from text anxiety and failing an intelligence test. He received a 'C' in his first college introductory psychology class. His teacher commented that there was a famous Sternberg in psychology and it was obvious there would not be another. At university Sternberg dropped out of psychology because of his poor grades and switched to mathematics. But later, with determination and hard work he graduated with honours from Stanford University with exceptional distinction in psychology, summa cum laude. In 2002, Sternberg became President of the American Psychological Association. Sternberg published 750 books and articles in the fields of intelligence, creativity and love.

• As growing boys, the Wright Brothers flew kites just as every other boy had done. But they drew some valuable knowledge from their kites. Finally, they concluded after discussion and experimentation that a man could be kept aloft on the principles of flying kite, if an engine could be developed that would sustain the flying kite. Their idea was scoffed at by others. But they kept working on their idea. In *The New York Times* in September 1903 two physics professors explained why airplanes could not possibly fly. The article appeared just three months before the Wright brothers split the air with their Kitty Hawk. *The New York Times* editorial on December 10, 1903 questioned the wisdom of the Wright Brothers who were trying to invent a machine heavier than air that would fly. One week later, at Kitty Hawk, the Wright Brothers took their famous flight. Flying kite was simply an idea conceived in the minds of the Wrights who had not even finished their high school. Believe it or not, they did not have a University degree in Aeronautical Engineering, Mathematics, Physics or any other subject. They were not scientists in the true sense of the word. A true example of translating dreams into reality.

- Albert Einstein was not able to speak until he was almost four years old and was not able to read until he was seven. His parents thought he was 'sub-normal' and one of his teachers described him as 'mentally slow, unsociable and adrift forever in foolish dreams". He was expelled from school and was refused admittance to the Zurich Polytechnic School. Einstein eventually learned to speak and read. He declared, "Do not worry about your difficulties in Mathematics. I can assure you, mine are still greater". He faced even more difficulties when it came to finding a job. But he persevered in all his attempts. Einstein has contributed more than any other scientist to the modern vision of physical reality. The touchstones of the modern era – the Bomb, the Big Bang, Quantum Physics and Electronics – all bear his imprint.
- Isaac Newton was the man who discovered the *Law of Gravity* which completely revolutionised our understanding of the Universe. Newton's father was a farmer who died shortly before his son was born. It was intended that Newton should carry on the paternal farm. The little Isaac was not expected to survive due to his bad health. It is said that he could be fitted into a quart pot. When Isaac was three, his mother remarried a rich man from the next village and went to live there, leaving Isaac behind with his grandmother. Isaac showed little promise in academic work. His school reports described him as 'idle' and 'inattentive'. His mother thought that her eldest son was the right person to manage her affairs and her estate. Isaac was taken away from school but soon showed that he had no talent or interest in managing an estate. He turned out to be a total failure as a farmer. Newton suffered from depression for most of his life and had two major emotional breakdowns. According to biographers that may be the reason for his reluctance to publish his work while he was alive. His accomplishments in Mathematics, Optics and Gravitation laid the foundation of modern science and revolutionised our understanding of the Universe.
- Thomas Alva Edison, one of the most famous and prolific inventors of all time has profoundly affected the modern life through inventions such as the incandescent light bulb, the phonograph and the motion picture camera. Edison's teachers said he was "too stupid to learn anything". He was thrown out of school when he was 12 because he was thought to be dumb. He was noted to be terrible at Mathematics, unable to focus and had difficulty with

words and speech. He was fired from his first two jobs for being 'non-productive.' Over the course of his career Edison patented 1,093 inventions. Edison believed in hard work, sometimes working twenty hours a day. He has been quoted as saying, "Genius is one per cent inspiration and 99 per cent perspiration." Every failure had become a stepping stone for Edison. In his attempt to invent the electric bulb he had failed hundreds of times. Still he could say smilingly, "I learnt 999 times how not to make an electric bulb..." In 1914, Edison lost two million dollars worth of equipments and the precious record of many years' work, when his laboratories were gutted by fire. The next morning, walking among the ashes of his hopes and dreams, aspirations and ambitions, the 67-year-old Edison said, "There is great value in disaster. All our mistakes get burnt down. Thank God, we can start anew."

- As a young cartoonist, Walt Disney faced many rejections from newspaper editors who said he "lacked imagination" and had "no original ideas". One day a minister at a church hired him to draw some cartoons. Disney was working out of a small rodent-infested shed near the church. Disney carefully observed the different movements of the mouse and began to draw them. That was the beginning of *Mickey Mouse*. Disney did not stop at drawing cartoons alone. He started his own small studio in a garage. His very first cartoon production went bankrupt. During his first press conference, a newspaper editor ridiculed Disney because he had no idea about film production. Today, Disney's company, known as *The Walt Disney Company* makes an average revenue of US $30 billion annually. The name Walt Disney is today synonymous with creativity and innovation. He won a record breaking 59 nominations to the Academy Award and was honoured with 29 Oscars.
- When he was forty-six years of age, Oscar Hammerstein had worked with thirty different composers. Nothing took off. There was no successful song. It was a despairing, dispiriting time for him. Finally, Oscar Hammerstein tied in with Richard Rodgers. The following year they wrote the musical Oklahoma. He was a success. In fact his success was so enormous in its impact that he went out and bought a full page ad in Variety magazine. To keep himself humble, he bought this headline: 'I've done it before and I can do it again!' he then listed every single one of his failures.

A man is not finished when he is defeated.
He is finished only when he quits.

- The Beatles were rejected by Decca Recording Studios, who said, "We don't like their sound" and "they have no future in show business".
- Steve Jobs at the age of 30 was left devastated and decompressed after being unceremoniously removed from the company he started.
- Oprah Winfrey was demoted from her job as a news anchor because she was considered "unfit for television".
- In 1982, JK Rowling, the famous author of Harry Potter series books appeared the entrance exams for the Oxford University but was not accepted. When she wanted to publish her first book on Harry Potter, 12 publishing companies rejected the manuscript. Today, she is the only author who has become a billionaire just from writing books.
- Margaret Mitchell's classic novel, *Gone with the Wind* was rejected by over 25 publishers. The general feeling was that the public was not interested in Civil War stories.
- The tragic failure of the British ship *Titanic*, which struck an iceberg in the North Atlantic killing at least 1,500 people, brought about at least one good effect: *The International Ice Patrol* was formed to prevent similar tragedies.

Just see where you belong:

"I won't" – is a tramp.
"I can't" – is a quitter.
"I don't know" – is lazy.
"I might" – is waking up.
"I will try" – is on her feet.
"I can" – is on her way.
"I will" – is at work.
"I did" – is now the boss

6.13 Build a Positive Weltanschauung

Stan Toler, an author and host of the television programme *"Leadership Today"* says, "We live in a battery-powered world. From your PDA to your MP3 player, the Energizer Bunny is working overtime. Batteries work great unless they're inserted in your electronic device the wrong way. They must be installed according to the positive and negative signs that are usually stamped on the device." This principle runs parallel in life. It doesn't work if you put negative where there should be a positive. A positive perspective always makes things work better. Positive people are energisers. You might also notice that they are usually in leadership positions.

Look for the best in every situation. There is always something to learn and there is something to share it with. Look for the best in others. Look past their faults to their finer characteristics. Look for the best in yourself. One of the best things you can do for yourself is to discover your goal and be positive that you will surely achieve one day. Be positively positive towards your goal and on the day of your achievement you will create a positive repercussion around you.

> Life is a matter of perspective (outlook). Two shoe salesmen were sent to Africa by a particular company to check the potential international market there. Like the two spies who returned to Joshua in the Old Testament after reviewing the Promised Land, the salesmen returned to their shoe company with their report. One salesman had a negative report. 'There is no market there', he said. 'Nobody wears shoes in Africa.' The positive salesman reported, 'On the contrary, it's a fantastic opportunity – no one has bought shoes yet!' So, life is a matter of positive outlook.

The opposite of positive outlook is negative outlook. One can look at the goal and say, "I think this is not meant for me or I can't." This indicates the person is already defeated before he even tries. Such an attitude can cripple a person all through his life and renders him as a perennial underachiever. The worst feeling that can bog down a person completely in life is the feeling of being defeated. This makes a person incapable of trying anything. Who told you that you are defeated? Be positive! One can remain undefeated even when one loses. Can I not win the person who wins me? Or Can I not defeat the person who defeats me? I can and you can. What is important is an attitudinal victory! Defeatism is an obnoxious incapacitator. Never allow it to control you. Never allow yourself to be defeated at least before you try. The way of the people who succeed in life are strewn with a series of failures. But they have accepted failures as stepping stones. Here is the story of a man who never succumbed to his failures:

> Richard M. Nixon was the 37th President of the United States really captivates me. Perhaps, he is one of the most fascinating political figures of the 20th century. Nixon was the son of a grocer. He grew up in a poor family. He nearly died twice as a child, the first time as a result of a head wound and the second time from pneumonia. Every morning before school, he would set up the display in his father's grocery store. Nixon's political career nearly came to an end after he was defeated for re-election as Governor of Carolina. He later ran for President against John F Kennedy but lost. It was thought that Nixon seemed too stuffy next to the

energetic and charismatic Kennedy. This too nearly stopped his career. But he did not succumb to these failures. He wrote a number of books and travelled widely. "A man is not finished when he is defeated. He is finished when he quits," goes the maxim by Richard M. Nixon.

Norman Vincent Peale in his book *The Power of Positive Thinking* relates this incident. He says:

A man 52 years of age consulted me. He was in great despondency. He revealed his utter despair. He said he "was all through." He informed me that everything he had built up over his lifetime had been swept away.

"Everything?" I asked.

"Everything," he repeated. He was through, he reiterated. "I have nothing left at all. Everything is gone. There is no hope and I am too old to start all over again. I have lost all faith."

Naturally, I felt sympathetic towards him, but it was evident that his chief trouble was the fact that dark shadows of hopelessness had entered his mind and discoloured his outlook, distorting it. Behind this twisted thinking his true powers had retreated, leaving him without force.

"So", I said, "suppose we take a piece of paper and write down the values you have left."

"That's no use", he sighed. "I haven't a single thing left. I thought I told you that."

I said, "Let's just see anyway." Then I asked, "Is your wife still with you?"

"Why, yes, of course and she is wonderful. We have been married for thirty years. She would never leave me no matter how bad things are."

"All right, let us put that down – your wife is still with you and she will never leave you no matter what happens. How about your children? Got any children?"

"Yes," he replied, "I have three and they are certainly wonderful. I have been touched by the way they have come to me and said, "Dad, we love you and we'll stand by you".

"Well, then," I said, "that is number two – three children who love you and who will stand by you. Got any friends?" I asked.

"Yes," he said, "I really have some fine friends. I must admit they have been pretty decent. They have come around and said they would like to help me, but what can they do? They can't do anything."

"That is number three – you have some friends who would like to help you and who hold you in esteem. How about your integrity? Have you done anything wrong?"

"My integrity is all right," he replied. "I have always tried to do the right thing and my conscience is clear."

"All right," I said, "we will put that down as number four – integrity. How about your health?"

"My health is all right," he answered. "I have had very few sick days and I guess I am in pretty good shape physically."

"So let's put down as number five – good physically health. How about the United States? Do you think it's still doing business and is the land of opportunity?"

"Yes", he said. "It is the only country in the world I would want to live in."

"That is number six – you live in the United States, land of opportunity and you are glad to be here." Then I asked, "How about your religious faith? Do you believe in God and that God will help you?"

"Yes", he said. "I do not think I could have gotten through this at all if I hadn't had some help from God."

"Now", I said, "Let's list the assets we have figured out:

"1. A wonderful wife–married for thirty years.

"2. Three devoted children who will stand by you.

"3. Friends who will help you and who hold you in esteem.

"4. Integrity–nothing to be ashamed of.

"5. Good physical health.

"6. Live in the United States, the greatest country in the world.

"7. Have religious faith."

I shoved it across the table at him. "Take a look at that. I guess you have quite a total of assets. I thought you told me everything had been swept away."

He grinned ashamedly. "I guess I didn't think of those things. I never thought of it that way. Perhaps things aren't so bad at that," he said pensively. "Maybe I can start all over again if I can just get some confidence, if I can get the feel of some power within me."

Well he got it and he did start all over again. But he did so only when he changed his viewpoint, his mental outlook. What this man failed to see was the positive remnants of his possessions which are more worth than what he has lost. He was so engrossed in what he has lost so much so that he forgot what he had.

In life, things turn out to be in topsy-turvy for those who meet with a series of defeat or failure. Believe that you can win against all odds. Rise up to your occasion and make the most out of your living. Understand and accept the fact that nothing can be changed but at least tell yourself that you can win against all odds. Know that there are many broken hearts like you, suffering, dependant and getting prone to sympathies of people day after day. Wake up! No, you don't need an injection of adrenaline to walk on your feet; just a NEVER SAY DIE attitude will suffice in order to turn things around. This is the attitude of those who win. They are never defeated even when they fail or lose. Feel that you have to lead a normal life even after knowing that you cannot. You have to tell your story to the human race and to the people ailing with their respective drawbacks and earning their daily sympathy and disappointment. Help your fellow beings, encourage them to live more, remember the trauma you have experienced, absorb it from those ailing in a similar fashion like you.

> Don't you know Lance Armstrong? He is a seven times *Tour de France* champion. He was diagnosed with testicular, brain and lung cancer in 1996. Only with minute chemotherapy, his ability to fight back and faith gave him the confidence to combat the disease and today he is a living example of one who survived Cancer. Lance declared himself not a cancer victim but a cancer survivor. The doctors told him he had no chance. However, a formidable combination of faith and grit took him to an almost incomprehensible seven times victory of the sport's premier event, the *Tour de France*. Indeed he said, "Cancer is the best thing that could have ever happened to me." He also established the *Yellow Ribbon Cancer Foundation* in the heart of United States helping thousands of people each year.

It is good to learn from the extraordinary efforts of ordinary people. Let your life be a new rung of the ladder to climb higher for those who feel that there is no more rung for their foothold to climb. Try to live for what you want to be and never give an opportunity to people trying to show some sort of sympathy towards you while pursuing your goal. Always remember, 'when the going gets tough, the tough gets going'. This will perpetually help you to fight against all obstacles. Amidst all the obstacles persistently focus on your goal. Know that the more the difficulty, the greater will be the success.

"People never change, only their perspectives,"

– *Sarah Crowder*

6.14 Budget Your Time

Time is free, but it's timeless.
You can't own it, but you can use it.

You can't keep it, but you can spend it.
Once you have lost it, you will never get back.

Thomas Alva Edison says, "Time is really the only capital that any human being has and the things he can least afford to waste or lose". Time is your most limited asset. You have only 24 hours in each day and 365 days in each year. You have no idea how many of those years are in the bank? Spend your time wisely. Each day consists of 1440 minutes. That is more than 10,000 minutes a week. This is a gift given to you. So, how are you going to spend your time today? Sleeping? That is about 480 minutes. Work? That is another 480 or so. What about the rest? Stan Toler says, "Imagine minutes were dollars. Would you watch television for four hours today if it cost you $240? Would you play video games for two hours if you had to rent the machine for $120?" Imagine if a second were to cost one dollar, I think nobody would dare to waste. If you waste an hour a day, you would be wasting $3,600. In a week, you would be wasting $25,200. In a month you would be wasting $7,56,000. In a year you would be wasting a whooping amount of $90,72,000. If you truly realise the value of time, you won't waste and yet one second is much more precious than one dollar. A dollar cannot buy time. In reality you just can't buy time because it is of immeasurable value.

Your minutes are more precious than your money. And your success depends largely on how you manage every minute of your time. Minutes are the building blocks of life. You can use them to construct whatever you want. But they can be also wasted. Remember! Wasted money can always be regained but wasted time is gone forever.

> "Time is given to us to be happy and for no other reason.When we waste time, we waste happiness."
>
> —*L. Frank Baum*

The clock is running. Make the best use of your time:

To realise the value of one year,
Ask a student who has failed his final exam.

To realise the value of one month,
Ask the parent of a premature baby.

To realise the value of one week,
Ask the editor of a weekly newspaper.

To realise the value of one day,
Ask a daily wage labourer who has a large family to feed.

To realise the value of one hour,
Ask lovers who are waiting to meet.

To realise the value of one minute,
Ask a person who has missed the train, the bus or a plane.

To realise the value of one second,
Ask a person who has survived an accident.

To realise the value of one millisecond,
Ask the person who has won a silver medal at the Olympics.

Budget your time just as you budget your money. Spend your time in the areas of highest priority. Plan your days – even your days off – so that even these can be a means of accomplishing what is most important in your life – your DREAM. Go minute by minute and it will lead you to your dream.

> "It is only when we truly understand that we have a limited time on earth that we will live each day to the fullest"
>
> —*Elizabeth Kubler Ross*

One of my favourite music artists and English songwriter is Llyod Cole who has a song that reminds us that 'time is a lot like an airplane, flying by too fast'. Therefore, don't blink and waste your time. Time slips through our fingers like grains of sand. Give your best at work and do all that you can because one day, your time will run out.

6.15 Concentrate on Your Dream

You need to use the "Magic Key" to unlock the doors of all positive things that will help you to attain your dream. Napoleon Hill in his book "*The Law of Success*" says that the "Magic Key" is nothing but "*concentration*". According to him, concentration means the ability, through fixed habit and practice, to keep your mind on one subject until you have thoroughly familiarised yourself with that subject and mastered it. In other words, it means the ability to *control your attention and focus it on your dream until you have achieved it.* Strength comes from concentration. When you focus on many things your energy gets dispersed and you are not able to garner your attention. Concentration allows your energy to flow in one direction and it flows with a strong force. Here, all your energy is concentrated or congregated for the realisation of your goal. Because of this, the *Rishis* of the old and spiritual masters emphasise the importance of meditation. Meditation is nothing but the process of controlling one's mind to a single object or goal. In other words, it is an undisturbed concentration on a particular object or goal without any distraction or divided attention.

6.16 Cultivate the Habit of Listening

A doctor once said, "I don't have to diagnose my patients. They diagnose themselves. All I have to do is listen carefully when they tell me about themselves." This same principle can be applied in all areas of life. Listeners are learners and learners are winners. Listen to your friends; you will find out about their dreams and how they work at it. Listen to those who have experienced in a field; you will learn their trade. Listen to your parents; you can learn from their mistakes and experience. Listen to your boyfriend or girlfriend; you will discover their character. Everything you need to know, someone will tell you if you are willing to listen. A listening ear is more worth than giving advice to someone. You will learn more in listening than giving a word of advice and this will give you *direction in life.* You will see your dream becoming clearer and clearer.

> *Listening and Talking*
>
> There is a dichotomy between listening and talking. When you listen, you learn more. Listening is a window through which knowledge and information flows in. The more you listen, the more you learn. Don't you know a student learns by listening to his teacher? Listening increases your knowledge bank and makes you rich. Robin Sharma in his book "*The Greatness Guide 2*" says, "We are influenced by the ideas we hear and the people we meet. (Big idea: Every person you meet knows at least one thing you don't; don't let them leave without learning it). Listening is a master skill for personal and professional excellence... When we go deep into listening to the person we are communicating with, when we allow them to share what they know, we have the opportunity to get behind their eyeballs and learn, grow and evolve into our highest and best". While, talking makes you to give out whatever you have deposited in your bank. Some people give even what they don't have or what they are not sure they have – fabrications, presumptions, etc., funny! In talking, you are closing your window. Because of this, wise people don't talk much. They are reticent and calculative even when they talk.

6.17 Be Judicious about Mass Media

It is pertinent to ask yourself this question: Do you use the media or do the media use you? Television, Internet, movies, music and other media enrich our lives to a great proportion. Can you imagine living without them? How much more corrupt would our society be without the watchful eye of the news media? Yet, since the mass media dominates our attention so effectively, it is easy for the tail to begin wagging the dog – for the media to control rather than merely enrich our lives. It has been estimated that the average person watches television for more than twenty hours a week. That's far too much time for most healthy, productive students and adults. Limit the time you spend in front of the tube. Use it for entertainment and information, not vegetation.

The internet allows the free flow of useful information all round the world. At the same time, it also allows the free flow of harmful and dangerous things into our minds. Make a contract with yourself; agree that you will not allow yourself to view things over the Internet that you would not feel comfortable within other settings – pornographic content etc. The news media offers helpful, accurate information about everything from weather forecasts to world conflicts. Yet it can also provide distorted views and biased opinions. Let others gather the facts but learn to interpret those facts for yourself.

Mass media is of great utility and at the same time it is potentially dangerous in the path of realising your goal if you do not use judiciously. It can be a source of distraction and has the power to bewitch you to digress from your dream.

6.18 Be Realistic

The saying *"Rome was not built in a day"* indicates the long and tedious duration of its construction. In the same manner you won't reach your entire life goal in a day either. In fact, you won't reach them in a week, a month or a year. That's why they are called "LIFE" goals: *it takes a lifetime to realise them.* Therefore, here comes the need to be realistic about what you can do today or tomorrow. Focus on baby steps, not giant leaps. If you think of each decision as an important step towards your goal, they won't seem trivial and boring. Your goal will make your everyday life worthwhile.

You can't complete your graduate degree in one day but you can enroll in a programme. You can't meet all of your financial goals today but you can put another 50 rupees into your savings account. You may not be able to get married today, but you can make some decisions about what kind of person you hope to marry. You can't meet all your career goals today but you can develop your skills and explore your interest fields.

Take your life one step at a time and you will worry less and achieve more. This will make you enjoy your journey towards your goal. Remember, in history all giant leaps began with a STEP.

6.19 Always Do Your Best

No one ever received a failing grade for doing one's best. Many bad grades have been handed out for lack of effort however. Effort is not just important at high school or university or in order to achieve your dream. It is important everywhere. By making an effort, by always doing your best, you give yourself an advantage. At times, life is unfair. People get jobs, promotions or relationships they seemingly don't deserve and sometimes without much effort. But as a rule, those who make an effort are those who make a difference. Do the best you can for there is no one who ever fail after trying his best.

Prepare yourself. Get all the education you can. Get all the training you can. And accept all the advice you can. The effort you put into your preparation will show up later in your performance. Stretch yourself. You can do it! You can become what you want to be by trying harder, working smarter and stretching yourself mentally, spiritually and physically. You can do more than you think you can!

> *Doing One's Best is More Important Than Success*
>
> To understand this is very important. Some parents and teachers stress so much on being 'successful' that they destroy many children. Train a child to do his or her best. Doing one's best is the surest way to success. In the mind of the child, hard work must be implanted not success. If you stress so much on success; the child may sink into despondency and he may even go to the point of committing suicide when he fails. Teach him to work hard. Sow the seed of hard work and gradually it will grow up and bear fruit. Success also may be possible without much hard work. But such success is never a success because the person does not deserve it. Success is sweetest when you earn it by doing your best. I have not heard anyone failing after doing his or her best.

One of the biggest ideas that I came across in one of the magazines comes from Chris Carmichael, the coach of seven-time Tour de France-winner Lance Armstrong who said, "The last one per cent most people keep in reserve is the extra per cent champions have the courage to burn". You need to spend every bit of your energy doing your best and creating world-class results. Offer every bit of your potential to all you do and awaken your talents and your inner fire. So at the end, you can say, "I gave it my all. I did my best".

> Tom Cruise, a Hollywood actor was born in the lap of penury. His father moved frequently searching for work and this affected his schooling. Tom, like his mother suffered from dyslexia and was put into the remedial classes at school. While, Tom was not

an academic success, he focused on athletics and competed in many sports. A knee injury derailed his hope of pursuing an athletic career. Tom then went to a Franciscan monastery to try for priesthood but left after a year. While in high school, he appeared in a number of plays and with his mother's encouragement and support, pursued a career in acting. Tom focused all his energy on developing his acting career, once again revealing his drive and steadfast determination. He never let his learning disability stand in the way of his success. Impoverished and barely scraping by, Tom began his ascent towards superstardom. Much of the early 1980s were spent on forgettable tecn flicks that did little to enhance his career. However, he persevered till he was recognised by the industry. "When I work, I work very hard. So, I look to work with people who have that level of dedication," says the star. Today, Tom has an enviable number of box-office busters.

6.20 Perseverance

Perseverance is a continuous steady effort to achieve your aim or goal. It is a steadfastness or holding on to a goal in spite of all the difficulties. Carlyle writes:

- "*Perseverance* is the very hinge of all *virtues*. On looking over the world, the cause of *nine-tenths of the lamentable failures* which occur in men's undertakings and darken and degrade so much of their history, lies not in *the want of talents* or the will to use them but in the *vacillating and desultory* mode of using them in *flying from object to object* in staring away at each little disgust and *thus applying the force* which might *conquer any one difficulty to a series of difficulties*, so large that no human force can conquer them. The *smallest brook* on earth, by *continuing to run* has hollowed out for itself a considerable valley to flow in. Commend me therefore to the virtue of perseverance. Without it all the rest are little better than fairy gold which glitters in your purse but when taken to market proves to be stale or cinders."

An Analysis of Carlyle's Statement:

(a) *Virtue:* Perseverance is one of the most important of all virtues. Virtue is a positive quality. It is a qualitative good which is indispensable for successful living. A person has to possess by all means if one wants to ccomplish anything. The virtue of perseverance is a must if you want to achieve your goal in life.

(b) *Cause... of the Lamentable Failures:* Most of our failures occur not because we do not possess talents but due to our *vacillating and desultory* manner of using them. In other words, people do not lack talents but they lack constancy and seriousness.

(c) *Flying from Object to Object:* This is a clear sign of a vacillating mind (inconstant mind). A fickle-minded person will never stick to one object (goal); he jumps from one goal to another. He has no clarity of goal. He or she will be like a butterfly that sits from one flower to another. He or she will be like a rolling stone that gathers no moss.

(d) *Thus Applying the Force...to a Series of Difficulties*: This speaks about wrong channelisation of one's energy. When we concentrate from object to object our energy is scattered. When there is no clear goal, our energy evaporates. Instead of applying our energy to a series of goals if we are to apply on one goal we would have easily achieved.

Let us see some of the great models of perseverance:

- Jackie Chan, the action hero of the silver screen is an epitome of great perseverance and endurance. When Jackie Chan was a baby, his parents could not afford to feed him due to abject poverty. They considered selling him off for US $26 to the English obstetrician who delivered him. At the tender age of seven, Jackie was apprenticed at the infamous Academy of Chinese Opera. For more than 10 years from five am to midnight, seven days a week, he endured a brutal programme of music, dance and traditional martial arts training. The training Jackie received was particularly harsh and cruel. The student was beaten and starved for not performing up to par. Later he appeared in some early Hong Kong films as a stunt man and worked his way up to stunt coordinator, then to director. When Bruce Lee died, Jackie along with many others were picked up to fill the vacuum. Jackie failed miserably. "Very hard, very hard," he said, "so instead of trying to be Bruce Lee, I decided to be myself." Jackie's first American movie was considered a failure. He had very little control over the stunts, although he'd been choreographing Kung Fu in Hong Kong for almost 10 years. As the years went by with further efforts and determination Jackie achieved his dream of being a superstar in America. Today, Jackie is indisputably the greatest action hero in movie industry. His earnings stand at US $50 million a year.
- In all of Hollywood history, there cannot be a better example of 'the Self-Made Man' than Arnold Schwarzenegger. The Guinness Book of World Records depicts him as, "the most perfect developed man in the history of the world." After watching the dedicated bodybuilders in a gym, Arnold was fascinated. Growing up in a small, isolated village in Austria he turned to bodybuilding as his ticket to a bright future. In those days, bodybuilding was viewed as a rather oddball sport and even misunderstood as a 'freak show' by the general public. Even his own father discouraged him from pursuing the sport. But Arnold was determined and gave himself fully excel in the sport. Due to his untiring efforts, Arnold won the title of Mr Universe seven times. It is said that as part of his

workout routine, he would frequently go into the corner of the gym and visualise himself winning the title again. This famous bodybuilder, Hollywood action hero, successful businessman, generous philanthropist and California's thirty eighth Governor has only one things to say, "Strength does not come from winning. Your struggles develop your strengths. When you go through hardships and decide not to surrender, that is strength."

- One cannot forget Daniel Defoe, the author of one of the most popular adventure novels *Robinson Crusoe.* Dafoe had a very tough life. His father was a poor butcher. Dafoe tried his hand at many businesses and saw many ups-and-downs in his life. The market fluctuations affected Dafoe's business and he even became bankrupt. He was also imprisoned for a few reasons. But misfortune and imprisonment were powerless to tame his indomitable spirit or check his restless energy. He kept up the fight within the walls of his prison, writing controversial pamphlets. Dafoe wrote *Robinson Crusoe* and took it to 20 publishers before he finally got it printed. Amazing perseverance! It has been a best-seller for over 250 years and has been translated into many languages. Finally, this is what Dafoe had to say, "In the school of affliction I have learned more philosophy than at the academy, and more divinity than from the pulpit. I have seen the rough side of the world as well as the smooth."

> "I hated every minute of training. But I said, 'don't quit, suffer now and live the rest of your life as a champion."
>
> —*Muhammad Ali*

6.21 Persistence

Persistence is the courage to continue working at your goal with determination in spite of difficulty, opposition or argument or failure. Persistence is a stronger form of perseverance. It is a positive obstinacy with a goal attached.

- In the early 1970s, Dr. Folkman proposed an idea in cancer research that did not fit what scientists "knew" to be true – that tumours did not generate new blood vessels to "feed" themselves and grow. He was convinced that they did. But colleagues kept telling him, "You're studying dirt," meaning his project was futile science. Dr Folkman disregarded the catcalls of the research community. For two decades, he met with disinterest or hostility as he pursued his work in angiogenesis, the study of the growth of new blood vessels. At one research convention, half the audience walked out. "He's only a surgeon, what does he know?" he heard some say: But he always believed that his work might help find ways to grow blood vessels where they were needed – like around clogged arteries in the heart. Dr. Folkman and his colleagues discovered the first angiogenesis inhibitors in the 1980s. Today, more than lakhs of cancer patients are benefiting from the research he pioneered. His work is now recognised as being on the forefront in the fight to cure cancer. "There is a fine line between persistence and obstinacy," Dr. Folkman says, "I have come to realise the key is to choose a problem that is worth persistent effort."

• Sir Charlie Chaplin Spenser is undoubtedly the greatest pantomime actors in history. He is recognised as an icon of the silent film era and certainly no other creative talent did as much as he to elevate screen comedy to a high standard. Charlie was born in a poor district of London. His mother, a talented singer was suffering from mental illness and spent most of her life in and out of mental hospitals. His father was a fairly successful singer until he took to alcohol. After his parents separated, Charlie spent most of his childhood in orphanages, where he often went hungry and was beaten up when he misbehaved. Barely able to read and write, Charlie left school to tour with a group of comic entertainers. Later he began to star in comedy acts. He was initially rejected by Hollywood studio chiefs because his pantomime was considered 'nonsense'. But he had his own way of going about and he was totally persistent in trying out his histrionic skills. Nothing could deter him. Today, Charlie Chaplin is considered as one of the greatest film actors in the history of American cinemas. His movies were and are still popular throughout the world.

• The driving force behind most of the inventions is due to consistent persistence. This is what proves the life of Chester Carlson. Carlson, the only child of an itinerant barber, used to work after school and on weekends as the chief support of his family. His father was crippled with arthritis and his mother died of tuberculosis when he was 17. As a young man, Carlson worked as a patent analyser for an electrical component maker, a job that required multiple copies of documents and drawings which he had to duplicate by hand. He thought of the idea of reproduction technique based on photo-conductivity. Frustrated by lack of time and suffering from painful attacks of arthritis, Carlson decided to dip into his meager resources to pursue his research. Carlson took his idea to more than 20 companies and they all turned him down. Even the National Inventors Council dismissed his work. He wrote later, "Several times I decided to drop the idea completely. But each time I returned to try again. I was thoroughly convinced that the invention was too promising to be dormant." After seven long years of rejections, a small company agreed to purchase the rights for his invention which developed into the Xerox Machine. The astounding success of xerography is all the more remarkable because it was given little hope of surviving its infancy. Today, xerography is the foundation stone of a gigantic worldwide copying industry.

Persistence is putting up with your work in spite of difficulties. You feel like giving up but you have refused to surrender because you know that you have started not for giving up. Rochelle E. Goodrich in her book writes, "*Eena: The Tempter's Snare*" thus:

"Don't ever give up.
Don't ever give in.
Don't ever stop trying.
Don't ever sell out.
And if you find yourself succumbing to
One of the above for a brief moment,
Pick yourself up, brush yourself off,
Whisper a prayer and start where you left off.
But never, ever, ever give up."

6.22 Endurance

According to Oxford Advanced Learner's Dictionary, 'endurance' means the ability or the *willingness* to *suffer patiently* and without complaining or to tolerate a difficult situation *for a long time*. From this definition we can elicit three important points. They are:

(a) Willingness
(b) Suffer patiently
(c) For a long time

In order to achieve your goal, you need the above three elements. You must first willingly choose your goal and be ready to suffer patiently for a long time till your goal is achieved. Many people are very enthusiastic in pursuing their goals; they are willing to suffer but not for a long time. This is the difference between achievers and quitters. Achievers willingly suffer to the end till they achieve; while quitters give up on the way when it is too hard to endure. If you are not willing to endure, you will never get anywhere in life.

- Mel Fisher is known around the world as "the king of the treasure hunters". He is one of the most ordinary men of our times who spent the most part of his life looking for one single treasure and found it. Mel's dreams of treasure began in childhood with the reading of Robert Louis Stevenson's *Treasure Island*. The Spanish galleon, *The Atocha*, sank in a storm over 350 years ago. It was a vessel worth hundreds of millions of dollars. It could have gone down anywhere over hundreds of square miles of the South Coast of Florida. Mel invested all he had on this quest, underwent untold hardships and even lost his own son and daughter-in-law. The sea claimed their lives. With little boats and a crew Mel scoured the bottom of the ocean day after day, year after year. When he was over 60 years old, he had spent over 12 million dollars (mostly borrowed) and barely had enough money to meet his payroll for two or more weeks, his voice crackled over the radio from his little salvage boat, "We have found *The Atocha.*" With it Mel recovered mountains of silver and gold bars and precious jewels valued at over 400 million dollars. After having found the greatest treasure, this is what Mel had to say, "I think that endurance has paid. That's one of the main things, just hang in there and do your thing and when people try to tear you down or get jealous, just let it go in one ear and out the other and keep going."

- Imagine about sailing the open sea and being on the sea for weeks, months and years at a time with neither the land in sight nor the navigation systems to help guide the adventure. Christopher Columbus who discovered the New Land (The United States of America) began his travels under such conditions. Everyone believed the world was flat but, not Columbus. The experts of Spain concluded that Columbus' plan to discover a new and shorter route to the Indies was virtually impossible. Columbus' great part of the time was passed in almost hopeless solicitation, amidst poverty, neglect and taunting ridicule; that the prime of his life had wasted away in the struggle and that when his endurance was finally crowned with success, he was in about his fifty-sixth year. With three voyages behind him and age finally catching up with him, Columbus in his late 50s was suffering from arthritis and opthalmia. He and his men had to face lots of adversities on their voyages. Diseases spread in the ship; people were sea sick and the food was getting old. They ran out of drinking water. However with "I can make it happen" attitude Columbus persisted. If Columbus had turned back, no one could have blamed him, considering the constant adversity he endured. Of course, no one would have remembered him either! And America would have had to wait longer to be discovered!

- The Telecom giant of India Sunil Bharti Mittal had to endure patiently to reach the stage he is now. Sunil Bharti Mittal is the managing director of the Bharti group, which owns India's largest GSM-based mobile phone service. He is one of the key persons behind cellular revolution in India. After graduation, Mittal along with his friend formed a small bicycle business with borrowed capital in Ludhiana. Soon he realised that his ambitions could not be fulfilled there and so he moved out to Mumbai. By 1982, Mittal had started a full-fledged business selling portable generators imported from Japan. Business was good in the beginning but it ran into rough weather when the government banned the import of generators as two Indian companies were awarded licences to manufacture them in India. 1976 to 1985 was a period of great struggle and a period of great pain for him. The blows were hard yet with great endurance he overcame. Mittal's romance with telecom started in 1985. When he began his entrepreneurial venture, he was ignored and laughed at. In 1995, he founded Bharti Cellular

Limited (BCL) to offer cellular services. Mittal named the telecommunication brand Air-tel which gained a large success within a few years of its launch with over more than fifty million customers. "I didn't go to a B-school, instead learnt lessons on the streets and at every opportunity. Everything begins with a small step, but you have to dream big to take a leap," recalls Mittal.

Remember, the Latin phrase "*fortitudine vincimus*" which means 'by endurance we conquer'.

If You Can Keep Your Head

If you can keep your head when all about you
Are losing theirs and blaming it on you,
If you can trust yourself when all men doubt you,
But make allowance for their doubting too;
If you can wait and not be tired by waiting,
Or being lied about, don't deal in lies,
Or being hated, don't give way to hating,
And yet don't look too good, nor talk too wise:
If you can dream – and not make dreams your master;
If you can think – and not make thoughts your aim;
If you can meet with triumph and disaster
And treat those two impostors just the same;
If you can bear to hear the truth you've spoken
Twisted by knaves to make a trap for fools,
Or watch the things you gave your life to, broken,
And stoop and build'em up with worn-out tools:
If you can make one heap of all your winnings
And risk it on one turn of pitch-and-toss,
And lose, and start again at your beginnings
And never breathe a word about your loss;
If you can force your heart and nerve and sinew
To serve your turn long after they are gone,
And so hold on when there is nothing in you
Except the Will which says to them: "Hold on!"
If you can talk with crowds and keep your virtue,
Or walk with Kings – nor lose the common touch,
If neither foes nor loving friends can hurt you,
If all men count with you, but none too much;
If you can fill the unforgiving minute
With sixty seconds' worth of distance run,
Yours is the Earth and everything that's in it,
And – which is more – you'll be a Man, my son!

– *Rudyard Kipling*

6.23 Be Decisive

A person devoid of decisiveness will find his thoughts and dreams like vapour blown in the wind. He or she will go nowhere until he or she decides. Decision is very crucial in achieving your dream. Life is made up of little decisions and big decisions and how a man decides determines the direction of his life. Decision is the spark that ignites action. Until a person makes a decision nothing happens in his or her life. Decision is the courageous facing of issues, knowing that if they are not faced, problems will remain unanswered forever.

Decision can lead a person to mountain top to realise his goals. It can also cause a person to fall to the valley below. But without decision no mountains are climbed, no dream is achieved and no success ever follows. It is better and courageous to risk a wrong decision rather than to make no decision at all.

Decision is not a blind chance. It is focusing the power of intelligence, meditation and prayer on the thing to be decided. Decision should not be made impetuously or randomly. Deciding to delay making a decision is a decision itself. When it comes to choosing your goals in life, it is also good to consult an expert who can enlighten you more on the area.

- "There is so much about my fate that I cannot control, but other things do fall under the jurisdiction. I can decide how I spend my time, whom I interact with, whom I share my body and life and money and energy with. I can select what I can read and eat and study. I can choose how I'm going to regard unfortunate circumstances in my life – whether I will see them as curses or opportunities. I can choose my words and the tone of voice in which I speak to others. And most of all, I can choose my thoughts."

  –Elizabeth Gilbert

- An indecisive person is one who lacks mental clarity.
  An indecisive person is a timorous person afraid to take risk for fear of the presumed consequences.
  An indecisive person is one who tries to please everyone.
  An indecisive person is a spineless man, not able to stand on his own.

- It is better to take a wrong decision than not take decision at all. Anyway take decision, if you are right it helps and contributes. And if you are wrong, there is always enough time come back And begin again and you learn a lot.

- Great movers of history are all *decisive people.*

6.24 Live in the 'Now'

"Do you know a better time than the present for igniting your dreams?"

—Carolyn Tody in "*A Whimsical Holiday for Children*"

The past is not real. Neither is the future. Both are simply manifestations in your brain. The past is a memory you experience by reliving it in the present and the future is a projection you invent in your mind. You only live in the present – *the now.* Master the art of living right now. Thinking right now; acting right now. Successful people understand that living in the moment allows them to take action and focus more intensely because they are not distracted by fears of the future or regrets of the past.

Do it NOW. Sometimes
"LATER" becomes "NEVER".
Yesterday is history
Tomorrow is a mystery
Today is a gift. That is why it is called PRESENT. So, accept it with gratitude.

Begin *hic et nunc (here and now)*
Desire *hic et nunc*
Work *hic et nunc*
And sure is your *Success.*

The present is all you have and you have to make the most of it. Living in the 'now' does not mean you are completely oblivious of your future goals. No, you know what you want to be but if you live in that state of what you want to be, then your 'now' does not exist anymore. The 'now' is to be filled with action that points to your goal. Otherwise without a goal your energy can be a waste.

"One day you will wake up and there won't be any more time to do the things you have always wanted. Do it NOW".

–Paulo Coelho

6.25 Cultivate the Habit of Initiative

Napoleon Hill says that the place to begin developing the habit of initiative is in the small, commonplace things connected with my daily work therefore, I will go at my work each day as if I were doing it solely for the purpose of developing this necessary habit of initiative. Practicing the habit of taking initiative in connection with my daily work will help me in developing that habit. Developing a good habitual action that corresponds to my dream is *sine qua non* to the realisation of my dream.

6.26 Take One Step a Day

Foolish people with all their other thoughts, have this one too: *They are always getting ready to live but never living.* Your success will start when you begin to pursue it. To reach your goal or to attain success, you don't need to know all of the answers in advance. You just need to have a clear idea of what your goal is.

- Don't procrastinate when faced with difficult problems. Break your problems into parts and handle one part at a time.
- Develop the proclivity to take action. You can make something happen RIGHT NOW.
- Divide your big goal into small STEPS.
- Take the first step right away.

Everyone who ever got where they are, had to begin where they were. Your big opportunity is where you are right now. Don't you know, a journey of a thousand miles begins with one step? Take it. Martin Luther King Jr once said, "If you can't fly, then run, if you can't run, then walk, if you can't walk, then crawl. But whatever you do, you have to keep moving forward."

Cicero wrote to Atticus thus:

"Si dormis, expergiscere;
si stas, ingredere;
si ingrederis, curre;
si curris, advola
(If you are sleeping, wake up;
If you are standing, walk;
If you are walking, run;
If you are running, fly).

6.27 At Least Give a Try

There are some students who give up before even trying. According to their mental arithmetic, they feel that they cannot. They are being handicapped by their mental defeatism. Before trying, they are already incapable in their mind. How can such people know 'what they are good at?' They are afraid to try. They feel cocksure in their mind that they CAN'T. This is the most harmful attitude towards accomplishing any goal. Brian Herbert in his book, "*House Harkonnen*" writes, "*If you surrender, you have already lost. If you refuse to give up, though no matter the odds against you, at least you have succeeded in trying*".

In June 1985, two British mountaineers Joe Simpson and Simon Yates made the first-ever climb of the West Face of the 21,000 foot snow-covered Siula Grande mountain in Peru. It was an exceptionally tough assault – but nothing compared to what was to come. Early in the descent, Simpson fell and smashed his right knee. Yates could have abandoned him but managed to find a way of lowering him down the mountain in a series of difficult drops blinded by snow and cold. Then Simpson fell into a crevasse and Yates eventually had no choice but to cut the rope, utterly convinced that his friend was now dead. In the subsequent book on the climb entitled "Touching the Void", Joe Simpson wrote, "As I gazed at the distant moraines, I knew that I must at least try. I would probably die out there amid those boulders. The thought didn't alarm me. It seemed reasonable, as a matter-of-fact. That was how it was. I could aim for something. If I died, well, that wasn't so surprising, but I wouldn't have just waited for it to happen. The horror of dying no longer affected me as it had in the crevasse. I now had the chance to confront it and struggle against it. It wasn't a bleak dark terror any more, just fact, like my broken leg and frost-bitten fingers and I couldn't be afraid of things like that. My leg would hurt when I fell and when I couldn't get up I would die". The survival of Yates himself was extraordinary. That Simpson somehow found a way of climbing out of the crevasse after 12 hours and then literally crawled and dragged himself six miles back to camp, going three days and nights without food or drink, losing three stone and contracting ketoacidosis in the process, would be the stuff of heroic fiction if it was not so true. Indeed, six operations and two years later, he was even back climbing. All because, against all the odds, he tried...("Touching the Void" by Joe Simpson).

Here is the man who saved himself because he gave himself a chance to AT LEAST TRY. When Barack Obama got re-elected to the presidency of the United States of America for the second term, in his winning speech he said, "*It doesn't matter whether you're black or white or Hispanic or Asian or Native American or young or old or rich or poor, able, disabled, gay or straight, you can make it here in America if you're willing to try.*" What matters is not your background or status but your willingness to try.

Don't Quit!

When things go wrong, as they sometimes will,
When the road you're trudging seems all uphill,
When the funds are low and the debts are high,
And you want to smile, but you have to sigh,
When care is pressing you down a bit,
Rest if you must; but don't you quit.

Life is queer with its twists and turns,
As every one of us sometimes learn,
And many a failure turns about.

When he might have won had he stuck it out;
Don't give up, though the pace seems slow;
You might succeed with another blow.

Often the goal is nearer than
It seems to a faint and faltering man,
Often the struggler has given up
When he might have captured the victor's cup.
And he learned too late, when the night slipped down,
How close he was to the golden crown.

Success is failure turned inside out;
The silver tint of the clouds of doubt;
And you never can tell how close you are,
It may be near when it seems afar;
So stick to the fight when you're hardest hit;
It's when things seem worst that you mustn't quit!

—*Unknown*

6.28 Transform Your Comfort Zone into 'Discomfort Zone'

Comfort zone is a paracosm where you feel secured and comfortable. It is your micro-personal world where you embrace complacency and satisfaction. If you feel that what have done so far is enough, how can you progress further? When you want to really accomplish your goal, you can never feel complacent and satisfied with what you have done. There should be a thirst for more that drives you crazy. If you are dreaming for greater things in life, you can't afford to sit back and be self-complacent about it'. Your comfort zone can be one of the biggest hindrances towards achieving your goal. For dream makers, comfort zone is never a good place to be. Maintaining a comfort zone can cause stagnation and as a result, you won't feel the need to fight or struggle further.

Transforming your comfort zone into 'discomfort zone' is what you need to focus. You need to destroy your comfort zone. Your perpetual assault on the comfort zone will create a kind of dissatisfaction within you to strive for more. But it is not enough to transform your comfort zone into 'discomfort zone'; you need to value the discomfort zone. The Greek word '*oikos*' means 'house' or 'place to live'. You need to shift your house or your place of dwelling – from the comfort zone to the discomfort zone. Changing a dwelling place is very uncomfortable and inconvenient. Furthermore, changing your dwelling and getting settled in a new dwelling place which is less comfortable than the first is still more challenging. But embracing the latter will pay you big dividends. Living in the discomfort zone will accelerate your ascent towards your goal. Therefore, you need to be comfortable in the discomfort zone. Since, you are so keen on achieving your goal, you prefer to embrace discomforts in the form of inconveniences, struggles and pains that are being littered on the way towards your goal.

6.28.1 What to Do in the 'Discomfort Zone'?

In the discomfort zone, you must *think fast* and *think forward*. *Thinking fast* means you should be quick in taking decisions at every step that will gradually lead towards the fast attainment of your goal. Decisiveness sustains your interest towards your goal. Being indecisive can cause delay and your interest will begin to wane. So, never delay and never procrastinate! Do not get mired in the discomforts. Discomforts are decision-making situations without which there will be no progress. You need to be fast and agile in responding to these situations. Discomforts act as raw materials that need to be churned up into refined advantages. *Thinking forward* means inventing new ideas or models in your discomfort zone that will enable you to move *forward* towards your goal. It is a post decision-making activity. It is how you act and proceed after you have taken a decision. All the actions and decisions taken in the discomfort zone should be geared up towards the goal.

6.28.2 Ecosystem

Ecosystem refers to the 'biological community of interacting organisms and their physical environment'. Human beings are a biological community that interacts with one another. This interaction is a very important factor in the field of attaining one's goal. There is no individual achiever. An individual's success is always the result of a collective effort. There is always the role of the other in one's achievement. Therefore, a person needs to interact more if he or she wants to achieve his or her goal. Interaction is a form of consulting, discussing, listening and learning from others. This will give you sometimes better insights and foresights and act as a gargantuan help towards the attainment of your goal.

6.28.3 Challenge Your Personal 'Comfort Zone'

In order to achieve your dream, you need to escape the conventional norms by taking on the new challenges beyond your personal comfort zones. The ordinary conventional way of doing things (comfort zone) will bring only complacency and nothing more. This is a stagnation syndrome which will further give birth to retardation where no progress leads to nowhere. Moving beyond the conventional way means accepting ideas and constructive criticism from outside. This will help you to progress towards your goal.

6.28.4 Never Stop Learning

If you really want to achieve your goal, you need to be a constant learner. A learner has to be humble. You should be willing to stoop if you want to gain new knowledge and insights from others. There cannot be an arrogant learner because such a 'better than thou' attitude will never pave the way for noematical amelioration. A pompous classification of yourself from others will make your ego grow oversised and a point will come when nobody will like to share their ideas with you. So, be an authentic learner and you will receive an influx of ideas and knowledge which will give you a better opportunity to realise your goal. In the discomfort zone, it is not *what* you know today that counts – it's *how* you acquire, refine and apply new knowledge for achieving your goal. In business parlance, you become 'a fine human resource'.

6.28.5 Find Opportunity in Your 'Discomfort Zone'

You need to get more comfortable with your discomfort zones and get through the obstacles that prevent you from achieving your goal. Being comfortable in the discomfort zone means you have learnt to accept the disorder, confusion, chaos, hardships and struggles that pertain to the attainment of your goal. Success comes only through discomforts. There is no easy sail towards success. It has to be earned through hardships, pain and struggle. See the discomfort zone itself as a fertile ground for opportunity.

6.29 Excerpt from the Book *The Law of Success*

You have to make a tough journey from turning your dream to a reality. Therefore, you need to form the habit of taking some definite action each day that will carry you one step nearer to your dream.

- You must know that procrastination is a deadly enemy of all who want to attain their dreams and you must eliminate this habit from your psychological make-up.
- Doing some or one definite thing each day that ought to be done, without anyone telling you to do it.
- Looking around until you find at least one thing that you can do each day that you have not been in the habit of doing and that will be of value to others without expectation of pay.
- Telling at least one other person each day, of the value of practicing this habit of doing something that ought to be done without being told to do it.

The muscles of the body become strong in proportion to the extent to which they are used, therefore the habit of initiative also becomes fixed in proportion to the extent that it is practiced.

6.30 The Seven Principles of an Eagle by Dr. Myles Monroe

Principle 1: Eagles fly alone at high altitude and not with sparrows or other small birds. No other bird can get to the height of the eagle. They stay away from sparrows and ravens. Eagles fly with Eagles. This is true in life too. If you want to do something great in life, learn to be alone and when you are with people, share your time with people of the same ambition and aspirations.

Principle 2: Eagles have strong vision. They have the ability to focus on objects up to five kilometres away. When an eagle sights its prey, it narrows its focus on it and sets out to get it. No matter the obstacles, the eagle will not move its focus from the prey until it grabs it. In the same way, in life too many obstacles will appear to distract you in life. Stay focused and never allow dissenting views and voices to deter you from your goals.

Principle 3: Eagles do not eat dead things. They feed only on fresh prey. Vultures eat dead animals but eagles will not. In the like manner, in life stale information will never do you good. Update yourself regularly with fresh information from reliable sources. Research your subject area and use it for maximum benefit. Be careful with what you feed your eyes and ears with. Stay clear of outdated and old information. Always try something new.

Principle 4: Eagles love the storm. When clouds gather, the eagles get excited. The eagle uses the storm's wind to lift itself higher. Once it finds the storm, the eagle uses the raging storm to lift itself above the clouds. This gives the eagle an opportunity to fly and rest its wings. In the meantime all the other birds hide in the leaves and branches of the trees. We can use the storms of life to rise to greater heights. Achievers relish challenges and use them profitably.

Principle 5: The Eagle tests before trusting. When a female eagle meets a male and they want to mate, she flies down to earth with the male pursuing her and she picks a twig. She flies back into the air with the male pursuing her. Once she has reached a height high enough for her, she lets the twig fall to the ground and watches it as it falls. The male chases after the twig. The faster it falls, the faster it chases it. The male eagle has to catch it before it falls to the ground. It then brings it back to the female eagle. The female eagle grabs the twig and flies to a higher altitude and then drops the twig for the male to chase. This goes on until the female eagle is assured that the male eagle has mastered the art of catching the twig which shows commitment. Then and only then, she will allow him to mate with her. In life too, if one wants to achieve a goal, one's commitment must be tangible.

Principle 6: When ready to lay eggs, the female and male eagle identify a place very high on a cliff where no predators can reach. The male eagle flies to earth and picks thorns and lays them on the crevice of the cliff, then flies to earth again to collect twigs on which the female lays in the intended nest. He flies back to earth and picks thorns laying them on top of the twigs. Then, flies back to earth and picks soft grass to cover the thorns. When this first layering is complete the male eagle runs more thorns, lays them on the nest; runs back to get grass it on top of the thorns, then plucks his feathers to complete the nest. The thorns on the outside of the nest protect it from possible intruders. Both male and female eagles participate in raising the eagle family. She lays the eggs and protects them; he builds the nest and hunts. During the time of training, the young ones begin to fly; the mother eagle throws the eaglets out of the nest. Since they are scared, they jump into the nest again. Next she throws them out and then takes off the soft layers of the nest, leaving the thorns bare. When the scared eaglets again jump into the nest, they are pricked by thorns. Shrieking and bleeding they jump out again this time wondering why the mother and father who love them so much are torturing them. Next, mother eagle pushes them off the cliff into the air. As they shriek in fear, father eagle flies out and catches them up on his back before they fall and brings them back to the cliff. This goes on for some time until they start flapping their wings. They get excited at this newfound knowledge that they can fly.

The preparation for the nest teaches us to prepare for change. The preparation for the family teaches us the importance of helping one another in order to realise one's dream. To realise our dreams and goals we need the help of many people. The being pricked by the thorns tells us that sometimes being too comfortable where we are or not willing to come out of our comfort zones may lead to ignorance of the reality and non-experience of life which retards growth and learning. The thorns of life teach us that we need to grow, get out of our nest and live on. We may not know it but the seemingly comfortable and safe haven may have thorns. The people who love us do not let us languish in sloth but push us hard to grow and prosper. Even in their seemingly bad actions they have good intentions for us.

Principle 7: When an eagle grows old, its feathers become weak and it cannot fly as fast as it should. When it feels weak and about to die, it retires to a place far away in the rocks. While there, the eagle plucks out every feather on its body until it is completely bare. It stays in this hiding place until it has grown new feathers, then it can come out. We occasionally need to shed off our old habits and items that burden us in order to realise our dreams and goals.

7

Students, Beware of Your Enemies!

The enemy is not an outsider or unknown; it is always an insider very close to you. Its nature is very subtle, unsuspecting and credulous.

Student-life is vulnerable to many negative forces that are destructive. If you are not circumspective, your enemies can purloin your dreams. Therefore, there is an urgent need to stir up your attention waves within yourself that will put you on the *qui vive*. The enemies are marauding around like a famished wolf to shallow and destroy people who are determined and focused in life. Your enemies are not strangers; they are the ones who function within the circle of your friendship.

7.1 Bad Companions: The Most Subtle Enemy

Never Plan a Future with Someone Who has no Future Plans for Themselves

One of the most fundamental choices of a student's life is choosing friends. Choosing a good friend will greatly enhance your life but choosing a bad friend will lead you to destruction. Remember the saying: "It is better to be alone than be in bad company". The most important priority of a student is to *study* and there is no other greater priority than this. If a student has some other priority greater than study, his academic performance will begin to dwindle. Since *study* is the most important priority of a student, he or she must guard himself/herself and keep wary of anyone who can disrupt this sacred duty. Your study is important not merely because you are going to get a good job tomorrow. It is phenomenally important because education is an all-round development of one's personality. In short, it is a positive construction of your *value system*. Your value system has to be rightly formed. Otherwise it can be destructive to yourself and to others. Education must be founded on ethics. Your education is going to affect the society. Your value system will affect not only you but your surroundings too. As a good person affects others positively and a bad person affects negatively, so too, your character and values will either affect others negatively or positively. So value-based education is very important as it trains you to develop values and not merely intellectual learning.

During student-hood, it is better to have friends as fewest as possible. Because having many friends would entail many appointments. If you have friends, you cannot say "no" to them, most of the time. Adolescence is a stage or a time during which a person trusts friends more than parents. Since you have made a pact with them, you also have to give some of your time. As a consequence, you will begin to grapple with the proper management of your time. A student can't afford to lose his time. A bad management of your time will affect your whole academic system. Your homework and other assignments are no longer done in time. When you don't do your duty, you may not feel like going to school any more. Therefore, it results in truancy. Finally, you will begin to feel that it is meaningless to go to school. You will begin to prefer your friends to school. If you have reached this stage and your friends have not corrected you, then it clearly shows you had made a wrong choice of friends.

True Friendship will greatly ameliorate your life but bad friendship will impede the positive unfolding of your life. When you choose somebody who is better than yourself – intelligent, purposeful, truthful, respectful, humble etc., you will learn and begin to pick up those values. If you choose someone worse than yourself, you have nothing much to gain. Eagles fly with eagles not with chickens. Remember the Latin phrase that says: "*Si claudo cohabites, subclaudicare disces*" (If you live with a lame man you will learn to limp).

> Once an eagle made friendship with a chicken and they use to walk and play together every day. The eagle was completely lost in the friendship of chicken. The chicken had greater influence on the eagle. So the eagle started following the ways of the chicken. Their friendship went on for years. One day the eagle looked up and saw another eagle soaring and enjoying in the high sky. The eagle said to himself, 'I think it is time for me to soar up high in the sky and enjoy the way of the eagle since I have been with chicken for so many years.' When the eagle began to fly, it could not fly anymore because the eagle had not been using its wings for so many years. It had already lost its power to fly due to disuse.

The eagle instead of progressing, it was regressing. Its mistake was its choice of friendship. The eagle chose a bird that would never fly and that affected him. If you have a friend better than yourself, you always have a chance to be better. So, choose better friends.

7.1.1 Defiance of Parental Injunctions

If you choose bad friends, parents will begin to notice because they know this by the changes that take place in your behaviour. They will begin to object your friendship. This objection is not because they don't like your friends; rather it is because they have a dream for you. When your parents realise that this dream is in danger, it is their bounden duty to protect it. Therefore, they will begin to shun your friendship more and more. They do this not because they hate you but they want you to reach your goal. Your parents want you to be somebody in life not because they want to reap the fruits of your labour later. Some of your parents will be gone by the time you finish your graduation and get a job. In most cases, parents are never self-centred. Your parents' wish is that you live a better and comfortable life after they are dead and gone. In reality, parents don't want to die till they see their children well-settled in life.

Many children today, shun parental injunctions. They have dubbed and branded their parents as "*out-dated*" or "*a quart in a pint pot*" or "*irrelevant*" to their contemporary age. They think that their parents don't fit into this highly advanced technological age. I think this is the greatest sin of this generation. Jesus called the people of his time "*adulterous generation*". I think the same term is applicable to this generation too. The word "adulterous" is a very apt word to describe the present generation. The word 'adulterous' would mean pollution as adultery pollutes marriage. This generation is also polluted with so many things unheard of in history. With the coming of internet everything is exposed and unlatched; no parents, no taboo or even religion is unable to withstand its onslaught. As a result, the gap between the secret and the open and the holy and the profane hardly exists.

Your parents may not be 'advanced' or 'intelligent' like you and this is precisely the reason why they sacrifice everything for you; so that you may see what they have not seen, you may know what they have not known and you may reach where they have not reached. Let us not call our parents "*outdated*" because they do not know the simple operations of modern electronic gadgets like mobile phone, iPhone, iPad, tablets, laptops, etc., or talk 'irrelevant topics' that do not relate to our times. These gadgets do not belong to their generation. How can they know what is not theirs? Let us not take the mickey out of our parents and our elders. Our life is better because of them. Fire was discovered by the primitive man. Can you call him uncivilised because he did not put on clothes? Most of us have not discovered anything. In what way are we better than the primitive man? Our life is easy and comfortable because of our past generations.

You may not listen to your parents when they talk about the modern gadgets like cellular phone, computer – internet, software and hardware etc. Most of our parents may not be aware of the basic knowledge of these things. But since they are ignorant of these things, that does not mean they are fools. When it comes to relationship problems and other experiences of life, they are an authority. We must listen to them. They saw life earlier than us. Their advice will be if not perfect, it will be always better than ours. If your parents oppose your friendship with someone, you need to give a thought. Our generation thinks that we are too clever. Remember, this generation is tech savvy but not relationship savvy–they are close to gadgets that they have no time for family and friends. Human management is more important than technological management. The most successful people in businesses are those who are adept in human management.

7.1.2 Defiance of Teacher's Injunctions

A teacher who corrects you always is the one who is interested in you. If a teacher does not correct you after he has seen your misdeed or involved in some bad habits, that teacher is not a teacher who wish your good but your enemy because a teacher who wants you to be good will never close his eyes over your mistakes. He will try to correct you. Such teacher is either consenting to your bad behaviour or he is allowing you to tread the path of destruction. The other reason could be that 'he has given up on you'. He may feel that you're beyond correction and that his advice would longer work anymore. A teacher who advices you is a teacher who wish your well being. Follow his advice and someday, you will climb higher than your teacher himself. The teacher who loves you will know you more than your parents. Your teacher will begin to notice the changes in your behaviour long before your parents notice. He will be able to diagnose you better than any others. Most of the time your behaviour changes because of peer influence. Listening to your teacher can help you a lot. Never contravene your teacher's admonitions.

7.2 Engaging in Dating and Courtship

Dating and courtship can be very detrimental to student's power to concentrate on his or her study. Once you fall in love with a boy or a girl (the significant other), the general tenor of your academic life is going to be affected. This new romance will take the upper slot in your priority list. Your study will fall from first in your priority list. Love is such a nice and dangerous thing. Romance is for mature people otherwise it can confuse and destroy your world. In romance, even mature people can become immature because the path of love can never be predicted. You do not lead but it leads you.

Adolescent students should not take to dating and courtship. I am not saying that dating and courtship are bad. But I would like to request you to delay or postpone. This will pay you big dividends. If you are a person with a great sense of direction and purpose in life, never ever risk your life in romance because once you fall in love, all your energy will begin to flow in that direction and you'll never be able to stop it and you'll not be able to channelise in the direction that you want to go. The most harmful thing is that your lover *begins to take control of your mind and heart, time and money and your relationship with others.* Your freedom begins to be constricted. Now, if someone else controls the most vital parts of your system, what else is left for you to accomplish other things in your life? Your mind and heart, your time and money and your relationship with others are the most quintessential elements for achieving your dream. Now, if you sell away all these vital elements to somebody else, what is left for you, to accomplish your GOAL? Such person may be able to climb small hills but will never climb great mountains.

> *"I see guys spending weeks, months trying to make a girl happy. I see girls waiting endlessly for their guys to call. Is that all your life is about? For your lover to validate you? Or to make a relationship work? Instead why not focus on yourself – working on your goals, learning something, being a more positive person and helping others. That will boost your self-esteem far more than any lover ever could".*
>
> *—Chetan Bhagat*

7.2.1 Consequence of Selling away Your Mind and Heart to the Significant Other

The mind and heart is the seat of concentration and other intellectual functions. Once this is occupied by the 'significant other' (lover), how can you concentrate on your books? For those who are engaged in romance, books are such a boring thing.

7.2.2 Time and Money

People say 'time is money' but I wish to disagree with such premise. The value of time is far beyond money. Money lost can be regained but not time. Many failures are the result of time mismanagement. If you prepare yourself in time, you will certainly succeed in time. Our lives begin in time, then continue in time and end in time. Successful man is one who uses his time judiciously. As a student, you are to invest your time in study but if you spend most of your time with your lover and other insignificant things, when are you going to study?

Money is of such a great value if you use well but it is equally destructive if abused. It is not enough you give your time to your significant other, your money too follows. You will not go to meet your lover without any money in your purse. As a student, you have not begun to earn, so where is the source of your income? Finally, you have to extort money from your parents. With the extorted money of your parents, you lavishly spend on your significant other. The amount you spend on your significant other could have been spent on buying the necessary books and other essential things. Since, you have not earned, your extortion rate increases and as a result, the tenor of your family atmosphere begins to be disturbed. This is the stage where you have already left your books but still registered in the school or colleges.

Now, your mind and heart are disturbed, your time and money are simply wasted, no more progress in the academic performance. Your academic progress report turns into regressed and depressed report. Finally, you have become an underachiever hero of love. What will you do next? We can prognosticate with surety that the next step you are going to take is in no way will lead to a positive success. You will soon be a dropped-out.

Let us learn from the Koreans. Korean students are extremely studious. Most of the students leave home at 5 am and return home well after 10 pm, then they go to special study schools and often remain there till 2 am. This is a common Korean saying, *"If you sleep three hours a day , you may get into one of the top universities; if you sleep four hours each day, you may get into other universities; if you sleep five or more hours each day, especially when you are in high school, forget getting into any university"*. Journalist W. Branigin of the *Washington Post* says, "Korean students are the most literate bunch and do exceedingly well in the areas of Science and Mathematics". The competition is very fierce there. Korean students do not mind sacrificing their social and family life to the supreme end of getting the best education. President Barack Obama has repeatedly panegyrised the South Korean system of education due to the number of engineers the country produces and the amount of time Koreans spend in school compared with America.

7.3 Misplacement of Priorities

Misplacement of priorities can be fatal to the life of a student. It will affect your academic performance which is a condition *sine qua non* to the attainment of your goal. Your dream and goal can be achieved only through proper prioritisation of the required activities. Prioritisation is the process of listing in order, the most important to the lesser important activities of your daily tasks which will ultimately lead you to achieve your long-term goal (dream). There are so many activities that a student has to perform daily. Some of them are: work, study, games, cooking, watching TV or movie, updating status on the facebook, surfing the internet and roaming in the cyber-world, socialisation etc. Among these, the student needs to schedule the most necessary activities according to their importance. Let us put the necessary items in order of their importance:

7.3.1 Priority List

(i) Study
(ii) Helping Parents
(iii) Work
(iv) Games
(v) Watching TV
(vi) Socialisation
(vii) Roaming in the Cyber World
(vii) Continuous face-booking

In the above given list, the most important priority of a student is 'STUDY'. This tops the priority list. Study is the most important activity of a student, the rest comes after. This is because study is directly connected with the student's ultimate dream. Human beings are created with a purpose not like animals that have no purpose. If you do not achieve what you want to be (dream/goal), you will never be satisfied, fulfilled and happy. That is why setting a dream or goal is of phenomenal importance for a happy living.

> A guard in-charge of a Lighthouse along a dangerous coast was given enough oil for one month and told to keep the light burning every night. One day a woman asked for some oil so that her children could stay warm. Then a farmer came. His son needed oil for a lamp so he could study. Another needed some for an engine. The guard saw each as a worthy request and gave some oil to satisfy all. By the end of the month, the tank in the lighthouse was dry. That night the beacon was dark and three ships crashed on the rocks. More than one hundred lives lost. The lighthouse attendant explained what he had done and why. But the prosecutor replied, "You were given only one and very important task: to keep the light burning. Every other thing was secondary. Derivation from your responsibility has caused loss of many lives and much property. You have no excuse." The guard's mistake was misplacement of priority. All that he did was all good activities but he misplaced his priority. Clarity of priority was missing in him.

Study is the most important but if you begin to change your priority list say No. VI becomes your first priority; then your academic performance will begin to deteriorate. Now your priority is 'Socialisation'. As a student, socialisation can never be your priority because this will begin to affect your study. Socialisation is the process of getting *au fait* with the life of the society—you begin to make friendship, involve in courtship and social programmes and celebrations etc. These activities are not evil *per se* but they affect your study. As a student if you begin to socialise when are you going to devote your time for your study? Socialisation is the thief of time—you will never know how time passes. Your academic performance will come down and finally a stage will come when you are no longer interested in study anymore. At this juncture, you will think of dropping out. This is misplacement of priority. You have made the insignificant activities top your priority list.

Vilfredo Pareto, an Italian economist opined the *Pareto Time Principle*. This principle simply states that within any system, some constituent elements yield higher returns than others, with 20 per cent of the total elements yielding high returns that produce 80 per cent of the work. The other 80 per cent of the elements produce 20 per cent of the work. In simple terms, the *Pareto Time Principle* means that on a particular day, if you have things to do and choose the two most important of the things to be done, your productivity would be 80 per cent. When you are able to do some of the other eight things, your productivity would proportionately rise higher. The important consideration would then be to choose the two most urgent and important things and also to prioritise the other eight so that your productivity will increase.

The *Pareto Time Principle* teaches us that one can increase one's personal productivity by learning to prioritise one's activities. It also assumes that it is not necessary to do everything because the time available may not be sufficient to do so. All that needs to be done is to learn to differentiate the most urgent, less important and insignificant activities. Concentrate on the most urgent. Some activities may be important but may not be urgent. Some activities are not significant at all; even if you don't do, it will make no difference. Then, why go for such futile activities?

7.3.2 Study Methodology

In everything you do, you need to be methodical. This will systematise your way of thinking and doing things and it will give you a good feeling that you are able to organise your life in an orderly manner. Study methodology will systematise the way you study. Mere hard work will not lead you to succeed in your examinations if your study methodology is wrong. Therefore, first construct a daily study time-table and then follow strictly.

Daily Study time-table (for High School Students)

Evening study at home (6:00 p.m. to 9:00 p.m.)

6:00 pm – 7:00 pm Mathematics
7:00 pm – 8:00 pm Science
8:00 pm – 8:30 pm English
8:30 pm – 9:00 pm Social Science

Spend also sometimes, watching BBC, CNN, NDTV, Discovery channel, Animal Planet or some other educative television programmes.

Morning (5:30 am to 7:30)

5:30 am – 6:30 am all the other subjects that you did not study in the previous evening.

6:30 am – 7:30 am revise all the important points of all the subjects.

This is only a tentative study time-table. You can make a time-table of your own with the proper time that is convenient for you. When you construct your study time-table first identify your weakest subject and allot more time for that particular subject and make that subject your priority.

For college students it is easier to make the daily study time-table as there are lesser subjects and they get more time than high school students.

7.3.3 A Few Important Things to be Kept in Mind before You Begin Your Study

(a) First and foremost, clean your environment–no mobile phone and no other distracting objects should be found on your study table or your study room.
(b) Try to first tackle your weakest subject.
(c) Follow your study time-table strictly without any alteration of the time allotted to each subject.
(d) Never change the order unnecessarily. Make up your mind to study the subject that you don't have any interest.

When you begin to study, you won't feel like studying the subjects which you find difficult. Your weakest subject will be the subject which you'll find the most difficult because you do not have predilection for the subject. Never break the order of your study time-table and the time allotted. Stick to the time. If it is one hour follow it through. What to do with this difficult subject say for example Mathematics? Follow the diagnostic method. Mathematics has different parts—Algebra, Geometry, Trigonometry etc. Of these topics you may find some more difficult than others. For example, if you find difficulty with Algebra; it may not be that you do not know everything. After the teacher has taught you at least you know something. Begin with this something that you know. Gradually, identify which area of algebra is difficult and work on in that area. But don't just look at the subject and say "I think, I don't know or I cannot." Mathematics needs to be done with pen. It needs more practice than intellectual gyration. While doing a problem, sometimes you're not able to proceed because you are not sure of it; identify and mark that. In the same way mark others which you're not sure. Then, when you come to the school find time to ask your teacher personally. He will be most willing to help you if you're putting a sincere effort. So identify which part of algebra you find more difficult and begin to tackle that area.

7.3.4 The Danger of Avoiding Your Weak Subjects

Following your daily study time-table will pay you big dividends. Follow strictly, no matter how difficult it may be. Slackening will affect your academic performance. Some students begin their study with the subject they find tough but give up very soon because it is difficult and boring. They switch on to the next and feel the same thing. Finally, they choose the subject that they like, e.g., say English. Then, they begin to spend their entire study time studying only one subject (English). Their daily study time is spent only on a particular subject or very less time is given to other subjects. This result can be very disastrous to the student's academic output. When the exam result comes, the student gets very high mark in English but the marks in other subjects are very less. His or her parents are flabbergasted at the result telling themselves, "He worked so hard, this can't happen". True, the person had worked very hard daily but his methodology was wrong and so could not pass the exam. Usually, the weak subject is the subject in which the student takes least interest.

7.4 Drugs

Drugs are one of the deadliest enemies of students. Once a student is into drugs it is almost impossible to come out of it. Drug is a substance which when absorbed by a living body even in small quantities stimulates the nervous system and alters the functioning of the body chemistry. There are some substances that changes even the mental behaviour of a person. Such drugs are called psychotropic drugs. Drugs intake alters a person's mind. The mind is the sanctuary of all intellectual works and therefore, it must be contravallated from all negative onslaughts. Once the mind is affected with drugs, it will not be capable of concentration and there will be a marked reduction in memory retention. Once you lose the power of concentration and memory, how can you study? Don't you know many drug users experiences "black out". This is a fatal stage during which one is no more capable of performing an orderly human action. Drugs are also not only harmful but very fatal. Once you are into it, it is almost impossible to come out. So, the best is to decide "NOT TO TRY". Beware of some of the reasons why many students ranging from high school to graduate are trapped by drugs.

7.4.1 How students get into Drugs?

Students don't just get into drugs, alcohol or tobacco overnight. Their starting points are very insignificant and look seemingly quite harmless. But in reality, it is not so. Most of the addicts never knew they would become addicts. They formulate a simple mental logic with a premise that runs: "Ah, this is only a talab" or "just a small tablet" or "just a peck" and draws a conclusion that "it will not cause any harm". These kind of simple premises are used for rationalising their entry into drugs. This is mostly the technique employed by peers to hook their friends. Once you enter into the world of drugs, you will soon reach a place of no-return. Let us see some of the seemingly harmless beginnings:

7.4.1.1 To Increase One's Confidence Level

Some young people feel that after taking drugs or drinks the effect seems to heighten their confidence level. It is thought, a student who is shy and reserved in character is suddenly able to gather courage to talk to a girl whom he has been admiring clandestinely. He feels that he is able to do what he could not do in his sober state. In other words, he just gets emboldened. He has also seen his friends doing it and got attention from girls. When he also does the same; he gets the same result. Since, the drug brings a desired result, he continues now and then and gradually this 'now and then' becomes 'a regular always'.

7.4.1.2 The Principle of Trying Once

"Try everything once" is the philosophy of the young. Young people even if they know that ganja or a tablet or an alcohol is harmful, they will still feel like trying once, "just once". Even the unwilling friend is also finally made to believe in the philosophy of "just once". They would say, "after all it is only once and we will never do again". Trying once is after all not a harmful thing. But know that trying once is the beginning of everything. Trying once will lead to trying twice and trying twice will lead to trying thrice and trying thrice will finally lead to trying dies. Now you know that this is no simple logic: Once leads to twice and twice leads to thrice and thrice to dies. In the beginning it impels and later it compels and finally it expels. This philosophy of trying once is attractive at first sight but fatal gradually.

7.4.1.3 The Young People Want to Belong to a Group

The young people wants a recognised 'group identity' that would make them stand apart from others. Because of this proclivity, they will begin to form gang groups to which they feel secured and free. Belonging to a group gives them security and freedom to work or realise the short-term common goals. Once they belong to a group they have to subscribe to the group ethos: *to feel what the group feels, to think what the group thinks, to eat what the group eats, to drink what the group drinks and do whatever the group does.* For example, John's friends are all drinking alcohol whereas he refrains from it in order to protect his moral rectitude. The group would never accept such a sanctimonious and moralistic attitude of John. A moral pedagogue is such a person who is always unwanted among friends. They do not want a saint or an angel among them. They want one who is like them and hate one who not like them. Since, many young people fear of losing friends just subscribe to the group ethos. This is how most of the young students get into drugs, alcohol, tobacco and other bad habits.

7.4.1.4 To get a Kind of Strange Elation or Thrill

Young people like anything that thrills. They try to get thrilled by smoking ganja or taking alcohol or a tablet. By doing this they get a short span of euphoric well-being for time-being. This is the thrill that they are searching for but it is only an illusion for it lasts only for a short time. They are soon transported back to the pre-thrilled stage of normality.

7.4.1.5 Low Frustration Tolerance

People who have low frustration tolerance often take recourse to drugs and alcohol. Young people are in the process of growing or becoming. They are growing psychologically, physically and emotionally. Since, they are in the stage of growth, their physique, psyche and emotions are very fragile. Due to their fragility, often they experience an emotional crunch at this stage. Their emotional crunch can be due to many reasons – failure in examination, love failure, rejection from parents, demands are not met by parents etc. So, in his struggle to become anorexic to his frustration he becomes an easy prey to the temptation of drugs.

7.4.1.6 To Satiate One's Curiosity

Young people are curious. They are curious because they are in the stage of knowing and discovering things for themselves and no taboo can control them. A person's curiosity is heightened when he hears his friends boasting about their previous experience of drugs or alcohol etc. Some of them took a sort of powder and got a sense of weightlessness. Others felt as though they were ethereal beings flying in the space. Yet others were able see beautiful colours, flying horse or round-square. Even an ordinary music becomes mellifluous. So, out of curiosity, a person wants to experiment for himself in his existential laboratory.

7.5 Alcohol

The World Health Organisation estimates that nearly 62 million people worldwide suffer from alcohol dependence. The illness implicates a broad cross-section of society and affects people from all walks of life, trapping young students, business executives, artists, poets, writers, priests, poets, physicians, engineers, skilled mechanics, labourers and sometimes homemakers. Alcohol abuse harms bodies, minds, families, societies and economies.

Alcohol is one of the greatest enemies to students. Alcohol contains "*ethanol.*" In small amounts "*ethanol*" stimulates the nerve cells in the brain and the cells gradually get damaged. Once these cells are damaged a person loses his power of association, i.e., a person is not able to associate the messages received through the sense organs. This is why learning process drastically slows down and hardly takes place. Once the brain cells are affected learning will be a great problem because the information received through the senses is not able to be processed by the brain.

When alcohol is regularly taken over years, the substance becomes toxic to the cells of the body especially the cells in the liver and this in turn lead to Cirrhosis of liver. This is the major killer associated with alcohol addiction. Liver cirrhosis is the terminal stage of the liver disease in which the liver becomes shrunk and fibrosed thereby losing all its function. This stage occurs after liver has undergone abuse and destruction for a long period of time. A person who begins taking alcohol today will be destined for tomorrow's liver cirrhosis.

7.6 Cigarette Smoking

"Cigarettes contain more than 4000 chemicals compounds and at least 400 of them are toxic substances. Of the 400 toxic substances, 42 are both toxic and carcinogenic. When you smoke, a cigarette burns at 70°C at the tip and around 60°C in the core. This heat breaks down the tobacco to produce toxins. As a cigarette burns, the residues are concentrated towards the butt. The damage caused by smoking is influenced by the number of cigarettes smoked, regardless whether the cigarette has a filter or how well **the tobacco has been prepared. Research has shown that smoking reduces** a person's life span by seven to eight years. On an average, each cigarette shortens a smoker's life by around 11 minutes. The number of people under the age of 70 who die from smoking-related diseases exceeds the total figure for deaths caused by breast cancer, AIDS, traffic accidents and drug addiction". Tobacco products are not only injurious but deadly to health.

Cardiovascular disease is the main cause of death due to smoking. Hardening of the arteries is a process that develops over years, when cholesterol and other fats deposit in the arteries, leaving them narrow, blocked and rigid. When the arteries narrow (arteriosclerosis), blood clots are likely to form. Smoking accelerates the hardening and narrowing process in your arteries. Cardiovascular disease can take many forms depending on which blood vessels are involved and all of them are more common in the people who smoke. Blood clots in the heart (coronary thrombosis) and clots in the brain (cerebral thrombosis). If the vessels to the brain are blocked it can lead to collapse, stroke and paralysis. If the kidney arteries are affected then high blood pressure or kidney failure will results. Blockage to the vascular supply to the legs may lead to gangrene and amputation.

Another disease caused by smoking is Chronic Obstructive Pulmonary Disease (COPD). COPD is a collective term for a group of conditions that block airflow and make breathing more difficult such as emphysema i.e., breathlessness caused by damage to the air sacs (alveoli), chronic bronchitis (coughing with a lot of mucus that continues for at least three months).

Everyone knows that smoking is harmful to health including those who manufacture. The government is well-aware of it as they have imposed a statutory warning on the cigarette package "Smoking is injurious to health." It is unthinkable that the government which is well aware of the ill-effects of tobacco allows tobacco products to be consumed by its citizens. This is another way of saying we don't need healthy citizens. The government does not really care about of its citizens. Now, the big question is: Why does the government allow tobacco products to be manufactured in spite of knowing the harmful effects on its citizens? Clearly, it is because of "*Tobacconomics*". The 35,000-crore tobacco industry employs about 40 lakh people and sales of tobacco products contribute 10 per cent of India's revenue–of which 90 per cent comes from cigarettes. And the Indian tobacco market will continue to grow, until the country is in a position to forgo revenue from tobacco and clamp down on smoking. (Excerpts from *Substance Abuse* by Stephen Touthang, Delhi: Maxford Books, 2011)

7.7 Mobile Phone

Mobile Phone or cellular phone or cell phone is an electronic device used for full duplex two-way radio telecommunications over a cellular network of base stations known as cell sites. It is one of the wonders of contemporary inventions that can instantly connect us to the other person by using the facilities provided by this mini-electronic gadget. We can exploit this gadget for calling, texting or messaging, photography and even high end technological access including internet, music and television streaming. It has made our communication system easy and instant. Thanks to Martin Cooper who invented the first handheld cellular phone in 1973. The practicability of this technology fascinates and inclines especially the young people to purchase it and make it a necessary attribute of their daily activities. Handy, fast, instant, cost-efficient, easy access and immediate results are the features of mobile technology. Together with these there are a number of small industries that manufactures and sells mobile games and *"mobisodes"*, video content designed specifically to be viewed on mobile phones. All these, compel especially the student community to possess a cell phone. The craze for mobile among young people is on the rise today.

One of the most important functions of cellular phone is *connectivity*. The young people want to be connected always to their friends. Cell phone enables them to connect even to an invisible unknown stranger. When their connectivity fails they find themselves in a fit of paroxysm. Most of them today are suffering from what is called *nomophobia* (the fear of being out of mobile phone contact), a new fear unheard of before the coming of mobile phones. This is an added fear to this generation. The day the cellular network fails their mood also changes. Sometimes, I wonder how this small electronic gadget commandeers a person's mood and feelings. All their attention, time and money are systematically consumed by this small device.

Today, this small technological device is controlling the student's time and their parent's money, their moods and feelings and their attention and focus. There are some people who love their mobile more than anything else. Such people are called *nomophiles* (people who have an obsession for mobile phone). These people often say, "I love my mobile more than anything else." They carry their mobile phone wherever they go. Mobile phone becomes their closest constant companion. In other words, they live a mobile-centred life. Their life is glued to a mobile phone. They spend more time on the mobile phone than their study. These people have insulated themselves and they just live happily in their micro-mobile world. This encourages a *leave-me-alone* attitude. Here the person moves from human relationship to electronic mechanical relationship. I think this is a dangerous culture. Gradually, this can metamorphose a person into electronic mechanical being. The person's world contains only him and his mobile. This will make the person adopt the *Laputan* culture (a life of insulation and no interaction with others) and live in his or her own microcosm.

Parents should decide for their children. Students should not be given a free hand on mobile phones. They should not possess or keep it with them. Because as it is said above, mobile contains a lot of entertaining facilities like calling, texting or messaging, gaming, photography and even high end technological access including internet, music and television streaming. They can access unethical sites like pornography etc. Due to these things, the student can be addicted to mobile phones as much as he or she can get addicted to drugs. Mobile can greatly harm their concentration power and proper management of their time. It affects their studies. Mobile phone is as addictive as drug. Mobile phone should not be found on their study table because most students would choose mobile readily over their books. Therefore, their access to mobile phone should be regulated by parents. Mobile phone is a wonderful invention which can also adversely affect the life of students.

7.8 Television and Video Albums

Entertainment media are very good for updating one's knowledge and give us a variety for relaxation. For students too there are many channels which are very useful for them. But too much interest in media will result in time mismanagement. Children would prefer to watch TV or video albums than sit boringly before their books. Watching TV and video albums should be well-regulated by parents. If not regulated, it will affect their study. Watching TV and video albums can be addictive like any other drugs. Most of the TV serials and video albums depict a highly romanticised love stories which can cause an adverse effect in the young minds. It arouses their romantic spirit and venture into courtship and dating prematurely.

7.9 An Appeal to Parents

Dear parents, the Bible says, "Children are a gift from the Lord; they are a reward from Him." Children are the greatest gift, God has given to every parent. This gift is no comparable with any other gifts. You may be a billionaire, having all the comforts and amenities that the world can provide. But what are all these to you, if you have no good, reliable and promising children. It is better to be poor and have good and promising children than be opulent and have unreliable, unpromising and hopeless children. More wealth will give you more worry and better children will give you better hope and the joy of living. If you want your child to be someone great in the future, you need give your time, love and care for them. Your earning, feeding and paying their school fees do not suffice. Even animals perform these biological responsibilities spontaneously to their young ones. Human beings are far superior to animals. Our actions and duties should manifest the supriority of our being over other beings. Therefore, to make a difference in the life of your children you need to go beyond all these banal, mundane and conventional chores of parental responsibility. Your children have to rise above who you are and what you are! You need to inspire them by your life, give them the courage to navigate through this life, instill in them the spirit to do their best, give them a sense of direction and purpose in life. It is better to have children weak in studies but sincere and hardworking than children who are clever but lazy. Don't be lugubrious because your child fails to get good grades in the examination or is not able to outdo your neighbour's child but be lachrymose if your child fails in character. All clever people are not always successful. The majority of the people who succeed in life are mostly hardworking and sincere people and not always the cleverest. Remember, the happiest parents are those whose children are climbing the ladder of life well. Invest on your children and you will get back what you have invested with enormous interest. Never do anything that can negatively affect your child.

- *Do not educate your child to be rich*
Educate him to be happy.
So that when he grows up,
He will know the value of things
Not the price.

Make Me into a Television

A teacher from a Primary School asks her students to write an essay about what they would like God to do for them. At the end of the day, while marking the essays, the teacher read one that made her very emotional. Her husband, who had just walked in saw her crying and asked her 'What happened?' She answered 'Read this. It is one of my students' essay.' The essay runs thus: "Oh God, tonight I ask you something special. Make me into a television. I want to take its place and live like the TV in my house. Have my own special place and have my family around ME. To be taken seriously when I talk. I want to be the centre of attention and be heard without interruptions or questions. I want to receive the same special care that the TV receives even when it is not working. Have the company of my dad when he arrives home from work, even when he is tired. And I want my mom to want me when she is sad and upset, instead of ignoring me. And I want my brothers to fight to be with me. I want to feel that family just leaves everything aside every now and then, just to spend some time with me. And last but not the least, ensure that I can make them all happy and entertain them. Lord I don't ask you for much. I just want to live like a TV.' At that moment the husband said, "My God, poor kid. What horrible parents!" The wife looked up at him and said "That essay is our daughter's!"

Dear parents,

Children are the keys of paradise. The best thing to spend on your children is your time, attention and love. Give a little love to a child and you will get a great deal back. Children have more need of MODELS than of CRITICS. A child mis-educated is a child lost forever. Love, care and attention are the basic needs of every human being and if these basic needs are not met, children will perennially suffer from psychological inadequacy which will later manifest in love and attention deficit syndrome which will in turn give birth to different forms of violence. If you want your children to be someone great, lay the foundation bricks properly so that they feel firm on the ground where they are standing in life. It is better and much more profitable to invest your time, love, attention and care on your children than on any other persons, things or objects. It will give you a lucrative payoff and towards the end of your lives, you will be satisfied and happy that you have done something for your children–then, you can then sing your *nunc dimittis*.

Something to Think About

A child who has been protected and habitually given whatever he wants, will develop an "entitlement mentality" and will always put himself first. He will be ignorant of his parent's efforts. When he starts work, he will assume that every person must listen to him and when he becomes a manager he will never know the sufferings of his employees and will always blame others. For, this kind of person maybe good academically and maybe successful for a while but eventually he will not feel the sense of achievement and fulfillment in life. He will grumble and be full of hatred and fight for more. If we are this kind of protective parents, are we really showing love or are we destroying our children instead?

You can let your children live in a big house, eat a good meal, learn piano, watch a big screen TV and ride the latest car. But when you are cutting grass or doing other manual works, please let them experience it. After a meal, let them wash their plates and bowls together with their brothers and sisters. It is not because you do not have money to hire a maid. You want them to understand and learn life lessons, no matter how rich their parents are, one day their hair will grow grey, same as the mother of that young person. The most important things are that your children learn how to appreciate the effort and experience the difficulty and learn how to work with others in life. If you fail to teach these values to your children, you have failed to train your children to face life. They will have a hard time to sail through this life.

Here is the Story of a Mother who Refuses to give up on the Education of her son:

> Jacob Barnett has an IQ believed to be higher than Einstein's, but at the age of two he was diagnosed with Asperger's Syndrome (a mild form of autism) and doctors told his mum he'd likely never speak or read. She refused to give up on his education and is now far advanced in his Indiana University studies that professors are lining him up for a Ph.D research role. Jacob Barnett is so far

ahead of his age group and is now developing his own theory on how the universe came into existence.

Jake, a teenage boy who was diagnosed with Asperger's Syndrome at a young age has risen to stellar heights after quitting the special education system with the help of his concerned mother. State therapy specialists claimed Jacob Barnett would never tie his shoes, read or function normally in society. But the boy's mother realised when Jacob was not in therapy, he was doing "spectacular things" completely on his own. She decided to trust her instinct and disregard the advice of the professionals. Instead of following a standardised special needs educational protocol, she surrounded Jacob with all the things that inspired passion for him–and was astonished at the transformation that took place.

Following a diagnosis of autism at age two, Jacob was subjected to a cookie cutter special education system that focused on correcting what he couldn't do compared to normal children. For years, teachers attempted to convince Kristine Barnett that her son would only be able to learn the most basic of life skills. When exposed to the state system of educational therapy, Kristine noticed Jacob would withdraw deeply and refuse to speak with anyone. Even though she found it "terrifying to fly against the advice of the professionals," she knew in her heart "that if Jake stayed in special education system, he would slip away," Kristine relates in her memoir, "*The Spark: A Mother's Story of Nurturing Genius*". So began a journey for Jacob that would lead to such unexpected achievement that the whole premise of standardised therapy for this 'special needs' child would be blown to bits.

A Path of Passion and Discovery: After years of frustration and little progress, Kristine made a radical decision in the eyes of the special education system – she took Jacob out of school and prepared him for kindergarten herself. As described in the *New York Daily Times:*

> She let him explore the things he wanted to explore. He studied patterns and shadows and stars. At the same time, she made sure that he enjoyed "normal" childhood pleasures–softball, picnics–along with other kids of his age. "I operate under a concept called 'muchness'," Kristine said. "Which is surrounding children with the things they love – be it music or art, whatever they're drawn to and love".

By the time Jacob reached the age of 11, he entered college and is currently studying condensed matter physics at Indiana University-Purdue University in Indianapolis. According to an email, astrophysics Professor Scott Tremaine, a world renown expert wrote to Jacob's family, "The theory that he's working on, involves several of the toughest problems in astrophysics and theoritical physics... Anyone who solves these will be in line for a Nobel Prize."

Jacob also has an IQ of 170–higher than that of Einstein. He is history's youngest astrophysics researcher and has spoken at a New York TED conference and appeared on a variety of news interviews, including *60 Minutes* and the *Time* magazine website. It is truly surprising for someone who was classified by state experts as so severely disabled that he would never tie his own shoes or learn to read. If Jacob had stayed within the system, the prediction may very well have come true.

I really admire Kristine Barnett for her insight to see the needs of her child and her courage to abandon the existing system and train her child all by herself. Jake is lucky to have such a mother.

"*Great mothers always produce great children*".

8

Architecturing a Positive Attitude

"The greatest discovery of my generation is that human beings can alter their lives by altering attitudes of mind."

—*Lee Iacocca*

8.1 What is an Attitude?

Psychologists define attitude as a learned tendency to evaluate things in a certain way. This can include evaluations of people, issues, objects or events. Such evaluations are often positive or negative but they can also be uncertain at times. For example, you might have mixed feelings about a particular person or issue. According to Hogg and Vaughan, an attitude is "a relatively enduring organisation of beliefs, feelings and behavioural tendencies towards socially significant objects, groups, events or symbols". For Eagly and Chaiken an attitude is a "psychological tendency that is expressed by evaluating a particular entity with some degree of favour or disfavour". Researchers also suggest that there are several different components that constitute attitude.

- *Affective (Emotional) Component*: This involves a person's feelings or emotions about the attitude object (person, issue or event). For example, "I am scared of spiders".
- *Behavioural (Conative) Component:* The way the attitude we have influences how we act or behave. For example, "I will avoid spiders and scream if I see".
- *Cognitive Component:* This involves a person's belief/knowledge about an attitude object. For example, "I believe spiders are dangerous".

This model is known as ABC model of attitudes. The three components are usually linked. However, there is evidence that the cognitive and affective components of behaviour do not always match with behaviour. Attitude can also be explicit and implicit. Explicit attitudes are those that we are consciously aware of and that clearly influence our behaviours and beliefs. Implicit attitudes are unconscious but still have an effect on our beliefs and behaviours.

8.2 Formation of Attitudes

Attitudes are the epiphenomenon of EXPERIENCE. They may emerge due to direct personal experience or may result from observation. Social roles and social norms can have strong bearing on attitudes. Social role relate to how people are expected to behave in a particular role or context. Social norms involve society's rules for what behaviours are considered appropriate.

Attitudes can be learned in a variety of ways. Consider how advertisers use *classical conditioning* to influence your attitude towards a particular product. In a television commercial, you see young, beautiful people having fun in on a tropical beach while enjoying causes you to develop a positive association with this particular beverage. *Operant conditioning* can also be used to influence how attitudes develop. Imagine a young man who has just started smoking. Whenever he lights up a cigarette, people complain, chastise him and ask him to leave their vicinity. This negative feedback from those around him eventually causes him to develop an unfavourable opinion of smoking and he decides to give up the habit.

Finally, people also learn attitudes by observing the people around them. When someone you admire greatly espouses a particular attitude, you are more likely to develop the same attitude. For example, children spend great deal of time observing the attitudes of their parents and usually begin to demonstrate similar outlooks.

8.3 How Attitudes Influence Behaviour

We always presume that people behave in accordance with their attitudes. However, social psychologists have found that attitudes and actual behaviour are not always perfectly aligned. After all, plenty of people support a particular candidate or political party and yet fail to go out to vcte. Researchers have discovered that people are more likely to behave according to their attitudes under certain conditions.

- When their attitudes are the result of personal experience.
- When they are an expert in the subject.
- When they expect a favourable outcome.
- When the attitudes are repeatedly expressed.
- When they stand to win or lose something due to the issue.

In some cases, people may actually alter their attitudes in order to better align them with their behaviour. Cognitive dissonance is a phenomenon in which a person experiences psychological distress due to conflicting thoughts or beliefs. In order to reduce this tension, people may change their attitudes to reflect their other beliefs or actual behaviours. Imagine the following situation:

> Mercy has always placed a high value on financial security, but she starts dating a man who is financially unstable. In order to reduce the tension caused by the conflicting beliefs and behaviour, she has two options: she can end the relationship and seek a partner who is more financially sound or she can de-emphasise the importance of financial stability. In order to minimise the dissonance between her conflicting attitude and behaviour, she either has to change her attitude or change her actions.

8.4 The Different Shades of Attitude

8.4.1 Introduction

Captain Jack Sparrow says, *"The problem is not the problem. The problem is your attitude about the problem"*. Attitude is everything. Our attitude is what we architect from our experience and is manifested through our behaviour. Our values and belief system (our experience of persons, objects, issues and events) are acquired during our formative years beginning from our childhood days. This process is in continuum. If the combination of your innate temperament and your experiences have produced a positive attitude, you are indeed fortunate. But, if you have acquired a negative attitude, whether by design or by default and you are stuck with it, do not get discouraged. Can you change? Yes, but it will be a gargantuan task. It is not going to be easy. Absolutely difficult but is it worth it? Yes!

"We can choose our attitude even though we cannot always choose our circumstances. The choice is either to act like a victor or a victim. It is not our position but our disposition that determines our destiny," says Shiv Khera.

8.4.2 Be Proactive

This is the "Habit 1" of Stephen R. Covey's international best seller book *"The 7 Habits of Highly Effective People"*. You need to take initiative in your life by realising that your decisions and how they align with life's principles are the primary determining factor for effectiveness in your life. Do not wait for people to push you into a situation but propel yourself into it and expect the best out of it. Your goal is important; begin today to realise tomorrow. Take responsibility for your choices and the consequences that follow. The antonym of "proactive" is "reactive". Do not be reactive in pursuing your goal. This will cause bitterness and discouragement. If you are reactive, people will begin to close their doors and you cannot have access to them. This will limit your chances and opportunities to get help from them in attaining your goal. On the other hand, if you are proactive, it will invite many people in your life and they would get involved in contributing their best towards the achievement of your goal.

8.4.3 Win-Win Attitude

Of the seven habits, "*Think-Win-Win*" is the fourth Habit of Stephen R. Covey's "*The 7 Habits of Highly Effective People*". It means one must genuinely strive for mutually beneficial solutions or agreements in your relationships. Value and respect others by understanding a "Win" for all, is ultimately a better long-term resolution than if only one person in the situation had gotten his way. This Win-Win attitude is very important for students who would like to achieve their goals. It is an attitude that is mutually helpful to each other in achieving their goals. I was very happy to hear from my friend who is preparing himself for the UPSC (Union Public Service Commission) examination that he and his friends (preparing for the same exam) used to have group study where they pool their knowledge and strategies together for achieving their goal. This group study is beneficial for all the members in achieving their common goal. This is a Win-Win attitude. Win and let others also win.

8.4.4 A Search for the Positive

Instead of looking for the negatives in others, try to see and find the positive. This will pay you bigger dividends in your life. Seeing only the negatives makes you incapable of interacting with that person. Interacting with more people will expand your horizon and you will gain more. If you see only the negative, you have no time to interact. If you look for the positives, you will learn a lot from others. A student needs to be in constant search for the positive. When you look for the positive in others, the positive qualities you see in others flow in to you. Ultimately, you benefit more than the person from whom you see the positives. If you inject yourself, all the positive qualities that you garner from others, without being aware, you will automatically become positive. Looking for the positive in others itself is a positive act.

8.4.5 Abundance Mentality

Covey coined the idea of 'Abundance Mentality' or 'Abundance Mindset', a concept in which a person believes there are enough resources and success to share with others. He contrasts it with the 'Scarcity Mindset' (i.e., destructive and propels unnecessary competition), which is founded on the idea that if someone else wins or is successful in a situation that means you lose; not considering the possibility of all parties winning (in some way or other) in a given situation. People with an 'Abundance Mentality' reject the notion of zero-sum games (i.e., where only one party wins) and are able to celebrate the success of others rather than feel threatened by it. Some people become selfish and are not willing to share what they have.

8.4.6 Zero-sum Game

In game theory and economic theory, a zero-sum game is a mathematical representation of a situation in which a participant's gain (or loss) of utility is exactly balanced by the losses (or gains) of the utility of the other participant(s). If the total gains of the participants are added up and the total losses are subtracted, they will sum to zero. Thus, cutting a cake, where taking a larger piece reduces the amount of cake available for others is a zero-sum game if all participants value each unit of cake equally. The zero-sum property (if one gains, another loses) means that any result of a zero-surn situation is Pareto optimal. Pareto optimality or Pareto efficiency is a concept in economics with applications in engineering. It is a state of economic allocation of resources in which it is impossible to make anyone further better off without making at least one individual worse off. Given an initial allocation of goods among a set of individuals, a change to a different allocation that makes at least one individual better off without making any other individual worse off is called Pareto improvement. An allocation is defined as "Pareto efficient" or "Pareto optimal" when no further Pareto improvements can be made.

In the process of realising your goal the concepts of zero-sum game or the Pareto optimality can be dangerous. It is dangerous because success in any field is always a collective contribution. An individual winner also had to depend on many people, ideas and knowledge which he gained from myriads of sources and therefore there is no concept called individual winner. Behind every successful person there are many bracing individuals. It is ethically wrong to succeed at the cause of somebody's loss. If my success is going to cause a failure to somebody, that success is morally unacceptable. In realising our dreams we need the help of others and we need to help others too in realising their goals.

8.4.7 Non-zero-sum Game

Non-zero-sum game is the antithesis of zero-sum game. Situations where participants can all gain or suffer together are referred to as non-zero-sum. Thus, a country with an excess of bananas trading with another country for their excess of apples where both benefit from the transaction is Non-zero-sum situation. This game teaches a big lesson for people who are daring to achieve their goal. Here both the countries give each other what they have for what they do not have. As a result, both had what they did not have. In the process of pursuing our goal, we need to give to the other what they do not have and take what we do not have from them. As a result, we will all have or realise our goals. For example, John who is good in Mathematics shares his knowledge with Peter who is weak in Mathematics and receiving from Peter who is good in Science, the subject in which John is weak. This will help both of them to score better marks in Mathematics and Science in their examination (goal).

8.4.8 Nash Equilibrium

This also is an economic theory which is a solution concept of a non-co-operative game involving two or more players, in which each player is assumed to know the equilibrium strategies of the other players and no player has anything to gain by changing only his own strategy unilaterally. If each player has chosen a strategy and no player can benefit by changing strategies while the other players keep theirs unchanged, then the current set of strategy choices and the corresponding payoffs constitute Nash equilibrium. Let's take example, Tom and Jerry are in Nash equilibrium if Tom is making the best decision he can, taking into account Jerry's decision and Jerry is making the best decision he can, taking into account Tom's decision. Likewise, a group of players are in Nash equilibrium if each one is making the best decision that he or she can, taking into account the decisions of the others.

Game theorists use the Nash equilibrium concept to analyse the outcome of the strategic interaction of several decision makers. In other words, it provides a way of predicting what will happen if several people or several institutions are making decisions at the same time and if the outcome depends on the decisions of the others. The simple *insight* underlying John Nash's idea is that one cannot predict the result of the choices of multiple decisions in isolation. Instead one must ask what each player would do, *taking into account* the decision-making of the others.

This theory stresses collectivism in bringing about a result. This is true in the pursuit of our lives' goals. We need to apply the Nash equilibrium. Each person's decision to contribute is of paramount importance for a better achievement. The more you involve others (who will be useful) in the pursuit of your goal, you have a better chance of attaining that goal. In the like manner, you also contribute your best to the attainment of the goal of the others. You take decision that will be beneficial to you and favourable to others. In this way, you can solve the problems of attaining your goal and that of the others'.

8.4.9 Persuasion

Persuasion is a powerful force in our daily life and has a major influence on the individual and society. Politics, mass media, news and advertisements are all influenced by the power of persuasion and they influence us in turn. Persuasion is not just a pushy salesman trying to sell you a car or a television commercial enticing you to buy the latest and greatest product. Persuasion can be very subtle and how we respond to such influences is of paramount importance. According to Perloff, persuasion can be defined as "*...a symbolic process in which a communicator tries to convince other people to change their attitudes or behaviours regarding an issue through the transmission of a message in an atmosphere of free choice*".

Every day we are confronted by persuasion. Food makers want you to buy their newest products, while movie studios want you to go and see the latest blockbusters. Because persuasion is such a pervasive component of our lives, it is easy to overlook how we are influenced by outside sources. The goal of persuasion is to CONVINCE the target, to internalise the persuasive argument and ADOPT this new attitude as a part of their core belief system. Persuasion can be both positive and negative. For example, you can be persuaded to watch pornography on a television. This is one of the examples of Negative persuasion. Advertising the harmful effects of cigarette smoking on the television is an example of positive persuasion. You need to avoid negative persuasion in your life. It can be a source of distraction and it can distort your attitude. Once your attitude is distorted, you have destroyed the base on which you construct your life structure.

8.4.10 It Pays to be Positive

There is a direct correlation between a positive attitude and better relationships, superior health and greater success. A positive attitude can boost your energy, heighten your inner strength, inspire others and garner the fortitude to meet difficult challenges. According to research from the *Mayo Clinic*, positive thinking can increase your life span, decrease depression, reduce levels of distress, provide greater résistance to the common cold, offer better psychological and physical well-being, reduce the risk of death from cardiovascular disease and enable you to cope better during hardships and times of stress.

9

Techniques to Develop a Positive Attitude

Attitude and not aptitude determines your altitude.

One of my favourite books that has touched my life so profoundly is "*Man's Search for Meaning*" written by Viktor Frankl, who survived confinement in the Nazi concentration camps. Many people around him perished giving up all hopes. They felt into despondency and then face death. But Viktor Frankl managed to get through the ordeal by his strong belief in the power and exercise of human freedom. Human beings have the ability to choose how we respond to and process any event that happens to us. In moments of despair and despondency, we can look for some good or we can become haunted by the bad. Frankl writes, "Everything can be taken from a man but one thing, the last of the human freedom to choose *one's attitude* to a given set of circumstances, to choose one's way". What matters most in our lives is to exude a positive attitude in every experience we encounter in our lives.

9.1 Surround Yourself with Positive People

Spend time with people who are positive, supportive and who energise you. Remember, if you get too close to drowning victim, he may take you down with him. Pick always a positive person in your life instead. It is quite tough, but try to surround yourself with people who support you, speak the truth and think positively. Try to avoid people who criticise often and are prone to negative thinking. Also avoid people who are jealous of you and impede your progress. It is true that if you go with negative people, you become negative someday and vice versa.

Surround yourself with the dreamers and the doers, the believers and the thinkers but most of all; surround yourself with those who see the greatness within you, even when you don't see it yourself.

9.2 Keep off the Negative Influences

With so much provocation, it's difficult to keep away negativity. Moreover, peer pressure is killing. Lack of self-esteem culminates in smoking, substance abuse, taking to alcohol, pornography and even resorting to profanity. But these are no permanent solutions. Rather, building self-esteem helps. Self-esteem is how we feel about ourselves and feeling good results in improved performance. On his 70th birthday, April 16th, 1959, Charlie Chaplin said,

"As I began to love myself
I freed myself of anything
That is not good for my health
– food, people, things, situations
And everything that drew me down
And away from myself.
At first I called this attitude
A Healthy Egoism".

The entire water of the sea can't sink the ship. Similarly, negativity of the world can't put you down unless you allow it to get inside you.

9.3 Be Positive Yourself

Learn to master your own thoughts. For example:

- When you visualise a goal, it makes you more likely to take actions necessary to reach it. Visualise yourself winning the race etc.
- Control your negative thinking. This can be accomplished in the following ways:
  - See the glass as half full than half empty.
  - Anticipate the best outcome.
  - Stay the middle ground. Don't view everything in extremes–as either fantastic or a catastrophe. This will help you reduce your highs and lows.
  - Mistakes happen. Negative people blame themselves for every bad occurrence whether it was their fault or not. Don't let this be you.

"A lot of things are inherent in life-change, birth, death, aging, illness, accidents, calamities and losses of all kinds — but these events don't have to be the cause of ongoing suffering. Yes, these events cause grief and sadness, but grief and sadness pass, like everything else and are replaced with other experiences. The ego, however, clings to negative thoughts and feelings and as a result, magnifies, intensifies and sustains those emotions while the ego overlooks the subtle feelings of joy, gratitude, excitement, adventure, love and peace that come from Essence. If we dwelt on

these positive states as much as we generally dwell on our negative thoughts and painful emotions, our lives would be transformed."
— Gina Lake, in "*What about Now? Reminders for Being in the Moment.*"

9.4 Set Realistic, Achievable Goals

There is nothing wrong setting a high bar—unless you beat yourself up for not achieving your goals. The key is to build confidence by setting realistic goals and by hitting a lot of singles rather than swing for the fences. Don't try to live up to the expectations of others. Do what you really want to do. Have positive and achievable dreams. You know your strength—what you can and what you cannot. Concentrate on what you can and try to aim high and when you really work at it, you will realise that you are greater than what you think, you can. Set a goal in which you really take interest, no matter how hard it may be. Make up your mind and tell yourself 'this is what I want to be and I will fight it out'. Do not set a goal which you can never achieve. For example, you want to become a flying eagle. How can you become a flying eagle? Or you want to become a doctor in two days. This is not being realistic. When you are realistic, you will be able to achieve your dream.

9.5 Start Liking the Things that Need to be Done

Some things need to be done irrespective of the fact whether we like them or not. So, when we learn to like the task, the impossible becomes possible. As St. Francis of Assisi once said, "Start by doing what is necessary, then what is possible and suddenly you are doing the impossible". What is "necessary" is what must be done. Most of the people are not able to achieve their dream because they do only what they like and not what is necessary. What is necessary needs not be what interest you most of the time. It is the core longing of your heart to achieve something in life—a goal. Sometimes it may bore you to death. But by persevering in doing what is necessary even when you have no interest will one day take you to arrive at your goal. Therefore, try to discriminate between 'what is necessary' and 'what is your interest' at the moment. These two can clash on the way to realising your dream. We are prone to doing what interest us at the moment rather than what is necessary. Follow 'what is necessary' because it always leads to success.

9.6 Consciously Resist Negative Thinking

Be cognisant of and mentally avoid negative thinking. This will help you modify your behaviour. If you don't resist negative thinking, it can poison your mind and such mind will never have a positive function and will only exude venom. Negative thinking can be the greatest barrier to the wholesome growth of a person. It retards the person's process of unfolding. Negative thinking sucks away the vital strength of a person and others' too. It does not allow the person as well as the others to grow. Negative thinking is internecine in character.

Robert H. Schuller Writes thus

One winter I took a trip up the Nile River to Aswan Dam. In the old tomb of the kings there are sketches of the pharaohs. It was fascinating to learn that every representation of pharaohs in the temples depicted the pharaoh with a bird and a snake around his head. The bird is a vulture and the snake is a wrapped cobra. The vulture eats rotten food and the cobra attacks and kills. These symbolised that the pharaoh had to guard the thoughts that went on his head. If rotten thoughts came, the vulture would consume them and if poisonous thoughts came, the cobra would kill them.

9.7 Do not Compare

Never, never compare yourself with other people. Comparing yourself with others is the most fatal thing you can do to yourself because comparison starts when you see the other better than yourself. If you see the other better than yourself, then you will never see yourself better than others. It points out the good parts in the other person and you begin to feel bad because you don't find those qualities in yourself. Just think of all the good qualities you have too. If you feel you don't have, developed one at least in which you are interested. Comparison is harmful to oneself. Iyanla Vanzant says, "Comparison is an act of violence against the self". When you compare, your attention is most of the time on the other and less on yourself.

9.8 Do not Worry about What Others Say

Stay upbeat. Don't let other people drag you down! What they say is ALWAYS their opinion. Do what makes you happy and isn't harmful. Anthony Hopkins says,

"It is none of my business
What people say of me and think of me.
I am what I am and I do what I do.
I expect nothing and accept everything.
And it makes life so much easier".

When people insult you, don't take offense and don't also take personally, but listen to their words. They are telling you, how they see the world and the exact negative qualities that they possess. Have compassion on such people for they have no other way than to express this way. They have no more options. This is the final culmination of what they are. The "Law of Mirrors" states that one can only see and express what's in them, regardless if it is what is actually present in reality or not.

> "Life is too short to waste any amount of time on wondering what other people think about you. In the first place, if they had better things going on in their lives, they wouldn't have the time to sit around and talk about you. What's important to me is not others' opinions of me, but what's important to me is my opinion of myself... The unhappiest people in this world are those who care the most about what other people think."
>
> —C. *JoyBell C*

9.9 Subtract Your Ego

Everyone has certain amount of Ego but too much ego can kill a person. Developing a false ego can cause a great havoc in your life. A person with strong ego will brag about themselves. His/her 'self' will be the reference point for everything. Bragging is a pompous classification of oneself from others. Such person will always feel that he/she is above others when in actuality he/she may not be. It is a way of deceiving oneself. Exhibition of an ego is ignorance of one's inadequacy within oneself.

It is good to develop *an attitudinal equalisation,* i.e., a process of constructing one's attitude by deeming oneself neither as lower nor higher than others. There should be a feeling of *equalness* or equality with others even when you or the other person is better off in talents and abilities. As you are good at one thing, the other person may be good at something. You know what the other person does not know and what the other person knows you may not know. No human being is omniscient and therefore, no one can claim that he/she knows everything. Therefore, keep a space for dialogue and interaction. This will build confidence and give you the need to interact with others and your whole life will improve. You will benefit more from this than telling yourself "I am better than others and have nothing to learn from them." Superiority complex will feed your ego to grow oversise and ultimately it will erupt and crush your whole self.

9.10 Keep it in Perspective

Life is about prioritising the things that matter most in your life and focusing your efforts in these areas. This means that trivial things that go wrong everyday shouldn't bog you down. Learn to address or ignore small issues and move on. It's time to sweat the big stuff. Arrange your priorities in order. Concentrate and give more importance to the things that top your priority list. Keep it in perspective. Never exchange the most important thing for the lesser ones. What is most important is always the most important and never compromise.

9.11 Metamorphose Challenges into Opportunities

Instead of letting challenges overwhelm you, turn them into opportunities. Rather than hitting the wall, climb over it or go around. Some people find that the dream they are to ascend is too high and therefore feel insurmountable before they begin the climb. Instead, tell yourself, 'If others can, why can't I?" Take it as an opportunity or a chance given to you and try it out. Such an attitude will change challenges into opportunities.

9.12 Develop an Attitude of Gratitude

Develop an attitude of gratitude. Everyone likes grateful people. Be grateful and give thanks for the special things in your life rather than taking them for granted. Be generous expressing gratitude to people even for the slightest good that they have done. Some people do this by giving thanks around the dinner table, keeping a written journal or posting one special item each day on Facebook. Remember, some of the greatest possessions in life aren't material – gratitude, sympathy, love, etc. Take every opportunity to make a wonderful new memory. If you want to achieve happiness, better health, stronger relationships and continued success, you may not have to look any further than the mirror. "The happiest people don't necessarily have the best of everything; they just make the best of everything they have." Do you see the glass half-full or half-empty? True happiness may depend on how you view the world and who you look to for inspiration. It pays great dividend to be positive.

9.13 Use often Positive Language

Avoid words like 'never', 'can't', 'won't' and don't always use a 'why'. Use phrases like 'I can', 'I want', 'I will', 'I need', 'I should' 'I must' etc. You need to constantly challenge yourself with these phrases like 'I can', 'I want', 'I will', 'I need', 'I should' or 'I must'. These words have the power and potency to actualise in a person who constantly uses them.

9.14 Don't Expect Anything in Return

Give away what you seek without expectation or measuring. When you seek success, help others also to be successful. When you seek happiness, help others also to find happiness. Helping others to succeed will help you to succeed in a better way. If you help others; even if you don't ask, others will help you. When you help, expect nothing in return. Expectation can be a sure means of frustration because in life many things happen not according to our expectation. When you don't expect anything, even small helps or little successes become great and they cause you such great joy and happiness. This will make your life interesting.

9.15 Maintain Proper Diet

Improving one's health will facilitate the architecturing of a positive attitude. Eat properly and carefully and have a well-planned and carefully chosen diet. Without health you cannot enjoy anything in life. Remember, health is wealth. A hitch in your health can cast dark clouds in your world. Proper diet will give a healthy body and only a healthy body can enjoy life fully. Health affects the whole world of a person. Therefore, take care of your diet.

9.16 Change Your Focus towards the Positive

Focus on only the positives in life. Begin by finding the good in others instead of looking for flaws. If you look for flaws in others, you will find in abundance. If you look for positive, you will find them too. Now, what is the use of finding and pointing out the negatives in others when it is not mutually beneficial? Do always what benefits you and others. If you point out the positives of others, they will do the same with you. Life is like a see-saw. If you lift the other up, they will also lift you up. Life is all about reaping what you have sown.

Keep your thoughts positive
Because your thoughts become your words.
Keep your words positive
Because your words become your behaviour.
Keep your behaviour positive
Because your behaviour becomes your habits.
Keep your habits positive
Because your habits become your values.
Keep your values positive
Because your values become your destiny.

—*Mahatma Gandhi*

9.17 Stop Procrastinating

Stop procrastinating and begin doing it now. Don't live for tomorrow, live in the "now". "Now" is the favourable time available to you. Tomorrow is not in your hands. Develop the habit of doing things now, so that you don't regret later. Procrastination often eats up your interest and enthusiasm. The completion of a task fills you with joy and energy. To be positive, get into the habit of living in the present and doing it now. Paulo Coelho, the famous writer says, *"One day you will wake up and there won't be any more time to do the things you have always wanted. Do it NOW."*

9.18 Begin Your Day Positively

Begin your day by being positive. After a good night's sleep, you need to get into that mood so that the whole day is positive. Morning mood sets the tone for the day, putting you in the right frame of mind to make every moment of the day positive. And to bring about change, make positive thoughts a part of your life. As William James of Harvard University once said, "If you are going to change your life, you need to start immediately and do it flamboyantly." Thus, you embrace positivity to chart your success.

9.19 Ways to Change Your Attitude

Are you a pessimist ? Do you have a tendency to point out the negatives in a situation without seeing the good? Do people reject or regret being in your company because of your attitude? Successfully changing your attitude is dependent on a change in mindset and successfully changing your mindset is dependent on whether or not you really want to change. Going from pessimistic to optimistic can be difficult but it will result in a brighter and more enjoyable life. If you really want to know how to change your attitude, here are some simple ways but effective pointers:

9.19.1 Stop Focusing on Yourself

A lot of pessimism arises from false or unreasonable expectations especially when those expectations involve yourself. Make an effort to reach out and help at least one person everyday expecting nothing in return. Over time, you may find more joy in giving rather than receiving. To change the focus on yourself, you must bring the image of others before you. Be other-oriented. When you focus on others, the rays and reflection that bounce back to you is potentially good for your growth.

9.19.2 Face Your Flaws

We all have something upon which we can improve so whether you're at work, at home, at school or college or anywhere else, be open to learning more. Make a list of all your weaknesses and flaws. At the beginning of every week, take one of these listed flaws and think about what you could learn concerning that weakness. Use the remainder of the week to learn even more. Have the courage to look at your weakness and see how you can overcome them. Don't pretend that you don't have any weakness; it is a common human phenomenon which cannot be denied. A coward person will pretend as if he does not have any flaw. Feeling that you don't have any weakness does not exonerate you from having flaws. Instead, be true to yourself and deal with your flaws courageously; this will help you to improve your life. Positively, deal with your weaknesses and it can be a source of strength to improve your life.

9.19.3 Look on the Bright Side

In every undesirable circumstance, there is always a way to look on the brighter side. This isn't to say that you should live your life dishonestly, always ignoring the bad in favour of a fake smile. Instead, accept the bad things but also think about how much worse it could have been. For example, may be you just got into a car accident and need to pay a lot of money for reparations and medical bills. One way to look on the bright side is to be grateful that you are still alive without permanent damage to your body or your brain.

> Once there were two persons. One looked up the sky and saw only the thick cloud enveloping the whole sky. The other person looked up and to his surprise he not only saw the cloud but also a special lining that decorated the cloud and beautify the sky. The first one is a pessimist and the second an optimist. The pessimist, when beset by problems and pains sees nothing except the problems and pains. In other words, he sees only the clouds. He thinks that once he is caught in the web of problems and pain, there is no escape and no solution. He feels that he is irredeemable and therefore not worth trying a solution. He has no hope and allows gloom to encircle him. On the contrary, the optimist always holds that every problem and pain has its brighter side. He perceives that life is beyond problems and pain. He is able to see the things beyond the thick clouds. He is able to rise above problems and pains. He hopes that every problem and pain will pass someday and they can be overcome and that there is a solution. He may not be able to overcome just now or today but he hopes that someday victory will dawn.

9.19.4 Count Your Blessings

Post up a blank sheet of paper on your wall or use as a journal. Every morning, as soon as you've woken up, think of one blessing in your life that hasn't already been written on the paper and write it down. Counting your blessings will help you see that your life isn't all doom and gloom that you have reasons to be happy and joyful. Keeping a record of the good things that happen to you can make you always grateful and this feeling will increase your positive image of yourself.

9.19.5 Find a Life Coach/Attitutors

Life coach or attitutors are professionals who help people find success in many forms including successful attitude adjustments. They have the experience of knowing what methods work best for the majority of people. You can contact life coach in person, attend workshops and seminars.

Even if you don't find a life coach, there are people who can help you. Seeking the help of such people will be of great help in your life.

9.19.6 Befriend Optimistic People

Sometimes a poor attitude is a result of being surrounded by people with poor attitudes. As it has been said, "Bad company corrupts good character." Consider befriending new people especially people who are optimistic and have a healthy attitude towards life. It is true that if you go with a runner, you will begin to run and if you go with a slow walker, you will begin to walk slowly. Even optimism and pessimism can be contagious. If you go with an optimistic person, you will learn to be optimistic and if you go with a pessimist, you will begin to be pessimistic in your outlook.

> "What I am suggesting is that each of us turns from the negativism that permeates our society and look for the remarkable good among those with whom we associate, that we speak of one another's virtues more than we speak of one another's faults, that optimism replace pessimism, that our faith exceed our fears. When I was a young man and was prone to speak critically, my father would say: 'Cynics do not contribute, skeptics do not create, doubters do not achieve.'
>
> —*Gordon B. Hinckley*

9.19.7 Ask Your Friends to Point Out When You are Pessimistic in the Future

This will help you to see how often your pessimism arises and in what situation it tends to arise. This can be done only by a strong character. A person with a strong character will have the guts to tell others to point out their weaknesses or negative points in their character so that he/she can improve. A weak character will be afraid to tell others to point out his negativities. If you can do courageously, this will help you to build a positive attitude. A person with a strong character will always welcome someone who points out his negativities because those are the ones he himself might not have seen. With this new realisation of his flaws, he can correct himself.

9.19.8 Ask the Right Questions

When you are in a right situation where you feel your unwanted attitude forcing its way through, take the time to ask a few questions of yourself to help you change your outlook. Examples,

- What can I do to change the way I feel?
- Is there another meaning I can discover from this situation?
- What could I do to make this situation more interesting or appealing?

- What could I do to benefit from this?
- What is that person's story? How did they come to behave like this? Could that be me or someone I love?

9.19.9 Do not be Afraid to be What You are and Who You are!

Do not be afraid to be what you are and who you are! Be a 'warrior of light' as Paulo Coelho says. Never lost the hope of ameliorating what and who you are! Your weakness should not bog you down; instead it should be a springboard on which you take a greater leap for greater heights. The following is an excerpt from "*Warrior of the Light*" by Paulo Coelho:

Every Warrior of the Light

Every Warrior of the Light
Has felt afraid of going into battle.

Every Warrior of the Light
Has at some time in the past, lied or betrayed someone.

Every Warrior of the Light
Every Warrior of the Light has trodden a path that was not his.

Every Warrior of the Light
Has suffered for the most trivial of reasons.

Every Warrior of the Light
Has at least once, believed he was not a Warrior of the Light.

Every Warrior of the Light
Has failed in his spiritual duties.

Every Warrior of the Light
Has said 'yes' when he wanted to say 'no'.

Every Warrior of the Light
Has hurt someone he loved.

That is why he is a Warrior of the Light,
Because he has been through all this
And yet has never lost hope of being better than he is.

10

Building Self-esteem

"People with high self-esteem are the most desired and desirable people in society."

—*Brian Tracy*

10.1 What is Self-esteem?

Self-esteem is how you feel about yourself as a person. Those with high self-esteem believe that they are adequate, strong and worthy of a good life, while those with low self-esteem feel inadequate and worthless. Low self-esteem can develop in childhood and continue throughout adulthood, causing great emotional chaos in one's life. Therefore, it is important to develop a healthy and positive sense of self.

Roberth H. Schuller in his book "*Be Extraordinary in an Ordinary World*" writes:

> Rene Dubos, a great scientist said, 'The human being has an infinite capacity to adjust downward,' to which I replied, 'Adjustment is always a downward movement. The upward movement is never an adjustment – it is always a commitment!' That commitment comes through self-esteem, pride and human worth. To my knowledge, the last article written by Rene Dubos was called *Survival*, and in it he said what I'm trying to say. If you lose your pride in being human, you lose your self-esteem. When that happens you'll no longer believe that it's possible to solve the problems. Self-esteem produces possibility thinking. Remove self-dignity and you remove self-confidence. But adopt the faith of possibility thinking (self-esteem) and then get set for a surprise'.

10.2 Wrong Conceptions of Self-esteem

Many people base their self-esteem on external factors such as how much money they earn, how much they weigh and whether people like and appreciate them. If one of the external variables changes, their self-esteem can be broadly affected. For example, if your self-esteem is based on the fact that someone else loves you, then you risk feeling extremely vulnerable and worthless if that person's love ends. By the same token, building self-esteem is not an easy task if you have been abused or have suffered years of personal or professional failure.

You cannot make people *value* you
All you can do is show them
who you are
What you *feel* and
What you *believe*
It is up to them to realise your *worth*.

10.3 Create a Positive Self Awareness

Building your self-esteem and creating a positive self-awareness comes from taking an inventory of your own strengths and abilities as a human being. Being at peace with who you are and what you have to offer the world is a major part of having high self-esteem. This 'inner peace' does not mean you are unaware of your weaknesses; it merely means that you accept what you are and genuinely like the person you have become.

10.4 Maintaining Self-esteem

You should think about yourself as deserving attention, admiration and proper maintenance. Avoid the pitfall of paying too much attention to the happiness and well-being of others and too little to your own. Maintaining self-esteem involves becoming fully aware of your strengths and seeing challenges as opportunities to employ those strengths. Low self-esteem is often linked to depression or anxiety. If your emotions are overpowering or out of control, one way to build self-esteem around this issue is to learn to manage your mood and gain control over your feelings. Some people are able to do this with the help of friends and family. Others need to work with a mental health professional to manage the problems that may lie beneath the surface of low self-esteem.

10.5 What is Self-dominion?

Self-esteem refers to 'how much you like yourselves'. How much you like yourselves forms the level of self-dominion. Self-dominion is our ability to get ourselves to actually do, what we want ourselves to do; in other words, self-discipline and self-trust. A person who has dominion over themselves has self-integrity—staying true to their words and commitments. Every time we fail to listen to our inner voice and do not take action in something that we need to, we lose trust with ourselves and our abilities.

This lack of self faith continues to spiral downwardly as we flounder to fulfill more commitments.

Learning to know and trust yourself is a long but worthwhile process. Throughout life you may need to search within yourself again and again to find your own empowerment and strength.

10.6 Techniques to Develop a Positive Self Esteem

Let us now see the different techniques of building self-esteem.

10.6.1 Be Nice to Yourself

Unfortunately some people say the meanest things to themselves. If you criticise yourself long enough, you will begin to believe it. This negativity can drag you down over time. It may be time to fire the critic and hire the advocate. Grooming yourself by taking care of your appearance can affect you too if you feel ugly. Stay natural. You should change your hair styles, clothing and if you wear it make up but that's it. This can help you feel great. Remind yourself most things are possible if you try hard enough. Set your goal and work to reach it.

10.6.2 Do not Worry about What Others Say

Stay upbeat. Don't let other people drag you down! What they say is ALWAYS their opinion. Allow others to exercise their freedom of speech. When somebody criticises you it is not your problem. It is their problem. They criticise you because you possess what they don't possess. It shows that they have a lot of negativity within them. Criticism is a way of letting out their negativity. If a person is positive, he won't criticise you. So, be sympathetic towards people who try to put you down. Instead do what makes you happy and isn't harmful.

10.6.3 Start Small

Start with something you can do immediately and easily. When you start with small successes, you build momentum to gain more confidence in your abilities. Each completed task, regardless of how small is a building block towards a more confident you. What are some small actions you can take immediately to demonstrate that you are capable of achieving goals you have set for yourself? For example, clean your desk, follow your time table or study your lessons and so on.

10.6.4 Create a Compelling Vision

Use the power of your imagination. Create an image of yourself as the confident and self-assured person you aspire to become. When you are this person, how will you feel? How will others perceive you? What does your body language look like? How will you talk? See these clearly in your mind's eye with your eyes closed. Feel the feelings, experience it and see things from that person's perspective. Practice doing this for 10 minutes every day. Put on music in the background that either relaxes you or excites you. When you are done, write a description of this person and all the attributes you've observed.

10.6.5 Socialise

Get out of your house and socialise with others often. But this should not be just a mere social exercise. You must socialise with those people who will enhance your self-esteem. Socialising with others will give you opportunities to connect with other people and practice your communication and interpersonal skills. Man is a social animal and learning takes place through the process of socialisation. The more you socialise with others, the more you will learn and gain. Different people have different varieties of experience and knowledge and by interacting with them you gain their experience and knowledge. Once your knowledge bank is stashed with enough experiences, you will begin to feel very confident. Thus, improving your self-esteem.

10.6.6 Do Something You are Good at

What are you especially good at or enjoy doing? Regularly doing things that you are good at reinforces your belief in your abilities and strength. One can be very efficient in completing errands or administrative work. Whenever you have a few hours filled with ways in which you've maximised your time, you will feel highly productive and this boosts the confidence you have in your abilities as an organised and efficient person.

10.6.7 Help Others Feel Good about Themselves

Help somebody or teach them something. When you help other people feel better about themselves and like themselves more, it will make you feel good about yourself too. See what you can do to make others feel good or trigger them to smile, maybe giving them a genuine compliment, helping them what you admire about them.

10.6.8 Get Clarity on Life Areas

Get clarity on the life area that needs the most attention. Your self-esteem in all the major areas of your life is important. Write down all the major categories of your life e.g., Health, relationships, finance etc. Then rate yourself on a scale of 1-10 in each area. Work on the lowest numbered category first, unless they are all even. Each area affects the other areas. The more you build up each area of your life, the higher your overall self-esteem.

10.6.9 Create a Plan

Having a goal alone won't do much. Get clarity on your action items. One of the biggest reasons people get lazy is because they don't have a plan to achieve their goals. They don't know what the next step is and start to wander off randomly. When you're baking a cake, it's a lot easier to follow a set of clear instructions, than randomly throwing ingredients together.

10.6.10 Get Motivated

Read something inspirational, listen to something empowering, talk to someone who can uplift your spirits, who can motivate you to become a better person, to live more consciously and to take proactive steps towards creating a better life for yourself.

10.6.11 Get External Compliments

As funny as this point suggests, go find a friend or family member, whom you really trust and ask them "What do you like about me?" "What are my strengths?" or "What do you love about me?" We often value other people's opinions more than our own. We are best at beating ourselves up for things not done well and we are the worst at recognising what we've done well. Hearing from another person our strengths and positive qualities helps to build a more positive image of ourselves.

10.6.12 Affirmations and Introspection

Use affirmations but in the right way. Some people think that when they're in a slump, using positive affirmations will help them get out of it. Affirmations are good but you have to use them in a way that is beneficial to you. Sitting on your couch and saying "I am highly motivated and productive" does nothing. Say something like "I am sitting here being very unproductive right now, is this the ideal me? What would be my best self?" Your affirmations have to be the TRUTH. Once you're honest, take the first step towards doing the thing, no matter how small. This will build you up.

10.7 Causes of Low Self-esteem

It is not possible to point the one cause of low self-esteem for everyone because everyone follows a different path through life. The formation of your *core beliefs* about yourself is a complex process. Your own inborn nature or temperament will play a role but your experiences and relationships with the people around you also have an important part to play.

Negative experiences in childhood are often particularly damaging to self-esteem. In your early years, your personality and sense of self is being formed and harmful experiences can leave you feel that you are not valued or important. You have not had a chance to build up any resilience, so this negative view can become the one that you believe about yourself. Significant negative experiences in adult life can also shake core beliefs and cause them to change. This will normally happen over time and you might not realise at first that your self-esteem is being lowered. Experiences that commonly impact on people's beliefs include:

- Being subject to abuse – sexual, emotional or physical and loss of control associated with this.
- Having your physical and emotional needs neglected in childhood.
- Failing to meet the expectations of your parents.
- Feeling like the 'odd one out' at school coming from a community which often experience prejudice, such as being an asylum seeker or being poor but living in a wealthy neighbourhood.
- Peer pressure to conform to social norms which you don't agree with.
- Bullying or excessive pressures at work trauma.
- Physical ill-health–its impact on your quality of life and activities.
- Facing redundancy or being unemployed.
- Social isolation and loneliness.

The way you feel about experiences such as these will depend on lots of other factors, but negative core beliefs about your intelligence, appearance and abilities will often be formed:

I think I'm ugly and unattractive. Other people are more intelligent, talented and interesting than me. Most people wouldn't want to spend any time with me because of these things.

When something happens that reminds you of these significant experiences, you expect the worst and are likely to be at the back of your mind all the time.

- You will probably feel anxious and might shake, blush and panic.
- You may also try to avoid the situation all together or behave in a way that you think will keep you 'safe' e.g., not going to social event on your own.

This reaction is likely to confirm the negative core beliefs you have about yourself and leave the feeling you have even less chance of coping with a similar situation in the future. This cycle might seem unbreakable but it is crucial to remember that these are beliefs not facts and they can be changed.

10.8 Perfectionism can be Harmful for Building Self-esteem

Is perfectionism a highly desirable trait that ensures high standards and utter reliability or a psychological handicap indicative of dithering, delay and delusions? Is it a healthy drive or self-destructive?

Perfectionists value and foster excellence and strive to meet important goals. In certain areas like sports and science, perfectionism is not just tolerated but encouraged. To some, perfectionism is about high standards, persistence and conscientiousness. Perfectionists are organised. They have self-imposed high standards and in the role of parent, teacher or mentor, they tend to impose those standards on others. Combined with ability and stability, perfectionists can, should and do reach their ultimate level of performance.

But there is a dark side: Perfectionism is seen as a cause and correlate of serious psychopathology. At worst, perfectionists believe they should be perfect – no hesitations, deviations or inconsistencies. They are super-sensitive to imperfection, failing and weakness. They believe their acceptance and lovability is a function of never making mistakes. And they don't know the meaning of "good enough". For them, it's always all or nothing.

Psychologists see perfectionism almost always as a handicap. They see perfectionists as vulnerable to distress, often haunted by a chronic sense of failure; indecisiveness and its close companion procrastination and shame.

The clinical take on perfectionism is that it can and does involve setting excessively high personal standards and stringently evaluating one's behaviour in light of them. It can also mean imposing one's standards on others and having equally high (often quite unrealistic) expectations of them. Perfectionists often believe that powerful others–bosses, parents, spouses–expect one to be perfect in all ways. They are harsh, punitive, unforgiving judges. Perfectionists are rigid.

So where does perfectionism come from? Parents, teachers, elders etc. They may have been critical and demanding. Most perfectionists in adulthood live with their parents' voice and their standards. The way psychologists measure perfectionism probably best explains how they conceive of it. Measurement is mainly done by questionnaire or interview. And tests are multi-dimensional, trying to capture the full range of issues:

- One issue is concern over mistakes, which reflects negative reactions to mistakes; a tendency to interpret mistakes as equivalent to failure and a tendency to believe that one will lose the respect of others following failure: *"People will probably think less of me if I make a mistake"; "I should be upset if I make a mistake".*
- A second issue is of personal standards, which reflect the setting of a very high standards and the importance placed on these high standards for self-evaluation: *If I do not set the highest standards for myself, I am likely to end up a second-rate person; I hate being less than the best at things.*
- The tendency to believe that one's parents set very high goals comprises the third issue of parental expectations: *My parents expected excellence from me; my parents wanted me to be the best at everything.*

• Fourth, the perception that one's parents are or were overly critical constitutes the parental criticism element: *As a child I was punished for doing things less than perfect; I never felt like I could meet my parents' standards.*

• Another feature is the doubting of actions, which reflects the extent to which people doubt their ability to accomplish tasks.

• Finally, excessive importance can be placed on order and organisation: Organisation is very important to me; I try to be a neat person.

So pity the poor perfectionist. They are driven by a fear of failure; a fear of making mistakes and a fear of disapproval. They can easily self-destruct in a vicious cycle of their own making:

"Such unreachable goals – fail to reach them – become depressed and lethargic – have less energy and a deep sense of failure – get lower self-esteem and high self-blame."

Pathological perfectionists are both unhappy and unproductive. They tend to have low self-esteem because they feel they are losers. And there is always the ghost of guilt and its fellow travellers, shame and self-recrimination. Most perfectionists struggle with depression, pessimism and low self-belief. They can easily become immobilised and without motivation. But when they are at it, perfectionists are marked by their compulsivity, obsessiveness and rigidity.

There is nothing wrong with setting high standards but they need to be reachable with effort. It's all about being OK; human not super-human; among the best, if not the best. Perfectionism can be a curse and perfectionists can carry criticism both of themselves and others. By setting standards at the wrong level, they are condemned never to achieve them.

11

Loving Oneself is the Bedrock of Self-esteem

"To love oneself is the beginning of a life-long romance."

–Oscar Wilde

The self is the starting point of one's actions and thoughts:

- the way I look at others,
- the way I relate,
- the way I talk,
- the way I respond/react

If you don't have a genuine and authentic love of your SELF, all your thoughts and actions will be negatively affected and thus paving way for low self-esteem. Therefore, loving yourself is one of the surest ways of building your positive self-esteem. One concrete way of showing your love to yourself is *"to tryst with yourself"*. But before you tryst with yourself, you need to do few things in order to facilitate smooth trysting with yourself. They are:

11.1 Remove Disturbances

Unplug your phone, power down the cell phone, shut down the computer, turn off the TV. Do not let your mind get distracted during your self-tryst. This is your time to just be with yourself. Cultivate the habit of being with yourself from your younger age onwards. It is a source of strength. Learn to live alone otherwise you will be seeking solace only in the presence of others. If you don't learn to be happy and comfortable with yourself, you will find life at times very hard and boring. Self-tryst is important. We need to be realistic about life. A day will come even your best friends will leave you. In such moments, how will you tackle your situation? Remember the saying, "Even your shadow leaves you when you walk in darkness."

11.2 Being Solo

It is important that you are on your own. Disconnect your social network. Try to be alone. The purpose of trysting with yourself is to get yourself *au fait* with the inner workings of your SELF. It is important to realise that this moment is a gift for yourself and you should only focus on your well being.

11.3 Forgive Yourself

Forgiving oneself is very significant in building self-esteem. If you have made mistakes in the past that had caused you to feel less worthy, then you need to forgive yourself. All of us make mistakes; so there really is no need to beat yourself up over them. Also, if you have been carrying around a baggage of emotional hurt because of a childhood trauma, learn to forgive yourself.

Write down on your journal or paper all the things you forgive yourself for. At times we tend to be harsh on ourselves and voluntarily blame ourselves internally for failures—failures to achieve, failures to act etc. Take this time to forgive yourself for all the harsh things said, for mistreatment of your emotional and mental and physical health etc.

> "To forgive is to set a prisoner free and discover that the prisoner was you."
>
> —*Lewis B. Smedes*

11.4 Eliminate Self Criticism

Never berate yourself over a peccadillo. Is there an inner voice that often tells you that you are not good because you are stupid or make mistakes often? If you find that you are self destructive and judgmental, make a conscious effort to stop such negativism. Tell yourself that you are not all bad. From just one good, you can build up all good.

11.5 Being Grateful

List out all the things in your life you are thankful for. Make an inventory of the things that others admire about you. What are some of the things they say that you are good at or have natural abilities towards? You pretend to be another person looking at yourself. Express gratitude for the person that you are. For instance, cultivate an appreciation for your strengths and gifts. Also, feel a sense of gratitude that you are alive and well and fully capable of making a difference in your life.

11.6 Inject Yourself with Fun-tonic

Inject some fun into your life. Life is meant to be enjoyed. Don't take life or yourself too seriously. If you can think of life in this manner, you automatically relax and quit worrying over things that do not matter. Do not allow birds to make nests on your head. Shirk off all the negative things that come to you and do not allow them to make nests on your head. This can choke your growth and well being.

11.7 Acknowledge Your Effort

It is not always about winning or coming up tops in everything that you do. Many times, it is the sustained effort that counts. Acknowledge that you have done your best, even if you have failed to produce tangible results. Being faithful may not necessarily lead you to success but it will give you the satisfaction that you have done your best. So, be happy that you have made an effort.

11.8 Be Kind and Positive

When you begin to think kindly and positively about yourself, the love you have for yourself just grows. Make it a habit to praise yourself every day as you stand in front of the mirror. Because of such thoughts, you naturally undertake empowering actions that support your development.

"I am always reminded that my blood type is Be Positive."

11.9 Trust Yourself

Have confidence in your abilities. Know that you have the ability to make important changes for yourself, for as long as you put your heart to it. You can also support yourself by visualising the desired outcomes.

"*Trust yourself. You know more than you think you do*".

—Benjamin Spock

11.10 Be Truthful to Yourself

Loving yourself requires you to be truthful about your own feelings. If you are happy, acknowledge the joy. If you are sad, acknowledge the sorrow. When you are truthful about your feelings, you do not try to lie to yourself or seek to bury your negative emotions. Instead, acknowledging what you feel provides a good guide to what your thoughts are. And as we all know, thoughts can be changed, so that healing and self growth can take place.

11.11 Make Positive Affirmations Everyday

Regularly pass positive affirmations on yourself. For instance, say this to yourself "I love and accept myself completely and unconditionally".

Tell yourself "well done!" over your little success and "Never say die" over your small failures. Do this exercise several times a day.

11.12 Look after Your Body

It is important that you strengthen yourself with proper nutrition and regular exercise. Your body is a temple and you should treat it with respect, love and care. It has been found that the lack of self love is often the root cause of conditions like eating disorder, obesity or even terminal diseases. If your body is not healthy, you can't enjoy other things.

"Take care of your body. It's the only place you have to live."

—*Jim Rohn,* American Author and Speaker

11.13 Avoid Narcissistic Attitude

Some of the manifestations of narcissistic attitude are as follows:

11.13.1 Unilateral Listening

What I want is all that matters. When we make decisions together, what you want, your concerns, your feelings etc., are mere whispers, inconveniences and irrelevancies. When we discuss issues, my opinions are right. Yours are wrong or else of minimal importance. If you expect to have input, you are undermining me. Instead of listening in order to be responsive, narcissistic listening listens to dismiss, negate, ignore, minimise, denigrate or otherwise render irrelevant other people's concerns. One specific indicator: frequent responses that begin with "But..." which is linguistically a backspace-delete key.

11.13.2 It's All about Me

I know more, I know better, I'm more interesting. When we talk it's mostly about me. In conversation, I take up most of the air time. Maybe that's why people say I suck up all the air in a room. When I wasn't something I need to have it. Never mind how you feel about it; it's all about me. I'm big and important and you are merely here, mostly to do things for me, like a third arm.

11 13.3 The Rules don't Apply to Me

Narcissists suffer from what is called "*Tall Man Syndrome*". They experience themselves as above others, so the rules don't apply to them. The rules are for others not for them.

11.13.4 Your Concerns are Really Criticisms of Me and I Hate being Criticised

Narcissists paradoxically manifest an inflated idea of their self-importance, yet are quick to feel deflated by negative feedback. They are hypersensitive to criticism.

11.13.5 When Things Go Wrong between Us, It is Always Your Fault

I can't be expected to apologise or admit blame. I'm above others and above reproach. Unwillingness to take responsibility for mistakes goes hand-in-hand with quickness to blame. This trait may come from confusing the part with the whole. If I have done one thing that is not right, then I must be all bad.

11.13.6 If I'm Angry, It's because of You

It's never my fault if things don't go well. I'm not responsible for the problem. They are quick to anger because they see that they are special and also remarkably thin-skinned. Any feedback that punctures their belief in total specialness can feel quite threatening. The immediate response will be to issue blame. This is a mechanism for protecting their self pride from further damage.

11.14 Consequences of Low Self-esteem

The impact of low self-esteem on your life can be significant; you may find that all areas of your life are affected in some way and confirm your core belief that you are of little value. Low self-esteem can cause mental health problem and exacerbate existing conditions and make you more vulnerable to develop other problems. It can also influence your day-to-day life.

11.14.1 Personal Relationships

If you have low self-esteem you might find that you form damaging relationships. You may feel you don't deserve to be treated with love and respect and so allow friends or partners to take advantage of you or control you.

11.14.2 Social Life

For some people with low self-esteem can be very difficult to hear criticism and you might find that you are overly-sensitive and upset very easily. You might, therefore, stay away from activities that can expose you to any type of judgment, leaving you to become isolated and frustrated. You will begin to live a life of insularity and put yourself in quarantine.

11.14.3 Negative Behaviours

You might find that to try and deal with your low self-esteem, you behave in ways that are damaging to you and those around you. You might find that you try to 'escape' from life and engage in risky behaviour like taking drugs, unsafe sex or drinking too much. You might also develop an aggressive or violent personality to try to hide your vulnerabilities and protect yourself from further damage.

No one is happy all the time and having high self-esteem does not mean you will always feel confident about work nor have successful relationships. However, good emotional health and positive self-esteem are strong predictors of happiness. If your core belief about yourself is mainly positive you may still associate with some of these behaviours but your ability to cope with them will be much better.

11.14.4 Be Assertive

Be assertive does not mean you need to be aggressive or difficult but it will help you set clear boundaries. It means you value yourself and others and can communicate with mutual respect. To behave in an assertive way you should try to keep your body language open and confident and try to express your feelings if you have been upset. You need to learn to begin to say 'no' to unreasonable requests or tell people that you need more time or support with tasks that you find challenging.

12

Building Self-confidence

"Confidence comes not from always being right but from not fearing to be wrong."

—Peter T. Mcintyre

12.1 Introduction

Self-confidence is not an overnight achievement. It takes determination and dedication to realise you are a good human being that is worthy of respect and love. Your perception of yourself will dictate how you live your life as a whole. Self-confidence is learning how to appreciate and accept yourself as you are. If your self-esteem is only dependent on how people see you and what they think about you, then your confidence will be short-lived. You will have self-doubts the moment people start saying negative things about you. You need to learn how to be happy and proud of yourself, your achievements and experiences even if others are not there to cheer you on. Once you learn to do this, then you will have a healthy self-esteem no matter what the situation is. You will never know what life will throw at you, but you need to start building your self-confidence to face life's toughest challenges. You need the self-assurance to make strong decisions and navigate through life on your way to success. Here are few tips to help you build your self-confidence.

12.2 Recognise Your Strengths

Recognise your strengths or talents and empower yourself with them. Learn to accept your weaknesses without allowing them to pull you down into a miasma of depression. Instead work on developing and improving yourself. The more you develop and improve your talents, your confidence level will grow higher and higher. Self-confidence is built on your self-worth. Your self-worth is largely composed of who you are. Who you are, is made up of what you have–talents, capabilities etc. Once you have recognised your talents and capabilities and developed them, they give you a feeling of self-worth and the people around you will begin to recognise them. This feeling is not pride but a recognition of oneself. If you don't have anything or develop any of your talents, your confidence level will be low. What you have does not refer to the external variables like money, wealth etc. These external variables give only false self-confidence.

12.3 Identify Your Insecurities

What does the voice in the back of your mind say? What makes you uncomfortable or ashamed of yourself? This could be anything from acne to regrets, friends at school or a past traumatic or negative experience. Whatever is making you feel unworthy, ashamed or inferior, identify it, give it a name and write it down? You can also tear these written pieces to start feeling positive on those points.

12.4 Conquer Self-defeating Thoughts

Stay positive and fill your mind with good things about yourself, people and the situation you are in. Even if things seem really bad right now, focus on how things could be better and the small steps you need to take to make that happen. Stop telling yourself, "I can't make it or do it", "It is not meant for me" or "I can't overcome this".

12.5 Be Honest to Yourself and Others

Don't try to put up an image of yourself that is not real; don't project someone you are not. Allow people to accept you for who you are and not someone who is just created to please others. Remember, the Latin phrase, "*esse quam videre*" which means 'to be rather than to seem'. Who you are, is the real you. Do not project who you are not. In other words, do not be two-faced. No one is perfect and sometimes people may show you who they appear to be; accept them and maintain your authenticity in such moments. Do not impetuous to make conclusions. Sometimes, perceptions of people can be deceiving as you only see a fragment of the whole person.

11.6 Talk with Friends and Loved Ones Your Diffidence

Diffidence is just the opposite of confidence. Wear it on your sleeve. Each day you should chip away at it; wear it down. There is no quick fix. Get to the root of the problem; focus on it and understand that you need to resolve each issue before you can move on. Check if it's an old past emotion and if it is really still relevant or applicable in your life today. And that doesn't mean you have to get rid of whatever makes you feel bad (many times you simply can't). You need to learn to accept yourself, your past, your circumstances as they are, without necessarily thinking of them as 'bad'.

12.7 Take Responsibility for Your Actions and Decisions

Empower yourself to make important decisions about life and your future. Stop allowing others to dictate the course of your life. Think about what it is that you really want to achieve. Even if that means you need to do something that would normally make you feel a little selfish. Remember that it's your life, not theirs. Who will suffer if things go wrong because you let others run your life? In all likelihood, you will suffer the most. The people who keep trying to control your life won't be directly affected by what happens to you.

Building self-confidence isn't something that can be done overnight. You need to work on it every day and the best way to do that is one step at a time, the smaller steps the better.

12.8 Bounce Back from Your Mistakes

Remember that no one is perfect. Even the most confident people have insecurities. At some point of your life you may feel you lack something. That is reality. Learn that life is full of bumps down the road. And that often these insecure feelings come and go depending on where you are, who you are with, the mood you are in, how you are feeling. In other words, they are not constant.

12.9 Identify Your Success

Everyone is good at something. So discover the things at which you excel, then focus on your talents. Give yourself permission to take pride in them. Give yourself credit for your success. Inferiority is a state of mind in which you've declared yourself a victim. Do not allow yourself to be victimised. Express yourself, whether it's through art, music, writing, etc., and find something you enjoy. Everyone is born with talents and strengths. You can develop and excel. If it's difficult to name things you have some ability in, think about things others do, that you would like to do too and take some lessons. When you're following your passion, not only will it have therapeutic effect, but you'll feel unique and satisfied, all of which can help build your self-confidence. Plus, adding a variety of interests to your life will not only make you more confident, but it will increase your chances of meeting compatible friends.

12.10 Be Thankful

Be thankful for what you have. A lot of the times, at the root of insecurity and lack of confidence is a feeling of not having enough of something, whether it's emotional validation, good luck, money etc. By acknowledging and appreciating what you do have, you can combat the feeling of being incomplete and unsatisfied, finding that inner peace will do wonders for your confidence.

12.11 Be Positive

Be positive even if you don't feel the same way. Avoid self-pity and the sympathy of others. Never allow others to make you feel inferior – they can only do so if you let them. If you continue to loathe and belittle yourself, others are going to do and believe likewise. Instead speak positively about yourself, about your future, and about your progress. Do not be afraid to project your strengths and qualities to others. By doing so, you reinforce those ideas in your mind and encourage your growth in a positive direction.

12.12 Accept Compliments

Accept compliments gracefully. Do not roll your eyes and say, "Yeah, right," or shrug it off. Take it to heart and respond positively ('Thank you!' and smile works well). A person with low self-confidence will not accept compliments easily. They take them as a kind of mockery or insult. This is because the person feels that he or she does not deserve or is not capable of receiving a compliment.

12.13 Look in the Mirror and Smile at Yourself

Studies surrounding what is called the "*facial feedback theory*" suggest that the expressions on your face can actually encourage your brain to register certain emotions. So, by looking in the mirror and smiling every day, you might feel happier with yourself and more confident in the long run.

12.14 Fake It

Along the same lines of smiling to make yourself feel happy, acting confident might actually make you believe it. Pretend you're a completely confident version of you; go through the motions and see how you feel! My own classmate who was a third class in almost all the exams is now doing very well. He completed his Master of Social Work (MSW) and began his own NGO and now the government of India is making use of his expertise. I never expect he would rise so high in life rating his academic performance. But one thing is true of him: "he is a person with a very high level of self-confidence." I think his high level of self-confidence has carried him high in life. I was all the more surprise, when ! heard he was going around giving talk to high profile politicians, IAS and IPS officers. Self-confidence is key to ascend the summit of your life.

12.15 Stick to Your Principles

It might be tough, but if you don't have something you can believe in, you don't have anything. If you don't stand for something, you will fall for anything. No matter what happens in your life, you can always lay claim to the fact that from this day forward, you have followed your principles to the best of your ability. Have principles in your life; stick to it no matter come what may. Through this your authenticity will be manifested. Once you prove yourself as a person of principles, your self-confidence level will grow very high. You will be able to command others to do what is right. You will have the strength and courage to correct those who err and people will listen to you.

12.16 Help Others

When you know you're kind to the people around you, and you are making a positive difference in other people's lives (even if it's just being kinder to the person who serves you coffee in the morning), you will know that you are a positive force in the world–which will boost your self-confidence. If you are other-oriented, people will know who you are. They will come to know that you are a person not for yourself. They will recognise you and love you. This can be a source of great confidence in you because you know that you are accepted by people. Acceptance greatly boosts confidence in a person.

12.17 Avoid Perfectionism

Perfectionism paralyses you and keeps you from accomplishing your goals. A perfectionist seeks perfection in everything. He wants his surroundings to be strewn with perfection. But this can't happen always and as a result he will be dissatisfied with many things. This will chip off gradually the trunk of his confidence. You need to strive for perfection but don't expect perfection in the striving. Striving is a process of imperfection and you must see perfection through imperfection. A perfectionist will find difficult to build self-confidence because he always feels inadequate.

12.18 Step Out of Your Comfort Zones

Do not be afraid to push yourself beyond your physical or mental limits. Such a pressure would help you see how easily things can be achieved and thereby helps you to hone your skills. Step out of your comfort zones. Unless you have the courage to step out of your comfort zones, you are not going to achieve great things in life. Leaving your comfort zones is itself a manifestation of courage. Be ready to take risk; this will help you to see life from a different perspective and you will also find the reality of life. Your readiness to step out of your comfort zones is the beginning of self-confidence.

12.19 Courage to Take Action is Confidence itself and Not After

One of my most favourite snippets of movie dialogue is one from the 1999 film "*Three Kings.*" In this scene Major Archie Gates (George Clooney) wants the small team to save a fellow soldier and steal Saddam's gold just after the first Gulf War has ended. The young soldier Conrad Vig (Spike Jonze) has his doubts about the plan:

Archie Gates: *You're scared, right?*
Conrad Vig : *Maybe.*
Archie Gates: *The way it works is, you do the thing you're scared shitless of and you get the courage After you do it, not before you do it.*
Conrad Vig : *That's dumb ass way to work. It should be the other way round.*
Archie Gates: *I know. That's the way it works.*

12.20 The *Best Me Technique*

You can provide yourself with an extra dose of confidence by using the *Best Me Technique of Self-hypnosis* to pre-experience the rewards of a long-term goal, thereby reducing the stress. The *Best Me Technique* is a form of hyperempiria or suggestion-enhanced experience, which involves your whole person in the content of a suggested event. Every letter in "Best Me" corresponds with an element of suggestion. These elements can be applied in a variety of ways, including visualisation exercise and other forms of hypnosis and self-hypnosis. Instead of merely picturing something in the mind's eye, the *Best Me Technique* enables you to paint upon the canvas of your experience almost any masterpiece you may desire.

12.21 Positive Self Talk will Boost Your Self Confidence

Self Talk is the way your mind speaks to you in all situations from daily routines to difficult life events. It is the voice that can either encourage you or chastise you. The good news is that by listening to your inner dialogue and shifting it to become more in line with what you really want, you can transform your life.

12.21.1 Become Conscious of Your Self Talk

Put an effort to become aware of the way you Self Talk in any given situation; pay attention to both Positive Self Talk and Negative Self Talk. The way to do this is just simply stand back and listen to the tone of your Self Talk without making any adjustment yet.

12.21.2 Decide What Kind of Self Talk You would Like to Hear

If you want to be more positive, look at the various situations throughout your day and see how you can bring about prospective changes or turn them into something that will be positive. You need to decide and choose what do you want to talk to yourself? Positive self-talk must arise from the situations and events of your daily life. Choose only those things that will boost your self-confidence.

12.21.3 Catch Yourself Whenever You Begin to Self Talk in a Negative Manner

By recognising the tone, you can shift to a less stress inducing thought pattern. Regulate your self talk. Try to avoid self talk in a negative manner. Convince yourself that this way of talking to yourself is not going to help you in any way. Be wary and alert as not to allow negative self talk to dominate your lonesome conversation. Never allow yourself to be dominated by negative self talk.

11.21.4 Work on Managing Your Self Talk Everyday

It is a learned process and it does take time to be patient with yourself. Give yourself some times every day to talk to yourself–how you are, how you feel and your day's experience. Giving time to yourself can be very good for your growth. Be friendly and amicable with yourself. Find time to play some games with yourself. Your 'self' is more important than others. Find time to be with yourself, talk and converse with yourself. This will pay you big dividends.

12.21.5 Figure Out the Positive Self Talk

Figure out what type of Self Talk will encourage and motivate you throughout the day and then strive to stay in that frame of mind. Find out your positive self talk – figure out all the good things you have spoken and done to yourself and congratulate and thank yourself for being good to yourself. When you are involved in positive self talk sometimes the negative self talk will try to sabotage the conversation. Never allow such attempts to destroy your positive auto-conference.

12.21.6 Discard Self Talk That is Self-defeating

Sometimes the voice within you may tell you that 'you are not good at anything and that it is not worth trying a thing.' Never be self-defeated without at least giving a try. Nobody has told you that you will never win. It is the negative voice that is telling you. Never listen to such voice for it is potentially dangerous to building your self-confidence.

12.21.7 Avoid Negative Self Talk

Negative Self Talk can make a situation seem far worse than it is, causing unnecessary stress and potentially more conflict. Once the negative voice within you dominates your inner atmosphere, it can cause a great havoc in your world. Negative self talk is the voice that is trying to destroy you. Never listen to such voice. Just tell to shut its mouth.

12.21.8 A Few Points for Reflection

- Start changing your Self Talk in small ways. Trying to change it all at once can be overwhelming by breaking it down into phases; you increase your likelihood of sticking to it and making a lifelong change.
- Observe the way others speak around you. Sometimes your peers contribute to the way you talk to yourself. Surround yourself with people who encourage you and who have the same outlook you wish to obtain.
- Write motivational phrases or words on sticky paper and post them in places that you look at every day, like your bathroom mirror or the dashboard of your vehicle. By looking at these, you will be able to change your mind set to positive thoughts.
- Make a list of the positive ways you wish to think. Include goals and proactive steps to achieving them. Whenever you need to shift you inner dialogue look at the list and remember what you are working for.
- Read materials that will help you maintain your positive Self Talk.

"Don't listen to anyone who tells you that you can't do this or that. That's nonsense. Make up your mind, you'll never use crutches or a stick, then have a go at everything. Go to school; join in all the games you can. Go anywhere you want to. But never, never let them persuade you that things are too difficult or impossible."

— *Douglas Bader*

12.22 Thirteen Things Highly Confident People Don't Do

Highly confident people believe in their ability to achieve. If you don't believe in yourself, why should anyone else put their faith in you? To walk with swagger and improve your self-confidence, watch out for these fifteen things highly confident people don't do.

1. They don't make excuses: Highly confident people take ownership for their thoughts and actions. They don't blame the traffic for being tardy at work; they were *late*. They don't excuse their shortcomings with excuses like "I don't have the time" or "I'm just not good enough"; they *make* the time and they keep on improving until they *are* good enough.
2. They don't avoid doing the scary thing: Highly confident people don't let fear dominate their lives. They know that the things they are

afraid of doing are often the very same thing that they *need* to do in order to evolve into the person they are meant to be.

3. They don't live in a bubble of comfort: Highly confident people avoid the comfort zone because they know this is a place where dreams die. They actively pursue a feeling of discomfort because they know stretching themselves is mandatory for their success.
4. They don't put things off until next week: Highly confident people know that a good plan executed *today* is better than a great plan executed *someday*. They don't wait for the "right time" or the "right circumstances", because they know these reactions are based on a fear of change. They take action here, now, today – because that's where progress happens.
5. They don't obsess over the opinions of others: Highly confident people don't get caught up in negative feedback. While they do care about the well-being of others and aim to make a positive impact in the world, they *don't* get caught up in negative opinions that they can't do anything about. They know that their true friends will accept them as they are, and they don't concern themselves with the rest.
6. They don't judge people: Highly confident people have no tolerance for unnecessary, self-inflicted drama. They don't feel the need to insult friends behind their backs, participate in gossip about fellow co-workers or lash out at folks with different opinions. They are so comfortable in who they are that they don't feel the need to look down on other people.
7. They don't let lack of resources stop them: Highly confident people can make use of whatever resources they have, no matter how big or small. They know that all things are possible with creativity and a refusal to quit. They don't agonise over setbacks but rather focus on finding a solution.
8. They don't make comparisons: Highly confident people know that they are not competing with any other person. They compete with no other individual except the person they were yesterday. They know that every person is living a story so unique that drawing comparisons would be an absurd and simplistic exercise in futility.
9. They don't find joy in people-pleasing: Highly confident people have no interest in pleasing every person they meet. They are aware that no all people get along and that's just how life works. They focus on the quality of their relationships instead of the quantity of them.
10. They don't need constant reassurance: Highly confident people aren't in need of hand-holding. They know that life isn't fair and things won't always go their way. While they can't control every event in

their life, they focus on their power to react in a positive way that moves them forward.

11. They don't avoid life's inconvenient truths: Highly confident people confront life's issues at the root before the disease can spread any father. They know that problems left unaddressed have a way of multiplying as the days, weeks and months go by. They would rather have an uncomfortable conversation with their partner today than sweep an inconvenient truth under the rug, putting trust at risk.

12. They don't quit because of minor set-backs: Highly confident people rise every time they fall down. They know that failure is an unavoidable part of the growth process. They are like a detective searching for clues that reveal why this approach didn't work. After modifying their plan, they try again (but better this time).

13. They don't require anyone's permission to act: Highly confident people *take action* without hesitation. Every day they remind themselves, "If not me, who?"

13

Motivational Reflections on Achieving Your Dream

View everything from the angle of your dream. Let your DREAM be the centre of your operation. In everything that you see and experience either from fellow human beings or nature, draw lessons that will take you forward to your DREAM.

13.1 Row, Row, Row Your Boat

"Row, row, row your boat
Gently down the stream
Merrily, merrily, merrily, merrily
Life is but a DREAM".

Reflecting on this nursery rhyme that I learned in my childhood gives me a lot of lessons on dream. I know this rhyme since my childhood but the meaning never struck me. It is a very inspiring rhyme that describes life as a dream. We have already learned in Abdul Kalam's understanding of dream that 'dream is not what you see during sleep but it is that which does not let you sleep'. This means that there is a kind of 'terrible disturbance' that has emerged from your inner system because you are convinced and overwhelmed by the feeling of achieving your dream. Your overwhelming enthusiasm to tryst with your dream has caused restlessness within you so much so that you can't wait anymore. You want it to happen at the earliest. That is what does not let you sleep. The Swedish word "*resfeber*" aptly describes this reality. *Resfeber* means the restless race of the traveller's heart before the journey begins, when anxiety and anticipation are tangled together; a 'travel fever' can manifest as an illness. In the same manner, your whole system is disturbed and restless because you want to arrive at your destination at the earliest. Your dream is so real and you want to achieve so much so that you are completely obsessed with how you can achieve it.

Dream is that which propels you down the stream. The rhyme says "*row, row, row your boat*". It means that rowing one's boat entails exertion of energy, a little sacrifice, a little struggle and a little pain. Your boat is yourself. You must be willing to be rowed down in the stream. The boat must be in good condition to be rowed upon. In other words, you must be ready and prepared yourself for any eventuality to be rowed down for a destination. "*Gently*' means you must keep yourself cool and calm. "...*down the stream*" means as you row your boat down the stream, the sail is not going to be smooth as streams usually have less water and its path is all twists and turns. In such situation, you need to maintain your sang-froid (composure). Otherwise you can lose your calm and you won't feel like proceeding any more. "*Merrily, merrily, merrily, merrily*" refers to the joyful feeling that you experience because you are convinced of your destination and that you are getting closer to it. It is a kind of anticipatory joy. The tough sail is not going to be forever. The feeling that you will surely one day arrive at your dream gives you strength and happiness in spite of the difficulties. "*Life is but a dream*" points that life cannot remain as life, it has to be transformed into dream. When it turns into a dream, life becomes complete and wholesome. All human beings are striving to transform themselves into their dreams but only a few have achieved because the rowing is difficult. Transforming yourself into your dream is your real self. When you achieve this, you will feel that your mission is accomplished. Then, you see that dream is really real and not just a mere figment of the mind. Your dream is your *transformed Self*.

IMAGINE with all your mind
BELIEVE with all your heart
ACHIEVE with all your might
The DREAM that YOU ARE!

13.2 Nurturing Your Personal Dream

Being surrounded by like-minded friends can be awesome or it can also be a major block to your personal dreams. It depends on what dream the group believes in. Sometimes, the group's dream can be positively good and worth pursuing. Yet, the group's dream can be at the same time, detrimental to the nurturing of your personal dream. There are great causes for a group's dreams too. This is a very crucial juncture in your life as to which side to fall – to choose and nurture your personal dream or fall for the group's dream. This is the point where two roads diverged. In the poem "*The Road Not Taken*" the poet Robert Frost says,

"Two roads diverged in the wood, and I –
I took the one less traveled by,
And that has made all the difference.

In these lines, the poet is at the crossroads but he chooses the road that is less traveled by. It is a kind of fresh venture which involves risk, uncertainty and insecurity. Yet, the poet chooses it. "The road less traveled by" refers to the unique unfolding of every individual by following one's inner voice. Every individual has a path which is different from others. No two persons travel the same road exactly in the same manner. Therefore, this unscripted path is unique to every individual and if one does not choose this, it'll remain the untrodden path. So listen, if there is a *whisper* within you; if there is a subtle nudge from within asking you to give up the group's dream with certainty, embrace and follow the *voice* within you. Step into the uncertainty of the unknown (the road not taken), then the group that believes the collective dream will try to convince you that you're wrong. Not because you are wrong but they want you to be part of the collective effort for the attainment of the group's ideal. They do this not because they are bad people. Their collective goal can be a very noble one. They are just caught in their dream and you stepping out of that dream and following your own dream can be perceived as risky and potentially disastrous to the realisation of the group's dream. So, folks will do whatever they can to convince you.

Here, we are not denying that group's dreams are bad. But if there is a voice within you that calls for a unique expression of yourself, then you must follow that path. If you follow your own dream, a new story will emerge. The story runs thus: I am a unique expression in the world. There is no one like me. My gifts, talents and goals are unique; no one can do them the way that I can. It is my right as a human being who is alive and living right now to express those gifts. I feel called to a great adventure and what I am willing to give is a resounding YES! I am here to love and be loved. I love myself enough to surround myself with people who also want to go on the adventure of life with me. I surround myself with like-minded dreamers, believers and doers. I love the group of my like-minded friends and their concern for me but I know that I find more certainty in embracing the unknown path of my dreams than follow the collective dream. I will garner all my strength and courage to move forward even though some steps may seem impossible to take and I shall make one. I live in possibility because the word impossible says "I'm possible." I take action to ground my dreams until they come true. To do my best is my lifestyle. I am a dreamer, a doer and a believer. I am here to be an expression of what's possible. I no longer let the fear of the unknown hold me back. I trust myself and take steps daily outside of my comfort zone. I am here to light my lamp so that those who are groping in darkness can see me living out my dream and this may give a ray of hope. I will continue to do this because this is what I am. This is what my life is about.

13.3 A Lesson from the Life of an Eagle

According to ornithologists, the Eagle has the longest life span among the birds. It can live up to 70 years. But to reach this age, the Eagle must take a hard decision and go through a painful process of metamorphosis. In its 40s, its long and flexible talons can no longer grab its prey which serves as food. Its long and sharp beak becomes bent. Its wings with thick feathers have become heavy due to senescence and get stuck to its chest and make it difficult to fly. Then, the eagle is left with only two options:

- Die or
- Go through a painful process of *change* which lasts for 150 days

This process of *change* requires that the eagle flies to a rocky mountain top and sits on its nest. There the eagle begins to knock its beak against a rock until it plucks it out. After plucking it out, the eagle waits for a new beak to grow and then it begins to pluck out its talons too. After getting its new talons, the Eagle starts plucking it's senescent and worn out feathers and waits for the feathers to grow. And after *five months*, the Eagle takes its famous flight of rebirth and lives for another 30 more years.

Exegesis

The Eagle is able to live up to 70 years because it is able to decide to go through the painful process of change. If the eagle were not willing to go through this painful process of change, its life's span could have ended at the age of 40. The eagle knows that if it goes through the hard and painful process of transformation, it would live another 30 years more and it does it. Here, the purpose of the eagle is to live up to 70 years. If the Eagle were not to have this purpose it would not have gone through the painful process of transformation. From this we can draw a few conclusions:

- *Clarity of Purpose or Goal:* The purpose of the Eagle was to live 70 years (long life). The Eagle is clear of its purpose. In life, you need to have a purpose or a goal to achieve. You need to be clear of what you want to be. Clarity of vision is very important and directs your energy to flow in that direction.
- *Decision:* If you don't decide, nothing will take place. The Eagle takes a painful decision to go through the hard process of change. The Eagle has to choose this hard process or die. The eagle is left with a Hobson's choice. If you want to achieve your purpose or goal in life, you must decide today that you are willing to go through any pain or struggle in order to achieve it. There is no short cut to success other than hard work. The degree of struggle and pain you employ will

determine the rate and magnitude of your success. The more you struggle; the greater will be your success.

• *Hard Work without Purpose is a Waste:* If you have no purpose to achieve, why should you struggle. Many of us don't struggle in life because we have no clear purpose. If you have a clear purpose, you will never sit idle. It will lead you to action and you will be most willing to struggle and go through pain in order to achieve your goal. Only Hard work alone cannot make you achieve your goal. A donkey is christened with the sobriquet "a beast of burden" for it works very hard-carrying heavy loads day after day but it does not achieve anything, *why?* Because it has no *purpose*. Hard work without purpose is a wasted energy. Therefore, find out first your dream or goal and be clear of this vision (goal) and once there is clarity of vision, hard work will follow suit because people with a clear purpose can never sit back. *Hardwork* is a medium through which a *Goal* is achieved. Without the *Goal* the medium is futile and without the *medium* the *Goal* is a mere *will-o'-the wisp* and can never be *achieved.*

Gregor Johann Mendel was an Austrian monk who experimented with garden peas and others plants in his spare time and discovered the fundamental principles of genetics. Mendel was the only son of a peasant farmer. At that time it was difficult for poor families to obtain a good education and for the young Mendel the only way to escape a life of poverty and to gain a good education was to enter monastery. Monasteries were centres of learning in those days. The monastery where Mendel joined was the Augustinian Order of St. Thomas, a teaching Order with a reputation as a centre of learning and scientific enquiry. To enable Mendel to further his education, the abbot arranged for him to attend the University of Vienna to get a teaching diploma. However, Mendel did not perform well. He was nervous and the University did not consider him a studious student. His examiner failed him with the comments, "He lacks insight and the requisite clarity of knowledge".This must have a devastating effect on the young Mendel who had to return to the monastery as a failure. As this was a teaching order, he had to decide whether to stay on at the monastery as a failed teacher or leave it for good. Mendel decided to act against his failure and began to work harder and never stoop before despair. His hard work finally came to fruition as he discovered the basic principles of genetics through his examination of garden peas. But his discovery was not accepted in his time. It was in 1900s that Mendel's work was rediscovered and is now the foundation of the science of genetics. Today, he is considered as the 'father of genetics'. This is the man who persistently labours hard to get his dream through. His dream did not stop with himself but it is being carried on by the subsequent generations.

Mario Cuomo, former Governor of New York, US says:
"I watched a small man with thick calluses on both hands work 15 and 16 hours a day. I saw him once literally bleed from the bottoms of his feet, a man who came here uneducated, alone, unable to speak the language, who taught me all I needed to know about faith and hard work by the simple eloquence of his example".

13.4 The Life of an Arabian Phoenix

The Arabian Phoenix was a fabulous mythical bird, said to be as large as an eagle with brilliant scarlet and gold plumage and a mellisonant voice. Making its home near a cool well, the Phoenix would appear at dawn every morning to sing a song so enchanting that even the Sun God Apollo would stop to listen to its song.

It was said that only one phoenix existed at any one time and it is very long-lived with a life span of 500 years, 540 years, 1000 years, 1461 years or even 12,994 years (according to various accounts). As the end of its life approached, the Phoenix would build a pyre nest of aromatic branches and spices such as myrrh, sets it on fire and is consumed in the flames. After three days the birth – or as some legends say rebirth – the Phoenix arises from the ashes. According to some sources, the Phoenix arose from the midst of the flames. The new or re-born Phoenix gathers the ashes of its predecessor into an egg of myrrh and takes it to Heliopolis, the city of the sun, to deposit it on the altar of the Sun God, Apollo.

The earliest reference to the Phoenix was made by Hesiod in the eighth century B.C., but the most detailed account is by Herodotus of Halicarnassus, the famous Greek historian in the fifth century B.C.

Lessons from the Story of Phoenix

The Phoenix bird is gifted with a dulcifluous voice and it sings every morning and it is very soothing to the listeners even the Apollo, the sun god would tarry awhile to listen. In life too, each one is also gifted in one way or other. You need to recognise your talents and make use every day for the betterment of others. Using our talents every day will take us to a higher plane of perfection.

The Phoenix bird prepares itself for its death but death is not the end, instead it becomes a new begirining. Life is a process of continuous preparation. Only a prepared person is a ready person. A student becomes confident and happy to write an examination after he or she has prepared well. When a person does not prepare, fear and diffidence constricts his life and as a consequence, life becomes a misery.

The Phoenix dies only to rise again. This law of nature holds true in life too. The Bible says, "Unless a grain of wheat falls to the ground, it remains a single grain; but if it does fall and dies, it bears much fruit." This principle has to be operative in your life as you pursue your dreams. In order to realise your dream, you have to die to many things in life – friends, pleasures, pastimes, enjoyments, romance etc. In other words, you need to sacrifice them not because they are bad but they are not helpful at the moment till you achieve your dream. There is a Latin adage that says: "*Catus amat piscem sed non vult tingere plantas*". It means 'the cat loves a fish but it does not wish to wet its feet'. If the cat wants to eat fish, it has to go and wet its feet into the water and catch the fish. Without getting wet how can the cat wait outside the water to catch the fish? In the same manner, how can you achieve your dream if you are not willing to take the pain? Just desiring and wanting to achieve your dream without struggle is only a mere *wish* which will never become a reality. It is only a pie in the sky bye and bye. Some people have great dreams but lack great zeal and hard work. In such case, their dream will never happen.

The Phoenix readily embraces death because it knows it is going to experience a new and better life. If you are prepared and ready to sacrifice even the last drop of your blood in order to realise your most cherished dream, will you not have it? The size of your sacrifice and pain will determine the size of your dream and its materialisation. If you are ready to embrace for the worst of sacrifice, you'll surely have the most joyous future.

13.5 "The Word Impossible Says, 'I'm Possible'"

This famous saying of Audrey Hepburn really captivates me. The subtle semantic nuances of vocabularies have always intrigued me. Sometimes, a single letter makes a world of difference. For example, the alteration from "can't" to "can" and from "impossible" and "possible." 'Impossible' is a word which can be altered into a sentence through punctuation. When you change it into a sentence the meaning becomes completely different from the semantic significance i.e., I'm possible. The difference between "impossible" and "possible" is two small letters at the start and they happen to be "I'm". From the word *impossible* we come to know who is this "I'm." "I'm" is ontologically something that is "*possible*". The word "possible" speaks the ontological nature of "I'm". Therefore, 'I am's nature is something that is always possible. Possible speaks about taking ownership and impossible releases you of any need to try.

The word impossible negates impossible itself because the word "impossible" speaks of "I'm possible". I'm has to believe that it is not impossible. The noun "impossibility" says "I'm possibility". I am's identity is possibility. If you are possibility how can you make yourself an 'impossibility'? If you are possibility why doubt that you are possibility. The word impossibility itself is a proof that 'I'm possible'. It is the error in your perception that steals away your belief that you're are 'possible'. Clear the error and you will truly see your real nature that you are possible. Most of the time, we see impossibility in the light of impossibility. Don't merely look at the word Impossibility; rather gaze it deeply and you will be gobsmacked to see that it is not impossibility but 'I'm possible'. The way you look at makes all the difference. So if you believe that something is impossible it probably will be; in fact, you may as well drop the word "probably"! Seeing possibilities encourages you to *empower yourself.* The real power comes when you see that you are possible.

The quintessence of success is to see possibility in impossibility. Some people see failure as the birthplace of impossibility. Their common parlance is "if I do also I will fail, so better not try." It takes courage to see possibility in failures. Like driving a car – you turn into a 'T' junction but you realise there is no through access so you turnaround and find another route. This is seeing possibility in impossibility. Know that in every impossibility, there is possibility. The word impossibility is pregnant with possibilities. If you know how to face impossibility, it will give birth to many possibilities.

How can there be miracles if there are no obstacles? How can you chase the storm if there was none? You need challenges to reveal your abilities. Success comes out of nothing; success emanates from the problems you face. Those who refuse to give in come out smiling. Problems are the most fertile ground for sowing the seed of success. Robert X. Perez says, "The seeds of success spring from failure's ashes."

Failure is not an end; it is a means to an end. Many people see the first failure as the end and the next try as impossibility. Failure is not defeat; it is the pointer to do better than what you did. You have to know that you are in a constant study of life. What you face is your training. Remember in life we gamble; the earth is a playroom full of obstacles and thrills, so let things flow and you'll find good reasons. Learn from it. Each failure is simply another chapter to the story of our lives. To fail is to understand what not to do. Remember it and don't give up until your goal is achieved. Life is difficult; things will come at your left and right.

What do you do when you face circumstances? When life throws shoes at you, at least pick through the best ones and try them on for size! Discover yourself in life by taking the pains to fit in it, no matter the situation. Take the punches, develop mental toughness. Mental toughness is to see the long-term gains rather than be put off by short-term pains. Once you have this toughness, you have the winning edge. Let us not stop with our failures in life; instead let us rise from the ashes of our failures. Seeing impossibility ends all our initiative and evaporates all your energy. Let us look at and tell impossibility that "I'm possibility." Larry Page, the co-founder of Google once said, "Achieving your goal is really about a healthy disregard for the impossible".

- Napoleon Hill is one of the greatest motivators whose writings have influenced more people into success than any other person in history. He was born in a family stricken by abject poverty. At the age of 10, his mother died and two years later his father remarried. As a young man he had the ambition to be a writer. To accomplish this objective he knew, he would need to become expert in the proper use of words. And since he was a poor boy and deficient in education, his friends assured him that his ambition was impossible. Young Hill saved the pittance that he earned and bought a dictionary and he meant to master words. But then he did a strange thing. He turned to the word "impossible" and with a fine scissors expunged it out of the dictionary and threw it away. Thereafter, he built his whole career on the premise that nothing is impossible to the person who wants to grow and outgrow. By the time Hill was 13, he was writing for local mountain newspapers to help save money for school. As part of a series of articles assigned to him, he went to interview Andrew Carnegie, a wealthy and powerful man. Carnegie commissioned Hill to interview more than 500 millionaires to find a success formula that could be used by an average person. Fighting against all kinds of disadvantages and pressures, Hill dedicated more than 25 years of his life to define the reasons by which so many people fail to achieve true financial success and happiness in life. In 1937, Hill came up with his ground-breaking motivational book, *Think and Grow Rich* in which he illustrates his philosophy that "whatever your mind can conceive and believe it can achieve". This book has helped millions across the world to succeed in life and continues to inspire many writers.

Believe the impossible is possible.

One day a protestant bishop paid an annual visit to one of the schools run by his church. After the visit he spent the night with the principal. After the dinner they began a conversation. The bishop said, "Man has unraveled the secrets of nature and has made a number of discoveries. Now, think the world will soon end." The principal disagreed and said, "There are many more mysteries to be uncovered within the next 50 years man will make many more new discoveries." "Can you mention at least one?" Challenged the bishop. "Man might soon learn to fly," said the principal. "Rubbish" exclaimed the bishop, "Only angels and birds can fly." The bishop's name was Wright. He had two sons named Orville and Wilbur. They are the famous Wright Brothers who invented the aeroplane.

When you stop believing everything is impossible.
"Some of the best music was composed by Beethoven, but he was deaf, some of the best poetry was written by Milton, but he was blind. Possible is always inside the impossible..."

—*Shibin Mohammed*

Frank Sinatra, an American singer and film actor found an unprecedented success as a solo artist from the early to mid 1940s after being signed by *Columbia Records*. His professional career had stalled by the early 1950s, but it was reborn in 1953 after he won the *Academy Award for Best Supporting Actor* for his performance in *From Here to Eternity*. One of the best songs he ever sung was "*The Impossible Dream*". The lyric is worth reflecting:

The Impossible Dream

To dream the impossible dream
To fight the unbeatable foe
To bear with unbearable sorrow
To run where the brave dare not go

To right the unrightable wrong
To be better far than your are
To try when your arms are too weary
To reach the unreachable star

This is my quest, to follow that star
No matter how hopeless, no matter how far
To be willing to give when there's no more to give
To be willing to die so that honor and justice may live
And I know if I'll only be true to this glorious quest
That my heart will lie peaceful and calm when

I'm laid to my rest
And the world will be better for this
That one man, scorned and covered with scars
Still strove with his last ounce of courage
To reach the unreachable star

13.6 Stochastic Probability Theory–Pregnant Deer Scenario

In a remote forest, a pregnant doe is about to give birth to a fawn. It finds a remote verdant grassy green field nearby a river and slowly moves there thinking it would be safe. As she moves slowly, she begins to suffer labour pain. Concomitantly, dark clouds begin to envelop that area and lightening starts a forest fire. Turning left she sees a hunter's arrow pointing at her from a distance. As she tries to move towards right, she spots a hungry lion approaching her.

Application of the Stochastic Probability Theory – Pregnant Deer Scenario

- What can the pregnant doe do as she is already under labour pain?
- What do you think will happen?
- Will the doe survive?
- Will it give birth to a fawn?
- Will the fawn survive?
- Will everything be burnt by the forest fire?

At that particular moment:

- Can the deer go left? – The hunter's arrow is pointing at her.
- Can she go right? – The hungry lion
- Can she move up? The forest fire
- Can she move down? The fierce river

These are the probabilities or possible inferences that one can illicit at the moment.

The answer to these is: The Doe does nothing. She just FOCUSES on giving birth to a new LIFE.

The sequence of events that happens at that fraction of a second is as follows:

In the spur of the moment, lightning strikes and the thick cloud begins to dim the whole area and mars the target of the hunter. At that moment, he releases the arrow which misses and zips past the deer. At that moment, the arrow hits and injures the lion severely. Then, it begins to rain heavily and puts out the forest fire. At that next moment the deer gives birth to a healthy fawn.

Life Application of the Theory

In life too, at times, you will face with negative onslaught from all quarters. You will be at times bogged down to a frazzle. That is the moment you have to be still and maintain your *sang-froid* and concentrate on what matters the most in your life. The doe is surrounded on all sides with a fatal onslaught yet she does nothing but concentrate on giving birth to a fawn, which is the most important thing she has to do at the moment. This is what you have to do exactly with your life. In life you have to face criticisms, opposition, betrayal, rejection and discouragement from all sides yet the most important thing is to forge ahead amidst all these by pursuing your priorities. If you start giving attention to each of these, all of your energy will vanish and it may take the whole of your life. If you start throwing stones at all the dogs that bark on your way, when will you reach your destination? Why waste your energy and attention? You are wasting your life. Do what you want to do with your life – fully concentrating and centralising all your energy to achieve your set goal. Your achievement will be the greatest defeat to your enemies. Clarity of one's priority will congregate your energy to flow in one direction.

13.7 What is Life?

What is Life?
They say it's from B to D.
From Birth to Death.
But what is between B and D?
It's a 'C'. So, what is 'C'?
It is a CHOICE.

Our life is a matter of *choices*. All of us are the same human beings but our *choices* make us different from each other. So, what is most important in our life is what we choose. We become what we choose. People who achieve great heights in life are those who *choose to climb, struggle and win*. It is of paramount importance, *what you choose today*. Your choice today will affect your life tomorrow. Therefore, If you want to win something in life,

- choose a worthy goal
- choose to tread the toughest path
- choose your friends wisely
- choose never to give up

then, you are a winner and your dream becomes a reality.

13.8 Difference between Winners and Losers

There is a marked difference between winners and losers. Let us see their differences:

Winners	*Losers*
Winners have dreams	Losers have schemes
Winners see the gain	Losers see the pain

Winners see the potential	Losers see the past
Winners say, "It may be difficult but it is possible."	Losers say, "It may be possible but it is too difficult."
Winners see possibilities	Losers see problems
Winners make it happen	Losers let it happen
Winners make commitments	Losers are apart from the team
Winners always has a programme	Losers always has an excuse
Winners say, "Let me do it for you."	Losers say, "That is not my job."
Winners say, "I must do something."	Losers say, "Something must be done."
Winners are always a part of the answer	Losers are always a part of the problem
Winners see an answer for every problem	Losers see a problem for every answer
Winners believe in win-win	Losers believe for them to win, someone has to lose
Winners after they have made a mistake say, "I was wrong."	Losers after they have made a mistake and say, "It wasn't my fault."

13.9 Your Dream will be Challenged

In life as you pursue your dream, you will find more people trying to discourage and sabotage your dream than people who would help and encourage you. The world is full of wet blankets and obscurantists, who are always ready to choke the growth of others. Some people are allergic to the prosperity of others. Such people are suffering from what I would call as the "Saul Syndrome". Saul, the first king of ancient Israel was engulfed by jealousy, which in the parlance of William Shakespeare is the 'green-eyed monster' against David who was more loved and appreciated by the people. As a result, Saul tried to do away with him. You need to be careful of people who suffer from the "Saul Syndrome". Such people enjoy obstructing people from realising their dreams. They take delight in the failures of others. They give vent to their sadistic proclivity.

So prepare yourself to face criticisms in your life. Criticisms can never kill you; instead it has an enormous force to build you up. If somebody tells you that you are not good or clever enough to pursue a particular goal, just do the opposite i.e., if he says, 'you're not good'. Then, the opposite is 'I have to be good'. Do not waste your energy in fighting back against him. Your opponent's aim in putting you down is to make you a failure. Register this in your mind and work all the more harder – congregating all your energy towards your goal. A day of your achievement will come and your achievement will be the greatest defeat for him. If you go on fighting critics, you will waste all your energy and time and when will you concentrate on your dream? Therefore, in chasing your dream, you will come across more people trying to discourage you than encourage you. Do the positive opposite. Let us see some eminent personalities who reacted positively towards their critics:

- Gabriel Ruelas has been a professional fighter since 1988 and he reached the pinnacle of his sport in 1994 when he captured the World Boxing Council (WBC) championship. Gabriel's iife started on a cattle ranch in a horribly poor section of Mexico where children normally began working about the same time they started walking. Things most people took for granted like electricity, TV and shoes were only dreams for Gabriel. Even after Gabriel and his young brother, Rafael, immigrated illegally to the US, success seemed to be a property that belongs to somebody else. Gabriel was selling candy door-to-door with his brother when he discovered Joe Goosen's gym. The brothers begged Goosen to let them box at his gym. Goosen, who had a stable of professional fighters to train, tried to discourage the Ruelas brothers but in vain. They pestered Goosen until he relented. At the age of 12, Gabriel impressed Goosen with his natural quickness and skill level. His success story began from then on. *"Follow your heart and don't listen to anyone who says you can't do it. Even if you lose a few fights, don't give up"*, advises the world champion.
- Ole Bull was a violin soloist of international fame. As a violin virtuoso, he was widely acclaimed for his innovative improvisations and for the rich tone of his play. Ole's father sent him to the University to study theology and forbade him to play his favourite violin. He promptly flunked out and defying his father's admonition, devoted all his time and energy to the violin. Unfortunately, though he had great ability, his teachers were relatively unskilled; thus by the time Ole was ready to start his concert tour he wasn't prepared. In Italy, a Milan newspaper critic wrote, "Ole is an untrained musician. If he be a diamond, he is certainly in the rough and unpolished." There were two ways Ole Bull could have reacted to such an acerbic disparagement. He could get angry with the newspaper critic or he could learn from it. Ole rightly chose the latter. He went to the newspaper office and met the critic. Ole spent the evening with the 70-year-old critic, asked about his faults and sought the septuagenarian's advice on how to correct them. Then Ole cancelled the rest of his tour, returned home and spent the next six months studying under really able teachers. He practiced hours upon hours to overcome his faults. Finally, he returned to his concerts and at 26, became the sensation of Europe.
- In the history of Christianity, no other cleric is more widely preached and read than Charles Spurgeon. People still know him as the 'Prince of Preachers'. In his lifetime, he preached to about 10 million

people. After having felt the call of God, Spurgeon decided to become a pastor and he started preaching in his early years. Since his first sermon in London, the crowds never ceased growing larger and larger. But there were many criticisms and objections aimed at him. "All his discourses are redolent of bad taste are vulgar and theatrical..." said a newspaper. Another paper described his preaching as "that of a vulgar colloquial, varied by rant. All the most solemn mysteries of our holy religion are by him rudely, roughly and impiously handled." But he continued to preach no matter what. Spurgeon often worked 18 hours a day. He affirmed, "We can only produce life in others by the wear and tear of our own being. This is a natural and spiritual law – that fruit can only come to the seed by its spending and be spent even to self-exhaustion." Such was his love for preaching. No wonder, with no formal theological training, Spurgeon became the most popular minister of the nineteenth century, regularly attracting crowds of 6,000 each Sunday. Spurgeon's sermons which were often spiced with humour were widely translated and are circulated even today.

Somebody Said!

"Somebody said it couldn't be done.
But he with a chuckle replied,
That maybe it couldn't, but he would be one
Who wouldn't say so till he'd tried.

So he buckled right in with a trace of a grin
On his face. If he is worried, he hid it,
He started to sing as he tackled the thing
That couldn't be done. And he did.

Somebody scoffed, "Oh, you'll never do that
At least no one ever has done it."
But he took off his coat, and he took off his hat,
And the first thing we know, he'd begun it.

With a lift of his chin and a bid of grin,
Without any doubting or "quit-it"
He started to sing as he tackled the thing
That couldn't be done. And he did it.

There are thousands to tell you it cannot be done.
There are thousands to prophesy failure.
There are thousands to point out to you, one by one
The dangers that wait to assail you

But just buckle in, with a bit of a grin;
Just take off your coat and go to it.
Just start in to sing as your tackle thing
That cannot be done – and you'll do it!"
—*Edgar A. Guest*

13.10 How to be Successful?

Charles Menezes describes how to be successful:

Be brave, be bold, dare and do. Nothing is impossible. No obstacle is insurmountable. Once your mind is made up and you stand firm as a rock, no one can stop you from gaining your goal and crowning yourself with success. With hope and ambition do give rein to your vision, look ahead and plan and above all, ACT. Do not waver, do not hesitate and do not rest till the job is done. Know what you want and go after it with single-minded concentration and solemn resolution.

Success comes when you get what you want or desire. The starting point, then, is to know what you want in life. If you don't know what you want the question of getting it does not arise at all. You must, therefore, have a goal, an objective or a target. You decide your goal according to your vision, day dream, inclination, ability, natural skill, knowledge and needs. Think big and not small. Aim at the star and shoot high. The sky is the limit for those who dare and do. Gandhiji was a frail man, a lone individual. Yet he challenged the mighty British Empire in which the sun never set. He had the vision and displayed the courage and confidence to go after his visionary goal with missionary zeal.

Visualise the image of what you would like to become in life. Do you want to be a king, a revolutionary leader, a business tycoon, a famous lawyer, a renowned professor, a skilled engineer or a great doctor? Let your ambition surface. Be true to your own self. Your aspirations may seem mere day dreams and wild castles in the air at the start. Never mind and never fear. What appears impossible today will become a reality tomorrow with your determination, dedication and application.

The secret of success, the source of strength, the spring of power, the foundation of wealth and royal path to name, fame and glory is yourself, your self-confidence and your own will-power born out of and sustained by knowledge. Know and realise that you and you alone are the master of your destiny and captain of your soul. You can fashion your fate the way you will it, lending you on to the success road.

See It Through

When you're up against a trouble,
Meet it squarely, face to face;

Lift your chin and set your shoulders,
Plant your feet and take a brace.
When it's vain to try to dodge it,
Do the best that you can do;
You may fail, but you may conquer,
See it through!

Black may be the clouds about you
And your future may seem grim,
But don't let your nerve desert you;
Keep yourself in fighting trim.
If the worst is bound to happen,
Spite of all that you can do,
Running from it will not save you,
See it through!

Even hope may seem but futile,
When with troubles you're beset,
But remember you are facing
Just what other men have met.
You may fail, but fall still fighting;
Don't give up, whate'er you do;
Eyes front, head high to the finish.
See it through!

–Edgar A. Guest

13.11 Do not Depend on Mood if You Want to Achieve Your Goal

Mood is deceptive. Do not become a slave to your mood. If you pay heed, it will begin to control you. The toughest part of pursuing your goal is to work consistently persisting even when you are not in mood. Your mood can be affected by many events within and without (environment). Even the weather, can affect your mood. If you work only when you are in mood, nothing is going to take you closer to your goal and your attempt to achieve your goal will be sporadic and intermittent. Therefore, defy your mood and subdue it by not paying an iota of your attention. Whether, you are in mood or not, you do what you are supposed to do; determine and commit yourself to your tasks consistently and persistently and it take you forward towards your goal.

Pearl S. Buck, writer, Nobel and Pulitzer Prize Winner says:

"I don't wait for moods.
You accomplish nothing if you do that.
Your mind must know it has got to get down to work."

13.12 You must have Chaos within Yourself to Give Birth to a Dancing Star

The great atheistic philosopher Friedrich Nietzsche once said, "*One must still have chaos in oneself to give birth to a dancing star.*" Nietzsche was a German philosopher who wrote and spoke on an elitist plane above the level of most of normal average mortals. Hitler also studied Nietzsche like crazy because Nietzsche talked a lot about super human qualities in the truly few elite people this world has to offer. So, someone like Hitler looking to build his own master race probably would have really like Nietzsche!

Let us analyse and break it down this saying of Nietzsche:

"*One must still have chaos in oneself...*" This means that we can't be contented with our present circumstances. Contentment with your present circumstances will bring a dead end to your further exploration and development. We have to be a little unsatisfied. Maybe we even have to be a little angry at our present circumstances if we want to improve our lives. This reminds me of something I heard a long time ago about the really good professional boxers. I heard the really good ones were all a little bit angry. Well, maybe we can all get a little angry too. Now, I am not talking about acting violently, but I am talking about the kind that drives you to take massive action and enables you to put a lot of sticks in the red-hot fire. In other words, I am talking about creating a life of *chaos.*

While most people run from chaos, I think Nietzsche would say that the elite run towards chaos. He or she who most deftly manages *chaos* in his or her life usually wins the game of life. Maybe a little chaos isn't such a bad thing after all! Chaos is being dissatisfied or disgruntled with the *status quo* with a view to ameliorate the present situation. There is an element of aggressiveness in trying to make the present situation better. Chaos is the result of dissatisfaction.

Let us see the second part,

"*...give birth to a dancing star.*" What exactly was Nietzsche saying here? This surely sounds like something really BIG. Does giving birth to a dancing star put us on some crazy high level similar to our Creator? Can humans really do something as grand and large and magnificent as, "giving birth to a dancing star"? Can we really *create* or give birth to our future in advance? Well, we ourselves can be our own creators. You need to be your own creator. Our potential forms the substratum out of which we can create ourselves what we want to be. Every one of us is living far below our true potential. Our true potential is so vast, encompassing and empowering that we can't even begin to understand our worldly or universal powers that lie dormant in almost all of us. Maybe we all just need to have a little more faith in ourselves and manage our chaotic lives just a little bit better and then just maybe we too can create something special and give birth to a dancing star! We are born to give birth to a dancing star. 'Giving birth to a dancing star' in short means developing and stretching our potential to the fullest. It is the blossoming of our talents. It is the process of re-creating ourselves and transforming ourselves into 'who' and 'what' we really should be!

3.13 Sustaining One's Attention

If one wants to achieve one's desired goal, one has to begin with paying attention or concentrating his energies to the operation of that task which would lead him to the realisation of his goal. But this is the beginning of a process and not the end. After beginning to pay attention, care has to be taken to sustain it for the required length of time. The person should be wholly absorbed in handling the task, unmindful of anything that might be going on in his environment, without getting distracted. This is the sustaining of attention. Woodworth says, "To sustain attention is to concentrate one's activity continuously upon some object or happening or problem."

Thus, in the case of sustained attention, there is no wandering. The individual attention always remains on track and the activity proceeds uninterruptedly and without serious distraction. The most striking examples of such sustained attention are the activities of a hunter who is waiting for the opportune moment to shoot or of an astronomer sitting with his eyes fixed on a particular star while looking through his telescope or of a mathematician working on a particular problem for a long time.

If one needs to achieve the required goals in a reasonable time, one must learn to pay sustained attention. One must concentrate upon the activity which one is involved in. A student who cannot keep his attention fixed for a reasonable length of time is sure to lag behind in his studies. An artist has to strive for sustained attention so that he can finish his desired piece of art. A writer, a poet, a musician – all have to put in sustained attention. In order to hold attention for a long time, it is essential to capture the genuine interest in the activities that will take one to the goal one wants to achieve. Factors which cause distractions and disrupt attention should be removed. For best results, the person whose attention is to be sustained should be provided with favourable environmental conditions to work in, and factors which may disturb him mentally and emotionally should be removed or at least minimised. The will power of the subject must also be adequately developed and he should be made to strive to attain the set objectives and higher ideals of life.

3.14 Distraction

When we are attending to an object or activity, there are things in the external environment as well as inside ourselves that tend to intrude and divert our attention from that object or activity. In the same manner, when you begin to seriously pursue a goal, there will be many things that will begin to dissuade your attention. These things which interfere with our attention are called distractors. Therefore, distraction represents interference with attention. H.R. Bhatia has defined Distraction thus:

> "Distraction may be defined as any stimulus whose presence interferes with the process of attention or draws away attention from the object to which we wish to attend."

The sources of distraction can be roughly divided into external and internal factors. External factors can be like friends, social entertainments, films, video albums, computer, mobile etc. The sources of distraction are very diverse and affect a person according to his own mental set and personality characteristics. Internal distractions such as emotional disturbance, ill-health, boredom, lack of motivation, feeling of fatigue or preoccupations unrelated to the matter in hand have more effect than the everyday external distractors. If one is in normal health and not suffering from unusual mental worries and emotional disturbances, no power on earth can distract one's attention in case one is determined to pursue one's goal. Most of us are in the habit of offering lame excuses in the name of outside distraction, for failures resulting from our unwillingness and lack of determination.

A person needs to struggle hard in order to overcome the external factors of distraction. He has to put in great effort to keep the object before his mind. Certainly there should not be misutilisation of energy which otherwise can be applied to achieve higher aims. Therefore, great care should be taken to do away with all possible environmental causes of distraction. The working situations and environmental conditions should be so modified and adjusted as to provide adequate working facilities and a healthy congenial environment for an individual whose attention in the work we wish to capture and sustain.

3.15 The Anatomy of Determination

Determination is one of the cardinal ingredients necessary for achieving your dreams. It is the most important predictor of success. Many think at the prima facie that it is intelligence that brings success. Everyone thinks that what makes startups succeed is intelligence. Intelligence makes a better story that a company won because its founders were so smart. The people and reporters who spread such stories believe them. But while it certainly helps to be smart, it is not the deciding factor. There are so many people as smart as Bill Gates but achieving nothing.

If determination is so important, let us analyse its various components. Some of the questions we can pose are: Are some of the components more important than others? Are there some you can cultivate?

The simplest form of determination is *sheer willfulness*. When you want something, you must have it, no matter what. Willfulness clearly has two subcomponents – *stubbornness* and *energy*. The first alone yields someone who's stubbornly inert. The second alone yields someone active. Stubbornness can be either positive or negative. Positive stubbornness is directed towards positive goal (that will enhance one's life). While negative stubbornness is directed towards a negative goal (that will be harmful to oneself and others). A good deal of willfulness must be inborn because it's common to see families where one sibling has much more of it than another. Circumstances can alter it but at the high end of the scale, nature seems more important than nurture. Bad circumstances can break the spirit of a strong-willed person but I don't think there's much you can do to make a weak-willed person stronger-willed. Being strong-willed is not enough, however. You also have to be hard on yourself. Someone who was strong-willed but self-indulgent would not be called determined. Determination implies your willfulness is balanced by *discipline*. The word "*balance*" is very significant here. The more willful you are, the more disciplined you have to be. The stronger your will, the less anyone will be able to argue with you except yourself. And someone has to argue with you, because everyone has base impulses and if you have more will than discipline you'll just give into them and end up on a local maximum like drug addiction.

We can imagine will and discipline as two fingers squeezing a slippery melon seed. The harder they squeeze, the further the seed flies, but they must both be squeeze with an equal force or the seed spins off sideways. If this is true it has interesting implications because discipline can be cultivated and in fact does tend to vary quite a lot in the course of an individual's life. If determination is effectively the product of will and discipline, then you can become more determined by being more disciplined.

Another consequence of the melon seed model is that the more willful you are, the more dangerous it is to be indisciplined. There seem to be plenty of examples to confirm that. In some very energetic people's lives, you see something like wing flutter, where they alternate between doing great work and doing absolutely nothing. Externally this would look a lot like bipolar disorder.

In fact the dangers of indiscipline increase with temptation. This means, interestingly, that determination tends to erode itself. If you're sufficiently determined to achieve your goal, this will probably increase the number of temptations around you. Unless you become proportionally more disciplined, willfulness will then get the upper hand and your achievement will revert to the mean. That's why Julius Caesar thought thin men so dangerous. They were not tempted by the minor perquisites of power.

The melon seed model implies it's possible to be highly disciplined. I think there probably are people whose willfulness is crushed down by excessive discipline and who would achieve more if they weren't so hard on themselves. One reason the young sometimes succeed where the old fail is that they don't realise how incompetently they are. This led them do a kind of deficit spending. When they first start working on something, they overrate their achievements. But that gives them confidence to keep working and their performance improves. Whereas someone clearer-eyed would see their initial incompetence for what it was and perhaps be discouraged from continuing.

There is another major component of determination: AMBITION. If willfulness and discipline are what get you to your destination, ambition is how you choose it. I don't know if it's exactly right to say that ambition is a component of determination but they're not entirely orthogonal. It would seem a misnomer if someone said they were very determined to do something trivially easy. And unfortunately ambition seems to be quite malleable; there's a lot you can do to increase it. Many people don't know how to be ambitious especially when they are young. They don't know what's hard or what they're capable of. And this problem is exacerbated by having few peers. Ambitious people are rare, so if everyone is mixed together randomly, as they tend to be early in people's lives, then the ambitious ones won't have many ambitious peers. When you take people like this and put them together with other ambitious people, they bloom like dying plants given water. Probably, most ambitious people are starved for the sort of encouragement they'd get from ambitious peers, whatever their age. Achievements also tend to increase your ambition. With each step you gain confidence to stretch further next time.

In short, we can say that determination seems to work: it consists of willfulness balanced with discipline, aimed by ambition. And fortunately at least two of these three qualities can be cultivated. You may be able to increase your strength of will somewhat; you can definitely learn self-discipline; and almost everyone is practically malnourished when it comes to ambition.

3.16 The Sunk Cost Fallacy

Two singers competed to stay on the talent competition in "*The Voice*" on NBC. Their fate was up to a single coach/judge who had worked with both contestants but with one, Julio, longer than the other. The "newer" singer was far more talented – at least according to the other judges and the viewers who had commented on NBC.com – but the coach/judge picked the inferior singer saying, "I have so much time invested in Julio, I've got to go with Julio."

This is an example of what behavioural economists and psychologists call the SUNK COST FALLACY. The "sunk cost" refers to time, money or effort that has already been invested in an activity or project and cannot be retrieved and the fallacy is that once we've made this type of investment we're more likely to stay with a choice, even if it no longer benefits us or just wasn't the best decision in the first place. The "sunk cost fallacy" is considered a negative mental bias but it can be turned into one's own advantage. We know that sunk costs increase the chances we'll stay with a decision, whether that decision is good or bad. A strategic person might see this as an opportunity. Perhaps we can learn to use the power of sunk costs to increase the chances of sticking with something that matters. Let's say you have a certain goal – to write a book, finish college or get regular exercise. You can strengthen your commitment to sticking it out by making regular investments that can't be retrieved. You might invest time into an ongoing writer's group. You might invest effort in developing who will hold you accountable. Or you might commit money to a strength-training class with like-minded friends. *Where your investments go, your commitment will grow*–and this can be used to your advantage in achieving your goal.

14

People Who Dare to Act on Their Dreams

Perveniri ad summa sine industria non potest
(One cannot reach the highest position without industry.)

14.1 The Olympic Motto: *Citius, Altius, Fortius*

Father Henri Martin Didon was a Dominican priest and Principal of Arcueil College near Paris. As an energetic teacher and sports enthusiast, he used the discipline of sports as a powerful education tool. One day, speaking to an interschool athletics meet, Fr. Didon ended his speech quoting three Latin words: *Citius, Altius, Fortius* (faster, higher, stronger). Struck by the succinctness of this phrase, Baron Pierre de Coubertin made it the Olympic motto, pointing out that "Athletes need 'freedom of excess.' This is why we gave them this motto, a motto for people who dare to try to break records." Coubertin also said, "These three words represent a programme of moral beauty. The aesthetics of sports are intangible."

The Olympic Creed is adopted from the sermon of Ethelbert Talbot, the Bishop of Pennsylvania during 1908 London Olympic Games. It reads thus:

> "The most important thing in the Olympic Games is not to win but to take part, just as the most important thing in life is not the triumph but the struggle. The essential thing is not to have conquered but to have fought well."

Today, our history is interspersed with many inspiring legends that run faster, climb higher and fight stronger than the majority of the crowd. This is because they DARE. Remember this Latin phrase *qui audit adiscipitur* (who dares win). Let us see some of the living legends of our times who dares to win.

14.2 Anand Kumar: A Mathematician par Excellence

Anand Kumar is an Indian mathematician and columnist for various national and international journals and magazines. He is best known for

Fig. Anand Kumar.

his *Super 30* programme which he started in Patna, Bihar in 2002 and which coaches economically backward students for IIT-JEE, the entrance examination for the Indian Institutes of Technology (IITs). By 2013, 281 of the 330 had made it to IITs and *Discovery Channel* showcased his work in a documentary.

His Early Life

Anand Kumar was born on 1st January 1973 in Patna, Bihar. His father was a post office clerk in Bihar. His father could not afford private schooling for his children and Anand attended a Hindi medium government school, where he developed his deep interest in Mathematics. During graduation, Kumar submitted papers on *Number Theory* which were published in *Mathematical Spectrum* and *The Mathematical Gazette*.

Anand secured admission in Cambridge University but could not attend because of his father's death and his financial condition, even after looking for sponsor in 1994 – 1995 both in Patna and Delhi. He would work on Mathematics during day time and would sell *papads* in evenings with his mother, who had started a small business from home, to support her family. He also tutored students in Mathematics to earn extra money. Since Patna University library did not have foreign journals, for his own study, he would travel every weekend on a six-hour train journey to Varanasi, where his younger brother, learning violin under N. Rajam, had a hostel room.

Thus, he would spend Saturday and Sunday at the Central Library, BHU and return to Patna on Monday morning.

Teaching Career and Super 30

In the year 1992, Kumar began teaching Mathematics. He rented a classroom for Rs.500 a month and began his own institute, the Ramanujan School of Mathematics (RSM). Within the space of year, his class grew from two students to 36 and after three years there were almost 500 students enrolled. Then in early 2000, when a poor student came to him seeking coaching for IIT-JEE, who couldn't afford the annual admission fee due to poverty, Kumar was motivated to start the *Super 30* programme in 2002, for which he is now well-known.

Every year in May, since 2002, the Ramanujan School of Mathematics holds a competitive test to select 30 students for the 'Super 30' scheme. Many students appear at the test and eventually he takes 30 intelligent students from economically backward sections, tutors them and provides study materials and lodging for a year. He prepares them for the Joint Entrance Examination for the Indian Institutes of Technology (IIT). His mother, Jayanti Devi cooks for the students and his brother Pranav Kumar takes care of the management.

During 2003 – 2013, 281 students out of 330 have made it to the IITs. In 2010, all the students of Super 30 cleared IIT-JEE entrance making it a three in a row for the institution. Anand Kumar has no financial support for *Super 30* from any government as well as private agencies and manages on the tuition fee he earns from the Ramanujan Institute. After the success of *Super 30* and its growing popularity, he got many offers from the private – both national and international companies-as well as the government for financial help but he always refused it. He wanted to sustain *Super 30* through his own efforts. After three consecutive 30/30 results in 2008 – 2010, in 2011, 24 of the 30 students cleared IIT-JEE. In 2012, 27 of the 30 students and in 2013, 28 out of 30 students cleared the prestigious IIT-JEE examination. Anand Kumar does not accept donation for the programme. His team creates the fund by organising evening classes in Patna.

Recognition

In March 2009, *Discovery Channel* broadcast a one-hour-long programme on *Super 30* and half a page has been devoted to Kumar in *The New York Times.* Actress and ex-Miss Japan Norika Fujiwara visited Patna to make documentary on Anand's initiative. Kumar has been featured in programmes by the BBC. He has spoken about his experiences at the Indian Institute of Management, Ahmedabad. Kumar is in the *Limca Book of Records* (2009) for his contribution in helping poor students crack

IIT-JEE by providing them free coaching. *Time* magazine has selected mathematician Anand Kumar's school – *Super 30* – in the list of Best of Asia 2010. Anand Kumar was awarded the S. Ramanujan Award for 2010 by the Institute for Research and Documentation in Social Sciences (IRDS) in July 2010.

Super 30 received accolades from United States President Barack Obama's special envoy Rashad Hussain who termed it the "best" institute in the country. *Newsweek Magazine* has taken note of the initiative of mathematician Anand Kumar's *Super 30* and included his school in the list of four most innovative schools in the world. Anand Kumar has been awarded by top award "Maulana Abdul Kalam Azad Shiksha Puraskar" by the Bihar government in November 2010. He was awarded the Prof. Yashwantrao Kellar Yuva Puraskar 2010 by Akhil Bharatiya Vidyarthi Parishad (ABVP) in Bangalore.

In April 2011, Anand Kumar was selected by Europe's magazine *Focus* as "one of the global personalities who have the ability to shape exceptionally talented people." Anand Kumar also helped Amitabh Bachan in preparing for his role in the film Arakshan. Many people from Bollywood including renowned directors and producers are interested in making movie on the life of Anand Kumar. Anand Kumar has been selected by UK-based magazine *Monocle* among the list of 20 pioneering teachers of the world. He was also honoured by government of British Columbia, Canada. Anand Kumar has been awarded by '*Baroda Sun Life Achievement Award*' by Bank of Baroda in Mumbai.

14.3 Antony Jinman: Polar Explorer, Educator and Conservationist

> "Being an explorer gives you a lot of time to think and to question your desire to continue, but true passion never lets you give up."
>
> —*Antony Jinman*

Fig. Antony Jinman.

Antony Jinman was born in Plymouth, United Kingdom. As a young man, aspiring to become an explorer one day, he served in the Territorial Army. When, at the age of 22, a terrible snowboarding accident broke

Anthony's back, instead of giving up on his dream he vowed to never leave a "what if" unexplored. Without any academic degree in exploration, Antony created his own path towards his goal. At the age of 23, he went on to be an adventure guide and two years later became an expedition leader. In 2007, Antony travelled across the Artic Baffin Island and with the expedition helped raise over £200,000 for vulnerable children through the *Mitchem Trust*. The more he traversed the globe, the more his knowledge and passion for conservation and the protection of our fragile ecosystem grew. In 2010, he and two team mates journeyed to the geographic North Pole to collect valuable scientific data for the University of Plymouth. Skiing, snowshoeing and sometimes even swimming, they trekked over 800 kms in order to arrive at their final destination. After 51 days, Antony's dream was fulfilled:

"Reaching the North Pole was the happiest day of my life. The saddest day though, was literally the day after, in the back of the helicopter that took us back. It took so much time and effort to arrange that project and suddenly it was all over."

Whilst this was an amazing feat in itself, Antony had meanwhile already begun working on what would soon become *Education Through Expeditions* (ETE), a not-for-profit school outreach organisation that aims to educate and inspire children. Primarily web based, it is a programme that creates interactive expeditions, fieldwork, research projects and related outreach school work, bringing real knowledge and experience of climate change and conservation issues into classrooms across the globe. In 2011, in recognition of his contributions generated through ETE, Antony received an Honorary Degree Doctor of Education from the University of the West of England. Moreover, his expeditions have also been endorsed by the Royal Geographic Society.

Today, besides exploration, Antony works as a public speaker and is the CEO of ETE. He is planning and preparing for his next adventure: an expedition to the South Pole through which he aims to highlight the need for healthy and sustainable eating. Through his work Antony continues to inspire, educate and strive to be remembered as an educator rather than as an explorer.

Facing Interview

Q. *What is the main message that you try to spread to your students?*

Ans. When I visit schools I aim to inspire all of the pupils I meet to learn about and explore the world around them and raise their aspirations to reach their personal goals and achieve them. I also work with higher education students who I encourage to share their own knowledge and experience with younger children in order that they may inspire a new generation of explorers and researchers.

Q. *What is the hardest part of preparing for a polar expedition and what is the most unique thing that you get out of such a dangerous journey?*

Ans. Sometimes, it feels like the easiest part of the whole expedition starts once I get on the ice. The most difficult part is the planning and logistics, preparation of academic and outreach work that will be taking place as part of the expedition and making sure all of the necessary communication arrangements are in place so that I can share my story with young people in real time from the ice. There is not just one unique thing I get from the completion of these expeditions rather a combination of feelings, sense of achievement, success, the excitement to go and share my stories with others and to inspire students, academics and explorers to use the information and data I have collected for their research and to explore part of the world themselves.

14.4 Anupam Kher: Bollywood Actor

The story of Anupam Kher is a typical story of the boy next-door. He came to Bombay like thousands of young people do every day, with stars in his eyes hoping to hit the big time. He was 26 years old, bald and divorced. No one would have given the boy from Shimla a second look.

Fig. Anupam Kher.

He rented a ramshackle room in a slum, where eight others like him shared his dreams. His landlady washed dishes in the building next door, to make both ends meet. Kher went from door to door begging for bread. The year was 1981. At this time Mahesh Bhatt a famous but struggling director was trying to make good commercial films and decided to cast Kher in the role of a 70-year old man in *Saaransh.* The film made Bhatt into a legend. Kher became an instant draw. An actor everyone raved about... no wonder at 35, Anupam Kher is the one actor in whose shoes everyone wants to be. Rich, famous, successful, all and all, from a scratch. If uncle Kher can achieve the height of success from a scratch, why can you give a try? Our poor background should never deter us from moving towards our goal. Instead, it should create a confidence in us that "there are people worst than my background who climbs the ladder of success."

Anupam Kher's Interview with the *Times of India* (November 14, 2010):

God: "I find God in simple things of life. God resides in everything that encompasses us. I find Him in the goodness of people. God is a faith for me and faith is the only thing in life that keeps us going. I believe in optimism and being positive. Optimism is godly for me."

Connecting to God: "I connect to God through focus, concentration, happiness and being good to other people. Prayers connect me to Him. I do not need a visa of meditation to get closer to God. It doesn't matter that I am stressed or happy. I can chat with Him any time I want."

Karma and Kismet: "I believe in *kismet*, but *karma* is more important for me. When I was young, my grandfather told me, 'Hard work is the only way to attain your goals'. And all through my life, I didn't try to prove him wrong. There is nothing in life that comes to you easily. I strongly believe and advocate the philosophy of Bhagavad Gita, *'Karam karo, phal ki iccha mat karao'*. For me karma is supreme."

True Contentment: "Being kind to people, to be able to bring joy to others' lives signifies contentment to me. Being compassionate towards what you do, enjoying it and being happy is important too. You can't make others happy, if you do not enjoy yourself. So live, laugh and enjoy!"

Once a taxi driver from Pakistan refused to take money from Anupam Kher. The taxi driver told him, "Your movies have given us so much happiness. Don't spoil it by paying me."

14.5 Bai Fangli: The Unsung Hero

Bai Fangli was a Chinese pedicab driver who has donated 350,000 Yuan to enable more than 300 poor students continue with their studies. For almost twenty years, to save up for his donations, Bai Fangli peddled his pedicap everyday. His devotion started in 1987 when he retired from his pedicab driving and returned to his village. On his return to the village he saw many children working in the field. Bai's daughter, Bai Jinfeng said, "Her father had asked why the children didn't go to school. And our relatives told him that it was because they were too poor and couldn't afford to pay tuition fees. My father was worried so he decided to donate 5,000 yuan to the schools in our hometown. But for him, it was all he owned."

At that time he was 74 years old and he decided to go back to his job of driving a pedicab in Tianjin. All of his earning went to support the needy students. His sons and daughters tried to persuade him to change his mind as they wanted him to enjoy a relaxing life. But their father turned a deaf ear to them. Bai Jinfeng also said, "At that time, he went out at dawn and wouldn't return until darkness fell. He earned 20 to 30 yuan each day. After returning home, he put his earnings in a place carefully."

Fig. Bai Fangli.

Bai had always felt regretful that he was illiterate. So he hoped the next generation could change their destiny with education. A little later on, to increase his effort to assist students in need, Bai moved to a simple room near the Tianjin Railway Station. He waited for clients 24 hours a day, ate simple food and wore discarded second-hand clothes he found.

At the age of 82, to his childrens' surprise, Bai made another decision. He founded an education support fund with the help of loans. But his driving of pedicab continued.

Xu xiuxiang, one of the workers of Education Support Fund said, "He never forgot when to give money to the schools and often urged us to give his earnings to the school. Each time he gave the money he felt very happy and said he had completed his mission again."

In 2001, he drove his pedicab to Tianjin YaoHua Middle School, to deliver his last installment of money. Nearly 90 years old, he told the students that he couldn't work anymore. All of the students and teachers were moved to tears. Bai Fengli said, "I hope the students could study hard and get a good job and then make contributions to our country". A long journey of supporting and aiding students lasted two decades.

In 2005, he was diagnosed with terminal lung cancer and he died in the same year at the age of 93. Although he had kept none of his earnings for himself, he was left with his selfless spirit and love.

14.6 Ben Underwood: The Boy Who could "See" with His Ears

Ben Underwood was diagnosed with retinal cancer at the age of two and his eyes were removed at the age of three. He discovered echolocation at the age of five. He was able to detect the location of objects by making frequent clicking noises with his tongue. He used it to accomplish such feats as running, playing basketball, riding a bicycle, rollerblading, playing

Fig. Ben Underwood.

football and skateboarding. Underwood's child eye doctor claimed that Underwood was one of the most proficient human echolocators. Ben's ability to navigate in his sightless world is, say experts, extraordinary. "His skills are rare," says Dan Kish, a blind psychologist and leading teacher of echomobility among the blind. "Ben pushes the limits of human perception".

To most people's amazement upon meeting him, he seemed completely unfazed by his lack of sight defying common stereotypes about blindness as a disability. So how did he do? The answer is echolocation. Echolocation is an ability to detect objects in their environment by sensing echoes from those objects. By actively creating sounds – for example, by tapping their canes, lightly stomping their foot or making clicking noises with their mouths – people trained to orientate with echolocation can interpret the sound waves reflected by nearby objects, accurately identifying their location and size. This ability is used by some blind people for acoustic way-finding or navigating within their environment using auditory rather than visual cues. It is similar in principle to active sonar navigation technique used by bats, dolphins, toothed whales and several other mammals and some birds. As Underwood moved about, he habitually made clicking noises with his tongue; these sounds bounced off surfaces and with each return, added to Underwood's perception of his surroundings.

He was so good at it that he could tell the difference between a fire hydrant and a rubbish bin, distinguish between parked cars and trucks and – if you took him to a house he had never been to before – he would tell you he could 'see' a staircase in that corner and a kitchen in the other. He could even distinguish between different materials.

Ben built an enduring legacy after his story became public in *The Bee* in May 2006. He became a worldwide celebrity, an Internet sensation and an inspirational speaker. "He motivated people who wanted to see again, wanted to live again," Aquanetta Gordon (Ben's mother) said. "Ben was blind, but he saw more than most". A cancer called retinoblastoma took both of Ben's eyes when he was a toddler, but he never let his blindness prevent him from navigating the world. For the past two years, Ben has appeared on television programmes across the country and far beyond, travelling from Japan to Great Britain to tell his story and deliver inspirational speeches. He swam with dolphins in San Diego, surfed in Hawaii, danced with Ellen DeGeneres and charmed Oprah Winfrey. He became friends with iconic musician Stevie Wonder, who visited him in Elk Grove.

An unflinching faith in God guided Ben and his mother during his last few months as cancer spread to Ben's brain and spine. In his final days, Ben was enjoying listening to gospel music and getting neck and back messages. He seemed more concerned about his mother's emotional state than his own pain, forgoing medications and assuring her that he was fine. "Ben was perhaps the most inspirational patient I've seen in more than 20 years in medicine," said Kaiser Permanente, a paediatric eye surgeon. He eventually died on January 2009 at the age of 16.

14.7 Casey Neistat: Autodidact Filmmaker and Provocateur

"I value experience over just about everything else."

—*Casey Neistat*

Casey Neistat is from New London, USA. He dropped out of high school at the age of 15 and never returned to an educational establishment since; he worked his way up in a different way. For the next three years, he lived in a trailer park in Connecticut. He first worked as a dishwasher and short order cook and at one time was on welfare. Having a strong passion for filmmaking, Casey bought an iMac DV – the first PC which allowed consumers to edit videos. Being determined to use the opportunity that this feature of the iMac DV presented for filmmakers, he moved to New York to make movies.

In the Big Apple, his first job was a bike messenger but he ultimately teamed up with his brother Van and began making all kinds of short videos. Their first film that went viral was a three minute video called "iPod's Dirty Secret" that focused on Apple's policy on replacing iPod batteries. In 2008, HBO released "The Neistat Brothers"; an eight episode show that portrayed the brothers' adventurous lifestyles. One year later. After having worked on hundreds of video projects as a team, Van moved to Los Angeles and Casey began making films on his own. Through his creative filmmaking approach, energetic and fun personality, Casey soon accumulated an international following on YouTube. "Different people relate to different

Fig. Casey Neistat.

things in my movies, whether it is the handmade style, the simple way I try to communicate ideas or they relate to me as a person." Despite Casey's work gained great popularity, he has always refused to place ads in front of his videos and consequently never monetised his YouTube account.

In 2012, Casey made his most viral video ever: "*Make it Count*". A Nike commercial that depicts him and a lucky friend travelling around the world burning the budget received from the company. Until this date, the video has been viewed over nine million times.

Today, Casey continues to entertain his audience by regularly uploading his movies on his "*numero uno channel*" YouTube and was recently hired by Mercedes-Benz to shoot the new CLA car commercial. He also writes and directs short films for the website of the *New York Times*.

Facing Interview

Q. *Why do you exactly value experience over just about anything else?*

Ans. Experience expands your understanding of life. Little experience means a small life. I have been very very poor, I have been hungry and not had money for food, I have also had dinner with the president and flown on private planes. This range of experience has shaped who I am and my appreciation for the world around me and shaped my values and priorities.

Q. How did you come up and develop your movie making style?

Ans. My movie style is the product of never learning the "right way" of making films. Having never been taught, I was forced to find my own way. This yielded my style.

14.8 Chris Burkard: Adventure Photographer

"Do not follow where the path may lead, go instead where there is no path and leave a trail."

–Emerson

Fig. Chris Burkard and His Creation.

Chris Burkard was born and raised in sunny California, USA. As a teenager, he unsurprisingly spent most of his free time surfing and exploring the beautiful coastline with his friends. Shortly after graduating from his school, Chris dedicated a lot of his time to another passion of his: art. He experimented several types of creative expression but it was not until he adventured into photography that he felt genuinely inspired. He loved the fact that with this art form he could let his creativity flow in different environments and it did not take him long to find himself shooting his favourite setting–the ocean. Chris started documenting his surfer friends and eventually–armed with a waterproof housing for his camera–started shooting them from amidst the waves. The mix of adrenaline, weightlessness and powerful sound experienced whist shooting in the water became one of the aspiring photographers' favourite feelings; he was hooked.

"When I realised that I did not want to live with any regrets, I decided to go after it as a career. I never wanted to wonder, 'what if?'"

Eagerly dedicating his time to improving his skills and shooting as much as he could, Chris managed to soon shoot images that went on to become appreciated internationally. He concentrated on capturing photographs that he personally really loved which resulted in him getting less advertising jobs, but eventually enabled him to shoot amazing editorial pieces. Putting effort into capturing timeless moments, Chris' career ultimately took off big time. This enabled him to travel to some of the most beautiful, remote and untouched places on Earth; Iceland, Kamchatka and Patagonia just to name a few. The 26 year old has since won numerous photo contests such as the highly coveted *Red Bull Illume* award and worked for the most prestigious surf and adventure magazines in the world.

Today, Chris's passion and admiration for landscape photography have resulted in his creation of an own style and composition. The unique feeling conveyed through his images has made it possible to instantly recognise a "Burkard Photo". He continues to shoot around the world and capture moments that motivate people across the globe to pick up surfboards and head for the waves.

In his interview with the amazers.org he says: *"My goal has always been to inspire others through my work."*

Q. *What does photography mean to you?*

Ans. Photography first and foremost is a passion of mine and an expression of how I see moments take place around me. It is a way to experience and interact with the world around me and has provided opportunities to visit so many unique places and tell so many stories that I never thought I would have the opportunity to document. I feel fortunate that I can do work that I am passionate about and love to do all while being able to provide for a family. Though it has turned into a job for me, it will always be first and foremost about telling stories and capturing moments that hopefully get other people inspire enough to go out and live their own stories.

Q. *There are so many photographers out there. What can you suggest an inspiring photographer to do, in order to stand out?*

Ans. In this day and age social media is such a huge component of any business and photography is no different. My suggestion to most aspiring photographers besides constantly shooting photos is to find a professional photographer in your and intern or assist them. Learning the business side of photography is so a huge leg up. Find unique stories to tell and as your photography improves people will begin to take notice, but take every opportunity to improve and make connections within the industry.

14.9 Conor Mccreedy: Artist, Entrepreneur and Conservationist

"Action is the foundational key to all success. Be proactive!"

—*Conor Mccreedy*

Fig. Conor Mccreedy and His Creation.

Conor Mccreedy was born in Johannesburg, South Africa. Being a very curious kid from an early age, Conor grew up having broad interests: he had a strong connection to animals, enjoyed playing sports and was passionate about art. At the age of 18, he decided to leave South Africa and go to the US to attend college on a golf scholarship. A year later, fueled by his prevailing love for art, Conor decided to drop his golf clubs for a painbrush.

He then moved to New York to attend the Pratt School of Art and Design, but soon choose to abandon this new path to instead try to directly live and work as an artist. It was easier said than done; scraping together only a meagre living, Conor started selling his work in the streets of New York's Union Square Park. There, in order to secure his spot for the busy Saturdays, he was often forced to spend the night outside. Times were hard– "sometimes I would not make a sale or I would make a $10 sale or a $50 sale; I used to get so despondent and sad" – but learning the hard way shaped Conor's mindset forever. Pushed by nothing but his entrepreneurial drive, Conor relied on his business savvy to get him known in New York's art-scene.

Only a year after he had fully dedicated himself to art, his proactive style presented him with a chance encounter that ultimately led him to become the youngest artist to ever display a solo exhibition at the prestigious National Arts Club. After the successful exhibition, Conor's career took off. His work has since been appreciated and displayed in galleries and collectors homes all across the globe. Some of Mccreedy's pieces have exceeded prices for artists under the age of 30. In the last few years, his unique art has become characterised by an almost exclusive use of a particular blue pigment known as the "Mccreedy Blue".

Today, Conor continues to work in the art world and lives between South Africa, The Big Apple and Europe. Besides art he is devoted to supporting people through several charities and is an international ambassador for The Ubuntu Educational Fund and Faces of Hope Foundation. Conor's heart still beats in Africa; he is an active conservationist, owns a lion named Mohlatsi and recently found P.A.L. – an organisation that aims to protect African lions from extinction.

In an Interview he was Asked the Following Questions:

Q. *What is your primary suggestion or advice to someone who would like to become an artist?*

Ans. First of all, aspiring artists have to expose their work to the right clients. They should drop their ego and don't worry about failure. I got turned down by at least 15 galleries; it is no problem if you get turned down as galleries will still want you in the future when you do well. You have to be a big hustler to make it in the early stage of your career and to have a chance to expose your work. No one works for you for free so you have to do the hard work on your own. If you want to make a living as an artist, you just have to sell your art. That is why, it is important to build a strong team, stay focused and keep grinding away because it's about progression not perfection. Proactivity is key.

Q. *Why did you create the Protecting Africa Lions Foundation?*

Ans. I created the foundation because I was upset to see that the number of lions in Africa is strongly diminishing. We need to start protecting these animals because if we do not protect them in ten years they will be extinct. As a kid I have always liked cats. I grew up going back and forth the safari house so I was exposed to wild animals at a very young age. I have had many dangerous encounters in the wild and have learned to respect Mother Nature and its forces especially wild African lions. I also acquired my own lion five years ago and watched it grow up. This made me realise how special and powerful lions are and that we really must look after them.

4.10 Craig Tracy: Fine Art Body Painter

> "It is my intent to continue to explore and expand the perceptions and boundaries of this most ancient, alluring and contemporary art form of body painting."
>
> —*Craig Tracy*

Craig Tracy is a creative genius who has chosen to dedicate his life to the ancient art of body painting, ultimately taking it to a complete new level. Craig Tracy was born in New Orleans, USA. He was raised in a loving nonconformist family during the hippie movement. An ever rambunctious child, he could only be calmed down when given something to draw with. At the age of three, Craig was diagnosed with a degenerative eye disease that caused him blurred vision and difficulty in focusing on near objects. This was a shock to his entire family and forced Craig to wear really big glasses that he soon started despising. Nevertheless, he never let his condition stop him from doing what he enjoyed most, which was still painting and drawing.

As a kid, Craig started selling hand-drawn maze puzzles to his classmates and for the first time in his life, made some money through his art.

"There was never any question regarding my being or becoming a professional artist. It was always just obvious and understood. I remember people calling me an artist since as long as I can remember."

Craig's artistic horizon particularly expanded during his teenage years when he received an airbrush from his parents and began painting on numerous different surfaces. He spent an incredible amount of his free time perfecting his skills and eventually started selling airbrushed T-shirts.

Fig. Craig Tracy and His Creation.

He then went on to attend Art School in Fort Lauderdale and once he graduated, got a job as a professional illustrator. But sadly, it soon became evident to Craig that this new profession would not bring him the satisfaction he expected. Creatively limited and forced to make art that was meant to sell, he felt lost and out of place.

After five years of unhappily working as an illustrator, he finally found the courage to follow the direction he truly wanted and listening to his heart, turned back to being an independent artist. Regaining the freedom of making art for both himself and his admirers, he went back to painting on a wide variety of surfaces and quickly fell in love with painting on the human body. "It really clicked, from the very first time that I painted a face". Craig spent the next few years of his life researching and studying this ancient art and in 2005, finally created his first series of 15 body-painted photographs that he named "The Nature Series". These pieces which represented a unique and never before seen concept of body painting, became quickly appreciated across the globe. That same year, Craig attended the World Body Painting Festival in Austria and to his own surprise, was named World Champion. His determination had finally proved worthwhile –Craig's passion had brought him to an artistic level, which considering the fact that was close to blind, was thought to be unreachable.

Today, Craig runs his own art gallery in his hometown New Orleans. There, he continues to create breathtaking works of art that amaze people worldwide. Every week, he meets and talks to hundreds of visitors, inspiring them through both his art and story of hope and dedication.

Facing Interview

Q. *Where do you find your inspiration for new ideas and how do these evolve into a final body painted image?*

Ans. I allow my inspirations to come to me from all aspects of life and imagination. The natural world and the curves of the human body are my greatest inspirations. Sometimes I will see a certain curve on a body and I will feel compelled to explore it further with design and colour. Something as simple as a certain colour can motivate me to create. I am greatly inspired by aspects of culture, nature and intellectual constructs. Look at the variety of my work and you will see what looks like several different artists work. I have no definite style and that is very much on purpose. I love being free to explore as I wish without limits, restraints and conventional expectations.

Q. *What is the message you wish to convey through your art?*

Ans. I feel that art is without rules, definitions and constrictions. I also feel that art at its highest level does make people feel something. My favourite art makes me feel more alive. I try with much of my work to delight, surprising and intriguing the viewer and myself. Freedom is my philosophy and I express my freedom through the aesthetics of beauty, mystery, contrast, harmony and diversity.

14.11 Debbie Aung Din and Jim Taylor: Social Entrepreneurs

"Good design starts with empathy."

—Debbie Aung Din and Jim Taylor

Debbie Aung Din was born in Burma, her husband Jim Taylor was born in the US. Although raised in different corners of the world, the two grew up with the same aspiration: using their skills to serve others. Fresh out of college, Debbie and Jim met whilst doing development work in the Mississippi Delta. Together, in the mid 1980's, they moved to Cambodia which – after the destructive four year reign of the Khmer Rouge – was in great need of social help. They eventually returned to the US to start their family and complete MBAs at Harvard University. Jim went on to additionally complete an MBA and work in the private sector, whilst Debbie spent an increasing amount of time in her home-country consulting for the World Bank and the UN.

Fig. Debbie Aung Din and Jim Taylor.

In 2004, the Taylor's decided to settle permanently in Burma. With the aim of improving the lives of the country's rural population, they set up a social venture called "*Proximity Designs*". Realising that irrigation was a major problem for small plot farmers, Debbie and Jim focused on designing foot-powered water pumps that enable farmers to effectively collect water and hence extend the all-important growing season. However, they did not give away their products for free; instead they sold them at an affordable price. "For the poor, this way of aid is much less patronising and represents a relationship of mutual exchange and respect." With this approach, they built relationships with their customers upon empathy.

Through regular feedback, they were able to improve their offerings and launch a complete line of necessary products, amongst these, a lately released low-cost rechargeable solar light. In 2008, Debbie, Jim and the Proximity team played a heroic role when they mobilised their organisation in order to provide humanitarian aid to the survivors of Cyclone Nargis; a disaster that claimed over 140,000 lives. Proximity's field staff was the first at the scene of the affected areas and directly distributed recovery-kits, rice, seeds, water tanks and shelters. It is estimated that by the end of the relief process, Jim and Debbie's organisation had helped over 1.2 million people.

Today, Debbie and Jim's aspirations remain the same. They continue to passionately design products for rural families in Myanmar and since recent years also offer financing-services. Through their offerings, Debbie and Jim have so far managed to increase the incomes and improve the quality of life for over 500,000 Burmese people.

Facing an Interview

Q. *As Proximity is not a non-profit organisation, why do you sell your products, rather than give them away for free?*

Ans. Yes, we are not a non-profit organisation; we are social enterprise and we sell our products at cost, subsidising the R&D through donations and putting any small profits we might make back into the organisation. Selling our products helps us to know their worth, challenges us to always be delivering products that are relevant to the customers and enables us to have a two way relationship based on empathy rather than sympathy. As customers rather than beneficiaries, the power is in the hands of rural families in Myanmar. Anyone will take something for free and probably tell you that they like it even if they never use it, but you know you're really serving your customers if you've created something so useful that they're willing to invest their hard earned cash in it. If they do, as a customer, if they find fault with it, they feel like they have a right to give feedback and then we can use that to improve and serve them better. It's also a far more sustainable and inclusive way of helping people out. Because we sell things at cost, we're not totally reliant on donor dollars to operate. We're also able to sell products all across the country and to anyone who wants to buy them. There's no village hierarchy to bypass and no conflict over who receives something and who doesn't.

Q. *Do you believe that design, if used for the right purpose, could push development work further on a global scale? Have you ever thought of selling your products outside of Burma?*

Ans. We believe design to be important for all companies, especially if they're working with people. We'd like to see more human centered research happen in organisations serving underprivileged people. This means more listening, more empathy and a lot of prototyping of new ideas. Currently we're not looking to sell outside of Myanmar. Our reasons for this are that our products are designed especially for a Myanmar market and might not suit other climates, environments or users. Part of our success here is because we offer a full after sales service of repairs, replacements and spare parts that we couldn't ensure would be possible if we sold them abroad. We value knowing our customers as well as we can and we've invested a lot in doing that in Myanmar. This would be difficult to replicate in a new place.

14.12 Glenn Cunningham

A true story about athlete Glenn Cunningham who was horribly burned in a schoolhouse fire at the age of eight. Doctors predicted he would never walk again. Determined to walk, Glenn would throw himself off his wheelchair and pull his body across the yard and along fence. Twenty-two months later, he took his first steps and through sheer determination, learned to run despite the pain...

Fig. Glenn Cunningham.

The little country schoolhouse was heated by an old-fashioned, pot-bellied coal stove. An eight-year-old boy named Glenn Cunningham had the job of coming to school early each day so that he could use kerosene to start the fire and warm the room before his teacher and his classmates arrived. One cold morning someone mistakenly filled kerosene container he used with gasoline and disaster struck. When the teacher and his classmates arrived, they found the schoolhouse engulfed in flames, terrified on realising that Glenn was inside, they rushed in and managed to drag the unconscious boy out of the flaming building more dead than alive. He had major burns over the lower had of his body and was taken to a nearby country hospital. His brother Floyd died in the fire.

From his bed the dreadfully burned, semi-conscious little boy faintly heard the doctor talking to his mother. The doctor told his mother that her son would surely die–which was for the best, really–for the terrible fire had devastated the lower half of his body. But the brave boy didn't want to die. He made up his mind that he would survive. Somehow, to the amazement of their physician, he did survive. When the mortal danger was past, he again heard the doctor and his mother speaking quietly. The mother was told that since the fire had destroyed so much flesh in the lower part of his body, it would almost be better if he had died, since he was doomed to be a lifetime cripple with no use at all of his lower limbs.

Once more the brave boy made up his mind. He would not be crippled. He would walk. But unfortunately from the waist down he had no motor ability. His thin legs just dangled there, all but lifeless. Ultimately, he was released from the hospital. Every day his mother would massage his little legs but there was no feeling, no control, nothing. Yet his determination to walk was as strong as ever. When he wasn't in bed, he was confined to a wheelchair. One sunny day his mother wheeled him out into the yard to get some fresh air. This day instead of sitting there, he threw himself from the chair. He pulled himself across the grass dragging his legs behind him. He worked his way to the white picket fence bordering their lot. With great effort, he raised himself up on the fence. Then, stake by stake, resolved that he would walk. He started to do this every day until he wore a smooth path all around the yard beside the fence. There was nothing he wanted more than to develop life in those legs. Ultimately through his daily massages, his iron persistence and his resolute determination, he did develop the ability to stand up, then to walk haltingly, then to walk by himself and then to run. It was in the early summer of 1919 when he tried to walk again, roughly two years after the accident. He had positive attitude as well as a strong religious faith. His favourite Bible verse was Isaiah 40:43: "But those who wait on the Lord shall renew their strength; they shall mount up with wings like eagles, they shall run and not be weary, they shall walk and not faint".

He began to walk to school, then to run to school, to run for the sheer joy of running. Later in college he made the track team. Still later in Madison Square Garden this young man who was not expected to survive, who would surely never walk, who could never hope to run–this determined young man, Dr. Glenn Cunningham, ran the world's fastest mile!

He competed in both the 1932 Summer Olympics and took 4th place in the 1500 metres and in 1936 Summer Olympics; he took silver in the 1500 metres and set a world record in the 800 metres run. On June 16, 1934, Glenn Cunningham ran the mile in 4:06.8 minutes breaking the world's record. In 1938, he set a world record in the indoor mile run of 4:04.4. He retired from competition in 1940 (Roger Bannister was the first to break the four-minute mile in 1954). Cunningham's goal-unachieved was a four-minute mile. Many people tried that before and failed. Several theorists proclaimed it was impossible physiologically for humans. He won the Sullivan medal in 1933 for his various running achievements in middle distance.

His effort portrays that whatever you want to create in your life is yours for the making. As long as you desire, it's enough and allow your will to guide you, you can have and be whatever your heart desires. The only one that can put limits on our personal will is ourselves. Develop and encourage your will to create and all the forces of nature within and without will help you bring your desire to pass.

Life Summary of Glenn Cunningham

- Eight years old was horribly burned in a schoolhouse fire. Doctors predicted he would never walk again.
- 22 months later, took his first steps and through sheer determination learned to run despite the pain.
- In high school, set records for the mile and later attended Kansas University.
- While at Kansas University, refused all scholarship money preferring to pay his own way.
- By sophomore year, ran the 1,500 metre race at the 1932 Olympics but finished fourth due to severe cold.
- By senior year, set a world record for the mile of 4:06.8 and held seven of the top 13 fastest recorded times for the mile.
- In 1936, voted "Most Popular Athlete" by his fellow athletes.
- He went to earn his master's degree from the University of Iowa and later doctorate from New York University.
- While in New York won 21 of 31 races at Madison Square Gardens and set an indoor mile record there in 1938. His fastest mile time was 4:04.4 at a Dartmouth track meet in 1938.
- When the 1940 Olympics were cancelled, he retired from his running career and taught at Cornell College in Iowa.
- During World War II, he served two years in the Navy. Spent the remainder of his life running Glenn Cunningham Youth Ranch for troubled kids in Kansas, USA. It is estimated that he and his wife raised around 9,000 kids on their ranch in the years until his death in 1988.

14.13 Google Page Creators: Sergey Brin and Larry Page

14.13.1 Sergey Brin

Sergey Brin is an Internet entrepreneur and computer scientist who with Larry Page co-founded Google, one of the most profitable Internet companies. As of 2013, his personal wealth was estimated to be $22.8 billion. Brin was born on August 21, 1973 in Moscow, Russia. The son of a Soviet mathematician and economist, Brin and family immigrated to the United States to escape Jewish persecution in 1979. After receiving his degree in mathematics and computer science from the University of

Fig. Sergey Brin.

Maryland at College Park, Brin entered Stanford University where he met Larry Page, with whom he later became intellectual soul-mates and close friends. They crammed their dormitory room with inexpensive computers. Brin's focus was on developing data mining system while Page's was in extending "the concept of inferring the importance of a research paper from its citations in other papers", together, the pair authored a paper titled "The Anatomy of a Large-Scale Hypertextual Web Search Engine". The programme became popular at Stanford and they suspended their Ph.D studies to start up Google in a rented garage.

Combining their ideas, they began "cramming their dormitory room with cheap computers" and tested their new search engine designs on the web. Their project grew quickly enough "to cause problems for Stanford's computing infrastructure". The search engine listed results according to the popularity of the pages, after concluding that the most popular result would often be the most useful. They called the search engine "Google" after the mathematical term "Googol", which is a one followed by 100 zeros to reflect their mission to organise the immense amount of information available on the Web.

After raising $1 million from family, friends and other investors, the pair launched the company in 1998. Google has since become the world's most popular search engine, receiving more than 200 million queries each day. Headquartered in the heart of California's Silicon Valley, Google held its initial public offering in August 2004, making Brin and Page billionaires. Brin continues to share the company's day-to-day responsibilities with Larry Page and CEO Eric Schmidt. In 2006, Google purchased the most popular Website for user-submitted streaming videos, YouTube for $1.65 billion in stock.

The Economist newspaper referred to Brin as an "Enlightenment Man", and someone who believes that "knowledge is always good and certainly always better than ignorance", a philosophy that is summed up by Google's motto "*Organise the world's information and make it universally accessible and useful*".

14.13.2 Larry Page

Lawrence Larry Page is an American computer scientist and Internet entrepreneur who is the co-founder of Google alongside Sergey Brin. On April 4, 2011, Page became the chief executive officer of Google. As of 2013, Page's wealth is estimated to be US$ 23 billion, ranking him #20 on the Forbes 400 list of the 400 richest Americans. Page is the inventor of PageRank, the foundation of Google's search ranking algorithm and he and Brin own approximately 16 per cent of Google's stock.

Fig. Lawrence Larry.

Page was born on March 26, 1973 in East Lansing, Michigan, United States. Both his parents were computer science professors at Michigan State University. He holds bachelor's degree in computer engineering from the University of Michigan with honours and a Master of Science in computer science from Stanford University. While at the University of Michigan, Page created "an inkjet printer made of LEGO bricks". Page's attraction to computer started when he was six years old when he got to play with the stuff lying around. In an interview he said, "From a very early age, I also realised I wanted to invent things. So I became really interested in technology and business. Probably from when I was 12, I knew I was going to start a company eventually."

After enrolling in a computer science Ph.D programme at Stanford University, Page was in search of a dissertation theme and considered exploring the mathematical properties of the World Web Wide, understanding its link structure as a huge graph. His supervisor Terry

Winograd encouraged him to pursue this idea, which Page later recalled as the best advice he ever got. Page then focused on the problem of finding out which web pages link to a given page, considering the number and nature of such backlinks to be valuable information about that page, with the role of citations in academic publishing in mind. In his research project, nicknamed "BackRub", he was soon joined by Sergey Brin, a fellow Stanford Ph.D student.

To convert the backlink data gathered by 'BackRub' web crawler into a measure of importance for a given web page, Brin and Page developed the PageRank algorithm and realised that it could be used to build a search engine far superior to existing ones. It relied on a new kind of technology that analysed the relevance of the backlinks that connected one Web page to another. In August 1996, the initial version of Google was made available, still on the Stanford University Web site.

With their invention of Google, Brin and Page allowed billions of people access to the entire world's information at the user's fingertips. Created in 1998, Google has become the highest ranked website of all time. According to Compete.com, over 176 million people visit the site on daily basis. The word, "Google" itself has become a staple in today's vocabulary. If someone needs an answer to a question, it's common for someone to tell that person to "Google it."

14.14 Govind Jaiswal

An Impossible Journey of a Rickshaw-Puller's Son who Rose against the Odds to become an IAS Officer.

Fig. Govind Jaiswal and his father.

> "I am very sure that all the youngsters who are living in deprivation and facing consistent difficulties can accomplish anything and everything provided they have the will and courage."
>
> – *Govind Jaiswal*

Once an 11-year old boy, the son of an illiterate rickshaw puller went to play at his considerably rich and respected friend's house. Minutes later, he was insulted, disgraced and literally thrown out. The educated man yelled at him, "How dare you come here and mix with my son; don't you know who you are and where you belong?" A litany of vindictive taunts and phrases like 'however much you study; you will still be a rickshaw-puller's son, 'What is your worth?' 'you can only take your father's business a bit further', 'your father's one rickshaw can become two or three at the most tomorrow with your hard work', were hurled against him. His life's path was strewn with ignominious invectives. This type of incident happened almost on a daily basis. But these 'TAUNTS and INSULTS' steeled Govind Jaiswal's determination and initiated a dream journey for him to become an IAS officer.

A question, 'What to do so that people will respect me?' constantly knocked him deep and somebody told him, 'Either you request your father to change his profession or you become somebody great in life' created an inner tsunami in his life. It was impossible for him to change his father's profession and so he chose the second. An 11-year old Govind did not know what it took to become an IAS officer but he knew he had to do his every bit to see himself where he wanted to be. Govind started spending most of his time studying with cotton jammed in his ears to stop the extreme clattering noise of printing machines and generators of his neighbourhood. He says, "During noisy morning hours, I sat on the staircase practicing Mathematics. Since it is a practical subject, we can bear all chaos around." As the sound simmers down in the evening, he focused on the other subjects like Science, History and English. His father somehow managed Mathematics tuition for him by investing all his hard work, energy and courage to make his son's dream come true. He studied in government school and college and took advantage of the students' library. "I was very cautious of every act. I restrained myself getting carried away in momentary fun. I didn't allow anyone to intrude my privacy," says Govind.

Later, on completion of graduation, many suggested him to go for engineering. Govind once gave a thought but put it off as he could not afford to buy an application form costing Rs. 500. The other option remained IAS, which was a pauper's friend. The real struggle happened when he enrolled for IAS coaching – his dad's condition worsened and he had stopped pedaling his rickshaw. It was an emotionally shattering phase – but Govind managed to pull through. There was no other option but to move to Delhi for IAS coaching. His struggling father sold the only remaining plot of land for Rs. 30,000 for his expenses in the new city. Govind ensured his father's investment don't go in vain and studied 18 hours a day. He lived a very rigorous and abstemious life by often skipping one or two meals a day to save the pittance he got from his father. For IAS Mains, he dropped Mathematics as an optional paper for Philosophy and History because he could not afford coaching. He read them from scratch to understand the basic nuances. "No subject on the earth is tough. You should have the will power to crack it," he said.

In 2006, one of the most emotional and proudest moments came in his life when 23 year old Govind ranked #48 among 474 successful candidates in the Civil Services Examination. Unlike most of the toppers, it was his very first attempt.

In an interview to a TV channel, his sister Nirmala said, "My father had hardest time sending me money; he was exhausted and could not go beyond this year. It was becoming tough pulling rickshaw with his wounded legs. Govind was also earning Rs. 1,500 from tuitions, which is still less for living in a city like Delhi. I don't know what would have happened if he'd not have made it this year.... From 10 days before the results were to be announced, my father could not sleep a wink".

"Anyone who can understand my hardship and circumstances will realise that I had no other option. Neither I could go for a lower government jobs as they are mostly fixed nor I could start a business as I had no money for it. I went for the option I was left with: work hard on studies" Govind said after successful medical procedure which is mandatory for IAS. His success dramatically changed his life forever.

Today, Govind Jaiswal is a respected IAS officer whose success story inspires and motivates thousands of youths across India.

While our country India has been suffering from lack of accountability, corruption and violence on a daily basis, Govind's thoughts are enflamed by the honesty and idealism of youth. He is grateful to his hardships and struggles and is determined not to soil his immaculate character and honesty or be influenced by anything negative in the future. It is apparent when he says, "Today, I am thankful to my circumstances and hardships through which I have evolved and curved progress. Now that I am an officer my character has been put to the test and that is a proof for me to see what a real man I am."

Lessons from Govind Jaiswal's Story

- Do not be ashamed of your humble background: Don't break down if someone tries to show where you belong. Give them a meaningful answer not by your words by your actions and courage. These people are ignorant about your worth and potential.

• An unflinching WILL power: Will power is the key ingredient of any accomplishment. Be so determined that nobody could stop you from moving ahead. There are and will be a bunch of negative people on your way of destination, ready to sabotage your dream by saying 'No' and this is the time when your perseverance is put to the test–break it and prove that you can achieve what you dream of.

• Never give a chance to Idleness: Never take your idleness for granted under the pretext of hardships that bring life lessons and help you to find the right way to accomplish anything you want. Remember, every great personality emerged through their hardships.

• Never take shelter in any lame excuses: Don't take shelter in some lame excuses as it keeps you from overcoming challenges and making things possible. There is a very good saying, *"Ninety-nine per cent of the failures come from people who have the habit of making excuses."* – George Washington.

• Don't waste your energy: Don't waste your energy on worthless and insignificant events. There were many times when Govind Jaiswal felt like hitting negative people who were consistently taunting him but he always maintained his composure. Instead of reacting, he used all his energy in pursuing his dreams. Those who try to put you down and those who are working against you; do not worry about them. Instead work hard quietly and one day when you achieve, they are already defeated. *Your achievement is the greatest defeat to your enemy.*

14.15 Hannah Cockroft

A British wheelchair athlete specialising in sprint distances in the T34 classification. She holds the Paralympic and world records for both the

Fig. Hannah Lucy Cockroft.

100 metres T34 and 200 metres T34. Competing for Great Britain at the 2012 Summer Paralympics, she won two gold medals.

Let us listen to Hannah Lucy Cockroft how she narrates about her life:

I was born on 30 July, 1992 and within 48 hours of birth, I had suffered two cardiac arrests which went on to leave me with brain damage on two different parts of my brain, deformed legs and feet and weak hips. This meant that doctors predicted that I wouldn't be able to walk and would rely on a wheel chair to get around for life. But my parents had other ideas and so the years of physiotherapy, standing frames, walking frames, splints and twisters began and at three years old, I took my first steps. Although this opened up new problems with mobility, balance and the use of my fine motor skills, it was a huge step to make. This fighting spirit has been a recurring theme throughout my life and so has seen me go on to attend mainstream nursery, primary and secondary schools, being the first disabled student at all three and coming out with top grades, showing the world that nothing was going to hold me back. As long as my family is behind me, I've always been determined to go on to great things.

In early life, I was like any other little girl. I started out wanting to be a ballerina. Not the most realistic of dreams but once again, my parents stepped up and scouted the area for a dance school that would accept me. Eventually, they found Dance four all who let me join their creative dance classes and I stayed there for 13 years of shows, lessons and hard work, being awarded the 'outstanding achievement' in dance award in 2007. The dance lessons helped with my mobility and flexibility and acted as a more enjoyable physiotherapy session as I was with friends. But dreams change and I went on to want to be in the police force, an actor, a singer and finally I settled on, 'anything to play violin, completed my Bronze Duke of Edinburg award, and became a Rainbow, a Brownie, a Sunday school leader and a member of Halifax Young Singers.

But when I moved up to senior school, I found a love for sports. An enthusiastic sports teacher introduced me to the local wheelchair basketball coach and at 13 years old, I began to play for the Cardinals wheelchair basketball team. At school, I got involved with the disabled sports team and also began my journey in athletics. At 15 years old, I represented Yorkshire in both basketball and seated discus. After winning a silver medal at the UK School Games Athletics Talent ID day at Loughborough University I met Dr. Ian Thompson, husband of Baroness Tanni Grey-Thompson, who gave me my first taste of wheelchair racing and as they say the rest is history.

"Ian let me have a go in his Wheelchair and I loved it. I'd Never experienced anything Like it before. You go and You don't stop."

Ian coached me for the first year of my career, guiding me onto the Great Britain Paralympic development team. I went on to drop both basketball and discus as I moved up the team and onto a new coach, Peter Eriksson. Eriksson is regarded one of the top wheelchair racing coaches in the world, having taken his athletes to over 119 world and Paralympic medals. With this experience, in three years he took me from novice to elite in the Paralympic world. In 2010, I broke my first world record in the T34 400 metres. I now hold 21 world records over the T34 100 metres, 200 metres, 400 metres and 800 metres. In June that year, I broke seven world records in eight days, at the same time as becoming prom Queen, completing my a-level exams and competing in my first year international overseas competition. In 2011, I was selected for the IPC World Athletics Championships in New Zealand. In my senior debut on the Great Britain team I brought home two gold medals and 'Hurricane Hannah' was born. This then made me a solid contender on the start line of the 2012 London Paralympic Games. Although it was my first games, the pressure was wasted on me and the nation's 'sweet heart' thundered into the record books, bringing home double gold and breaking four Paralympic records in the T34 100 metres and 200 metres. Following this victory, I was named on the Queens New Years Honours list in 2013.

So *'anything to be famous just takes five years of dedication and very hard work and the ability to dream very big'*. Now, I'm riding the wave of a 'celebrity' life, taking every opportunity as it comes and loving every minute. I've worked the red carpet at the Pride of Britain awards, BBC Sports Personality of the year awards and the National Television Awards. I've done fashion photo shoots for Marie Claire magazine and Fabulous Magazine and I've appeared on programmes such as Celebrity Mastermind, eight out of ten Cats and Countryfile. In 2013, Eriksson stepped down as my coach after a promotion to head coach of the Olympic team and so Jenni Banks has taken the reins and is putting me through my paces so I remain number one in the world, in summer 2013.

14.16 Harsha Bhogle

"If failure could ruin people, I would never be in TV"

–Harsha Bhogle

Harsha Bhogle is a television anchor, cricket commentator and journalist. He was born in a Marathi speaking family in Hyderabad. Bhogle recently became a freelance presenter. Harsha Bhogle attended Hyderabad Public School and subsequently studied chemical engineering at Osmania University at Hyderabad. He did his post graduate programme PGDM at Indian Institute of Management, Ahmedabad. After post-graduation he joined an advertising agency and worked there for two years, following which he completed another two-year stint at a sports management company. Bhogle began his career as a commentator at the age of 19 with All India Radio, while living in Hyderabad. In 1991 – 1992, he became the first Indian commentator to be invited by the Australian Broadcasting Corporation during India's cricket series before the 1992 Cricket World Cup. He has

Fig. Harsha Bhogle.

since worked for ABC Radio Grandstand during India's Australian tours and for eight years worked for BBC as part of their commentary team in the 1996 and the 1999 Cricket World Cups. Since 1995, he has been presenting live cricket from all round the world for ESPN STAR Sports and was part of the 'Few Good Men' commentary team that included Ravi Shastra, Sunil Gavaskar and Alan Wilkins along with Geoff Boycott etc.

He covered the 2011 – 2012 series in Australia solely for ABC Radio-- the first time in decade he has not been part of an ESPN Star broadcast. Harsha has been covering all Indian Premier League seasons since 2009 and is an expert cricket analyst on CNN-IBN. He has hosted television programme such as Harsha Online, Harsha Unplugged and School Quiz Olympiad for ESPN and Star Sports. He even had a Television programme named after him "Harsha ki khoj"/ "Hunt for Harsha", that strived to find broadcasting talent in India. Bhogle was voted the favourite commentator by *Cricinfo* users based on a worldwide poll. Bhogle has also anchored BBC's travel serial Travel India and Business Today Acumen Business Quiz and Debate competitions. He has published and authored a number of books including a biography of Mohamad Azharuddin and a collection of columns in *Indian Express; Out of the Box – Watching the Game We Love* and is also columnist for the Chennai based *"The Sportstar"* a subsidiary of The Hindu group of publications under the title "Hitting Hard" by Bhogle. He has presented the programme *Travel India with Harsha Bhogle* on Discovery Channel and TLC.

Bhogle's Own Account of His Career

After so many years in the profession it might seem unusual to say – but I should never have been in television. I didn't have what it took and for a better part of my career I was defined by who I wasn't rather than by who I was! I wasn't a test cricketer, I didn't look like a suiting model (far from it!), I had no sense of fashion or colours. I wore large glasses, I had a face for radio and after the first programme of a new series for ESPN, the producer said (though I must admit, not at the time) that there was everything wrong with it, including the anchor. Worse still I had no one to look up to. Live television was very young in India and Doordarshan was the only channel. I guess you could say that, as a result, I knew what not to do but didn't always know what was right. And so I had no choice but to learn by making mistakes. I did what I thought was right and if it was wrong, I tried not to do it again.

Great Blunders

I made many mistakes. I once ended a presentation ceremony at the end of a high profile tournament halfway through because I thought the director was telling me to move on when in reality he was telling someone else. I had very little idea of how to use the ear-piece through which the presenter gets instructions from the director. So when he said, "After this we will go to an interview" I assumed he was talking only to me and not to the crew so after that particular award had been given, I turned to camera and said, "That's it from the presentation." When I turned there were million eyes boring holes into me. I crept up to where the producer was, feeling as terrible as anyone could and said, "Sorry Rik, I promise it will never happen again." He put me at ease but I knew I had committed a blunder.

Making Mistakes isn't a Crime, Repeating Them is!

Indeed the year before that, I was first asked to present the telecast and I said, "Yes" without having a clue about what it meant. So before leaving for Chennai, my wife and I went to buy couple of jackets. We only knew one store so we went to the Raymond shop and it turned out they only had double breasted jackets so those were what we bought! One of those was a black and white striped jacket, the kind you should never wear in television because the picture jitters. But I learnt one thing about mistakes and about failure. It is not a crime to commit them, but it is criminal not to learn from them and ensure they are not repeated. If you make one mistake it tends to be pardoned but if you keep making it, no one is interested in you anymore.

Look, Failure is a Necessity: Little failures are like potholes on a road. After a while you know where not to drive. Also, you learn what not to do and it was thus that I learnt what I did about television. So if you fail, don't think it is the end of the world. Ask yourself why you failed and promise yourself that you will never do it again. You will actually emerge tougher. In a programme my wife and I did some years ago, an Australian sports psychologist told us that when they put together elite squadrons in Australia, they don't pick you if you've never failed because if you have never been face-to-face with failure you may not know what to do when confronted by it. If however, you have looked failure in the eye, vanquished it and returned stronger, you are considered a better candidate.

The one thing we should all try to do in life is to convert a problem into an advantage or opportunity. Since I didn't have much to start with, I tried much harder than anyone else, I was never afraid of learning. I learnt to be professional from the cameramen and the editors on the crew, I learnt what colours are good for television from Navjot Sidhu, I learnt how to knot a tie from my friend whose camera I had to look into, I learnt how to iron a jacket from someone else.

Unfortunately, in India we condemn failure too strongly; we attach a social status to it and clothe failures with a stigma. Stay away from such people or better still, try harder to prove them wrong. Failure can sometimes drive you towards getting even better than you would have if you hadn't failed.

We Fail When We Fear Failure: Failure can be a friend only if you learn from it and never repeat it. There are hundreds of stories around you of what the human spirit can do. Failure is not an enemy, failure is not fatal so don't fear it because the more you fear it, the more you attract it. I found that the day I stopped being afraid of failing, I grew much more relaxed. I told myself, 'what is the worst thing that will happen?' I would have to apologise on air, in front of all those viewers but I would only be apologising for a mistake, I wouldn't be committing a crime.

Very often we fail because we are afraid of failing, because we fear the aftermath of failure. I didn't do well at all in my first term at Indian Institute of Management (IIM), Ahmedabad because I spent more time fearing a D or an F than actually studying – which would have saved me in the first place. So I relax, if you fear failure, it will encircle you.

"If failure, if mistakes, could ruin people, then I would never be in television," says Harsha Bhogle.

14.17 Huang Guo Fu: An Armless Chinese Artist with an Indomitable Spirit

Huang Guo Fu of Tong Nan, China has been painting with his feet since he was 12 years old. A freak electrocution accident at the age of four left him armless. But that did not deter him from chasing his dreams.

Unable to attend school, Guofu spend his days at home flipping through comic strips. Eventually, a brush ended up in his possession and gradually he taught himself how to paint with his feet. After years of diligence, by age seven, Guofu was drawing the figures he saw in the comics and by age 12, he began receiving formal lessons from professor Zhao Yi for two years.

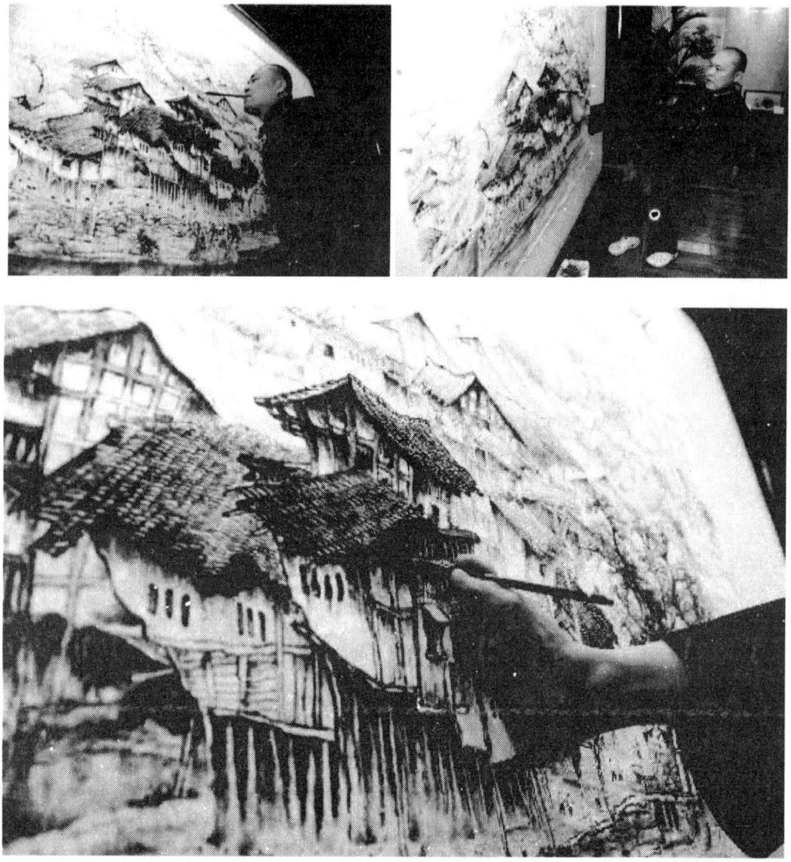

Fig. Huang Guo Fu and His Creation.

In 1986, his father was stricken with bone cancer and Guofu took to the streets to draw and sell his works to raise funds for his father's treatment. He quit his studies and started travelling to other Chinese cities, creating beautiful paintings on the side of the streets, selling them to the passers-by. During his travels, he learned to paint with his mouth, which he found to be a more elegant method than using his right leg.

A flood in Hu Nan in 1993 compelled Guofu to take to the streets again for a week straight, raising roughly five to six thousand RMB, all of which he donated to the devastated area.

Now, at the age of 41, he's the vice-curator of Chongqing Talents Museum, creating masterpieces using paintbrushes held in his mouth and between his toes. This museum has become a Mecca for artists. Awarded the position for both his artistic achievements and determined spirit, he has inspired other mouth-and-foot painters to join the museum. During one of the travels when he traveled to a city in China's Sichuan Province, he met Hu Guoui. When Hu Guoui saw him and learned about his successful journey full of struggles, she was very much impressed with the real story and felt in love with hm. She expressed her love in front of him and proposed the painter. Huang Guofu was struck dumb coupled with inner joy. She said, "I have never seen such a strong and dedicated man. I loved him at first sight. Guofu is very humble, gentle and sympathetic and we understand each other without words. And yes, the lack of hand does not affect our relationship." Both of them married in the year 2000 and since that day, Hu Guoui became his assistant and accompanies her husband in all his travels in China. "I do not have hands, but with my loving woman who more than compensates for this deficiency," says Guofu. His loving wife travels with him in different parts of China and helps him to carry the painting tools like the canvas, brushes, spreads paint, in general perform all the most menial jobs. Her husband also feels so relaxed from his wife's help.

"We compensate each other and without her help I would have simply not been able to create such a picture" – continues to praise his faithful wife. Haung says that his wife was not only assistant but the muse – the source of his inspiration. The love of art, natural talent and strong-willed character helped Guofu become one of the most famous artists in China. Huang was even invited by the expo committee to present his skills in front of all during the 2010 Shanghai World Expo.

"When life closes one door to you, it must have opened another at the same time", says Huang. "I want to let the younger generation know that there are no real obstacles in life. The only obstacle is if you want to do it." He also says, "Look at me! I had a goal to which I went in spite of everything. Today, I live a full life; I have a family and favourite work! I am happy and grateful to God for losing my arm, not my head."

14.18 Ibrahim Djan Nyampong: Bamboo Bike Frame Builder and Entrepreneur

"With my bamboo bikes, I want to create a better tomorrow."

–*Ibrahim Djan Nyampong*

Ibrahim Djan Nyampong was born in Accra, Ghana's capital and its most famous city. Since his early childhood, Ibrahim was very creative; he had cleverness for building things from scratch and a strong passion for music. As a young man he was employed by the Centre for National Culture in Accra where he was working as crafts artist. There, he developed his engineering skills and started building professional drums that he went on to export to Europe and the United States. In 2007, Ibrahim was told by

Fig. Ibrahim Djan Nyampong.

a friend that a famous bicycle engineer from California named Craig Calfee and two scientists were travelling to Ghana to do feasibility studies on bamboo. Without hesitation, Ibrahim eagerly sent an e-mail to Calfee who, impressed by the young man's straightforwardness and kindness, suggested meeting the very next day.

After welcoming the visitors in their hotel in Accra, Ibrahim was briefed on the details of the team's project. Striking everyone with his enthusiasm and knowledge, Ibrahim was asked to bring the researchers to a nearby forest to look at bamboo the next day. Two weeks later, the team left Accra and promised to stay in touch with the Ghanian. The American bicycle engineer kept his word and less than six month later, proposed Ibrahim with a partnership agreement. For the next three years, whilst still working at the art centre, Ibrahim received training in bamboo bike frame engineering. Every three months or so Calfee tripped down to Accra to teach and guide Ibrahim through the fulfilling of his new ambition. After three years of hard work, Ibrahim sent his custom built bamboo frame to a technical proof laboratory in Germany. The fame passed the test and marked a new beginning for the aspiring engineer; Ibrahim got a two-year contract with Calfee Designs and started supplying the company with his handmade creations. At the end of his contract, Ibrahim decided to start a new entrepreneur challenge. He founded his own company Africa Items, set up his own modest manufacturing plant and started building and shipping his frames around Ghana and abroad.

Today, Ibrahim continues to vigorously expand his business and now produces up to 15 bikes frames per month. He happily shares his engineering expertise with many others, teaches bike frame manufacturing to teenagers and promotes the use of bicycles across Accra. He continues to passionately pursue his dream and is still very good friend with Calfee.

Facing Interview

Q. *How strong was your life impacted by that one e-mail that you sent to the bicycle engineer?*

Ans. That e-mail has really changed my life. It has improved my livelihood and has really helped me to achieve a lot of my goals. It has enabled me to own my personal company and train a lot of Ghanians which thus also improved their livelihood. That e-mail also exposed me to a world of countless creative possibilities and global exposure in my quest to be successful bamboo bike frame builder.

Q. *What do you want to achieve with your company and what are the next steps? How do you see the future of bamboo bikes?*

Ans. My main goal is to make 'Africa Items' bamboo bikes to become the No. 1 bike building company in the world. To have an ultra modern jigs and assembly plant and to get at least one bamboo bike per household in the world. I can see the future is big. People are warming towards the bamboo bike X games and also bamboo bike circus'.

14.19 Jessica Cox: A Story of What a Determined Person can Do!

Jessica Cox is the world's first licensed armless pilot as well as the first armless black-belt in American Taekwondo Association (she now has two black belts in Taekwondo). She was born without arms due to a rare birth defect. None of the prenatal tests her mother took showed there was anything wrong with her. And yet she was born with this rare congenital defect but also with a great spirit. The psychology graduate can write, type, drive a car, brush her hair and talk on her phone simply using her feet. Ms Cox, from Tuscon, Arizona, USA is also a former dancer. She has no restrictions in driving license, she flies planes and she can type 25 words a minute.

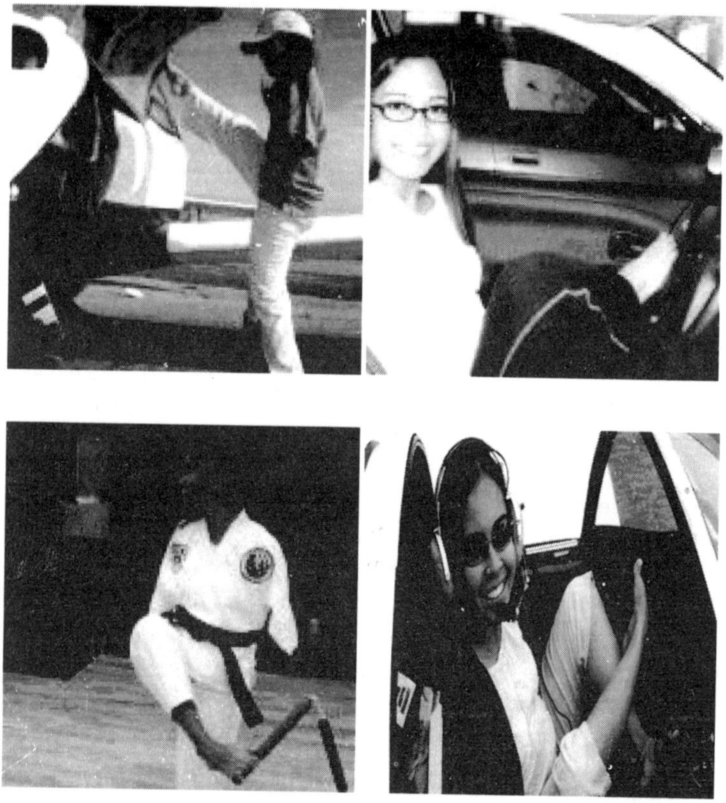

Fig. Jessica Cox.

The plane she is flying is called an *Ercoupe* and it is one of the few airplanes to be made and certified without pedals. Without rudder pedals Jessica is free to use her feet as hands. She took three years instead of the usual six months to complete her lightweight aircraft license, had three flying instructors and practiced 89 hours of flying, becoming the first pilot with no arms.

Born in 1983 in Sierra Vista, Arizona, USA, Jessica has learned to live her life with her feet. Born without arms and all doctors did not know why. There were many questions at the time about whether Jessica would be able to live a normal life. However, Jessica's father said he never shed a tear about her birth condition. He had full confidence in her potential.

With the support of her parents and family, Jessica became confident in herself as an adult and continued to explore the world with her feet.

As a child, Jessica studied dance in her hometown. When the first performance arrived, she asked to be put in the back row. Her dance teacher told her there was no back row. Tentatively, she took the stage with the other students and performed her routine. When she finished, the applause from the audience gave her encouragement and the confidence to continue dancing for 14 years. Jessica's parents eventually met a Taekwondo instructor named Jim Cunningham. His response when told of her birth condition was that she would be more than physically able and that only her attitude could hold her back. At the age of 14, Jessica earned her first Black Belt in the International Taekwondo Federation.

After graduating from high school, Jessica attended the University of Arizona where she earned bachelor's degree in Psychology. When talking about her degree, she frequently explains that psychology credits the way people think has a greater impact on their lives than a physical limitation. Jessica's most famous accomplishment was learning how to fly. It took three states, four airplanes, two flight instructors and a discouraging year to find the right aircraft; a 1946 415C Ercoupe Airplane. She received the Guinness World Record for being the first person certified to fly an airplane with only her feet.

Awards Received:

- Guinness World of Record: The Only Pilot to Fly With Her Feet, US
- Inspirational Awards for Women 2012: Most Aspirational.

When she received a Susan G. Komen Inspiration Award, 2012, Jessica challenged the audience, *"If I can fly a plane, what can you do?"*

Jessica is a woman of extreme courage and accomplishment. But she says that many places in the world the disabled face so much prejudice that even extreme courage and faith are not enough. In some places in Africa for example, people with disabilities are often perceived as "unwanted", punished by angry ancestral spirits. Shunted aside by society, they are rarely accepted into the mainstream world and become beggars. This is the kind of adversity Jessica wants to confront and to change. In 2013, she had planned to travel to Ethiopia in partnership with acclaimed NGO Handicap International. She will be visiting schools where children with disabilities are being incorporated into the mainstream school and engaging the local media to spread a message of acceptance and opportunity. This is part of her mission in life to change "ostracism" into "acceptance".

Jessica now works as a motivational speaker and advocate for the differently abled. She travels around the world sharing her story and encouraging people to be creative and innovative with the mantra "Think outside the shoe."

So the next time when you feel "You can't..." remember this amazing young woman.

14.20 JK Rowling: An Author

Joanne "Jo" Rowling born on 31 July 1965 popularly known as JK Rowling is a British author who is best known for the *Harry Potter Series* won multiple awards and sold more than 400 million copies. They have become the best-selling book series in history and been the basis for a series of films which has become the highest-grossing film series in history.

Fig. JK Rowling.

Rowling has led a "rags to riches" life story in which she progressed from living on state benefits to multi-millionaire status within five years. The 2008 *Sunday Times Rich List* estimated Rowling's fortune at 560 million pounds ranking her as the 12th richest woman in the United Kingdom. *Forbes* ranked Rowling as the 48th most powerful celebrity of 2007 and *Time* magazine named her as a runner-up for its 2007 *Person of the Year*. In October 2010, Rowling was named the "Most Influential Woman in Britain" by leading magazine editors. She has become a notable philanthropist, supporting such charities as *Comic Relief, One Parent Families, Multiple Sclerosis Society of Great Britain* and *Lumos*.

As a child, Rowling often wrote fantasy stories which she would usually read to her sister. As a young teenager she says that her life was not a happy and she described as a "dreadful time of life." During this time she had a difficult home life; her mother was ill and she had a difficult relationship with her father (she was no longer on speaking terms with him).

In 1982, Rowling took the entrance exams for Oxford University but was not accepted and read for a BA in French and Classics at the University of Exeter, which she says was a "bit of a shock" as she was expecting to be amongst lots of similar people – "thinking radical thoughts." This was her expectation at entering Oxford University. Martin Sorrell, the then professor of French at the University of Exeter said about Rowling: "a quietly competent student, with a denim jacket and dark hair, who, in academic terms, gave the appearance of doing what was necessary."

Inspiration and Mother's Death: In 1990, while she was on a four-hour-delayed train trip from Manchester to London, the idea for a story of a young boy attending a school of wizardry "came fully formed" into her mind. She told *The Boston Globe* that "I really don't know where the idea came from. It started with Harry, then all these characters and situations came flooding into my head." When she had reached her Clapham Junction flat, she began to write immediately. In December of that year, Rowling's mother died after ten years of suffering from multiple sclerosis. Rowling commented, "I was writing Harry Potter at the moment my mother died". And her death heavily affected her writing.

Marriage, Divorce and Single Parenthood: An advertisement in *The Guardian* led Rowling to move to Porto in Portugal to teach English as a foreign language. She taught at night and began to write during the day. While there, she met Portuguese television journalist Jorge Arantes in a bar and shared their mutual interest in Jane Austen. They married and later had a child named Jessica Isabel Rowling Arantes. They separated in 1993 after a lot of abuse from her husband, who said in an interview with *The Daily Express* that on their final night together he had dragged her out of their home at five in the morning and slapped her hard. Rowling and her daughter then moved to be near Rowling's sister in Edinburg, Scotland.

Seven years after graduating from university, Rowling saw herself as "the biggest failure I knew". Her marriage failed, she was jobless with a dependent child but she described her failure as liberating:

> "Failure meant a stripping away of the inessential. I stopped pretending to myself that I was anything other than what I was and began to direct all my energy to finishing the only work that mattered to me. Had I really succeeded at anything else, I might never have found the determination to succeed in the one area where I truly belonged. I was set free, because my greatest fear had been realised and I was still alive and I still had a daughter whom I adored and I had an old typewriter and a big idea. And so rock bottom became a solid foundation on which I rebuilt my life"
>
> —J.K. Rowling, "*The Fringe Benefits of Failure*", 2008.

During this period Rowling was diagnosed with clinical depression and contemplated suicide. It was the feeling of her illness which brought her the idea of Dementors, soul-sucking creatures introduced in the third book. Rowling signed up for welfare benefits describing her economic status as being "poor as it is possible to be in modern Britain, without being homeless". Rowling was left in despair after her estranged husband arrived in Scotland seeking her and her daughter. She obtained an order of restraint and Arantes returned to Portugal with Rowling filing for divorce in August 1994.

Rowling began a teacher training course in August 1995 at the Moray House School of Education at Edinburg University after completing her first novel while having survived on state benefits. In 1995, Rowling finished her manuscript for *Harry Potter and the Philosopher's Stone* on an old manual typewriter. The book was submitted to twelve publishing houses, all of which rejected the manuscript. Another disappointing moment for Rowling; all her hard earned production was rejected. A year later she was finally given the green light by editor Barry Cunningham from Bloomsbury, a publishing house in London. Although Bloomsbury agreed to publish the book, Cunningham says that he advised Rowling to get a day job since she had little chance of making money in children's books. Soon after, in 1997, Rowling received an 8000 pounds grant from the Scottish Arts Council to enable her to continue writing. In June 1997, Bloomsbury published Philosopher's Stone with an initial print run of 1,000 copies, 500 of which were distributed to libraries. Five months later the book won its first award, a *Nestle Smarties Book Prize*, then won the prestigious British Book Award for Children's Book of the Year and later the Children's Book Award. In early 1998, an auction was held in the United States for the rights to publish the novel and was won by *Scholastic Inc.* for $105,000. In Rowling own words, she "nearly died" when she heard the news. But later she regretted and she was helpless because she was not financially sound at that time.

Fig. Harry Potter.

Rowling began to meet success in her subsequent books on Harry Potter. The sixth book, Harry Potter and the Half-Blood Prince, was released on 16 July 2005. It too broke all sales records, selling nine million copies in its first 24 hours of release. While writing, she told a fan online, "Book six has been planned for years, but before I started writing seriously I spend two months revisiting the plan and making absolutely sure I knew what I was doing". On 21 July, 2007, the seventh book, Harry Potter and the Deathly Hallows was released and it broke its predecessor's record as the fastest selling book of all time. It sold 11 million copies in the first day of release in the United Kingdom and United States.

In an interview with Oprah Winfrey, Rowling gave credit to her mother for the success of the series saying that "the books are what they are because she died...because I loved her and she died".

In 2004, *Forbes* named Rowling as the first person to become a US-dollar billionaire by writing books, the second-richest female entertainer and the 1,062nd richest person in the world. In February 2013, she was assessed as the 13th most powerful woman in the United Kingdom by Woman's Hour on BBC 4.

14.21 John Roebling: An Engineer Who Conceived the Idea of the Famous Brooklyn Bridge

John Augustus Roebling was a German-born American civil engineer. He is famous for his wire rope suspension bridge designs in particular, the design of the Brooklyn Bridge. The real life story of engineer John Roebling building the Brooklyn Bridge in New York, USA back in 1870. The bridge was completed in 1883, after 13 years. In 1883, a creative engineer named John Roebling was inspired by an idea to build a spectacular bridge connecting New York with the Long Island. However, bridge building experts throughout the world thought that this was an impossible feat and told Roebling to forget the idea. It just could not be done. It was not practical. It had never been done before.

Fig. John Roebling.

Roebling could not ignore the vision he had in his mind of this bridge. He thought about it all the time and he knew deep in his heart that it could be done. He just had to share the dream with someone else. After much discussion and persuasion he managed to convince his son Washington, an up-coming engineer that the bridge, in fact, could be built. Working together for the first time, the father and son developed concepts of how the obstacles could be overcome. With great excitement and inspiration, and the headiness of a wild challenge before them, they hired their crew and began to build their dream bridge.

The project started well, but when it was only few months underway a tragic accident on the site took the life of John Roebling. Washington was also injured and left with a certain amount of brain damage which resulted in him not being able to talk or walk. *We told them so, "Crazy men and their crazy dreams."* Everyone had a negative comment to make and felt that the project should be scrapped since the Roeblings were the only ones who knew how the bridge could be built.

In spite of his handicap Washington was never discouraged and still had a burning desire to complete the bridge and his mind was still as sharp as ever. He tried to inspire and pass on his enthusiasm to some of his friends but they were too daunted by the task. As he lay on his bed in his hospital room, with the sunlight streaming through the windows, a gentle breeze blew the flimsy white curtains apart and he was able to see the sky and the tops of the trees outside for just a moment.

It seemed that there was a message for him not to give up. Suddenly an idea struck him. All he could do was move one finger and he decided to make the best use of it. By moving this, he slowly developed a code of communication with his wife. He touched his wife's arm with that finger, indicating to her that he wanted her to call the engineers again. Then he used the same method of tapping her arm to tell the engineers what to do. It seemed foolish but the project was under way again.

For thirteen years Washington tapped out his instructions with his finger on his wife's arm until the bridge was finally completed. Today, the spectacular Brooklyn Bridge stands in all its glory as a tribute to the triumph of one man's indomitable spirit and his determination not to be defeated by circumstances. It is also a tribute to the engineers and their team work and to their faith in a man who was considered mad by half the world. It stands too as a tangible monument to the love and devotion of his wife who for thirteen long years patiently decoded the messages of her husband and told the engineers what to do.

Perhaps this is one of the best examples of a never-say-die attitude that overcomes a terrible physical handicap and achieves an impossible goal. Often when we face obstacles in our day-to-day life, our hurdles seem very small in comparison to what many others have to face. The Brooklyn Bridge shows us that dreams that seem impossible can be realised with determination and persistence, no matter what the odds are.

14.22 Kalpana Chawla: An Indian Born American Astronaut

Kalpana Chawla (March 17, 1962–February 1, 2003) was born in Karnal, Haryana, India. She was the first Indian American astronaut and first Indian woman in space. She first flew on Space Shuttle Columbia STS-107 in 1997 as a mission specialist and primary robotic arm operator. In 2003, Chawla was one of the seven crew members killed in the Space Shuttle Columbia disaster when the spacecraft disintegrated after re-entry into the Earth's atmosphere.

Fig. Kalpana Chawla.

Chawla studied aeronautical engineering at the Punjab Engineering College in 1982 and thereafter, she went to the United States and earned her Master's degree in aerospace engineering from the University of Texas. She took her doctorate from the University of Colorado. The NASA used to announce candidates every two years, selecting about a hundred men and women out of thousands of applicants. Chawla cracked the NASA entry exam, which is one of the toughest exams in the world and was selected.

After having been selected by NASA, Kalpana Chawla reported to the Johnson Space Center as an astronaut candidate in the 15th Group of Astronauts. After completing a year of training and evaluation, she was assigned as crew representative to work technical issues for the Astronaut Office EVA/Robotics and Computer Branches. Her assignments included work on development of Robotic Situational Awareness Displays and testing space shuttle control software in the Shuttle Avionics Integration Laboratory. In November, 1996, Kalpana Chawla was assigned as mission specialist and prime robotic arm operator on STS-87. In January 1998, she was assigned as crew representative for shuttle and station flight crew equipment, and subsequently served as lead for Astronaut Offices Crew Systems and Habitability section. She flew on STS-87 (1997) and STS-107 (2003), logging 30 days, 14 hours and 54 minutes in space.

Chawla's first mission to space began on November 19, 1997 as part of the six astronaut crew that flew the Space Shuttle Columbia Flight STS-87. STS-87 was the fourth U.S Microgravity Payload flight and focused on experiments designed to study how the weightless environment of space affects various physical processes, and on observations of the Sun's outer atmospheric layers. Two members of the crew performed an EVA (spacewalk) which featured the manual capture of a Spartan satellite, in addition to testing EVA tools and procedures for future Space Station assembly. STS-87 made 252 orbits of the Earth, traveling 6.5 million miles in 376 hours and 34 minutes. STS-107 *Columbia* (January 16 to February 1, 2003). The 16-day flight was a dedicated science and research mission. Working 24 hours a day, in two alternating shifts, the crew successfully conducted approximately 80 experiments. The STS-107 mission ended abruptly on February 1, 2003 when Space Shuttle *Columbia* and the crew perished during re-entry into the Earth's atmosphere, 16 minutes prior to scheduled landing.

Chawla was the first Indian-born woman in space, as well as the first Indian-American in space. She was the second person from India to fly into space, after cosmonaut Rakesh Sharma who went into space in 1984 in a Soviet spacecraft.

Kalpana Chawla was posthumously awarded the Congressional Space Medal of Honour, the NASA Space Flight Medal, and the NASA Distinguished Service Medal.

From then on, she has been an inspiration to many young Indians and Americans to become astronauts. Her success continues to inspire many young people to aspire for high goals in life.

14.23 Karoly Takacs

You might not have heard of this man. However, in Hungary, he is elevated as a national hero-everyone there knows his name and his incredible story. Karol Takacs was the first shooter to win two Olympic gold medals in the 25 metre rapid fire pistol event; the first using his right hand and after a serious injury, the second with his left.

Takacs was a world-class pistol shooter but he was denied a place in the Hungarian shooting team for the 1936 Summer Olympics on the ground that he was a sergeant and only commissioned officers were allowed to compete. This prohibition was lifted in Hungary after the Berlin Games and Takacs had expectations of success at the 1940 Summer Olympics, scheduled to be held in Tokyo.

Fig. Karoly Takacs.

In 1938, Karol Takacs of the Hungarian Army was the top pistol shooter in the world. He was expected to win the gold in the 1940 Olympic Games scheduled for Tokyo. Those expectations vanished one terrible day, just months before the Olympics. While training with his army squad, a hand grenade exploded in Takacs' right hand and Takacs' shooting hand was blown off.

Takacs spent a month in the hospital depressed at both the loss of his hand and the end to his Olympic dream. At that point most people would have quit. And they would have probably spent the rest of their life feeling sorry for themselves. Most people would have quit but not Takacs. Takacs was a winner. Winners know that they can't let circumstances keep them down. They understand that life is hard and that they can't let life beat them down. Winners know in their heart that quitting is not an option. Takacs did the unthinkable he picked himself up, dusted himself off and decided to learn how to shoot with his left hand! His reasoning was simple. He simply asked himself, "Why not?"

Instead of focusing on what he didn't have – a world class right shooting hand he decided to focus on what he did have – incredible mental toughness and a healthy left hand that with time, could be developed to shoot like a champion. For months Takacs practiced by himself. No one knew what he was doing. Maybe he didn't want to subject himself to people who most certainly would have discouraged him from his rekindled dream. In the spring of 1939 he showed up at the Hungarian National Pistol Shooting Championship. Other shooters approached Takacs to give him their condolences and to congratulate him on having the strength to come and watch them shooting. They were surprised when he said, "I didn't come to watch, I came to compete." They were even more surprise when Takacs won!

In 1940 and 1944 Olympics were cancelled because of World War II. It looked like Takacs Olympic Dream would never have a chance to realise itself. But Takacs kept training and in 1944 he qualified for the London Olympics. At the age of 38, Takacs won the Gold Medal again at the 1952 Helsinki Olympics. Takacs – a man with mental toughness to bounce back from anything.

Although most associated with rapid fire pistol, Takacs also won a bronze medal at the 1958 ISSF World Shooting Championships in 25 metre center-fire pistol. He also won 35 Hungarian national shooting championships.

After his shooting career, Takacs became a coach. He trained Hungarian Szilard Kun, who won the silver medal at the 1952 Summer Olympics. He ended his army career as a lieutenant colonel.

Winners in every field have a special trait that helps them become unstoppable. It is a special characteristic that allows them to survive major setbacks on the road to success. Winners recover *quickly.* Bouncing back is not enough. Winners bounce back *quickly.* They always find an alternative way. The reason *quick recovery* is important is that if you recover quickly, you don't lose your momentum and your drive. Takacs recovered in only a month. If he had wallowed in his misery and had stayed 'under the circumstances' or if he had played the martyr and felt sorry for himself much longer, he would have lost his mental edge – his "eye of the tiger" and he never would have been able to come back.

14.24 Kumi Naidoo: Activist, Humanitarian, Executive Director of Greenpeace Int.

> "Great struggles in history require decent men and women to put their lives on the line."
>
> –*Kumi Naido*

Kumi Naidoo was born in Durban, South Africa. Growing up during apartheid and witnessing inequalities of all sorts, Kumi felt a strong urge to fight for equality and freedom from a very young age. When he was 15, he joined the Helping Hands Youth Organisation and was expelled from high school due to his anti-apartheid involvement. He became active in neighbourhood organisation, youth work in his community and mass mobilisations against the apartheid regime. Fighting for liberation, Kumi was arrested several times and police harassments eventually forced him to go underground at the age of 21.

To get him out of the country, certain progressive professors encouraged the young activist to apply for a Rhodes Scholarship in Oxford. "To be honest, I did not know much about Oxford. I was 21 years old and standing trial for violating the state of emergency." The day Kumi heard his application was accepted, his home was raided. "For the next four months, until I fled to Oxford, I was basically on the run." During the

Fig. Kumi Naidoo.

night of his arrival in the British university, it snowed and the next morning a friendly lady knocked on Kumi's door and offered him breakfast; this was not the life he was used to. During his time at university, in addition to focusing on his academic work, Kumi was heavily involved in several student anti-apartheid organisations. Those years were very repressive period for South Africa; Kumi's thoughts never left his country. After the release of Nelson Mandela, he returned home to work on the legalisation of the African National Congress. Since, then, he participated and held leadership positions in countless non-governmental organisations. He led a variety of initiatives in education, development, human rights and social justice. In 1997, driven by his motivation to take action against the high rate of violence towards women in South Africa, Kumi organised the 'National Men's March against Violence on Women and Children'.

Today, Kumi keeps on eagerly dedicating his time to activism and inspiring the younger generations; he is recognised internationally as a strong advocate for gender equality, human rights and environmental protection. Atop many institutions such as *Civicus* or the *Global Call for*

Climate Action, Kumi serves as the head of Greenpeace International where his goal is to expose global environmental problems and to promote solutions that are essential to a green and peaceful future.

Facing Interview

Q. *To which extents were your actions in life inspired by Nelson Mandela?*

Ans. I was 15 years old when I first heard of Mandela. His whole public persona and personal history, even his face, were censored in the public domain. During the apartheid regime I participated in my first protest opposing inequality in education, fighting apartheid education. Over the course of our campaign questioning and opposing inequality in education, we first heard of the "Free Mandela" campaign. Mandela became a major source of inspiration because when he said that "the struggle is my life" I realised how powerful and true his statement really was. The struggle to eradicate climate, gender and social injustice take a lot of effort and time. As Mandela put it: the struggle for justice is a marathon, not a sprint, we all found inspiration and motivation in Mandela who was a model for all of us. Mandela also said that the struggle for justice is not a popularity contest and that injustice will carry on until decent men and women say enough is enough and no more, we are prepared to go to prison, we are prepared to put our lives on the line if necessary. Even today, his words and actions remain an inspiration to young people everywhere.

Throughout your life, what were the driving forces that – in addition to human rights activities – lead you to focus on environmental issues and ultimately join Greenpeace?

I grew up in Apartheid South Africa and used to think that environmental activism is the privilege of the rich. In the mid 90's I started to realise that environmental issues cut across all other issues. For me, climate change is not only about the environment–climate change is an issue of survival, economy and equity. Because of that growing consciousness I started to volunteer for various environmental organisations. In my experience in the international development sector I saw how development projects that sought to address poverty and succeeded were rolled back because of environmental degradation and climate impacts. I understood that the struggle to end environmental and climate injustice and the struggle to end social and economic injustice are two sides of the same coin. We have to ensure a balance between ecology, economy and equity. Greenpeace seemed like a logical place to make a contribution and there were two things about the organisation that relies on millions of people around the world who contribute modest sums of money and help raise resources for our campaigns. We don't take money from corporations or governments –

and this gives us the independence to speak truth to power. Secondly, Greenpeace is drawing key lessons from history about how social change happens: those who profit from the *status quo* will not give up power unless there is a visible mobilisation. Greenpeace is committed to non-violent direct action and civil disobedience —we can only move forward in winning big struggles for justice when decent men and women stand up and say enough is enough and no more. Greenpeace is a life-loving organisation; nevertheless it does have that spirit of being prepared to take action.

14.25 Liz Murray: From Homeless to Harvard

Elizabeth "Liz" Murray is an American inspirational speaker who is notable for having been accepted by Harvard University despite being homeless in her school years. Elizabeth "Liz" Murray was born on September 23, 1980 the Bronx, New York to poor drug-addicted, HIV-infected parents.

Fig. Liz Murray.

She became homeless just after she turned 15, when her mother died of AIDS, and her father moved to a homeless shelter. Murray's life turned around when she began attending the Humanities Preparatory Academy in Chelsea, Manhattan. Though she started high school later than most students and remained without a stable home while supporting herself and her sister, Murray graduated in only two years. She was awarded a New York Times scholarship for needy students and accepted into Harvard University, matriculating in the fall semester of 2000. She left Harvard in 2003 to care for her sick father; she resumed her education at Columbia University to be closer to him until 2006 when he died of AIDS. As of May 2008, she was back at Harvard working towards her degree with plans to graduate with a degree in Psychology in June 2009.

Her life became a movie in 2003 and she now works as a professional speaker, representing the Washington Speakers Bureau. That same gutsy strength that pulled her from the streets now transforms the lives of others from student groups to business audiences in need of inspiration to overcome their own obstacles.

Let us Listen to Liz's Story in her Own Words

(*Abridged from 'Breaking Night' by Liz Murray*)

"It was three years old when I first realised that my mother and father shared strange habits. They would retreat into the kitchen of our New York apartment and spread spoons and other objects across the table while communicating in quick, urgent commands. I was not supposed to bother them, but I watched from the hallway. Water was needed – just few drops from the tap – and so were shoelaces and belts. Then, at the very last minute, they would shut the door, blocking my view entirely. One evening, when the door was closed on me again, I didn't budge but sat and waited outside. When my mother finally emerged, I raised my arms in the air and said, in a singsong voice, 'Al-l-l do-ne'. Taken off guard, my mother asked disbelievingly, "what did you say, pumpkin?' "Al-l-l do-ne', I repeated. She yelled at my father: "Peter, she knows!' and Daddy laughed while Ma stroked my hair. Thrilled to have found my place in their game, I sat outside the kitchen whenever they spread the spoons from then on. Eventually, they left the door open.

I have just one black and white photograph left of my mother when she was younger. She was 17 when it was taken and beautiful with wispy curls and eyes that shone like dark marbles. But I also know that by then she had been using drugs for four years. The eldest of four children, she was raised by an alcoholic father and mentally ill mother and she had started smoking grass to escape the violence and abuse of her home life. Later she ran away and between sleeping rough and earning her living through prostitution, she moved on to speed and heroin. Daddy was one of her dealers. They began hanging out together when she was 22 and he was 34. Daddy was also the child of a violent, alcoholic father but his middle-class mother had tried to secure her only child's future by holding down two bookkeeping jobs in order to send him to private school. Midway through a psychology degree, however, he had abandoned his studies for the drug trade.

He and Ma connected immediately, but instead of going on dinner dates they would take cocaine to Central Park, where they would sprawl in the moonlight and get high anchored in each other's arms.

A year or so after my parents met in 1977, my elder sister Lisa was born. By the time I followed in September 1980, Daddy was serving a three-year prison sentence for a fraud racket involving prescription painkillers. Amazingly, instead of falling apart, my mother proved to be a sober and house-proud single parent. But once Daddy returned home, dirty dishes sat untouched in the sink for days and we rarely went to the park any more. Ma was legally blind due to a degenerative eye disease she'd had since birth. This meant she was entitled to welfare and our lives revolved around the first day of every month when her payment was due. On that day, food would be abundant. Lisa and I would dine on Happy Meals in front of the TV to the sound of spoons clanking on the kitchen table. We knew what they were doing. Within five days, the money would be gone and for the rest of the month we lived on egg and mayonnaise sandwiches. Lisa and I hated them but they got us through the hours when our stomachs burned with hunger.

I started school in the summer of 1985 and from the outset, I tried to be a good student. It just didn't work out that way. Maybe getting more sleep would have helped but there was too much going on. At nights, Ma would go to the local bars and beg until she had gathered the five dollars she needed for a hit. Daddy would then slip out to a dealer while Lisa screamed at both of them: "we didn't eat dinner and you're going to get high?' I knew what she was saying made sense. But things weren't always so clear for me. Ma and Daddy had no intention of hurting us. They simply did not have it in them to be the parents I wanted them to be. I remember once Ma stole five dollars sent to me from my father's mother inside a glittery birthday card. I was furious and demanded that she gave me back my money. She responded by flushing the hit she had bought down the loo. 'I'm not a monster, Lizzy', she cried. 'I can't stop. Forgive me, pumpkin'. So I did.

I forgave her again when she sold the Thanksgiving turkey provided by the church so that she could buy another hit. And I forgave her when she attempted to sell Lisa's winter coat. The drug dealer refused to take a child's coat on principle, so Ma went back out later the same night and sold the toaster and my bike to get her cocaine instead.

At school I was clearly different. My dirty clothing hung heavily off my body and I was aware of the stench I gave off, so I knew the other pupils must have been aware of it, too.

'Who cares what people think?' Daddy said. But the shame gnawed at me. I pleaded with Ma and eventually she allowed me, against what she called her better judgment, to stay at home sometimes.

One morning, on one of the days I didn't go to school, there was a knock at the door. I was the only one awake. From the hallway, I heard a woman and a man talking. They knocked again before sliding a piece of paper under the door. When they had gone, I picked it up. The letter ordered the parent(s) or guardian of Elizabeth Murray to phone Mr. Doumbia regarding her truancy from school. I ripped it into tiny pieces and shoved it in the bin.

As well as being blind, Ma turned out to have the same mental illness that her mother had had. Between 1986 and 1990, she suffered six schizophrenic bouts, each requiring her to be institutionalised for up to three months. The combination of her illness and her and Daddy's chronic drug use pushed their relationship to breaking point. As their fights became increasingly bitter, Lisa and I locked ourselves in our rooms, her with her music and me with my books – or rather Daddy's ever-growing supply of unreturned library books. Slowly, I read through his collection of true crime, biographies and random trivia. Eventually, I began reading fast enough to get through one of his books in a little over a week.

Just after my 11th birthday, I woke in the early hours to find Ma sitting at the end of my bed, a beer bottle in her hand. 'I love you, pumpkin,' she was saying as tears streamed down her face.

'Ma, please, what's wrong?'

'Lizzy, I'm sick, I have AIDS'.

A hot quiver shot up from my stomach.

'Are you going to die, Ma?'

Abruptly, Ma stood up and reached for the door.

'Forget it, Lizzy. We'll be just fine', she said before walking out. I cried to her to come back. But she didn't reappear.

A year or so later, Ma and Daddy finally separated and Ma moved in with a new boyfriend. His name or the nickname that everyone knew him by was Brick. He was a security guard at a fancy art gallery in Manhattan. Ma liked the fact that he didn't use drugs–he just drank to ease his nerves sometimes. He had his own apartment in a neighbourhood much nicer than ours and Lisa moved there with Ma but I couldn't bear to leave Daddy on his own.

Being alone with Daddy meant my truancy worsened. I spent most days on the sofa eating cornflakes and watching *The Price is Right* while Daddy slept or went on a drug run. On the rare occasions my teachers saw me, some of them didn't even know my name.

Shortly, after I turned 13, Child Welfare took me into care. I was sent to a residential centre where girls with behavioural problems were 'evaluated'. My time there comes back to me now only in flashes of smells, images and sounds. I was, for that period, a witness more than a participant in my life.

After six months, it was decided that I would go and live with Ma and Brick and Lisa after all. Ma registered me at a new junior high school. My class had already been together or two years and were in tight cliques. But one pretty Latina girl offered to hang out with me. Her name was Sam and we fast became friends.

Sam was bold–she could make an ordinary day suddenly thrilling. But she confided that she had trouble at home, although she made me promise not to tell anyone what was going on. I told her she could stay with me, even though Brick had banned me from having friends to stay over. It was easy to sneak Sam into my bedroom. All we had to do was open and then slam the front door in the evening, to give the impression that she had gone home.

During the day, Sam and I started skipping school together with a gang of other truants. We would discuss between us whose parents were out working and in whose apartment we could therefore hang out for the day. It was rare for any of us to drink or do drugs, though. I was repulsed by both. Several times, Ma had pleaded with me, 'Lizzy, don't ever get high baby, baby. It ruined my life'. Witnessing what she and Daddy had been through was probably the most compelling anti-drug message anyone could have given me.

Ma was now dying from AIDS, but I was in denial about how sick she was. The more fun I had with my friends, the harder it was to come home. Then, one night, Brick found Sam hiding in my room and screamed at her to get out. She had nowhere else to go and I wasn't going to let her go on to the streets by herself. So we both left. We slept on the subway, on park benches under the stars and at friends' apartments and to begin with, it was a great adventure. But every so often an image of a sick and weary Ma would come into my mind and I would fight to push it away. After several weeks, I finally called Brick's number. Lisa picked up the phone.

'Where are you?' She asked.

'Not that far away. I was just wondering about you... and about Ma.'

'Lizzy, Ma's in hospital. She's been asking for you'.

Ma had tuberculosis. I arranged to meet Lisa at the hospital that night. Ma's skin was yellow, her cheeks sloped dramatically inwards and her eyes were wide open but fixed on nothing. I spent just a few minutes at her bedside, feeling powerless. I had no idea that it would be the last time I ever saw her. She died three weeks later, just before Christmas 1996. At her charity funeral she was buried in a pine box with her name misspelled on top. Daddy, who was living in a homeless shelter by then, didn't make it. Through that long, hard winter, I carried on sleeping at friends' apartments and yearning for home. The trouble was, I no longer had any idea where home was.

One night while staying with my friend Danny, he introduced me to his new girlfriend. Paige was 22 and a former runaway who now had a steady job and her own apartment. Ma had always said that she and Daddy were going to turn their lives around, but they never did. I asked Paige how she had done it and she told me about her 'alternative high school. It's a place like a private school, but for anyone who is really motivated to go, even if they don't have the money. The teachers really care about you', she said. My entire education was pitiful. But if Paige had made things happen for herself, then maybe so could I.

I researched as many alternative high schools as I could find and went for interviews. After several rejections, I felt my resolve slipping. But then I met Perry Weiner, the founder of the Humanities preparatory Academy or Prep. Immediately, I trusted him. I told him about my past and he agreed to give the chance that changed my life. Two years I spent at Prep unfolded like an urban-academic-survival-study marathon. Unknown to Perry, I remained homeless – crashing at friends' apartments whenever I could. But I always arrived on time or even early, for classes. I pictured myself as a runner on a track, with hurdles to jump along the way. And every morning, I knew Perry was waiting for me, as were the other teachers who became my compass in an otherwise dark and confusing world.

With their encouragement, I grew to love Shakespeare (I played Hamlet and Macbeth in school plays), joined student committees and learned that my voice mattered. Gradually, I took my hair out of my face and started looking people in the eye. My growing confidence was reflected in my academic achievements – I became a straight-A student, completing a four-year high school programme in just two years. When the time came to think about what I might do next, Perry selected me, along with nine other top pupils for a trip to Boston.

He took us to Harvard University and as I looked at the students reading on the open lawns I was filled with a deep longing for something I could not explain. The feeling must have shown on my face because Perry leaned over and said, "Hey, Liz, it would be a reach, but it's not impossible... Ever think about applying to Harvard?' Back in New York, my teachers advised me to apply for a scholarship offered by *The New York Times* worth $12,000 a year. I looked at the application form. It asked for an essay in which I was to describe any obstacles that I may have had to overcome in my life in order to thrive academically. My eyes widened. It was so ridiculously perfect that I laughed. Taking a blank sheet of paper, I poured everything I had on to the page. My frustrations, my sadness, my grief – the essay wrote itself. Three thousand high school students applied for the six scholarships offered by The New York Times. Had I known that– and had I known how difficult it was to make it to Harvard – then I may never have applied for either the scholarship or my college place... But I didn't know my chances of success; I only knew that I was going to carve out a life for myself that was in no way limited by my past".

Liz went to Harvard on a New York Times scholarship and graduated in 2009. She took a break in the middle of her studies to care for her father who died in 2006 from AIDS, age 64. He had been sober for eight years and led a drugs relapse prevention group before being taken ill. Liz's sister Lisa also went to university and became a teacher of autistic children. Now 30, Liz is an award-winning motivational speaker and runs workshops designed to help others change their lives for the better.

14.26 Lizzie Velasquez: The Ugliest Woman in the World Who Teaches True Beauty

Lizzie Velasquez was born in Austin, Texas on March 13, 1989. Born four weeks prematurely, her birth weight was only two pounds 11 ounces (1,219 grams). Her age was reported as 23 in September 2012, a time when

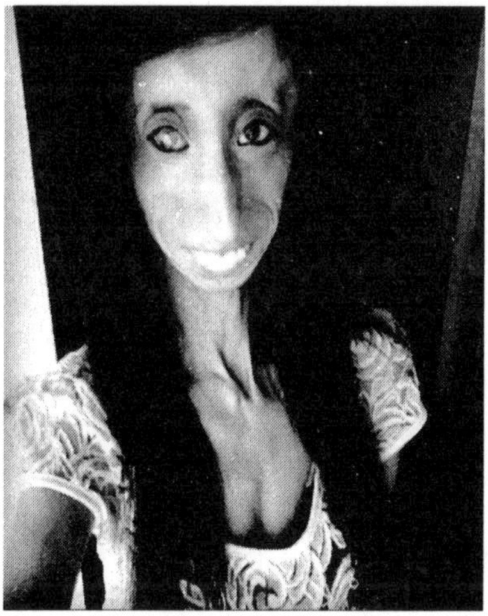

Fig. Lizzie Velasquez.

she was nearing graduation from Texas State University majoring in Communication studies. She is a Roman Catholic and she has spoken out in terms of her belief in God who has "blessed me with the greatest blessing of my life, which is my syndrome." Her extreme medical condition has led her to become an author and motivational speaker.

A few years ago, Lizzie Velasquez, a 23-year-old from Texas was labeled "the ugliest woman in the world" in a YouTube video that received more than four million hits. When Lizzie got the world's ugliest title she responded in an incredibly beautiful way. She became a motivational speaker and author of two books about true beauty, the one that is not always perceived by the eye. She has her own website and a channel on You Tube, where she addresses the same topic.

Skinny Bones Syndrome: Over the years, Lizzie has been through a long uneven journey. She suffers from a condition so rare that it is to this day undiagnosed. She calls it "skinny bones" and there are only two other people in the world who have it. The main symptom of it is that she's not able to gain weight. Lizzie was born four weeks prematurely, weighing just two pounds 11 onces and has never weighed more than 60 pounds.

Although she eats whatever she wants every 15 minutes, her body just can't store fat or build muscle. That's why she wears size 000 clothes. In addition, Lizzie is blind in one eye and has limited vision in the other. In one of the videos available on her website, her mother Rita Velasquez, remembers that newborn Lizzie "fit in the palm of my hand", and oscillates between laughter and tears when she remembers that she and husband Guadalupe had to buy doll clothes for their baby girl. Doctor told them not to expect anything from her, as Lizzie was so fragile she probably could not move, maybe even think. "To see what she's doing now is just awesome," says this proud and brave mother.

Facing Cyber-bullies: Following that first and humiliating video, the comments were sickeningly cruel. Someone even said, "Do the world a favour and put a gun in your head," and many referred to Lizzie as "it" and "monster". She received e-mails saying things like *"I was just looking at your picture and you are very ugly. How are you a cheerleader?"* Initially, she wanted to make cyber-bullies feel as low as she could, but she finally decided against it. She emerged from the ashes and realised that her purpose in life was to *"become a messenger of hope and comfort."* She has recorded a video titled *Courage and Determination*, where she shares her goals with the world.

"Every day is a struggle," the video begins. "Being judged by strangers is not easy." She continues by revealing she read every single comment to the 'Ugliest woman in the world' video. Then, after overcoming the pain, she set four goals for herself:

- Motivational speaking
- Publishing a book
- Graduating college
- Having a family and a career of her own

This is something beyond reckoning for someone who, doctors said would amount to nothing. She has gone far beyond the limits set by her doctors. Today, Lizzie is an experienced motivational speaker and during the last six years she has appeared at more than 200 workshops. She's the author of the book *Lizzie Beautiful* (where she tells her own story) and has just launched her second book, *Be Beautiful, be you*. She will soon graduate from college and in the meantime even uploads videos on how to style hair.

As her Courage and Determination video concludes, "In the battle between the world's ugliest woman against video, I... I think I won."

14.27 Mark Zuckerberg: The Facebook Creator

Born on May 14, 1984, Mark Zuckerberg is a technology innovator, CEO, Internet mogul and philanthropist who earned multibillionaire status in his mid-20s. As a co-founder, chairman and CEO of Facebook, Zuckerberg redefined the social media market and connected people in ways never thought possible before. He recently topped a list of "Highest Rated CEOs" from online career community Glassdoor. The list was the result of employee reviews over the past 12 months.

Technology Prodigy: Mark Zuckerberg was born in a well-educated family in New York. He developed an interest in computers at an early stage. He created his own messaging programme at the age of 12 and dubbed as "Zucknet" which his father used in his dental office. He would

Fig. Mark Zuckerberg.

create games and programmes under a private computer tutor, who later told reporters that it was hard to stay ahead of the technology prodigy.

Fig. Mark Zuckerberg with wife Priscilla Chan.

While still in high school, companies like AOL and Microsoft expressed interest in buying his software and hiring him, which he declined.

Life at Harvard: Mark Zuckerberg enrolled at Harvard and soon he developed a reputation as a strong programmer and software developer. He created programmes like *CourseMatch* which helped students choose their classes based on the selections of their peers and *Facemash*, which compared pictures of two students and allowed users to vote on who was more attractive. While popular, none of these programmes matched to the later success of Zuckerberg's development of Facebook. He then, began working on a project called *The Havard Connection*, a sort of dating site for the Havard elite. He later dropped out of Harvard and began working on his own site with friends Dustin Moskovitz, Chris Hughes and Eduardo Saverin. This site which started as the facebook.com, allowed users to create their own profiles, upload photos and network with users at specific universities. Run out of a dorm room at Harvard until June 2004, the facebook.com thrived and Zuckerberg dropped out to pursue it full time. By the end of 2004, Facebook boasted one million users.

The site began to evolve. At first, it was only available to certain schools. Thanks to investments from venture capital firms, the site eventually opened up to other schools, then to the general public. Early on, Zuckerberg was turning down offers from Yahoo and MTV Networks.

"The thing that we are trying to do at Facebook is just help people connect and communicate more efficiently," he said. Instead of taking lucrative offers (Yahoo! Reportedly offered Zuckerberg $1 billion), Zuckerberg focused on expanding the site to bring as much value to users as possible. But legal troubles from his early dealings with The Harvard Connection plagued him, as depicted in the Academy Award-nominated movie "The Social Network". Zuckerberg later noted that much of the story was exaggerated for Hollywood. "I just think people have a lot of fiction," he said, "*But the real story of Facebook is just that we've worked so hard for all this time. The real story is actually probably pretty boring, right? We just sat at our computers for six years and coded.*" Despite some of the negative depictions in the movie and the lawsuit filed by the Winklevoss twins, Zuckerberg and Facebook continued to thrive. He was named *TIME* magazine's Person of the Year in 2010 and FORBES has ranked him at No. 36 on its 400 list, estimating his net worth at $13.3 billion as of March 2013.

Zuckerburg who now resides in Palo Alto, single handedly changed the face of social media forever with Facebook's "like" button, "status updates", "relationship statuses" and now the new "timeline". He does not seem to be slowing down either. Facebook is going public and he bought Instagram for $1 billion.

Risk-taker: Taking risk is one of the secrets to Zuckerberg's success he says; risks that include dropping out of Harvard and forging forward with the Facebook strategy. "*The biggest risk is not taking any risk,*" he said. "*In a world that's changing really quickly, the only strategy that is guaranteed to fail is not taking risks*".

In May 2012, Facebook had its initial public offering, raising $16 billion and becoming the biggest Internet IPO in history. Though plagued by several problems and heavily criticised for being overhauled, the IPO was the icing on the cake that was Zuckerberg's success at such a young age – he was only 28 at the time. But while still young, he was not impulsive when it came to business decisions. Though part of Zuckerberg's entrepreneurial strategy is to take risks, he also emphasises not blindly committing to something. "I have this fear of getting locked into doing things that are not the most impactful things you can do," he said.

Philanthropist: Mark Zuckerberg donated 18 million Facebook shares to education initiatives, worth nearly $500 million and donated $100 million to save the failing Newark Public Schools system. Joining Bill Gates, Warren Buffet and George Lucas, Zuckerberg signed "The Giving Pledge" and promised to donate at least 50 per cent of his wealth to charity over the course of his lifetime. He encouraged other young entrepreneurs to do the same with their wealth.

"With a generation of younger folks who have thrived on the success of their companies, there is a big opportunity for many of us to give back earlier in our lifetime and see the impact of our philanthropic efforts" he said.

Mark Zuckerberg's Quotes

- "Our mission is to make the world more open and connected. We do this by giving people the power to share whatever they want and be connected to whoever they want, no matter where they are."
- "We don't build services to make money; we make money to build better services. And we think this is a good way to build something."
- "When people are writing nice stuff about us, it's important to get in front of the company and say, 'Don't believe all this.' When they write negative stuff, it's important to get in front of the company and say, 'Don't believe all this".
- "I mean, I wear the same thing every day, right? I mean, it's literally, if you could see my closet..."

In her book, "*Think Like Zuck: The Five Business Secrets of Facebook's Improbably Brilliant CEO Mark Zuckerberg*" (McGraw-Hill Professional; January 15, 2013) social media trailblazer Ekaterina Walter answers the question -What are Mark's five business secrets and why are they secrets?

The Five P's described in the book are:

- PASSION – Keep your energy and commitment fully charged at all times by pursuing something you believe in.
- PURPOSE – Don't just create a great product, drive a meaningful movement.
- PEOPLE – Build powerful teams that can execute your vision.
- PRODUCT – Create a product that is innovative, that breaks all the rules that changes everything.
- PARTNERSHIPS – Build powerful partnerships with people who fuel imagination and energise execution.

14.28 Maricel Apatan: A Chef without Hands

This is a true story of a young woman named Maricel Apatan, who went through the most gruesome fire. Maricel Apatan was an 11-year old girl from Zamboanga city, Mindanao, Philippines. She was not born with

Fig. Maricel Apatan.

disability. She was attacked on September 25, 2000 in Zamboanga City where she lived on her family farm. Some men were trying to force them off their farm for long and they turned up with machetes. On that day, this little girl went with her uncle to draw water. Along the way, four men with machetes in their hands met them. They told her uncle to face down to the ground and they hacked him on the neck and killed him. Maricel was in total shock especially that the men were their neighbours. She tried to escape but the men ran after her. She cried, *"Kuya, 'wag po, 'wag n'yo akong tangain! Maawa po kayo sa akin!"* ("Don't kill me! Have mercy on me!"). But they didn't listen to her plea. With long knife, a man attacked her and finally slashed her on the neck too. Maricel fell to the ground and lost consciousness.

When she woke up, she saw a lot of blood. She also saw the feet of the men around her but she pretended to be dead. When they walked away, Maricel ran back home. But along the way, she saw that both her hands were falling off because the men hacked them too. She cried but she kept running. Sometimes she would faint and fall to the ground. But she'd regain consciousness and run again. When she was near her home, Maricel called her mother. Upon seeing her daughter, her mother screamed in terror. She wrapped her bloodied child in a blanket and carried her to the hospital.

From her house to the highway was 12 kilometres walk. It took them four hours just to reach the highway. When they arrived in the hospital, the doctors thought Maricel was going to die. But tor five hours, they operated on her. It took 25 stitches to stitch together the long knife wounds in her neck and back. Maricel barely survived. And she lost both of her hands. Ironically, the next day was Maricel's birthday. She was 12 years old. But the tragedy didn't end there. When they went home, they saw their home was gone. It was ransacked and burned down by the goons.

Being in abject poverty, Maricel's family also didn't have money to pay their hospital bills. However, Archbishop Antonio Ledesma, a distant relative paid for hospital bills and helped them bring the criminals to court. They were sentenced to prison. Today, Maricel is staying with the nuns at *Regina Rosarii* with Sr. Eppie Brasil, O.P.

In spite of all these, the incredible miracle is Maricel kept running instead of self-pity. Instead of cursing God why she had no hands; she now uses her wrists in incredible ways that will boggle your mind. Maricel was cited as the most industrious, best in computer and most courteous in the School for Crippled Children. She enrolled in a Hotel and Restaurant Management course in Cagayan de Oro City. She was the only disabled student in that batch but that did not deter her at all and she took part in class competitions too. In 2008, she graduated from a course and went back to Manila. When she was in Manila, the media zeroed in on her and that was when she got her break. The managers at the Edsa Shangri-La Hotel spotted her on television and approached her for their Care for People project. At first they were apprehensive but she was a hard working girl and she made it clear that she did not require any 'special treatment'. She is now a successful chef in this Hotel. She even received a Gold Medal for Arts and Crafts. Nothing could stop this young lady from achieving her dreams. Today, she believes that dreams do come true if one works hard and prays and that is why she does not lose hope.

14.29 Martin Peniak: A Cognitive Robotics Researcher and Artificial Intelligence Ph.D

> "When I look at the stars, I see the past. When I look inside the mind, I paint the future."
>
> *-Martin Peniak*

Martin Peniak was born in Slovakia. He was a child that had a true fascination for technology and always loved to take things apart to see how they worked. Additionally, one of his early favourite practices was inline skating. At the age of 19, Martin accompanied his then girlfriend to England who had secured an au pair in Plymouth. At their arrival, she was picked up by her family; Martin instead, having no place to go, spent the night on a bench. He spoke little English so it took him a while to find a job but he eventually found one in a fish processing factory. Three months of hard work later something happened that changed his life forever.

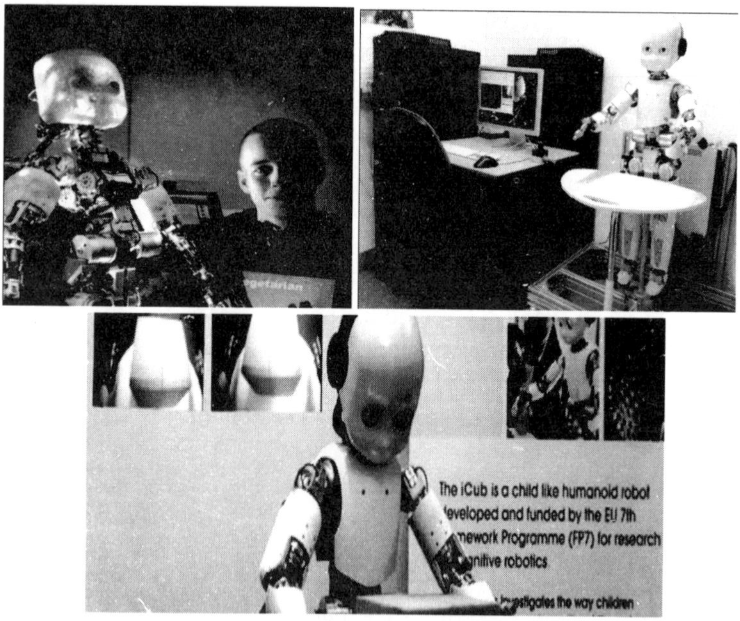

Fig. Martin Peniak and His Works.

It was in the evening of Martin's twentieth birthday when he struck up a conversation with a man on the street with which he started discussing astronomy; the stranger – who was a professor of Biological Sciences – asked him why he didn't consider going to university.

"I began to think that maybe I could study in the day and fund myself by working at night, so I went back to Slovakia to complete my civil service and started to learn English."

A year later, with a reference from that same professor, Martin applied to study computer science in Plymouth. He got accepted and his tough dual life began; studying during the day, working during the night. During his last year of studies, Martin worked on a project that would again drastically impact his career. He developed a programme that simulated the artificial evolution of neural network controllers for Mars rovers and presented a paper on it at the ASTRA European Space Agency conference. His outstanding work led to an official collaboration between his University and ESA. Martin was consequently offered an opportunity to undertake a cognitive robotics Ph.D at the University of Plymouth which he went on to happily accept. In 2012, he managed to secure himself an internship at the headquarters of the prestigious semiconductor manufacturer NVIDIA which helped him to further expand his knowledge.

Today, Martin is finishing his Ph.D. his work ethics and exceptional networking skills are taking him to participate in interesting projects across the globe. Martin never forgot where his passion for astronomy took him; he now believes that anything is possible and continues to aim for the stars.

Facing Interview

Q. *So what does a cognitive robotics researcher do? What are you currently working on?*

Ans. Cognitive robotics lies at the intersection of cognition and robotics and it's all about doing robotics dealing with cognitive phenomena such as perception, attention, anticipation, planning, memory, learning and reasoning. I have been fascinated by this subject ever since I was a kid and now I am doing research using *iCub* – one of the most advanced humanoid robots in the world. I have developed a software architecture for cognitive robotics called Aquila, which I now use to develop biologically inspired systems for actions and language acquisition.

Q. *What kind of role do you think robots will start playing in our society within the next 10, 20 to 50 years?*

Ans. Robots are already playing an essential part in our lives. Whether it's for industrial mass-production, high-precision surgical equipment, mobile robots for terrestrial and planetary exploration, robots are able to do jobs that are not possible or feasible for human beings. Some of these robots will have certain degree of autonomy, which allows them to make certain decision for themselves. This is great for specific, well-defined tasks. However, we have still a lot of work to develop machines that are capable of learning, reasoning and acting in real-world environments. Having said that, I think that we're on the right track and making a great progress! This is not only because our field involves collaboration with researchers from multiple disciplines (e.g. computer science, neuroscience, developmental psychology, linguistics etc.) but also because of the recent advancements in super-computing. For example, we have started developing hybrid-heterogeneous software that compute complex artificial neural networks on massively parallel GPU processors, which are inherently more powerful than standard CPU processors when it comes to parallel data processing. Thanks to NVIDIA GPU hardware and CUDA programming model we are now able to conduct novel experiments that were not previously feasible due to computational limits. Way too many people have made predictions about robotics and artificial intelligence that nowadays sound so funny that I would not like to make the same mistake. Our team has projects that are developing robots that help children in hospitals, elderly people and we have other projects that bring together the most outstanding scientists from all around the world to develop robots capable of learning and understanding actions and language. I have to add that this is not solely about developing intelligent robots, it is also about understanding ourselves and how we acquire motor and cognitive skills, which is very interesting in itself! I expect that in the years to come we will see more of this work being applied in the real-world scenarios. Technological and scientific progress accelerates and ever increasing phase. In addition to this sudden paradigm shifts are likely to occur, which makes the future progress of cognitive robotics rather unpredictable. Therefore, I prefer not to focus on predicting the future but rather on helping creating it!

14.30 Mike Oliveri: Inspirational Blogger, Motivator and Life Coach

> "I think it is worth to risk anything for life. To live a completely fulfilled life you have to take risks."
>
> —*Mike Oliveri*

Mike Oliveri is a young man with a rare condition who has made it his life's purpose to inspire others not to take anything for granted and live life to the fullest. Mike Oliveri was born in New Jersey, USA. He grew up in Jakarta, Indonesia and was an active kid who loved playing outside and always had a smile on his face. At the age of six, things unfortunately changed – at least momentarily. Mike was diagnosed with a rare condition called muscular dystrophy–a progressive skeletal weakness.

Faced with the consequences of his illness, Mike started going through a very rough time–both mentally and physically. Nonetheless, despite his constant and painful treatments, he never let his condition limit him from staying active. As he got older and his body increasingly weaker, Mike faced his darkest times; he was often bitter about everything, psychologically shattered and afraid of soon being forced to use a wheelchair. But luckily, his courage and positive outlook eventually took over:

Fig. Mike Oliveri.

"I started to look at things differently and believe that my illness was a gift. An opportunity to appreciate life, to embrace what I had and not take anything for granted, more than anything, I finally stopped feeling sorry for myself."

Subsequently, again motivated to live to the fullest, Mike began travelling and having as much fun as possible. Next to zip lining and parachute jumping, he also went skydiving and even broke record with a H.A.L.O. further goal of his when – thanks to his sister who saved up for it – he went on a zero gravity flight and for the first time in his life felt like he was not disabled. Mike's next challenge came in 2008, when – inspired by a disabled friend named Bob – he decided to live independently and moved to California documenting his entire trip. Once in Los Angeles, whilst dealing with the difficulties of living alone and financing his life, he kept on filming his daily adventures and common misfortunes. Eventually, Mike started meeting and connecting with lots of interesting people. He even got to know the guys of his favourite band TOOL and became friends with celebrities such as Paris Hilton and Mark Hamill. All these things fueled Mike's drive of inspiring the world and thus led him to produce a video that presented his latest dream of becoming the first disabled man in space. He addressed the video to one of his greatest idols, Sir Richard Branson and put it on the internet. Confidently believing that it would eventually reach him, he waited for an answer and persevered to flight his illness.

Today, Mike is not waiting for an answer anymore; he is about to meet Richard Branson and hence one step closer to getting to space. He is the living proof that no dream, is too big and that if you believe in it, anything is possible. Although his condition is very precarious, Mike fights his condition with his 'never give up' attitude. He continues to smile, live and try to inspire the world through his story; day after day, video by video.

Facing Interview

Q. *What lessons have you learned through your condition?*

Ans. Mainly it is the ability to accept. True acceptance means to fully accept something for what it is, as it is. I thought for many years like "Oh yeah, I got it"... but I was still depressed. And I was still thinking about horrible things that I imagined my future would look like. Somebody once told me: "You have not accepted your condition yet because you are still thinking about it." I then started to accept my situation and realised who I was and what I was supposed to do. I finally accepted my disease. I started seeing my life from a different perspective. For its awesomeness, realising that it is still great, just in its own way. I started to appreciate everything that I have, including what I don't have. I started to look at life like: "I am just Mike in a chair and this is just my life. If anything, it is more fun because now I can pop wheelies, and have hot first sit on my lap, get to do different things and go VIP and get backstage." True acceptance really set me free: "I felt as if I had just got a Ferrari!" Another thing I learned is that I am not handicapped, I am "*handicapable*". I have come to realise that muscular dystrophy has given me a perspective that most people only receive it during the later years of their life, so therefore I want to offer it to as many people as possible. Then, I gained my acceptance and everything has been possible ever since. I started to love life, living it up balls to the walls and having as much fun as I can... while I can. The real question is: "Why not?" Just because I am in a wheelchair does not mean I can't have just as much fun as anyone! I keep proving that to myself. I also try never to look back in my life. Back is bad. It does not exist, technically. I just try to live with the lessons that I have learned along the way. My lessons are my greatest gifts!

Q. *If you manage to go to space, what is your next big dream?*

Ans. A "bigger" dream would be to go to the actual Russian Space Center; to actually go to outer space. Also I want to climb Mt. Everest. And speaking not in the direction of a specific "dream", my aim would be to realise my potential as Mike Oliveri, the person that I am. There are so many people out there that get the spotlight, and get put on TV with ten million followers and get all the attention from the world; I want to be one of those people and get that kind of attention. Why? I want to bring something real to mainstream. I want to bring handicap into the world where it is no longer viewed as "handicapped", but more as in "Hey, we are out here, we are there, we are everywhere." The goal is pretty much to get handicapped people out of the house, help to inspire as many people as I possibly can – since this is apparently what I do – and take it to the maximum my main dream is to inject my happiness into as many people as possible and make them smile.

14.31 Mile Stojkoski

Mile Stojkoski was born on May 4, 1965. He is a Macedonian athlete and humanitarian known for going on long distance marathon runs (ultramarathons) in his wheelchair preceding the Summer Olympic Games.

Fig. Mile Stojkoski.

In 1996, he suffered a spinal cord injury from a motorcycle accident leaving him paraplegic, losing the use of both his legs. After much emotional struggle and learning about living with his disability he got involved in sports and humanitarian non-profit organisations.

Choosing Ultramarathon: He chose athletic activity of ultramarathon because it combines both physical strength and persistence. This eventually led him to focus on ultramarathons in his wheelchair with primary goal to raise public awareness and funds in support of people with disabilities in Macedonia. Since 2004 he completed a 704 kilometre ultramarathon in his wheel chair from Prilep to the Summer Olympic Games in Athens, Greece. Without much resource, Stojkoski successfully completed the marathon in 20 days at the official opening of the Athens Olympics in 13 August 2004. He has gone on nine marathons (four ultramarathons) gaining public recognition and awards. In 2012, he completed his tenth ultramarathon from Krushevo, Macedonia to London for the 2012 Summer Olympics Games.

He says, "I am Mile Stojkoski, a person with physical disability that chose a different life dedicated towards helping other people with disabilities. I travel long distance marathons with my wheel chair and team of people who support the same goals as me. My vision is to show that we deserve to live rich and full lives equally as everyone else".

Manager Vladimir Pandovski Says about Mile's Ultramarathon Journey: An ultramarathon is a sport activity where an athlete endures physical stress for a longer time and distance. Mile's 3,500 km ultramarathon is equal to doing 83 Virgin London Marathons and the biggest physical endurance comes not in the last leg of the day but in the very early morning waking up at five am facing again another 50 to 80 km to run. The numbers are mind boggling even to the best Paralympic athletes, especially if you consider this is done on normal motorways in a regular every-day wheel chair by 47-year-old Mile Stojkoski supported by only two other teammates.

"Where are the other competitors?" is the frequent question given by stunned spectators. There is no other like him. This is it. Every sport holds in its essence heroism and courage to run faster, jump higher and throw further. The only person that Mile Stojkoski can compete within this given circumstances is himself. It is a feat that normal people would not do. So he told us to hold on tight and witness him breaking his five-year-old record of an 86 km ultramarathon in one day in a regular wheel chair. The old record was set on his journey towards the Beijing 2008 Olympic and Paralympic Games in 2007 and included the length between Adapazari and Duzce, Turkey on eighth September, 2007 (National Holiday in Macedonia and the day he had his fatal accident that left him paraplegic). And the new personal record for Mile was official.

After Torino, as we were crossing from Lombardia to Piemonte Region, the scenery began to change drastically from blue skies to green mountains with snowy white peaks. The average uphill terrain began to exceed 12-15 per cent and the temperature on the asphalt passed the 34°C mark. The constant uphill and the burning sun rays made Mile admit this was his most difficult leg of the total ultramarathon to London.

Mile completed 23 km of constant Alpine uphill terrain in eight hours including breaks. We convinced him not to force tempo and save his strength considering the Alps will follow us through lower France and all of Switzerland. Up there among the Alpine peaks near Chivasso we were receiving tweets of photos and videos of Claire Lomas completing the London Marathon as well as the impressive British competitor in wheel chair racing Hannah Cockroft breaking records in the new London Arena.

Mile didn't stop for a second. Rain continued till eight pm as night fell and Police began to alert us to stop with the marathon because of large traffic congestion we had generated and because of the increased danger due to reduced levels of visibility. We agreed despite the danger to run for another seven miles because at that point Mile had completed 94 kms. In two hours' time the marker hit 101.1 km as we entered suburbs of Monza.

Awards and Recognition

- 2004 – Recognition for supporting people with disabilities awarded by the City of Prilep.
- 2004 – Vulkan Award for humanitarian achievements by Polio Plus.
- 2004 – Mother Teresa Award for humanitarian achievements by the Mother Teresa Foundation – Scopje.
- 2005 – Gert Jan Van Apeldoorn Award for Sustainable Development by MCIC.
- 2005 – 3ti Noemvri Life work award from the City of Prilep.
- 2007 – Honorary member of Lions Club - Scopje.

14.32 Nando Parrado: Andes Airplane Crash Survivor

Nando Parrado is one of the survivors of the dramatic airplane crash on October 13, 1972 when the plane carrying the Uruguayan old boys

Fig. Nando Parrado.

rugby team over the Andes Mountains lost its bearings in bad weather and crashed in the remote mountains. On impact, 13 passengers were instantly dead while 32 others were badly wounded.

Nando had invited his mother and sister on the trip to witness the match. When the plane crashed, he sustained a head injury and was in a coma for four days. He awoke to the grim reality that he was in a plane wreck, he had lost his mother and some of his friends, and his sister was on the brink of death. He held her in his arms as she died. Hoping to be rescued, the survivors waited in the freezing -37 ^{0}C temperature, melting snow for drinks and sleeping side by side to keep themselves warm. Food was so scarce, everyone had to pool whatever food they could find for a rationed pool. Nine days after the crash, due to dire desperation and hunger, the survivors called for an important meeting. One member proposed that they eat the dead. The two hours meeting ended with a conclusion: "If any of them died in the Andes, the rest had the permission to use the corpse as food". After two weeks, their hope of being rescued dashed when they found out via their radio transistor that the rescue effort was called off.

Despite spending 60 days on a glacier at 18000 ft, without suitable clothing, training, equipment or supplies and against all odds, Nando and two of his companions decided to walk out of the mountains to raise alarm to save their stranded companions. They took this 'do or die' decision because Nando saw that they were all dying. On the 60th day after the crash, they walk through the icy wilderness for the redemptive mission of their friends. Of the three friends, one went back. By the time they left, Nando Parrado said, the crash site was "...an aweful place, soaked in urine, smelling of death, littered with ragged bits of human bone and gristle". Wearing three pairs of jeans and three sweaters over a polo shirt, he and his friends trekked the mountains with human flesh as their ration. Knowing that they must search for rescue, the team endured frozen snow, exhaustion and starvation, walking and climbing for ten days before finding their way to the bottom of the mountain. The team was finally helped by a Chilean farmer who called the police for help. Parrado then guided the rescue team via a helicopter to the crash site. On the 22nd December 1972, after enduring 72 brutal days, the world found out that there were 16 survivors who cheated death in the mountain of Andes. Eight of the initial survivors died when an avalanche cascaded down on them as they slept in the fuselage. During the ordeal, Nando Parrado lost 40 kg of his weight.

Nando's Life Today: Nando now lives in Montevideo, Uruguay and has rebuilt his life to become a very successful businessman. He is the owner of a cable television channel, he produces six television programmes and he also runs family business in the United States and Europe. He has become a motivational speaker. Nando now candidly talks about his experiences in the Andes and how it has affected him. He offers audiences a very close and personal account of the events after the crash and explains how camaraderie and relationships is the key to survival. He continues to inspire people with his incredible story. Recalling his life on the crash site he says "the thirst was as horrible as in the Sahara desert" – and how they developed painful blisters and sores on their lips and mouths from eating snow. He recalled sub-zero temperatures and the way the men huddled together and breathed on each other as the only source of warmth. They made a pact to give their bodies to be eaten if they perished in order to help others survive. When Parrado was fielded with a philosophical question whether he would delete this episode of his life if he could, his answer was: "If you delete the bad things of your past, you will also delete the present. That other life does not exist". He also says that his philosophy has changed since the crash: "I wake up every day and live in the present".

Lessons that we can Learn from Nando's Experience

Nando's most heart-rending experience was that he had to bury his mother Eugenia and sister Susana with his own hands in an arid and freezing glaciers. His mother died instantly. Susana survived the impact but died few days after due to the injuries she had. She died in his brother's arms.

The Crashed Airplane.

Nando says "The hardest thing to me was burying my mother and my sister with my own hands in the ice". From this heart-rending experience Nando has drawn great lessons in his life and making them part of his life.

- To overcome the tragedy of survivors he had to learn how to work in teams
- To be always attentive to the good and innovate ideas
- To make decisions in extreme pressure conditions

"The biggest lesson for me had to do, mostly with taking decisions", says Nando. "It seems ridiculous what I'm going to say, but generally taking a decision doesn't take me more than 30 seconds, no matter how hard it is. Because at the Andes I decided in 30th way in which I was going to die. When I was at the mountains and saw what I had in front of my eyes 'I was dead'".

He was remembering his crossing to be rescued. He remembered the moment when, after climbing to the summit of the highest mountain that could be seen from the place where the fuselage was, he realised that they weren't where he thought—at the West, near Chile – but the only things they had ahead were more snow, more stones, more nothing.

"It was at that moment that I decided to die walking and no watching into my friend's eyes (Canessa). Any other decision compared with the decision of how are you going to die is a joke. So every time I have to decide something I remember that moment".

Being decisive is a great virtue. It is a virtue that especially today's businessmen, who are immersed in a competitive world, need to possess. Those who don't decide, die. "If I take the wrong decision I have time to correct it", says Nando. "It is far better to decide and make mistakes than not taking decisions, because there is always time to go back". Nando learnt a lesson which is essential in the business world. The biggest risk of all is, decide not to take risks. Nothing is more dangerous than the *status quo*.

Decision-making: The first lesson, Nando sets an example: "What we had to eat (human flesh)" is a perfect example of decision-making. This was the logical consequence of that moment, of the way in which your mind begins to think there. There were just three options:

1. Wait and die all together in the plane's fuselage looking at each other's eyes, but nobody wanted that opinion.
2. Commit massive suicide, go hand in hand and jump into a crevasse.
3. Eat human meat and survive at least for some time.

Although it was a dramatic decision, they all decided in group to opt for the third option.

But Nando has not only learnt about taking decisions. He learnt as well that although taking decisions democratically is a good option for some moments, there is a time in which somebody had to decide, because it is not always easy for a group to reach a decision. The person who decides, that becomes the leader of that organisation.

True Leadership: Leaders are not born leaders but they develop their skills on the way. They develop their actions. Important lesson for today's leaders who believe and expect to be the next leader of a company should not be just for being so-and-so or for having relationship with every Tom, Dick and Harry. Such person would be wrong. The experiences, the execution, the results, all of these make you a leader. If you don't have these qualities you're not going to exercise a good leadership. Nando's words concerning this: "Leaders are normal people who have extraordinary actions in difficult situations". To Nando a leader must have personality, he has to be charismatic without knowing it, in that way people will believe in him and finally he must do things properly. Nobody follows a leader if he doesn't do the right things. In other words, leaders are those who achieve good results and those who reach their purposes.

Teamwork with a Purpose: You achieve good results only if you do things together. Coordination is key to achieving a goal. A team however, doesn't function just because they do. They need to have an objective. It is useless having the best group of people, the most coordinated one, the best executor if they don't know where they are going to. For them, the objective must be not only unique but also shared. Every member of the group must be totally convinced of the objective and that they are going to achieve it. "Our goal was to survive...all our instinct, all our strength, all our intelligence, the teamwork, all designated to a unique and only objective: get out of that place on our own (because we had heard on the radio that nobody was going to rescue us). In my personal case I knew that I should keep all my strength for the summer (the plane crashed in October, winter at the southern hemisphere) because we couldn't even try to get out of there with that cold, you sink into the snow up to your waist. I used to say: 'If I become sad and cry, I'm going to lose salt through my tears. So, I can't afford the luxury of losing that energy. I closed my mind to all suffering and I turned into a survivor machine. My only objective: getting out of there alive". It was that obsession with the objectives and results that kept Nando and his friends alive. That obsession and visualisation is what keep companies alive.

The Most Important Lesson

Nando says,

"Today I can define which things are important and which ones are not. I like business and I want to be successful but only if the other aspects of my life are O.K. We can't deny that today our families are the most important thing for us. A hundred per cent of the people who were at the Andes wanted to come back to their families, not to their contracts, studies or money. We burnt all the money of the plane (7,000 dollars); we burnt it to obtain warmth. That means that money is important only if the other things are on its right place. I'd rather be a successful family than a successful businessman".

14.33 Nick Vujicic: A Man with no Limbs Who Teaches People How to Get Up

Nick Vujicic is a Serbian Australian evangelist and motivational speaker born with tetra-amelia syndrome, a rare disorder characterised by the absence of four limbs. As a child he struggled mentally and emotionally as well as physically but eventually came to terms with his disability and at the age of 17, started his own non-profit organisation, *Life Without Limbs*. Vujicic presents motivational speeches worldwide, on life with a disability, hope and finding meaning in life. He also speaks about his belief that God can use any willing heart to do his work and that God is big enough to overcome any disability.

Fig. Nick Vujicic.

In the high school, Vujicic became the target and butt of the school bullies because of his lack of limbs. This caused him to sink into deep depression. Following this depression, at the age of eight, he contemplated suicide and even tried to drown himself in his bathtub at the age of ten. However, a key turning point in his faith came around when his mother showed him a newspaper article about a man dealing with severe disability. Vujicic realised he was not unique in his struggles and began to embrace his lack of limbs. After this, he realised that his accomplishments could inspire others and became grateful for his life. Vujicic gradually figured out how to live a full life without limbs, adapting many of the daily skills limbed people accomplish without thinking. He writes with two toes on his left foot and a special grip that slides onto his big toe. He knows how to use a computer and can type up to 43 words per minute using the 'heel and toe' method. He has also learned to throw tennis balls, plays drum pedals, get a glass of water, comb his hair, brush his teeth, answer the phone and shave, in addition to participating in golf, swimming, soccer and sky-diving.

Vujicic currently lives in Los Angeles, California. On February 12, 2012, he married his fiancée, Kanae Miyahara and they already had their first son. Vujicic graduated from Griffith University at the age of 21 with a Bachelor of Commerce with a double major in accountancy and financial planning. Subsequently, he became a motivational speaker, travelling internationally and focusing on teen issues. Having addressed over three million people in over 24 countries on five continents, he speaks to corporate audiences, congregations and schools. His maiden book *Life Without Limbs: Inspiration for a Ridiculously Good Life* (Random House, 2010) was published in 2010. He starred in the short film *The Butterfly Circus,* which won the *Doorpost Film Project's* top prize of 2009 and Best Short Film award at the Method Fest Film Festival, where Vujicic was also awarded Best Actor in a short film. *Butterfly Circus* also won the best short film award at *The Feel Good Film Festival* in Hollywood in 2010.

Let us listen to what Nick has spoken about himself to his friends:

"My name is Nick Vujicic and I am thankful to have been born 30 years ago with no arms and no legs. I won't pretend my life is easy, but through the love of my parents, loved ones and faith in God, I have overcome my adversity and my life is now filled with joy and purpose. I reside now in California with my wife, Kanae and we both love seeing people's lives changed for the better or touched in some way. It is my hope that your life is positively impacted by my story.

I was born and raised in Melbourne, Australia and it was a shock to my parents that I arrived without limbs. There is no medical reason for it. My parents did their very best to keep me in the mainstream school system and gave me every opportunity to live to the fullest. I was blessed to have a brother and a sister as my best friends too. We later moved to Brisbane,

Fig. Nick with Wife and his Child

Australia, where I lived for 14 years before I made the move to California. At age eight, I could not see a bright future ahead and I became depressed. When I was ten years old, I decided to end my life by drowning myself in a bathtub. After a couple attempts, I realised that I did not want to leave my loved ones with the burden and guilt that would result from my suicide. I could not do that to them.

I wasn't depressed my entire childhood, but I did have ups and downs. At age thirteen, I hurt my foot, which I use for many things like typing, writing and swimming. That injury made me realise that I need to be more thankful for my abilities and less focused on my disabilities.

When I was fifteen years old, I sealed my faith in God and from there it has been an amazing journey. A janitor at my high school inspired me to start speaking about my faith and overcoming adversity when I was seventeen. I spoke only a dozen times to very small groups over the next two years. Then I found myself in front of three hundred somophore (grade 10) students and I was nervous. My knees were shaking. Within the first three minutes of my talk, half the girls were crying and most of the boys were struggling to hold their emotions together. One girl in particular was sobbing very hard. We all looked at her and she put her hand up. She said, "I am so sorry to interrupt but can I come up and hug you?"

She came and hugged me in front of everyone and whispered in my ear, "Thank you, thank you, thank you. No one has ever told me that they loved me and that I am beautiful the way I am". Her gratitude inspired me to go across 44 countries and speak 2,000 times. I realised that we all need love and hope and that I was in a unique position to share that with people around the world.

While majoring in both accounting and financial planning at a university, I also worked on developing my abilities as a speaker. I worked with a speaking coach who helped to cultivate me as a presenter. He especially worked on my body-language as my hands flew everywhere at first!

I spoke on motivational topics after creating the company, 'Attitude is Altitude'. I also launched a non-profit ministry, life without limbs, to spread my messages of faith and hope around the world.

Whoever you are, wherever you're from and whatever you are dealing with, I hope that you will be inspired by my story and my message....

Dream big my friend and never give up. We all make mistakes but none of us are mistakes. Take one day at a time. Embrace the positive attitudes, perspectives, principles and truths I share and you too will overcome".

14.34 Oprah Winfrey

Oprah Gail Winfrey is an American proprietor, talk show host, actress, producer and philanthropist. Winfrey is best known for her multi-award-winning talk show *The Oprah Winfrey Show* which was the highest-rated programme of its kind in history and was nationally syndicated from 1986 to 2011. She has been ranked the richest African-American of the 20th century, the greatest black philanthropist in American history and was for time the world's only black billionaire. She is also according to some assessments, the most influential woman in the world.

Fig. Oprah Gail Winfrey.

Her Early Life: Winfrey was born in Kosciusko, Mississippi to an unmarried teenage mother, Vernita Lee, who was a housemaid. After Winfrey's birth, her mother travelled north and Winfrey spent her first six years living in rural poverty with her grandmother, Hattie Mae Lee, who was so poor that Winfrey often wore dresses made of potato sacks, for which the local children made fun of her. Her grandmother taught her to read before the age of three and took her to the local church, where she was nicknamed "The Preacher" for her ability to recite Bible verses. Her grandmother brought her up with strict discipline.

Her Imperfect Family: Her family was a broken mess as her mother had children who became Winfrey's half sister and half brother. One of her half sister died of cocaine addiction and another was given for adoption due to financial straits. Her half-brother died of HIV/AIDS. In 1962, Lee was having difficulty raising her daughters so Winfrey was temporarily sent to live with Vernon in Nashville, Tennessee.

Her Struggles: Winfrey has stated that she was molested by her cousin, uncle and a family friend, starting when she was nine years old, something she first announced to her viewers on a 1986 episode of her TV show regarding sexual abuse. At the age of 13, after suffering years of abuse, Winfrey ran away from home. When she was 14, she became pregnant but her son died shortly after birth. She later stated she felt betrayed by the family member who had sold the story to the *National Enquirer* in 1990. She then began going to Lincoln High School; but after early success in the Upward Bound programme, was transferred to the affluent suburban Nicolet High School, where she says her poverty was constantly rubbed in her face as she rode the bus to school with fellow African-Americans, some of whom were servants of her classmates' families. She began to steal money from her mother in an effort to keep up with her free-spending peers, to lie to argue with her mother and to go out with older boys.

Her frustrated mother once again sent her to live with Vernon in Nashville, Tennessee, though this time she did not take her back. Vernon was strict but encouraging and made her education priority. Winfrey became an honours student was voted *Most Popular Girl* and joined her high school speech team at East Nashville High School, placing second in the nation in dramatic interpretation. She won an oratory contest, which secured her full a scholarship to Tennessee State University, a historically black institution where she studied communication. Her first job as a teenager was working at a local grocery store. At age 17, Winfrey won the Miss Black Tennessee beauty pageant. She also attracted the attention of the local black radio station, WVOL, which hired her to do the news part-time. She worked there during her senior year of high school and again while in her first two years of college.

Winfrey: Gradually Unfolding her Career: Winfrey's career choice in media would not have surprised her grandmother, who once said that ever since Winfrey could talk, she was on stage. As a child, she played games interviewing her corncob doll and the crows on the fence of her family's property. Winfrey acknowledged her grandmother's influence, saying it was Hattie Mae who had encouraged her to speak in public and gave me a positive sense of myself. Working in the media, she was both the youngest news anchor and the first black female news anchor at Nashville's WLAC-TV. She moved to Baltimore's WJZ-TV in 1976 to co-anchor the six o'clock news. She was also recruited by other local talk shows.

In 1983, Winfrey relocated to Chicago to host WLS-TV's low-rated half-hour morning talk show, *AM Chicago*. Within months after Winfrey took over, the show went from last place in the ratings to overtaking Donahue as the highest rated talk show in Chicago. The movie critic Roger Ebert persuaded her to sign a syndication deal with King World. Ebert predicted that she would generate 40 times as much revenue as his television show, *At the Movies*. It was renamed *The Oprah Winfrey Show*, expanded to a full hour and broadcast nationally beginning in September 8, 1986.

Winfrey's syndicated show brought in double Donahue's national audience, displacing Donahue as the number-one daytime talk show in America. Their much publicised contest was the subject of enormous scrutiny. Gradually, she became queen of media talk shows. *TIME* magazine wrote:

"Few people would have bet on Oprah Winfrey's swift rise to host one of the most popular talk shows on TV. In a field dominated by white males, she is a black female of ample bulk. As interviewers go, she is no match for, say, Phil Donahue (...) What she lacks in journalistic toughness, she makes up for in plainspoken curiosity, robust humor and above all empathy. Guests with sad stories to tell are apt to rouse a tear in Oprah's eye (...) They in turn, often find themselves revealing things they would not imagine telling anyone, much less a National TV audience. It is the talk show as a group therapy session".

Newsday's Les Payne observed, "Oprah Winfrey is sharper than Donahue, wittier, more genuine and far better attuned to her audience, if not the world." Winfrey has become one of the most recognisable faces in the world. According to *"Forbes"* her net worth has reached 2.7 billion and she is the fourteenth most powerful woman in the world. Not only is she successful television mogul but she has given millions to charity, built her own All Girls School in Africa and endorsed Barack Obama in the 2008 election which some say gave him the leverage he needed to win.

Her Success and Influence: Winfrey was the highest paid TV entertainer in the United States in 2006, earning an estimated $260 million during a year. By 2008, her yearly income had increased to $275 million. She was called "arguably the world's most powerful woman" by *CNN and Time.com,* "arguably the most influential woman in the world" by *The American Spectator,* "one of the 100 people who most influenced the 20th Century" and "one of the most influential people" from 2004 to 2011 by *TIME.* Barrack Obama said she "may be the most influential woman in the country". *Forbes* named her the world's most powerful celebrity in 2005, 2007, 2008, 2010 and 2013. In 2010, *Life* Magazine named Winfrey one of the 100 people who changed the world alongside such luminaries as Jesus Christ, Elvis Presley and Lady Mary Wortley Montagu. *Vanity Fair* wrote: "Oprah Winfrey arguably has more influence on the culture than any university president, politician or religious leader, except perhaps the Pope."

Oprahfication: The Wall Street Journal coined the term *"Oprahfication",* meaning public confession as a form of therapy. By confessing intimate details about her weight problems, tumultuous love life, and sexual abuse and crying alongside her guests, *Time* magazine credits Winfrey with creating a new form of media communication known as "rapport talk" as distinguished from the "report talk" of Phil Donahue. Observers have also noted the "Oprahfication" of politics such as "Oprah-style debates" and Bill Clinton being described as "the man who brought Oprah-style psychobabble and misty confessions to politics."

Philanthropy: In 2004, Winfrey became the first black person to rank among the 50 most generous Americans and she remained among the top 50 until 2010. By 2012, she had given away about $400 million to educational causes. In 2013, Winfrey donated $12 million to the "*Smithsonian's National Museum of African American History and Culture.*"

14.35 Randy Pausch: Inspired Thousands of People with his Dying Speech

Randolph Frederick "Randy" Pausch (October 23, 1960 – July 25, 2008) was an American professor of computer science and human-computer interaction and design at Carnegie Mellon University (CMU) in Pittsburgh, Pennsylvania. Pausch learned that he had pancreatic cancer, a terminal illness in September of 2006 and in August 2007 he was given a terminal diagnosis: "three to six months of good health left". He gave an upbeat lecture entitled "The Last Lecture: Really Achieving Your Childhood Dreams" on September 18, 2007 at Carnegie Mellon, which became a popular You Tube video and led to other media appearances. He then co-authored a book called "The Last Lecture" on the same theme, which became a New York Times best-seller. Pausch died of complications from pancreatic cancer on July 25, 2008.

Fig. Randolph Frederick.

Really Achieving Your Childhood Dreams (also referred to as "*The Last Lecture*") was a lecture Pausch gave on September 18, 2007 and it received a large amount of media coverage and was the base for the *Last Lecture*, a *New York Times* best-seller book co-authored with *Wall Street Journal* reporter Jeffrey Zaslow. During the lecture Pausch was upbeat and humorous, alternating between wisecracks, insights on computer science and engineering education, advice on building multi-disciplinary collaborations, working in groups and interacting with other people offering inspirational life lessons. Pausch's "*Last Lecture*" received attention from both the American media as well as recognition from news sources around the world. The video of the speech became an Internet sensation, being viewed over a million times in the first month after its delivery on social networking sites such as YouTube, Google video, MySpace and Facebook. Professor Pausch also gave an abridged version of his speech on *The Oprah Winfrey Show* in October 2007.

Here is a professor at the top of his field, designer of the *Alice* software that has been downloaded a million times to aid 3-D animation. He is co-founder of the *Entertainment Technology Center* at Carnegie Mellon, enabling students in science and art to work together on projects in education and industry. He is a visionary imagineer with experience at *Disney and Electronic Arts*. He is also a loving husband and father to three young children, ages five, two, and one. He's leading an extremely happy and productive life when cancer struck him. Instead being like Job, questioning why is this happening to me, Randy's talk did not veer off to religious or philosophical ponderings. He talked about his childhood dreams of winning stuffed animals at carnivals, authoring an article in the World Book Encyclopedia, being in zero gravity, working as Disney Imagineer. With hard work, determination, and persistence, he achieved them all. "Brick walls are there for a reason," he said. "They let us know how badly we want something". He was able to climb over the walls, not with talent alone, but with the help of mentors and friends.

He kept his childlike wonder, worked hard, showed gratitude, and being earnest. He tells the students "I'll take an earnest person over a hip person every day, because hip is short term. Earnest is long term." Find the best in everybody and be fulfilled when you help others achieve their dreams. At the end, Randy tells the audience that the talk is "not about how to achieve your dreams. It's about how to lead your life. If you lead your life the right way, the *karma* will take care of itself. The dreams will come to you." And the talk is not for the students in the audience, but for his kids. Someday when they are older, they'll appreciate what kind of Dad they had. Randy began his talk with his CAT scans showing the ten tumors in his liver, but he did not talk about his cancer. I admire Randy's stoic attitude to look death in the face and celebrate life and the joy of living. He did this so beautifully at the end of his lecture, telling everyone that yesterday was his wife Jai's birthday. So a giant birthday cake was wheeled onto the stage and shared with 500 people as all sang "Happy Birthday to You". Birth and mirth summed up Randy Pausch's Last Lecture—

no wonder it was downloaded over a million times on the Internet. Here is a man of true courage with life lessons for us all. This web page is dedicated to him for he has much wisdom to share. Randy's Mom took great relish in introducing him as "this is my son, he's a doctor but not the kind that helps people." Randy's "Last Lecture" has transformed countless people all over the world in living a good life.

Excerpts of the Lectures of Professor Pausch: The Lecture was part of the Cornegie Mellon University programme which was titled "*Journeys*" – lectures in which members of the community will share reflections and insights on their personal and professional journey". Before Professor Pausch began his lecture he was introduced by his close friend and co-worker Steve Seabolt.

Steve Seabolt, "It's a pleasure to be here, thank you very much. I'm going to start by covering Randy's credentials... So he spent a summer in residence at EA and I was his primary contact point. We were in my view the odd couple."

- Steve Seabolt, "Randy's dedication to making the world a better place is self evident to anyone who has crossed paths with him".
- Steve Seabolt, "For those of you who know Randy, Randy brings a particular zest for life and humour, even while facing death. To Randy, this is simply another adventure".
- Randy Pausch in response to Steve Seabolt's words says, "Make me earn it".
- "And as you get older, you may find that Today's talk is about my childhood dreams and how I have achieved them. How I believe I've been able to enable the dream of others, and lessons learned..."enabling the dreams of others" thing is even more fun."
- "When you see yourself doing something badly and nobody's bothering to tell you anymore, that's a very bad place to be. Your critics are your ones telling you they still love you and care."
- "Experience is what you get when you didn't get what you wanted."
- "The brick walls are there for a reason. The brick walls are not there to keep us out. The brick walls are there to give us a chance to show how badly we want something. Because the brick walls are there to stop the people who don't want it badly enough. They're there to stop the other people."
- "I created a course called Building Virtual Worlds... You make whatever you want. Two rules: no shooting violence and no pornography. Not because I'm opposed to those in particular, but that's been done with VR, right? And you'd be amazed how many 19-year-old boys are completely out of ideas when you take those off the table."

- [Referring to his creation of 'Alice', a software programme that teaches computer programming and 3-D animation that has been downloaded over a million times, with a new version coming out in 2008] "I, like Moses, get to see the Promised Land, but I won't get to set foot in it. And that's OK, because I can see it. And the vision is clear."
- "This is a dormitory in Thailand that my mom and dad underwrote. And every year about 30 students get to go to school who wouldn't have otherwise. This is something my wife and I have also been involved in heavily. And these are the kind of things that I think everybody ought to be doing. Helping others."
- [On Humility] "My dad had fought in World War II in the Battle of the Bulge, and when we were going through his things [after he died], we found out he had been awarded the Bronze Star for Valor. My mom didn't know it. In 50 years of marriage it had just never come up."
- "After I got my Ph.D., my mother took great relish in introducing me as, this is my son, he's a doctor but not the kind that helps people."
- "When I was in high school, I decided to paint my bedroom [shows slides of bedroom]. I always wanted a submarine and an elevator... And the great thing about this is they let me do it. And they didn't get upset about it. And it's still there. If you go to my parent's house it's still there. And anybody who is out there who is a parent, if your kids want to paint their bedroom, as a favour to me let them do it. It'll be OK. Don't worry about resale value on the house."
- [Lesson from his mentor Andy Van Dam, when Randy was his teaching assistant as sophomore at Brown University] "Andy put his arm around my shoulders and we went for a little walk and he said, Randy, it's such a shame that people perceive you as so arrogant. Because it's going to limit what you're going to be able to accomplish in life."
- "Decide if you're Tigger or Eeyore. Never lose the childlike wonder. It's just too important. It's what drives us. Help others."
- "Syl gave the best piece of advice pound-for-pound that I have ever heard. And I think all young ladies should hear this. Syl said, it took me a long time but I've finally figured it out. When it comes to men that are romantically interested in you, it's really simple. Just ignore everything they say and only pay attention to what they do. It's that simple. It's that easy. And I thought back to my bachelor days and I said, damn."
- "How do you get people to help you? You can't get there alone. People have to help you and I do believe in *karma*. I believe in paybacks. You get people to help you by telling the truth. Being earnest, I'll take

an earnest person over a hip person every day, because hip is short term. Earnest is long term."

- "Apologise when you screw up and focus on other people, not on yourself."
- "Remember brick walls let us show our dedication. They are there to separate us from the people who don't really want to achieve their childhood dreams."
- "Anybody can get chewed out. It's the rare person, who says, oh my god, you were right. When people give you feedback, cherish it and use it."
- "Show gratitude. When I got tenure I took all of my research team down to Disneyworld for a week. And one of the other professors at Virginia said, how can you do that? I said these people just busted their ass and got me the best job in the world for life. How could I <u>not</u> do that?"
- "Don't complain. Just work harder. [shows slide of Jackie Robinson, the first black major league baseball player] That's a picture of Jackie Robinson. It was in his contract not to complain, even when the fans spit on him."
- "Be good at something, it makes you valuable."
- "Work hard. I got tenure a year early. Junior faculty members used to say to me, wow, you got tenure early. What's your secret? I said, it's pretty simple. Call me any Friday night in my office at ten o'clock and I'll tell you."
- "Find the best in everybody... you might have to wait a long time, sometimes years, but people will show you their good side. Just keep waiting no matter how long it takes. No one is all evil. Everybody has a good side, just keep waiting, it will come out."
- "So today's talk was about my childhood dreams, enabling the dreams of others, and some lessons learned. But did you figure out the head fake? [dramatic pause]. It's not about how to achieve your dreams. It's about how to lead a life. If you lead your life the right way, the *karma* will take care of itself. The dreams will come to you."
- "And be prepared. Luck is truly where preparation meets opportunity."

Closing Remark by Andy Van Dam: Randy is the person, the *Mensch*, as we say in Yiddish. Your manifold accomplishments as a model academic, especially as a mentor to your students. You exemplify undaunted courage and grace under pressure. The most terrible pressure one can imagine. Randy, you have been and you will continue to be a role model for us. Thank you so much for all you have done for us. And to allow us to tell you privately and in such a public way how much we admire, honour, and indeed love you.

Randy was given three months of life, he lived three more years.

14.36 Roz Savage: Ocean rower, Environmentalist and Writer

"Whatever you do, put your whole heart into it."

—*Roz Savage*

Roz Savage was an ex-businesswoman who decided to follow a path of adventure and since became a world record breaking ocean rower. Rose Savage was born in Cheshire, England. A teenager with big dreams, Roz decided to study law at University College, Oxford. There, on the riverbank instead of in the library, she found her true passion: rowing. After getting her degree, Roz moved to London to start a career as a management consultant. Despite rowing during her free time, Roz's work life eventually took over. Eleven years later, in her mid-thirties, Roz started looking back at her career in disillusion and began asking herself a question: "What am I supposed to be doing in my life?" she sat down one day and sketched out two versions of her own obituary; the one she was headed for and the one

Fig. Roz Savage.

she wished she would. Comparing the two, Roz was awestruck to realise how far away she had slipped away from living the life she truly wanted. Determined to chase her dreams, Roz went on her first expedition and travelled to Peru. Feeling alive and inspired, Roz felt ready to give up a normal life and commit to her everlasting passion: rowing. In 2004, she thus announced her intentions to row across the Atlantic Ocean – solo. One year later, Roz began her epic journey and departed from the Canary Islands direction Antigua. She was at sea for 103 days, propelled by nothing else then her own strength:

"There were so many times I thought I had hit my limit but no choice but to carry on and try to figure out how I was going to get to the other side."

After a euphoric arrival in the Caribbean Island it did not take long until Roz announced her next goal: crossing the Pacific Ocean. His first attempt failed, but in 2010, three years after leaving San Francisco and splitting her route in three separate journeys, Roz arrived in Papa New Guinea becoming first woman to ever row the Pacific. "I had battled 20 feet waves, sleep deprivation, self doubt and depression. But I had never been happier." In addition to self-fulfillment, Roz's incredible journey through the Pacific provided her an imperative cause: at the point where all the waters met, Roz crossed a surreal large collection of marine debris, the so called Great Pacific garbage patch. After that experience, Roz ultimately crossed the Indian Ocean and hence became the first woman to conquer the world's three largest oceans–one stroke at a time.

Today, Roz, travels extensively giving inspiring talks worldwide. Her main message focuses on the infinite possibility that lies within every human being and the all-important need for respecting the ocean and diminishing plastic consumption. Her ex-normal life has become one of adventure, inspiration and environmental outreach.

In an Interview She was Asked the Following Questions:

Q. *Name three of the most important lessons that you learned during your oceanic journeys?*

Ans. Wow, there were so many but I will try to narrow it down to three that have had the most impact on my life. Firstly, no matter how big the challenge, no matter how great the distance between where you are and where you want to be, you can get there if you just take it one oar stroke at a time. One stroke does not get you very far but with consistency and perseverance you will get there eventually. Secondly, the size of your sense of accomplishment is proportionate to the size of the challenge. Rowing the Atlantic was by far the hardest thing I had ever done. It was so tough it nearly broke me. But the sense of achievement when I reached Antigua after 103 brutal days alone at sea was the best feeling I have ever had in my life. Lastly, the only constant in life is change, so don't get too despondent about tough times or high about the good times. In the early days on the Atlantic I became obsessed with the weather forecast – if it was good, I'd expect to make good mileage. If it was good, I'd expect to make good mileage. If it was bad, I'd get anxious about an incoming storm. Most of the time the forecast was wrong anyway. I expended a lot of mental energy hoping or worrying and it was all pointless. I had to focus instead on the thing I could control–namely, I had to keep on sticking my oars in the water.

Q. *How did you use your rowing adventures as a means to spread your environmental message?*

Ans. I thought about raising money but I decided that what the earth needs is not money, it is attention and love and awareness. So I was really more focused on trying to make people more aware of the challenges that we are facing but also to believe that they are playing an important part in this, that it is not just the government's problem or companies' problem or somebody else's problem. Actually, every single one of us is making a difference and it all adds up. So I used my blogs, podcasts, speeches and books to try and make this point—the human population has doubled in my life time and we are consuming more than ever and we know for sure that the Earth can't continue to sustain this. To me, the real tragedy is that all this over-consumption isn't even making us happy. We need to rediscover the real causes of happiness–family, friends, having purpose in life, learning new things and having new experiences–so that we can live more sustainably and be happier and more fulfilled at the same time. Sounds good to me!

14.37 Runa Khan: Social Entrepreneur, Author and Educator

> "When suffering is eased, one starts hoping. And there are no better means to hope, than education."
>
> —*Runa Khan*

Fig. Runa Khan

Runa Khan was born in the capital of Bangladesh, Dhaka. At the age of 12, she was sent to a convent in Pakistan. There, in the early 1970's, she lived through the Independence war that Pakistan fought against her home country; an experience that impacted her very deeply. When Runa was 15, she moved to India to attend university. She studied geography in Calcutta and after graduating returned to Bangladesh.

In Dhaka, in her early twenties, she began to teach children with learning disabilities; a practice she understood well and had a natural talent for. Runa went on to successfully publish a series of educational children books on geography and history. In 1992, she embarked on an entrepreneurial path during which she administered her family's business, worked for UNICEF and set up a security service company supervising 140 guards. Runa's life and career took a major unexpected shift when in 1994 she met a French sailor named Yves Marre who had sailed a retired oil barge all the way from France to Bangladesh. The Frenchman wished to see the vessel used for humanitarian purposes and eventually met Runa's father who suggested transforming the ship into a floating hospital that would provide healthcare to the poor. Believing in the concept, Runa took it upon herself to turn her father's idea into a reality and subsequently founded an organisation named 'Friendship' in 1998. She spearheaded the building of an innovative and successful healthcare system that aimed to help the hard-to-reach communities of Bangladesh by serving them through hospital ships.

"We are dealing with the poorest of the poor, those who are below the documented poverty line; those who earn 0.25$ a day".

At Friendship, Runa created a framework that provides health-care and education, builds schools and trains community medics and micro-entrepreneurs. In the last 15 years, she and the people at her organisation have served more than six million individuals and provided medical care to 1.7 million people – over one per cent of Bangladesh's population.

Today, Runa travels extensively giving talks on female entrepreneurship and on sustainable development. She continues to passionately lead Friendship with the mission of uplifting the quality of life of the ultra poor and empower the unprivileged to build their future on their own.

Facing Interview

Q. *What was the hardest challenge that you faced while setting up the hospital-ship concept?*

Ans.The hardest challenge setting up the hospital ship was that nobody believed it was possible. There were a lot of constraints to set up a hospital ship and people tried previously but did not succeed. Moreover, I was completely new in the field and we knew we had to do it differently to have an effective impact. Despite the idea was well-liked, the concept of a floating hospital had to contend with a fair share of skeptics as there was no prototype to follow. We had had to gather friends, advocates and well-wishers who could continuously help reach significant milestones.

Q. *What do you feel is the most rewarding side of your work at Friendship?*

Ans. The most rewarding side of my job is the smile on the people's face that is brought through the work of Friendship. And also the way we all work collectively towards one common goal; it is a self-fulfillment all together.

14.38 Ryan Seacrest

Ryan John Seacrest is an American radio personality, television host and producer. He hosts *American Idol*, a talent competition and also *On Air with Ryan Seacrest*, a popular morning radio show on *KIIS-FM*. He won *Emmy* nominations for *American Idol* and won an *Emmy Award* for producing the ABC show *Jamie Oliver's Food Revolution*.

Fig. Ryan John.

Seacrest was born on December 24, 1974 in an Atlanta suburb, Dunwoody Georgia, the son of Constance Marie, a homemaker and Gary Lee Seacrest. At the age of 14, he attended Dunwoody High School. As his school's regular morning public address system announcer, he was known as the "Voice of Dunwoody High School". At age 16, while still attending high school, Seacrest won a hard-to-get internship at WSTR (FM) in Atlanta with Tom Sullivan, who trained him in the many aspects of radio. When the regular DJ called in sick, Sullivan put him on the air for the very first show of his broadcasting career. He was given the weekend overnight shift at WSTR.

Seacrest continued to work on air at WSTR until graduating from Dunwood High School in 1992. He went on to study journalism at the University of Georgia. He continued his radio show at a local Athens station: Seacrest left the university at age 19 and moved to Hollywood to pursue his broadcasting career.

American Idol: In 2002, Seacrest accepted the position as co-host of a new *Fox* reality television series *American Idol* with comedian Brian Dunkleman. *American Idol* went on to success, putting Seacrest in the national spotlight. The following year, he became the sole host. When the show increased in popularity, seen by some 26 million viewers weekly, Seacrest became recognisable around the world. In 2003, Seacrest hosted the spin-off show *American Juniors.* In July 2009, Seacrest inked a deal with *CKX* for $45 million to continue to host *American Idol* making him the highest paid reality television host to date. In 2012, Seacrest signed a two-year, $30 million deal to stay on as host of *American Idol.*

His Credits

Radio

- *On Air with Ryan Seacrest*: Host, executive producer of this syndicated daily show airing on over 150 stations in North America alone, with affiliates worldwide
- *American Top 40:* Host of this syndicated weekly countdown show.
- *2003 Radio Music Awards*: Co-host
- *102.7 KIIS-FM* Los Angeles: Since 2004, Morning Drive Personality with co-host Ellen K
- Former*: KYSR and WSTR* On-Air Personality
- *98.7 FM* 1 pm to 4 pm

Film

- *Knocked Up* as a parody of himself
- *Get Smart* as himself (Host of American Top 40)
- *Shrek Forever* After a voice of the father of Butter Pants
- *New Year's Eve as himself* (host of Dick Clark's New Year's Rockin' Eve)

Television

- *American Idol:* Co-host (Season 1); Host (Season 2 – present)
- *American Juniors*: Host (2003)
- *Bank of Hollywood:* Producer (2009 – present)
- *Channel 1 News:* News Anchor/Reporter. Co-anchor Maria Menounos
- *Click:* Host
- *CNET Central:* Co-host
- *Dick Clark's New Year's Rockin' Eve:* Host (2005 – present), executive producer
- *E! News:* Co-host
- *Super Bowl XLII (2008):* Host for pregame and halftime shows
- *Gladiators 2000:* Co-host
- *Wild Animal Games*: Host

- *Ultimate Revenge*: Host
- *Fear Factor*: Contestant
- *Reality Check:* Jack Craft
- *The NBC Saturday Night Movie*: Host
- *Hey Arnold: Fighting Families*: Host
- *Larry King Live*: Guest host, substitute host
- *Walt Disney World Christmas Day Parade*: (2005-present): Host
- *America's Party: Live from Las Vegas*: Host
- *Good Day Live:* Guest host
- *Disneyland 2000: 45 Years of Magic*: Host
- *Robot Chicken*: (2005) Himself
- *59th Primetime Emmy Awards*: Host
- *Mind of Mencia:* (2005) Himself
- *Blind Date:* Himself
- *Punk'd:* Himself
- *Keeping Up with the Kadarshians:* Executive Producer
- *Denise Richards: It's complicated*: Executive Producer
- *2009 Academy Awards*: Host on E!
- *Jamie Oliver's Food Revolution*: Executive Producer
- *Shahs of Sunset*: Executive Producer
- *Melissa and Tye*: Executive Producer
- *Married to Jonas*: Executive Producer

Starting out of a co-host on American Idol, Seacrest has become show businesses most popular personality. Not only is he still hosting American Idol, he is a producer for *Keeping Up With The Kardashians, Dick Clark's New Year's Eve* predecessor and Host of the morning show on *KISS FM* Los Angeles. Seacrest seems to have his hands in every area of show business.

14.39 Sean Swarner: First Cancer Survivor to Complete the Seven-summits of the Highest Peaks of the Seven Continents

> "*The human body can survive about 30 days without food. The human condition can sustain itself for about three days without water, but no human alive can survive 30 seconds without HOPE, because without hope we truly have nothing.*"
> *—Sean Swarner, Co-Founder of the Cancer Climber Foundation*

The 29,035-foot giant known as Mount Everest tortures its challengers with life-threatening conditions such as 100 mph winds, the dramatic loss of oxygen, snowstorms and deadly avalanches. Climbers of Everest are faced with incredible dangers but for Sean Swarner the obstacles he overcame prior to his summiting make his story even more compelling.

Sean Swarner was born in Ohio, USA. An active child with aspirations of becoming an Olympic swimmer, Sean encountered great struggles at a very early age due to cancer.

Fig. Sean Swarner.

Sean is not just a cancer survivor; he is truly a medical marvel. He is the only person in the world ever to have been diagnosed with both Hodgkin's disease and Askin's sarcoma. He was diagnosed in the fourth and final stage of Hodgkins' disease at the age of 13, when doctors expected him to live for no more than three months. After ten months of intensive treatment Sean went into remission. His illness had turned his life upside down but he was alive. A routine check-up less than one year later sadly uncovered a tumour in Sean's lung. This second unrelated attack by the more aggressive Askin's Disease was sure to end the 16 year old life. He was given 14 days to live. Instead of giving up, Sean bravely chose to fight again and did so for 13 long months during which he lost the function of his sick lung. He astounded the medical community for a second time when he ultimately defeated cancer once again. It was now clear to Sean that after having survived battles with two deadly cancers, no challenge in his future would ever be too great. Determined to start over and chase his dreams, Sean decided to go to college. There, he was rather known as a swimmer and outdoor enthusiast. He says,

"I wanted people to know me for who I was, not what I had been through. I did not want pity; none of the 'poor Sean' stuff."

Realising how helpful his words could be for others, Sean became increasingly open about his past. Wanting to help people who were going through what he did, in 2001 he and his brother established '*The CancerClimber Association*', a non-profit organisation that offers and gives adventure support grants to cancer survivors. After finding out that no cancer survivor had ever climbed Mount Everest, Sean decided to take it upon himself to be the first who did. Only eight months of training later, he reached the summit of Mount Everest and in the name of his organisation buried a flag on the top that bared the names of people touched by cancer. Driven to make an even larger impact, Sean set his goal to climbing the Seven Summits – the highest mountain on each of the world's seven continents. After five years of climbing, 2007, Sean finally achieved his incredible goal planting his seventh Cancer Climber flag on Alaska's Mount Denali. This was still not enough. In 2008, Sean accomplished another unbelievable feat; he completed The Iron Man World Championship in Hawaii.

Today, Sean continues his quest of inspiration by travelling across the globe giving life-changing talks. He is still an avid mountaineer and is now aiming to travel to the North and South Poles – always spreading his "keep climbing" message. He has written about his life story in his book *"Keep Climbing: How I Beat Cancer and Reached The Top of the World"* (2007). He is the recipient of the *Don't Ever Give up Award* presented by the Jimmy V Foundation and ESPN in 2007.

Sean shares his own story:

When I was only 13 years old, I was diagnosed with Advanced Stage IV Hodgkin's Lymphoma and given only three months to live. I went through a year of chemo, lost all the hair on my body, lost all my friends, gained 60 lbs and when I was placed in remission, I had to start my life all over again. I lived life to the fullest by joining my friends playing soccer, swimming, cross-country and track. It was a wonderful life but it was short-lived. About 18 months in remission, I was going in for a check-up for the Hodgkin's and in less than 24 hours they found a tumour on an X-ray, did a needed biopsy, took out a lymph node, cracked open my ribs, removed the tumour, inserted a drainage tube and started chemotherapy. I was 16 and the doctors gave me less than 14 days to live. I went through three months of intense chemo, one month of radiation and then 10 more months of chemo. The medicine this time around was so harsh; the doctors actually put me in a medically induced coma. I literally don't remember being 16 years old.

When I was finally placed in remission, I celebrated and am still celebrating my survivorship by trying to give people something I never had... hope. I started trying to give hope to others at a very young age, when during my first cancer experience I was approach by the Make A Wish Foundation and my wish was to give it to others else so that they could enjoy something. To this day, I've been told I am still the only person who has ever given his or her wish to someone else. As an adult I wanted to help more than just one or two people. Because of my past and my goal of giving everyone affected by cancer hope, my brother and I founded The Cancer Climber Association, where we help others by sharing inspirational stories, giving survivors an opportunity to join us on a climb, providing a mobile camp for kids with cancer and facilitating personal visits to patients by survivors.

At the end of the day it's about enjoying each day you have with the ones you love and celebrating life. Cancer may have been the worst thing that has ever happened to me, but it also ended up being one of the best things to have survived. My book is dedicated, to all those affected by cancer. I couldn't have done anything without you... including climbing the highest mountain on each continent (the 7-summits) and completing the Hawaii Ironman... all with only one functioning lung. Thank you for being my inspiration, my hope and the driving force behind everything I've done in my life. At the end of the day, for anyone affected by cancer, it's about cherishing the time with those you love and powering through every day. Embracing your survivorship is one of the greatest experiences you could ever imagine. It's a new lease of life and can be absolutely anything you ever wanted. Keep Climbing!

Sean Swarner shares a part of his journey, excerpted from his book: "*Keep Climbing: How I Beat Cancer and Reached the Top of the World*".

The funny thing is, even with all these months of preparation, training and planning, I'd naively assumed mine would be the only flag up here. It's not; the top of Everest is like one of those roadside shrines you see everywhere these days, where someone has died in a horrible accident. Only, instead of teddy bears and plastic daisies, you see prayer flags, pickets and Perlon stacked in an unceremonial, if colourful, heap on the snowy, narrow summit.

I ignore the tackiness, the gaudiness and admire the flag anyway. People climb Everest for dozens of reasons but for me this is more than some mere personal odyssey. The flag, tattered though it soon may be, represents the hopes, the dreams and in some cases the dying wishes of countless people diagnosed with cancer.

I know I'm one of the incredibly lucky ones.

It's 9:32 AM on the sixteenth of May 2002 and I'm standing at the highest point on the planet. The summit of Everest: 29,035 feet. Below me is the globe that thing you spin in elementary school never looking past the big, red star that marks the capital of your home state.

That's the view from the top.

The silk-screened flag flaps in the stiff breeze at the top of the world. Its sound is subtle, instantly recognisable and reassuring. It brags, "You made it, Sean. You did it. You've made history. First cancer survivor to summit the world's tallest mountain." Then it whispers, "And we climb with you, all of us. Every name on this flag, every person ever affected by cancer in any way; we're here with you, here for you, right now and always".

Facing Interview:

Q. *What gave you the strength to fight when all the odds were so stacked against you?*

Ans. There were many times I wanted to give up and if I said I was constantly positive, that would be a lie. Everyone living has ups and downs, trials and tribulations but there has to be something within each person that keeps them moving forward, keeps them struggling, fighting and wanting more. I found that strength through, humor, and a never-say-die attitude that was instilled in me through my parents. Everyone has the ability to "Keep Climbing!" and reaching their own potential, just as I have... and more.

Q. *What would you say to people whose life situation is "normal" to inspire them to become more?*

Ans. Everyone is motivated by different factors... money, fame, love, power... whatever motivates you, it's ultimately your choice to move forward with your goals and stay in line with what you want to do. I can help motivate you, I can help you set goals and help you accomplish those goals, however, you have to continue burning that fire yourself. That desire must be done personally. I help people around the world with goal setting; motivating them and helping them climb their own Everest. If you'd like help with becoming the best you can be, please let me know and I'll help you make it happen, but remember, it must come from inside YOU.

14.40 Shah Rukh Khan

Shah Rukh Khan is an accomplished Indian film actor popularly known as "Badshah of Bollywood", "King Khan" and "King of Romance". Khan

Fig. Shah Rukh Khan.

has acted in 75 Hindi films in genres ranging from romantic dramas to action thrillers. His contributions to the film industry have garnered him numerous accolades and achievements including fourteen Filmfare Awards from thirty nominations. His eight Filmfare Best Actor Award win made him the most awarded Bollywood actor of all time in that category, tied only with actor Dilip Kumar. In 2005,.the Government of India honoured him with the Padma Shri for his contributions towards Indian cinema.

After graduating with a bachelor's degree in economics, he started his career appearing in theatre and several television serials in the late 1980s and later made his Hindi film debut in 1992 with Deewana and the subsequent films catapulted him to the height of success and fame. He is also the co-owner of the Indian Premier League cricket team Kolkata Knight Riders. Khan is often labeled by the media as "Brand SRK" due to his various brand endorsement and entrepreneurship ventures. He is also a regular stage performer and award ceremony host and has been involved in philanthropic endeavours related to healthcare, relief funds and children's education for which he was honoured with the UNESCO's Pyramide con Marni award in 2011.

Khan is considered to be one of the biggest film stars in cinematic history, with a fan following claimed to number in the billions; in 2011, the *Los Angeles Times* called him "the world's biggest movie star." In 2008, Newsweek named him one of the 50 most powerful people in the world. Khan has an estimated net worth of over US $600 million.

Let us recall some of the points of the talks that he delivered to Yale University students:

- I Walk, I Run, in the Direction of My Dreams
  As for my destination, I don't think I ever knew one. I walk, I run, in the direction of my dreams. Things change along the way, people change, I change, the world changes, even my dreams change. I don't have a place to arrive, I just keep doing what I know how to do the **best that I can do it.**

- 'To Survive, Hang on to Who you are Inside'
  I momentarily lose my ability to give and close up. And here's where the trick is — when you are in this place of despair, where the world is staring you down into yourself. There's only one thing you can do to survive — hang on to who you are inside. The world will be unkind to you; it will not be able to see you. You must learn at such times, to be able to see yourself.

- 'It never was about the cars or houses'
  For you have to remember....

Creativity is your gift to the world. It was never meant to be bartered for anything, not even appreciation. You have to dig deep, I do it while drinking vodka after vodka... listening to self pitying, loser songs... you should find a less destructive way... however you do it... but you have to believe... that you create only because this is the biggest gift you have to give to your world. Maybe that's why we even say God is a creator. It's not about the cars or houses...it never was... those are peripherals. They never come about because of your talent or your creative outpourings... they come out of a business that people around you do. Those people are in the business of barter — not you. Yours is the business of giving and learning. Your work of art may never be complete in your lifetime. Your fulfillment will always lie in your creative expression not in its products.

'Do not be Afraid to Defy Conventions'

So look beyond the brickbats... the critics and know within you that you always have a choice between barter and creation. Life as a creator will always be a tight rope. So...

1. Do not try to feed your stomach with creativity; it is food for your soul, not your stomach.
2. Do not be afraid to defy conventions.
3. Do not be afraid to destroy systems that kill art and your souls.
4. Do not be afraid to be hungry.
5. Do not be afraid to walk alone if necessary. Because on a tightrope we all walk alone. Remember....if you are a creator you are a funambulist and not very many people know that word...let alone be it.

Just as my life has centered on creativity, like every fellow human being's, it has also centered around the wish to find happiness. Your age is the age when we most confuse happiness with gratification so I will say quite plainly: if you are smart, if you want to survive life's relentless onslaught of challenges, you will sooner or later understand that the things that made you happy ten years ago will end up being the ones that make you happy when you hit the geriatric superhero stage. Kids...start collecting your action figures, now!

I have everything I could have aspired for at your age, I have success, I have fame, I have wealth and I have three play stations... one for the house... one for shootings and one just because I can have it. But none of these have any consequence to my happiness, the only thing that does is the love of my children.

You don't have children (I hope), but you have parents, you have people you love and nothing in this world of everything means more than that.

Happiness, in other words, lies in the things you will never be able to count. **To me, it is no more than cuddling up to my kids and watching** *I Carly* or *the Family Guy*. Well most of the time anyway, the other day my son and I stumbled upon the Kama sutra on the net and I can tell you that experience was not very happy. He's 14 and he knew more about it than I did.

I want you to understand this business of happiness well because I know at one level, all parents are actually the same... some look sterner... some are less fun, some are embarrassingly weird but for each parent the bottom and the top line of their lives is this- your kids are their greatest source of happiness.

- 'You don't acquire wisdom from success'

I lost my parents very early in my life... and I miss them dearly. So all of you who still have yours... don't listen to them... fool them if you must... a bit of lying is also welcome... but make sure you cherish what you have because when you don't have them... like me... you really miss someone to be rude to... someone to you can take for granted... someone to say and do whatever you wish with... you miss the comfort of being loved unconditionally. I call parents unconditional and forgiving punching bags...who feel happiest when they get bashed up by their kids.

If you want to survive life, its best to begin to respect the gift of love right now.

As children, your first teachers of this acceptance are your parents. If you are unable to accept the love they give you, in whatever form it arrives (even if it is a tight slap across your face), then when you become a parent, you will end up having to learn this lesson somewhat more harshly from teachers you give birth to... and learning Kama sutra from my son is a not a great idea you would agree. Incidentally he studies in a school that Isha's mom runs in India....I have to say ma'm your syllabus is quite different from the one I had when I was in school.

- A Fiendish Friend Called Failure

Whether I like it or not, my life has also been in constant play with what the world calls "Success". Success is a wonderful thing, but it tends not to be the sort of experience that we learn from. We enjoy it; perhaps we even deserve it. But we don't acquire wisdom from it. And maybe that's why it cannot be passed on either...me being successful does not mean my children will also be so...how much ever I teach them what I did in my life and even if they follow it to the letter.

So I feel that talking about how to become successful is a waste of time...instead let me tell you very honestly...whatever happened to me happened because I have always been terrified of failure. I don't want as much to succeed as much as I don't want to fail. I come from a very normal lower middle class family. I saw a lot of failure. My father was a beautiful man and the most successful failure in the world. My mother also failed to stay with me long enough for her to see me become a movie star. We were quite poor actually and let me tell you...poverty is not an ennobling experience at all. Poverty entails fear and stress and sometimes depression. I watched my parents go through this several times.

- 'Repeated Failure has Taught Me to Stop Pretending'

At an early age after my parents died... I equated poverty with failure. I just didn't want to be poor. So when I got a chance to act in films it wasn't out of any creative desire that I did so... it was purely out of the fear of failure and poverty. Most of the films I signed were discards of better known actors and the producers could not find anyone else to do them. I did them all to make sure that I was working to avoid unemployment. The timing or something was right, and that made them happen. I became a big star... which means sometimes our success is not the direct result of our actions.... Success just happens. Really, it is accidental and we take credit for it... I know I have done this even out of embarrassment sometimes.

So I believe the true path to success is through the fear of failure. If you aren't scared enough of failing, you are unlikely to succeed. It's not pleasant to fail, it's tough. All of us experience it. You too will if you haven't already. Use it to succeed.

Here's how I have done so:

1. Firstly, it's not the absence of failure that makes you a success...it is your response to failure that actually helps to buffer the reverses that you experience. I personally have one response to failure is pragmatism– a recognition and belief that if one's approach does not work...then the other will or might.
2. Failure also gives me an incentive to greater exertion... harder work...which invariably leads to later success in most cases.
3. Repeated failure has taught me to stop pretending I am someone else. It's given me the clarity to stick to the things that really matter to me instead of distracting me from my core.
4. Failure also gets you to find who your real friends are. The true strength of your relationships only gets tested in the face of strong adversity.
5. Overcoming some of my failures has made me discover that I have a strong will and more discipline than I suspected. It has helped me to have confidence in my ability to survive.

- 'Failure is Your Fiendish Friend'

Failure is an amazing teacher...There is a well-known story of a bank president who was asked the secret of his success. "Right decisions," he replied. "How do you get to know how to make right decisions?" came the follow-up question. "Experience," was the answer. "Well, how do you get experience?" asked his interrogator. "Wrong decisions," he replied.

You have to know and learn that life is a not just a check list of acquisitions, attainments and fulfillments, your qualifications and CVs don't really matter. Instead life is difficult and complicated and beyond anyone's control. The humility to know this will help you survive its vicissitudes.

But I don't want to sound dark. My hope for all of you is that you retain a lifelong love of learning that you never cease to dream – exciting and inspiring dreams, and when you fail, you fail well enough to succeed the next time. Don't be afraid of being afraid; be afraid of not facing your fears and failures.

So remember you are fortunate enough to be a funambulist....who has an amazing set of punching bags, cherish them... and failure is your fiendish friend... keep him close.

14.41 Shiv Khera

"Winners don't do different things. They do things differently."

—*Shiv Khera*

Shiv Khera is a motivational speaker extraordinaire and author of 12 self-help books. He is best known for his book *You Can Win* which became

Fig. Shiv Khera.

an international bestseller. He was born with silver spoon but when circumstances took a bad turn at a tender age he had to seek work as a car washer. It was a grind before glory would embrace him. Forking off from his role of a speaker, educator and consultant, Khera is now launching a *Leadership and Management Institute*. He says that unlike most institutes, who entice students with placement assistance, he will steer clear of that, instead focus on empowering students. He also launched a movement against caste-based reservation in India and has founded an organisation called *Country First Foundation* whose mission is "to ensure freedom through education and justice."

Shiv Khera was born in a business family who owned coal mines at Kendua in Dhanbad. Soon after the nationalisation of coal mines by the

Indian government, he had to search for his own living. This is what he says, "Our family used to own coal mines but when the mines got nationalised, we were left fending for ourselves on the streets. My sister sponsored my tickets to Toronto and for two years there, I washed cars during the day and in the evenings I used to give demonstration for vacuum cleaners. One day I saw an advertisement of Norman Vincent Peale (author of 'The Power of Positive Thinking'), but I didn't have the money to buy the ticket. Somehow I managed it and for the first time I realised that people who get anywhere in life, they take responsibility. From that day, I started reading books too."

His School Life: Regarding his school life Shiv Khera says, "I was a student of Modern School, Barakhamba Road, Delhi. I was a back-bencher. When I was in nineth, I was forced into taking Science though I was least interested. As a result I failed and repeated the class. But I was into sports. I represented the school in Delhi State horse riding, when ! was Class 11, two months before my exam, I asked my parents to switch me to Arts. The teacher said that I will fail. Eventually, I got switch and got first division in the exams."

Karma: "People, who don't want to accept responsibility, believe in astrology, palmistry. Superstition weakens people. It is not our position but disposition that determines our destiny" says Shiv Khera.

How can we keep ourselves self-motivated?: He says, "We must feed the mind with positive thoughts. One should change thinking. Thinking is more lasting. Belief is the greatest motivator. Henry Ford said, "If you think you can do it, you can, if you think you cannot, you are right."

His Formula for Success

- *Attitude, values and vision:* With positive thinking, commitment to values and a vision, you can reach great heights. Your attitude, your values and your vision form the blueprint of your success. Anything is possible to achieve by psyching oneself with positive thinking. Positive thinking alone cannot guarantee success. It is a supplement, not a substitute for your action plan. Your positive action combined with positive thinking results in success.

- *Will versus Skill:* Mr. Khera says that it is will power more than skill that contributes to one's success. Even though technical skill and people skill are essential, it is PEOPLE SKILL that is vital as you climb higher in your career. By building relationships, many problems can be solved. Today's generation is tech savvy but on the flip side they have become uncomfortable with people. If people skill is lacking, they cannot taste success. Few are willing to pay the price for the preparation for success, but everyone wants to be successful.

• *Selling:* When it comes to selling, Mr. Khera says that success in life depends on our ability to sell. Integrity and courtesy is the key here. By distinctly understanding the difference between promises we make and commitment we stand for, one can be successful in selling.

• *Character:* For most of us negative thinking has become habitual. Positive behaviour has to be a reflex action. Develop good habits for it greatly contributes to positive habits and attitudes. Give importance to your reputation and most importantly your character. Keep up your self-esteem.

• *Tips for Students:* Do not give too much importance to your grades/ scores in exam alone. Do not confuse failure in exam with failure in life itself. Youngsters perceive the world to be highly competitive. But give it a thought, success is easier today and opportunities aplenty. Just be willing to work hard and all will be well.

Some of his key sayings:

- Avoid miscommunication. The price you pay for it is horrendous.
- Ego can destroy team work/effort.
- Set your goal. It helps you to know where you are heading.
- Have a vision. It is the ability to see the invisible. If you can see the invisible, you can achieve the impossible.
- Credibility and integrity are vital. Organisations with credibility make higher profits.
- It is better to be honourable than be honoured.
- Don't quit. Don't give up.

14.42 Sparky: The Loser Who Never Gave Up!

When he was a little boy his uncle called him "Sparky", after a comic-strip horse named Spark Plug. School was all but impossible for Sparky.

Fig. Sparky

He failed every subject in the eighth grade. He flunked physics in high school, getting a grade of zero. He also flunked Latin, algebra and English. And his record in sports wasn't any better. Though he did manage to make the school's golf team, he promptly lost the only important match of the season. Oh, there was a consolation match; he lost that too.

Throughout his youth, Sparky was awkward socially. It wasn't that the other students disliked him; it's just that no one really cared all that much. In fact, Sparky was astonished if a classmate ever said hello to him outside of school hours. There's no way to tell how he might have done at dating. He never once asked a girl out in high school. He was too afraid of being turned down or perhaps laughed at. Sparky was a loser. He, his classmates and everyone knew it. So he learned to live with it. He made up his mind early that if things were meant to work out, they would. Otherwise he would content himself with what appeared to be his inevitable mediocrity.

One thing was important to Sparky, however – drawing. He was proud of his artwork. No one else appreciated it. But that didn't seem to matter to him. In his senior year of high school, he submitted some cartoons to the yearbook. The editors rejected the concept. Despite this brush-off, Sparky was convinced of his ability. He even decided to become an artist. So after completing high school, Sparky wrote to Walt Disney Studios. They asked for samples of his artwork. Despite careful preparation, it too was rejected. One more confirmation that he was a loser.

But Sparky still didn't give up. Instead, he decided to tell his own life's story in cartoons. The main character would be a little boy who symbolised the perpetual loser and chronic underachiever. You know him well. Because Sparky cartoon character went on to become a cultural phenomenon of sorts. People readily identified with this "lovable boy". He reminded people of the painful and embarrassing moments from their own past, of their pain and shared humanity. The character soon became famous worldwide: *"Charlie Brown".* And Sparky, the boy whose many failures never kept him from trying, whose work was rejected again and again..., is the highly successful cartoonist *Charles Schultz*. His cartoon strip, *"Peanut"*, continues to inspire books, T-shirts and Christmas specials, reminding us, as someone once commented that life somehow finds a way for all of us even the losers.

Charles Monroe Schulz nicknamed 'Sparky' was an American cartoonist, best known for the comic strip *Peanuts,* which featured the characters Snoopy and Charlie Brown among others). He is regarded as one of the most influential cartoonists of all time. His uncle called him 'Sparky' after the horse Spark Plug in *Billy DeBeck*'s comic strip, *Barney Google*.

Cartoon Strips from Peanuts

- In the comic strip *Peanuts* there is the following transaction:
  Charlie Brown: "What would you do if you felt that no one liked you?"
  Linus: "I'd try to look at myself objectively and see what I could do to improve."
  Charlie: "I hate that answer."
- In another of the *'Peanuts'* cartoon strips we have the girl handling over to Charlie a list of his faults. Charlie challenges her: "Where do you get off handing out lists of people's faults." She replies: "I have high ideals, Charlie Brown. I want to make this a better world for me to live in."
- In another strip, Charlie Brown is looking at a drawing of a man that Linus has just completed. "I see that you've drawn the man with his hands behind his back," said Charlie philosophically. "That shows that you're basically very insecure." "I didn't put his hands behind his back because I am insecure," explains Linus. "I drew the man with his hands behind his back simply because I can't draw his hands."

14.43 Steve Jobs

Steve Jobs was born to Abdulfattah Jandali, a Syrian and Jaonne Carole Schieble, a Swiss-American who met each other as students at the University of Wisconsin. When Jobs was born his father had to put the baby up for adoption as he had no choice because his girlfriend's family objected to their relationship. So Jobs was adopted at birth by Paul Reinhold Jobs and Clara Jobs, an Armenian American.

Fig. Steve Jobs.

The Jobs family moved from San Francisco to Mountain View, California when Steve was five years old. His father showed Steve how to work on electronics in the family garage, demonstrating to his son how to take apart and rebuild electronics such as radios and televisions. As a result, Steve became interested in and developed a hobby of technical tinkering.

Jobs began to grow up and his life as a youth was riddled with frustrations over formal schooling. He played pranks in the elementary school on others. When he attended his junior high school he had a new friend Bill Fernandez who shared the same interest in electronics. Fernandez introduced Jobs to another, older computer whiz kid, Steve Wozniak with whom he would later create an Apple computer.

In 1972, Jobs enrolled at Reed College in Portland, Oregon. Reed was an expensive college which Paul and Clara could ill afford. Jobs dropped out of college after six months and spent the next 18 months dropping in on creative classes including a course in calligraphy. He continued auditing classes at Reed. During this time, due to financial straits of the family, he used to sleep on the floor in friends' dorm rooms. He would return Coke bottles for food money and he used to get weekly free meals at the local Hare Krishna temple.

In 1976, Jobs and Wozniak formed their own business which they named "Apple Computer Company" in remembrance of a happy summer Jobs had spent picking apples. Then, Jobs created Apple Computers with Steve Wozniak out of his garage. Their company began to grow recruiting CEOs and employees from other companies while Steve Jobs was a persuasive and charismatic director for Apple. Then, slowly he began to have misunderstanding with his CEO Sculley whom he had recruited from Pepsi-Cola Company. Sculley learned that Jobs–who believed Sculley to be "bad for Apple" and the wrong person to lead the company–had been attempting to organise a *boardroom coup* and on May 24, 1985, called a board meeting to resolve the matter. Apple's board of directors sided with Sculley and removed Jobs from his managerial duties as head of the Macintosh division. Jobs stopped coming to work. It was a moment of despondency. He applied for a job in the Space Shuttle as a civilian astronaut but he failed there also. So he resigned from the Apple company.

In his speech, Jobs gave at Stanford University in 2005, he said being fired from Apple was the best thing that could have happened to him: "The heaviness of being successful was replaced by the lightness of being a beginner again, less sure about everything. It freed me to enter one of the most creative periods of my life." And he added, "I'm pretty sure none of this would have happened if I hadn't been fired from Apple. It was awful-tasting medicine, but I guess the patient needed it."

Jobs founded *NeXT Inc.* in 1985 after he resigned from Apple. A year later he was running out of money. He then attracted the attention of billionaire Ross Perot who invested heavily in the company. Then he started a company that built workstation computers. The *NeXT* Computer became technologically advanced and known for its technical strengths, chief among them are its object-oriented software development system. Jobs marketed *NeXT* products to the financial, scientific and academic community. Tim Berners-Lee invented the *World Web Wide* on a *NeXT* computer at CERN. Jobs' work began to grow and success was just following him. He then released the revised second generation *NeXTcube* in 1990. Jobs touted it as the first "interpersonal" computer that would replace the personal computer. With its innovative *NeXTMail* multimedia email system, *NeXTcube* should share voice, image, graphics and video in email for the first time. "Interpersonal computing is going to revolutionise human communications and groupwork," Jobs told reporters.

Jobs began to work with the *Walt Disney Company* and later became the Company's largest single shareholder. He also became a member of the Board of Directors for the Company. In 1996, Apple bought *NeXT* for $427 million and this also brought back Jobs to the Apple Company which he co-founded. With his return, the Company began to branch out introducing and improving upon other digital appliances. With the introduction of iPod, portable music player, iTunes, digital music software and the iTunes Store, the company made forays into consumer electronics and music distribution. In 2007, Apple entered the cellular phone business with the introduction of the iPhone, a multi-touch display cell phone, which also included the features of an iPod and with its own mobile browser, revolutionised the mobile browsing scene.

36 years later, Apple Computer is the leader in computer, music and telephone technology. Their products are innovative and refreshing in the time when downloading music illegally was becoming a major issue with recording artists and their record labels, Jobs introduced the Ipod and Itunes which made paying for music a cool and convenient way of getting music, television, movies and podcasts.

In 2003, Jobs was diagnosed with a pancreas neuroendocrine tumour. Though it was initially treated, he reported a hormone imbalance, underwent a liver transplant in 2009 and appeared progressively thinner as his health declined. On medical leave for most of 2011, Jobs resigned in August that year and was elected Chairman of the Board. He died of respiratory arrest to his tumour on October 5, 2011. Jobs received a number of honours and public recognition for his influence in the technology and music industries. He has been referred to as "legendary", a "futurist" or simply "visionary" and has been described as the "Father of Digital Revolution", a "master of innovation", a "master evangelist of the digital age" and a "design perfectionist".

The statement announced by Apple on the death of Steve Jobs:

We are saddened to announce that Steve Jobs passed away today.

Steve's brilliance, passion and Energy were the source of countless innovations that enrich and improve all of our lives. The world is immeasurably better because of Steve.

His greatest love was for his wife Laurene and his family. Our hearts go out to them and to all who were touched by his extraordinary gifts.

Inspirational Speech by Steve Jobs to Stanford University Students

(Steve Jobs gave this amazing and inspirational speech to Stanford University graduates on June 12, 2005):

I am honoured to be with you today at your commencement from one of the finest Universities in the world. I never graduated from college. Truth be told, this is the closest I've ever gotten to a college graduation. Today, I want to tell you three stories from my life. That's it. No big deal. Just three stories.

The first story is about connecting the dots: I dropped out of Reed College after the first six months, but then stayed around as a drop-in for another 18 months or so before I really quit. So, why did I drop out? It started before I was born. My biological mother was a young, unwed college graduate student and she decided to put me up for adoption. She felt very strongly that I should be adopted by college graduates, so everything was all set for me to be adopted at birth by a lawyer and his wife. Except that when I popped out they decided at the last minute that they really wanted a girl. So my parents, who were on a waiting list, got a call in the middle of the night asking: "We have an unexpected baby boy; do you want him?" They said: "Of course." My biological mother later found out that my mother had never graduated from high school. She refused to sign the final adoption papers. She only relented a few months later when my parents promised that I would someday go to college.

And 17 years later I did go to college. But I naively chose a college that was almost as expensive as Stanford and all of my working-class parents' savings were being spent on my college tuition. After six months, I couldn't see the value in it. I had no idea what I wanted to do with my life and no idea how college was going to help me figure it out. And here I was spending all of the money my parents had saved their entire life. So, I decided to drop our and trust that it would all work out OK. It was pretty scary at the time, but looking back it was one of the best decisions I ever made. The minute I dropped out I could stop taking the required classes that didn't interest me and begin dropping in on the ones that looked interesting.

It wasn't all romantic. I didn't have a dorm room, so I slept on the floor in friends' rooms, I returned coke bottles for the 5c deposits to buy food with and I would walk the seven miles across town every Sunday night to get one good meal a week at the Hare Krishna temple. I loved it. And much of what I stumbled into by following my curiosity and intuition turned out to be priceless later on. Let me give you one example: Reed College at that time offered perhaps the best calligraphy instruction in the country. Throughout the campus every poster, every label on every drawer, was beautifully hand calligraphed. Because I had dropped out and didn't have to take the normal classes, I decided to take a calligraphy class to learn how to do this. I learned about serif and san serif typefaces, about varying the amount of space between different letter combinations, about what makes great typography great. It was beautiful, historical, artistically subtle in a way that science can't capture and I found it fascinating.

None of this had even a hope of any practical application in my life. But ten years later, when we were designing the first Macintosh computer, it all came back to me. And we designed it all into the Mac. It was the first computer with beautiful typography. If I had never dropped in on that single course in college, the Mac would have never had multiple typefaces or proportionally spaced fonts. And since Windows just copied the Mac, it's likely that no personal computer would have them. If I had never dropped out, I would have never dropped in on this calligraphy class and personal computers might not have the wonderful typography that they do. Of course, it was impossible to connect the dots looking forward when I was in college. But it was very, very clear looking backwards ten years later.

Again, you can't connect the dots looking forward; you can only connect them looking backwards. So you have to trust that the dots will somehow connect in your future. You have to trust in something – your gut, destiny, life, karma, whatever. This approach has never let me down and it has made all the difference in my life.

My second story is about love and loss: I was lucky–I found what I loved to do early in life. Woz and I started Apple in my parents' garage when I was 20. We worked hard and in 10 years Apple had grown from just two of us in a garage into a $2 billion company with over 4000 employees. We had just released our finest creation–the Macintosh–a year earlier and I had just turned 30. And then I got fired. How can you get fired from a company you started? Well, as Apple grew we hired someone who I thought was very talented to run the company with me and for the first year or so things went well. But then our visions of the future began to diverge and eventually we had a falling out. When we did, our Board of Directors sided with him. So at 30 I was out. And very publicly out. What had been the focus of my entire life was gone and it was devastating.

I really didn't know what to do for a few months. I felt that I had let the previous generation of entrepreneurs down – that I had dropped the baton as it was being passed to me. I met with David Packard and Bob Noyce and tried to apologise for screwing up so badly. I was a very public failure and I even thought about running away from the valley. But something slowly began to dawn on me—I still loved what I did. The turn of events at Apple had not changed that one bit. I had been rejected, but I was still in love. And so I decided to start over.

I didn't see it then, but it turned out that getting fired from Apple was the best thing that could have ever happened to me. The heaviness of being successful was replaced by the lightness of being a beginner again, less sure about everything. It freed me to enter one of the most creative periods of my life.

During the next five years, I started a company named NeXT, another company named Pixar and fell in love with an amazing woman who would become my wife. Pixar went on to create the world's first computer animated feature film, Toy Story and is now the most successful animation studio in the world. In a remarkable turn of events, Apple bought NeXT, I returned to Apple and the technology we developed at NeXT is the heart of Apple's current renaissance. And Laurene and I have a wonderful family together.

I am pretty sure none of this would have happened if I hadn't been fired from Apple. It was awful tasting medicine, but I guess the patient needed it. Sometimes life hits you in the head with a brick. Don't lose faith. I'm convinced that the only thing that kept me going was that I loved what I did. You've got to find what you love. And that is as true for your work as it is for your lovers. Your work is going to fill a large part of your life and the only way to be truly satisfied is to do what you believe is great work. And the only way to do great work is to love what you do. If you haven't found it yet, keep looking. Don't settle. As with all matters of the heart, you'll know when you find it. And, like any great relationship, it just gets better and better as the years roll on. So keep looking until you find it. Don't settle.

My third story is about death: When I was 17, I read a quote that went something like: "If you live each day as if it was your last, someday you'll most certainly be right." It made an impression on me and since then, for the past 33 years, I have looked in the mirror every morning and asked myself: "If today were the last day of my life, would I want to do what I am about to do today?" And whenever the answer has been "No" for too many days in a row, I know I need to change something.

Remembering that I'll be dead soon is the most important tool I've ever encountered to help me make the big choices in life. Because almost everything – all external expectations, all pride, all fear of embarrassment or failure – these things just fall away in the face of death, leaving only what is truly important. Remembering that you are going to die is the best way I know to avoid the trap of thinking you have something to lose. You are already naked. There is no reason not to follow your heart. About a year ago I was diagnosed with cancer. I had a scan at 7:30 in the morning and it clearly showed a tumour on my pancreas. I didn't even know what a pancreas was. The doctors told me this was almost certainly a type of cancer that is incurable and that I should expect to live longer than three to six months. My doctor advised me to go home and get my affairs in order which is doctor's code for prepare to die. It means to try to tell your ids everything you thought you'd have the next 10 years to tell them in just a few months. It means to make sure everything is buttoned up so that it will be as easy as possible for your family. It means to say your goodbyes.

I live with that diagnosis all day. Later that evening I had a biopsy, where they stuck an endoscope down my throat, through my stomach and into my intestines, put a needle into my pancreas and got a few cells from the tumour. I was sedated but my wife who was there told me that when they viewed the cells under a microscope the doctors started crying because it turned out to be a very rare form of pancreatic cancer that is curable with surgery. I had the surgery and I'm fine now. This was the closest I've been to facing death and I hope it's the closest I get for a few more decades. Having lived through it, I can now say this to you with a bit more certainty than when death was a useful but purely intellectual concept.

No one wants to die. Even people who want to go to heaven don't want to die to get there. And yet death is the destination we all share. No one has ever escaped it. And that is as it should be, because Death is very likely the single best invention of Life. It is Life's change agent. It clears out the old to make way for the new. Right now the new is you, but someday not too long from now, you will gradually become the old and be cleared away. Sorry to be so dramatic but it is quite true.

Your time is limited, so don't waste it living someone else's life. Don't be trapped by dogma – which is living with the results of other people's thinking. Don't let the noise of others' opinions drown out your own inner voice. And most important, have the courage to follow your heart and intuition. They somehow already know what you truly want to become. Everything else is secondary.

When I was young, there was an amazing publication called "The Whole Earth Catalog" which was one of the bibles of my generation. It was created by a fellow named Steward Brand not far from here in Menlo Park, and he brought it to life with his poetic touch. This was in the late 1960s. Before personal computers and desktop publishing, so it was all made with typewriters, scissors and Polaroid cameras. It was sort of like Google in paperback form, 35 years before Google came along; it was idealistic and overflowing with neat tools and great notions.

Steward and his team put out several issues of The Whole Earth Catalog and then when it had run its course, they put out a final issue. It was the mid-1970s and I was your age. On the back cover of their final issue was a photograph of an early morning country road, the kind you might find yourself hitchhiking on if you were so adventurous. Beneath it were the words: "Stay Hungry. Stay Foolish." It was their farewell message as they signed off. Stay Hungry. Stay Foolish. And I have always wished that for myself. And now, as you graduate to begin anew, I wish that for you.

Stay Hungry. Stay Foolish.

14.44 Suli Breaks: Spoken Word Poet and Writer

"I am not chasing a dream. I am chasing a reality disguised as a dream."

—*Suli Breaks*

Fig. Suli Breaks.

Darryll Amaoko aka Suli Breaks was born in London, United Kingdom. He was a gifted kid who enjoyed spending time reading books. With time, this early passion developed into an enthusiasm for art and aspiration to become an artist. In school, Suli cultivated his love for the English language and began writing stories and poems. Despite his natural and wider ranging flair for numerous types of artistic expressions, Suli dedicated his teenage years to his most beloved sport: basketball. He spent the majority of his time on the court, training and dreaming of one day becoming an NBA player, but was ultimately forced to give up on basketball when deciding to enroll in University. There, whilst studying law unexpectedly, his passion for art took over once again. He wrote lyrics and rapped with his friends until one day, after being dared to do so, he decided to participate in a poetry slam, which he did with no expectations. To everyone's surprise, his loud spoken words wrapped his entire crowd in awe–his natural talent was conspicuous. After the amazing response to his performance, Suli's life took a quick turn. He attended numerous poetry events and became more and more motivated to take this new passion of his to the next level.

After University, not wanting to become a lawyer anymore and in need of earning quick money, Suli got job in a supermarket. Working behind till he visualised his future and planned out the next steps of his artistic career.

"What changed everything for me was a book I read: The Alchemist. The book allowed me to see that there were people out there that thought the way I did and understood that the world is designed on a greater scale than what we can see in our surroundings."

Inspired and struck by the book's message, Suli decided to shift the style of his poetry away from entertainment and instead focus on providing his audience with empowerment.

For nearly two years, he worked tirelessly to fulfill this goal; he spent his days working as a cleaner and shoe salesman in order to earn money and committing his evenings and nights to his artistic aspirations. Next to attending numerous live performances, he worked on building an international audience on You Tube and gradually began making a name for himself. Suli's breakthrough came in 2012, when in collaboration with his director Kevin, he created 'Why I hate school but I love education'–a video that led to heated online discussions and was shared all over the web. After the success of his video, Suli was finally able to give up on his day jobs and fully commit to his passion for poetry. His words have since reached millions of people worldwide.

Today, Suli continues to reach out to his fans through his loud spoken poetry. His goal remains empowering the world's younger generations with the perspectives that can change the course of their lives and careers.

Facing Interview

Q. *Where did you find the courage to get a normal job and focus on your artistic career after graduating from university?*

Ans. It really wasn't courage, I felt as though I had no other choice but to succeed and felt that through my art was the only way I would ever be as great as I imagined that I could be. The only difficulty was people's negativity; I had to look into myself to really find strength against it. Eventually I just focused on the negative people and realised that they had not achieved what I wanted nor were they in the position to and that helped me feel a lot more confident in my position.

Q. *How do you think the educational system should be adapted?*

Ans. I think the educational system does not accommodate for individuals well enough, if it could be adapted to enable each individual to value themselves and their skills within it, I believe it would make a drastic change to the impact and results the system achieves.

14.45 Sun Jifa

Sun Jifa is a 51-year old farmer from Guanmashan, northern Jilin province in China, who lost both of his hands when a homemade fishing explosive detonated prematurely from his hands. When Sun Jifa lost his arms, he couldn't believe how expensive hospital-supplied artificial limbs were. So he went with a cheaper set and was flabbergasted at how useless they were. Sun Jifa then began to spend developing prototypes before deciding on his current bionic arms made from scrap metal bycobbling together different parts. The arms work using a series of wires and pulleys inside the arm shell. It uses the power of natural movements of the elbow to make the fingers move. "The only drawback is that steel is quite heavy so they're tiring to wear and get hot or cold in the extremes of summer and winter", explained Sun.

Fig. Sun Jifa.

For eight years, Sun worked on his set of prosthetics, tweaking them at his home. They're the pair he now wears today. But these are anything but dummies–the homemade bionic arms allow the 51-year-old to drive his vehicle, light a cigarette and even pick up tools and utensils. And they cost less than $500, which is merely a fraction of what the hospital charges. This has created demand and turned him into something of a local celebrity. To date, Sun has sold approximately 1000 of these to other people in need of low-cost, high-functioning artificial arms or hands.

Sun is no hardware developer or engineer, nor does he have any medical training or anatomical expertise. He is a simple farmer. In other words, you're looking at a man who simply figured out how to create bionic limbs with no formal technical training whatsoever.

Sun explains how they work: "The left arm transfers power from the natural movement of my elbow into the finger, allowing it to grab and hold... rotating the two bones that I have left in this arm allows my right hand to open and close." His prosthetics may seem rough around the edges compared to the advanced technologies available today, but they're still very impressive. Not only can Sun operate farm equipment and handle chores, but he can also handle the brand-new prosthetics business he has created to support his family and help other amputees. As the saying goes, "Necessity is the mother of invention", it holds true in the case of Sun. It is amazing what can happen when great need meets even greater ingenuity and tenacity. And it's an important learning lesson for anyone who has ever felt that they don't have the right training, opportunities, age, cash flow, etc., to make miracles happen.

For a man who works in the field every day, not being able to work with your hands is a real tragedy. But when Sun lost both his arms in a tragic accident he decided to take an innovative approach to the problem. This is something that elevates Sun Jifa from the average man. He turns problems into opportunity. When Sun found that the options that local hospitals offered were too expensive, he could have given up. But it was essential to Sun not to live off his family and be a 'freeloader'. So he took to his workshop to figure out how he could replace the arms on his own – and came up with a solution that cost less than the other options. It took him eight years and a lot of failed experiments but eventually he was able to find solution that worked. Now that Sun has found something that works for him, he's set out to create more arms for others. When the bones left in the arm rotate, it makes the hand open and close. According to the China Rehabilitation Research Center 24 million people have benefited from Sun's discovery. The company has developed more than 140 kinds of prosthetic products for rehabilitation purposes. He is a man of grit and determination.

14.46 Sylvester Stallone

The life story of Sylvester Stallone is one of the finest stories ever told in Hollywood. He is one of the biggest, most successful and famous American movie stars in history. He is not only an actor but is also a screenwriter, film director and producer. He was born on July 6, 1946, in New York City. Sylvester is one of the most popular action stars of all time and is best known for portraying two heroic characters on the big screen—boxer Rocky Balboa and Vietnam War veteran John Rambo. His trademark droopy visage was the result of a forceps accident at the time of his birth. A nerve was severed in the accident, which also left him with slurred speech. He wrote every episode of two eponymous franchises, and directed some of their installments as well. Stallone had a difficult childhood. Both he and younger brother Frank were adversely affected by their parents' hostile relationship, which later ended in divorce. Sylvester spent some time in foster care. He eventually ended up in Philadelphia, living with his mother and her second husband. There Stallone struggled emotionally and academically. After his expulsion from several schools, he attended a special high school for troubled youth.

Fig. Silvester Stallone

After graduation, Stallone eventually went on to college. First, he attended the American College in Switzerland where he studied drama. Stallone then went to the University of Miami, again choosing to focus on the dramatic arts. He left school before completing his degree to go to New York City to pursue an acting career.

While he waited for his acting career to take off, Stallone worked all sorts of jobs to make ends meet. He cleaned up the lions' cages at the Central Park Zoo, ushered at a movie theater, and even made an appearance in an adult film called *A Party at Kitty and Studs* (1970). He was paid $200 for two days' work. Stallone later explained that he had done the film out of desperation after being evicted from his apartment and finding himself homeless for several days. He has also said that he slept three weeks in the

New York City Port Authority bus station prior to seeing a casting notice for the film. In the actor's words, "it was either do that movie or rob someone, because I was at the end–the very end–of my rope". Stallone was a struggling actor in every definition when he began a career in acting.

His lowest point came when he tried to sell his dog at the liquor store to any stranger. He didn't have money to feed the dog any more. He sold it at $25 only. He says 'he walked away crying'. Two weeks later, he saw a boxing match between Mohammed Ali and Chuck Wepner and that match gave him the inspiration to write the script for the famous movie, 'ROCKY'. He wrote the script for 20 hours. He created a screenplay about a rough-and-tumble thug who struggles for a chance to make it as a professional boxer. According to several reports, Stallone refused to sell the script unless he was allowed to star in it. Despite having a pregnant wife and little money in the bank, he held out until he found two producers, Irwin Winkler and Robert Chartoff, willing to let him play the lead.

He tried to sell this script and he was offered $125,000. But he had put one condition: 'he has to be the main star in the movie'. But the studio said 'NO'. They wanted a real star. They said that Stallone 'looked funny and talked funny.' He left with his script. A few weeks later, the studio offered him $250,000 for the script. He refused. They even offered $350,000. He still refused. They wanted his movie but not him. Stallone wanted to be in the movie by all means. After a while, the studio agreed, gave him $35,000 for the script and let him star in it! The rest was history! The movie won Best Picture, Best Directing and Best Film Editing at the prestigious Oscar Awards. He was even nominated for BEST ACTOR. The movie ROCKY was even inducted into the American National Film Registry as one of the greatest movies ever!

After this, the first thing he bought with the money he got from selling the script, i.e., $35,000 was buying the dog he sold. Yes, Stallone loved his dog so much that he stood at the liquor store for three days waiting for the man to whom he had sold his dog. And on the third day, he saw the man coming with the dog. Stallone explained why he sold the dog and begged for the dog back. The man refused. Stallone offered him $100. The man refused. He offered him $500. And still the man refused. He even refused $1000. And believe it or not, Stallone had to pay $15,000 for the same dog he had sold at $25 only and finally he got back.

And today, the same Stallone who slept in the streets and sold his dog just because he couldn't feed it anymore is one of the greatest movie stars who ever walked the Earth.

No one knows what you are capable of except yourself. People will judge you by HOW you look and by WHAT you have. But fight on for your place in history. Fight for your glory. Never ever give up. Whatever your struggle is, it's okay. As long as you are still alive, your story is not over.

4.47 Taylor Conroy: A Social Entrepreneur and Humanitarian

"If I am not happy I will not be of good service and if I am not serving the world, well then I will not be happy."

—*Taylor Conroy*

Taylor Conroy was born in Cranbrook, Canada. Already as a teenager, he was a determined and hardworking individual; this enabled him to experience success at an early stage in his life. When he was just 20, he was hired as the youngest fire fighter in Canada. At the age of 23, to fill his free time off from the fire hall, Taylor got his real estate license. Only the year later, he retired from fire fighting to build a real estate business and went on to quickly become the highest grossing new agent in North America.

Fig. Taylor Conroy.

By the age of 26, Taylor had built the most successful condo sales company in his region and ultimately hit the millionaire mark. He thought that after becoming a millionaire he was set for life and eternal happiness, but his excitement ended the very next day when he began aiming for higher monetary milestones:

"I was like, damn! Did I take something I had been working towards for five years and enjoyed it for only 24 hours? From that moment on, I decided that I should rethink how I am doing things, because with this mentality, no amount of money or things will ever be enough".

Looking for fulfillment, Taylor settled to travel to Africa. The general poverty and large amount of orphans that he encountered in Uganda and Kenya changed Taylor's life forever. At the age of 28, he sold off half of his real estate business and travelled the world for a year to find himself. Back in Canada, Taylor set out on a mission to reinvent fund-raising. He sold the rest of his real estate business and nearly everything he owned to get his new company *Change Heroes* off the ground: a friend funding platform that enables anyone to raise $10,000 in crowd funding in order to build a school or library in developing countries. To this date, Taylor fulfilled his goal of making it possible for anyone to have a massive impact on the world. Through *Change Heroes,* he was able to build over 60 schools and libraries in nine countries for over 60,000 children.

Today, Taylor continues his quest to change the world for the better. He lives a fulfilled life regularly give very inspiring talks and dreams to see people from all over the world become "*Change Heroes*".

Facing Interview

Q. How did you successfully apply your "enough" rule to your life?

Ans.Well, it all started in December 2008. I had been working for years at accumulating real estate and building a big business with the dream of becoming a millionaire. I really thought that when I hit that goal I would be proud of myself, satisfied with where I was at, and that I would be happier as a person. Guess what... that all lasted about 24 hours before my mind popped in and wanted to set another goal. I realised that it would never be enough – any goal.

After achieving a few more goals and having the subsequent depression afterward upon realising that I wanted to just set another higher goal to work toward, I sat down and decided what my "enough" was. Enough cash, enough investments, enough success, enough everything. It was deeply liberating. I committed to being satisfied with my enough and not trying to make any more from the age of 28–32 and that I would revisit it on my 32nd birthday. I am 31 now. I stuck to it despite urges to go and strive after more financial and business milestones. The funny thing is that my enough has actually decreased and continues to do so. Not to get all woo-woo on ya, but back then, the reason I always wanted more and nothing was ever enough, is because I didn't think I was enough. My striving for financial goals, wanting to have the coolest truck, the fastest motorcycle, the biggest house... was because I did not feel like I was enough as a person. Once I decided my enough, meaning I stopped looking at what I could do for ME, the immediate reaction was that I started looking at what

I could do for the world instead. It was really finding my enough that got me truly started on the path I am on now.

Q. What is necessary to make people understand the need of philanthropy?

Ans. That's a big question with a lot of answers. For me, it was the realisation that we are all the same. In Canada, the US, Sweden, Norway, Kenya, Cambodia, Ecuador, Haiti... everywhere... we are all the same! If you knew your brother was starving, you would feed him. If you knew your family was living in poverty, you would do whatever you could to help them. Well, 1.2 billion of your family members are living in poverty – extreme poverty. I hope that we all recognise them as our family as soon as possible and use whatever we are AMAZERS in, to help them.

14.48 Terese Alstin and Anna Haupt: Industrial Designers and Inventors

"Delusions of grandeur are exactly what it takes."

—*Terese Alstin and Anna Haupt*

Terese Alstin and Anna Haupt were both born in Sweden. They met whilst attending the University of Lund where they studied Industrial Design.

Fig. Terese Alstin and Anna Haupt.

In 2005, they decided to work on their master thesis together; a decision that completely changed the course of their life. At that time a new law was just introduced in Sweden that made it obligatory for children up to the age of 15 to wear bicycle helmets. Quickly, all over the country debates arose on whether or not this law should be applied to adults too. Everybody was concerned about the thought of being forced to wear bicycle helmets but unlike the rest, Terese and Anna decided to do something about it. The two graduates set out to collaborate on their master thesis and find a better and new solution that would encourage people to wear their helmets. The two entrepreneurs were sure of one thing:

"It wasn't the bicyclists who needed to change, it was the product".

Undergoing surveys and asking people on the streets, it was clear that what most desired was something innovative and cool, something that you could fold up or that would not mess up your hair. Terese's and Anna's moment of eureka finally came when an interviewee mentioned one word: "invisible". Struck and inspired by the power that this word conveyed, the two students decided to achieve the unimaginable and build an invisible helmet. When sharing their idea with others, Terese and Anna were mostly discouraged and told it was impossible. This did not hold them back – quite the opposite; it fuelled their drive and made them dream even bigger. Seven years of research and hard work later, what had started out as an exam project became "Hovding": the invisible helmet. The two designers had invented the first cyclist-airbag and proving everyone wrong, accomplished the impossible. Not only does Terese's and Anna's invention work, it looks good too. In recent years, their invisible helmet has gained international acclaim and won numerous international awards.

Today, Terese and Anna continue to lead their company 'Hovding'. They now have 16 employees, each with unique skills and backgrounds. Their invisible helmet is being distributed all across the globe and represents the power of their perseverance and hard work.

Facing Interview

Q. What was the hardest thing to do during your seven years of research? Any tips for those for people with similar ambitions?

Ans. We had a lot of employees during our development time, from electrical engineers to airbag specialists and mathematicians, obviously they needed to get paid and this was very costly. So for us, finding good investors, the right investors were the hardest part; it took us a lot of time and effort. A tip would be to work for yourself or with small team, it is much better to do that from the star and not include investors in the early stage. This because the hard thing with investors is that they have a time line and they are quite stressed getting the product out in the market. It could be really time consuming to just keep them happy and in a good mood so that they support you. Do not use venture capital if you do not need to. Just believe in yourself because the capacity in every human is really really big.

Q. Were there times when things were difficult and you were afraid to fail or thought about giving up?

Ans. Yes, and there are still times that can be really hard actually. Now, we are in a phase where we are selling the products and there are always new challenges along the way. It can be that the future will be even harder as we focus on the development of future products, take care of our customers in the best possible way and at the same time also try to fund the right distributors in every country. At the moment it is really frustrating that due to the huge time and effort it takes we are not able to distribute to all our global demand; especially the one in Japan and the USA.

14.49 Viet Dang: A Dancer and Choreographer

Viet Dang is a dancer and choreographer whose unique determination has brought him on the stage of some of the world's greatest artists. Viet Dang was born in a refugee camp during his parents' escape from Vietnam. He and his family eventually managed to flee to Malaysia and from there immigrated to Europe to start off a new and safe life in Switzerland. Like anywhere else, growing up as a foreigner was not always easy. In school, not fitting in with the rest of the kids, Viet faced early challenges such as insecurity and bullying. Not even after finding his passion for dancing did his life get much easier; his parents wanted him to focus strictly on studies

Fig. Viet Dang.

and were, thus, really against it. Increasingly fighting for his right to dance, it was therefore only at the age of 16 that he found the courage to step into a dance studio. Six months later, after quickly becoming one of the best dancers in the group, Viet decided to participate in a national dance contest. On the day of the competition, Viet's mother locked him up in the bathroom and only let him out after promising to her that if he did not win, he would had to stop dancing for good. Without thinking too much about it, Viet attended the event and to his own surprise won it.

Galvanised and motivated by the joy of the experience, he started dreaming big:

"The stage was the only place in the world on which I felt celebrated. I wanted to travel across the globe and dance for major artists."

Whilst persevering in his studies at University for the sake of easing his parent's anger, Viet began working on his dancing career and at the age of 18, built his own dance school. Hosting shows, performing and doing choreography for numerous Swiss artists, it did not take long for Viet to become one of the notable dancers in the country. When he did, his father showed him a notebook containing tons of images and articles which meant that he was proudly following his son's career. Viet went on to work for the popular music channel *Viva Swizz* but ultimately came to realise that the opportunities he was striving for were not available to him in Switzerland.

In 2011, determined to chase his dreams, he thus moved to Los Angeles. Starting a career in Hollywood was all but not easy. He worked and trained tirelessly every single day and eventually got booked for major performances; his motivation and perseverance began paying off. Viet was since able to dance for artists such as Mick Jagger, Rihanna, Christina Aguilera and Justin Timberlake. There, on the big stages–where no one ever believed him would end up—he finally found his freedom.

Today, Viet lives in Los Angeles. He teaches at one of the city's most prestigious dance academies to perform for major international artists. Living his dream, Viet is chasing his last remaining goal: going on a world tour with Madonna or Lady Gaga.

In an interview he was asked the following questions:

Q. *What would you say to all those people who want to chase a dream but are limited from those around them in achieving it?*

Ans. It's always easy to blame others. What is harder is waking up one day and realising that it was you who let others take away your dreams. And that it is you who never took the courage to stand up for yourself and chase your dreams. So, all I am saying is find something that makes you happy and go for it. Don't let anyone or anything distract you along the way. Think big. Even if narrow minded people in your village don't appreciate your dream, it doesn't mean that the rest of the world feels alike. If you are a loner find like-minded people.

14.50 Warren Edward Buffet

Warren Edward Buffet is an American business magnate, investor and philanthropist. He is widely considered as the most successful investor of the 20th century. Buffet is the primary shareholder, chairman and CEO of Berkshire Hathaway and consistently ranked among the world's wealthiest people. He was ranked as the world's wealthiest person in 2008 and the third wealthiest person in 2011. In 2012, American magazine *Time* named Buffett one of the most influential people in the world. Buffet is also called the "Wizard of Omaha", "Oracle of Omaha", or the "Sage of Omaha" and is noted for his adherence to the value investing philosophy of and for his personal frugality despite his immense wealth. He is a notable philanthropist, having pledged to give away 99 per cent of his fortune to philanthropic causes primarily via the Gates Foundation. He says, "I want to give my kids just enough so that they would feel that they could do anything, but not so much that they would feel like doing nothing".

Fig. Warren Edward Buffet.

Warrant Buffet was born on August 30, 1930. He had a very humble beginning. As a child, Buffet went door to door selling chewing gum, Coca-Cola or weekly magazines. For a while, he worked in his grandfather's grocery store. Due to this he had shown an interest in making and saving money. While still in high school, he carried out several successful money-making ideas–delivering newspapers, selling golf balls and stamps and detailing cars, among them. Filing his first income tax return in 1945, in his sophomore year of high school, Buffet and his friend spent $25 to purchase a used pinball machine, which they placed in the local barber shop. Within months, they owned several machines in different barber shops.

His Philanthropy

He says:

"I don't have a problem with guilt about money. The way I see it is that my money represents an enormous number of claim checks on society. It's like I have these little pieces of paper that I can turn into consumption. If I wanted to, I could hire 10,000 people to do nothing but paint my pictures every day for the rest of my life. And the GDP would go up. But the utility of the product would be zilch and I would be keeping those 10,000 people from doing AIDS research or teaching or nursing. I don't do that though. I can't use very many of those claim checks. There's nothing material I want very much. And I'm going to give virtually all of those claim checks to charity when my wife and I die."

In June 2006, he announced a plan to give away his fortune to charity with 83 per cent of it going to the Bill and Melinda Gates Foundation. He pledged about the equivalent of 10 million Berkshire Hathaway Class B shares to the Bill and Melinda Gates Foundation (worth approximately US $ 30.7 billion as of 23 June, 2006), making it the largest charitable donation in history and Buffet one of the leaders of philanthropism. The Foundation will receive five per cent of the total donation on an annualised basis each July, beginning in 2006. (Significantly, however, the pledge is conditional upon the foundation's giving away each year, beginning in 2009, an amount that is at least equal to the value of the entire previous year's gift from Buffet, in addition to five per cent of the foundation's net assets). Buffet also will join the board of directors of the Gates Foundation, although he does not plan to be actively involved in the foundation's investments.

This is a significant shift from previous statements Buffet has made, having stated that most of his fortune would pass to his Buffet Foundation. The bulk of the estate of his wife, valued at $2.6 billion went to that foundation when she died in 2004. He also pledged $50 million to the Nuclear Threat Initiative in Washington, where he has served as an advisor since 2002. In 2006, he auctioned his 2001 Lincoln Town Car on eBay to raise money for *Girls' Incorporated* (which is a nonprofit organisation that focuses on giving confidence to girls). In 2007, he auctioned a luncheon with himself that raised a final bid of $650,100 for a charity. On June 27, 2008, Zhao Danyang, a general manager at *Pure Heart China Growth Investment Fund*, won the 2008 five day online *"Power Lunch with Warren Buffet"* charity auction with a bid of $2,110,100. Auction proceeds benefit the *San Francisco Glide Foundation*. The following year, executives from Toronto-based *Salida Capital* paid US$1.68 million to dine with Buffet.

In 2010, Buffet and Gates spearheaded *The Giving Pledge*, inviting the wealthy to donate 50 per cent or more of their wealth to charity.

Speaking to Berkshire Hathaway 1994 annual meeting, Buffet said investments in tobacco are: "fraught with questions that relate to societal attitudes and those of the present administration. I would not like to have a significant percentage of my net worth invested in tobacco businesses. The economy of the business may be fine but that doesn't mean it has a bright future".

His Simplicity and Frugality: Warren Buffet, one of the world's richest men today lives in the flat he bought 50 years ago. He drives his own car. He does not use a private jet (owns just one for compelling reasons). He does not compel the CEOs of his companies to do anything, sending them just one letter a year stating their annual objectives. To him, the most important aspect of running the organisation is never to lose the investor's money. This is rule number one. And rule number two is never to forget rule number one. Buffet begs to differ from the famous saying of the Bard, "All that glitters is not gold". He states that gold is not all that is alluring or glittering to his eyes! "It gets dug out of the ground in Africa or some place. Then we melt it down, dig another hole, bury it again and pay people to stand around guarding it. It has no utility. Anyone watching from Mars would be scratching their head", he remarked on the non-profit nature.

The summary of his life:

1. Warren Buffet bought his first share at the age of 11 and he now regrets that he started too late.
2. He bought a small farm at the age of 14 with earnings from delivering newspaper.
3. He still lives in the small three bedroom house in mid-town Omaha that he bought after he got married 50 years ago. He says that he has everything he needs in that house. His house does not have a wall or a fence.
4. He drives his own car everywhere and does not have a driver or security people around him.
5. He never travels by private jet, although he owns the world's largest private Jet Company.
6. His company, Berkshire Hathaway owns 63 Companies. He writes only one letter each year to the CEOs of these companies giving them goals for the year. He never holds meetings or calls on a regular basis.
7. He has given his CEOs only two rules. Rule No. 1: Do not lose any of your share holder's money and Rule No. 2: Do not forget Rule No. 1.
8. He does not socialise with high society. His past time after he gets home is to make himself some pop corn and watch television.
9. Bill Gates, the World's richest man met him for the first time only FIVE years ago. Bill Gates did not think that he had anything in common with Warren. So he had scheduled his meeting only for half an hour. But when Gates met him, the meeting lasted for 10 hours and Bill Gates became a devotee of Warren.

10. Warren does not carry a cell phone nor has a computer on his desk.
11. His advice to young people: "Stay away from credit cards and invest in yourself."
12. He has donated $ 31 billion (85 per cent of his fortune) to charity.

Some of His Famous Quotes

1. On earning: "Never depend on a simple income. Make investment to create a second source."
2. On spending: "If you buy things you do not need, soon you will have to sell things you need."
3. On taking risk: "Never test the depth of river with both the feet."
4. On investment: "Do not put all eggs in one basket."
5. On expectation: "Honesty is very expensive gift. Do not expect it from cheap people."
6. "I always knew I was going to be rich. I don't think I ever doubted it for a minute."
7. "It takes 20 years to build a reputation and give minutes to ruin it. If you think about that, you'll do things differently."
8. "It is better to hang out with people better than you. Pick out associates whose behaviour is better than yours and you'll drift in that direction."
9. "Risk comes from not knowing what you're doing."
10. "Rule No. 1: Never lose money. Rule No. 2: Never forget Rule No. 1."
11. "Someone is sitting in the shade today because someone planted a tree a long time ago."
12. "The business schools reward difficult complex behaviour more than simple behaviour, but simple behaviour is more effective."

14.51 William Trubridge: World Record Diver and Conservationist

"I have a relationship with the depths; they beckon me beyond my means, cold dark vacant pressure, forever night, endless dreams."

– *William Trubridge*

William Trubridge is a UK born New Zealander. He was raised with the sea at his feet and learned to swim at the age of one and half – as his

Fig. William Trubridge.

parents sold their house and sailed to New Zealand when he was just a couple of years old. Growing up on a sailing boat, William's playground was the Atlantic and Pacific Oceans. One of the things he loved doing most was snorkeling and diving with his older brother Sam who he always tried to emulate in their daily aquatic adventures. At the age of eight and ten, inspired by their father and several semi-mythical encounters with pearl divers, the two brothers were diving down to astonishing depths of 15 metres. As William grew up so did his passion for challenging the depths.

When he first heard that freediving was an official sport, William was already 22 years old but this did not stop him from trying to go at it professionally. He initially trained at the Italian Apnea Academy where he was mentored by the legendary freediver Umberto Pellizzari. In order to freedive great distances and push the boundaries of his body to extremes, William had to learn mastering the physical and mental obstacles that came along with the sport. "It is thanks to my mother, I believe in myself and the infinitude of our capacity at whatever we set our minds to and it is thanks to my father, I have never reneged on training session, or quit when results were discouraging." Three years of hard training later William became the first man to dive at Dean's Blue Hole; the world's deepest known seawater sinkhole, located in the Bahamas. It is in that exact spot, where he broke his first world record and reached 81 metres of depths with no propulsive assistance. William has since beaten that performance several times and in 2010 combined his record attempt with an environmental cause. He reached the current world record of 101 metres during 'Project Hector', an event he set up to raise awareness on the plight of New Zealand's critically endangered Hector dolphin species.

Today, William runs a diving academy named Vertical Blue where he teaches and inspires aspiring freedivers and continues to advocate his conservational message. He currently holds 15 world records and still explores his limits whilst dedicating his time to his unique passion: challenging the depths.

Facing Interview

Q. *What are the psychological skills required to be a free diver and how have these impacted your everyday life?*

Ans. Free diving is unlike a lot of sports in that it requires total calm and mental serenity during a performance. Adrenaline is its antithesis! So the skills we need to learn for deep dives have to do with showing the mind down and maintaining composure despite the urge to breathe, lactic muscles or the mental 'daemons' that try to convince you that you're not capable. This kind of discipline is invaluable in many other facets of life, from giving you the staying power to stick with a task through to its end to allowing you detach from negativity that may enter your world.

Q. *What is it that drives you to aim for deeper and deeper depths?*

Ans. I don't think it's the depths themselves – at least not the numbers or the world records. Rather I am more drawn to the process of discovery and the challenge of finding a path that brings me closer to that ineffable 'perfect dive', where I come as close as I can to my absolute potential underwater. That would be the academic answer but I think even beyond that I just love being underwater and the sensations it provides. There is nothing more beautiful than being immerged in liquid with 'your breath at your breast' and the sensation that you actually belong there amongst fishes.

At 10 minutes to seven on a dark, cool evening in Mexico City in 1968, John Stephen Akwari of Tanzania painfully hobbled into the Olympic Stadium–the last man to finish the marathon. The winner had already been crowned and the victory ceremony was long finished. So the stadium was almost empty and Akwari, alone, his leg bloody and bandaged, struggled to circle the track to the finish line. When asked why he had continued the grueling struggle, the young man from Tanzania answered softly, "My country did not send me 9,000 miles to start the race. They sent me 9,000 miles to finish the race."

All of us have to finish the race we have started. Keep running towards your DREAM. NEVER GIVE UP! NEVER QUIT!

Conclusion

Children are the greatest asset to every parent. Children can be a boon as well as a bane; it all depends on how you guide and train them up. There is no greater joy for parents than to see their children growing up well. So, the most important priority of every parent is to train their children in the way they should grow (The Bible, Proverb 22:6) and not money or wealth. What is the use of being a billionaire when all your children are ill-bred? If wealth is your priority, your children will always occupy a secondary position in your priority list. I don't think anyone will exchange their children for wealth and money. If anyone does that, he or she will be branded as a 'fool'.

One of the most important areas of training your children is to give them the right education. Education indicates a person's quality and status in the society. Children should be given both intellectual as well as value-based education but the latter is more important than the former. What is the use of your child possessing a very high IQ (Intelligence Quotient) when he or she is actually suffering from value deficiency syndrome? Value-based education emphasises the training of the heart; while intellectual education stresses the training of the mind. Our education system today stresses the intellectual education which prepares a student to be 'smart' but not 'good'. The popular slogan is 'smart people earn better'. In our contemporary society, we have so many smart people and less of good people. This is the reason why there is an alarming rise in corruption, violence and decadence of values in our society. The simple premise is 'smart people steal better'. How can a simple person steal crores of rupees? Now you know who the smart people in our country are. In the same way, why so much of rape and lack of respect for the sanctity of life? It is because we have failed to inculcate values in our families and schools. Teach a child to be good first and the rest depends on effort.

Once the value system of a student is built on a firm foundation, he will also choose a career that tallies with his value system. Values will guide him in pursuing his dream. A student whose character is founded on values will have greater chance to succeed in life than those who are value deficient. The choice of a goal, pursuing a goal and reaching it, all depends on one's value system. Being true to oneself, being honest, being determined and being hard working etc. are all values that will help a person to achieve one's goal. Now, how can a person truly achieve his or her goal if his or her value system is not properly formed? I was confounded and at the same time laetificated to see that *Paramount Coaching Centre Pvt. Ltd.* based in Delhi which prepares students for Competitive Examinations mentions in its syllabus the various jobs and its parameters. One of the parameters is 'corruption' and this corruption is rated in three categorical degrees as high/medium/low. They have indicated the degree of susceptibility to corruption that is attached to a particular job or post. Accordingly, if a person holds a particular job, he or she will be liable to this degree of susceptibility to corruption. The Coaching Centre mentions this, so that every student can choose a job which is less susceptible to corruption. This Coaching Centre is trying to inculcate values in the students.

Values are the foundations of life. The values that students imbibe and assimilate will determine their life goals. Dreams and goals are formed according to the values of a person. The magnitude of one's interest in pursuing one's goal also is dependent upon the person's value system. Therefore, there is an urgent need on the part of parents, teachers, educators and all those who have a philodemic concern for students to inculcate values in every student. This will help us to create a good and better human person, family and society. This is a high time we stress values more than intellectualism in our education system.

References

Books

1. Anupama Chopra, *King of Bollywood: Shah Rukh Khan and the Seductive World of Indian Cinema*, Grand Central Publishing, 2007.

2. Bhalla P. Prem, *101 Ways to Stay Motivated*, New Delhi: Goodwill Publishing House.

3. Boulding, Maria, *Gateway to Hope*, St. Bede's Publication, 1987.

4. Carolyn Tody, *A Whimsical Holiday for Children.*

5. Covey R. Stephen, *The Seven Habits of Highly Effective People*, Free Press Publishers, 1989.

6. Cyriac, Sajith ssp, *Never Give Up*, Mumbai: St. Paul's Publications, 2013.

7. Dr Ignacimuthu S., *Skills and Qualities for Effective Life*, Bombay: St. Paul's Publications, 2012.

8. Ernest Hemingway, *The Complete Short Stories*, Scribner, 1998.

9. Garson, Helen S., *Oprah Winfrey: A Biography* (Greenwood, 2004) p. 20.

10. Gina Lake, *What about Now?: Reminders for Being in the Moment.*

11. Hill, Napoleon, *The Law of Success*, Mastermind Books: Bangalore, 2002.

12. Hill, Napoleon, *13 Keys to Success: 13 Steps to Personal Achievement*, Maanu Graphics: New Delhi, 1994.

13. Kalam, Abdul APJ, *Ignited Minds*, New Delhi: Penguin Books, 2002.

14. Kalam, Abdul APJ et al., *Wings of Fire*, Hyderabad: University Press, 1999.

15. Khera, Shiv, *You Can Win*, India: Macmillan, 1991.

16. Kosta and Kallick, *Learning and Leading with Habits of Mind.*

17. Lewis, Hedwig SJ, *Mirrors For The Heart*, Gamdi Anand: Gujarat Sahitya Prakash, 2003.

18. Mangal, S.K., *Advanced Educational Psychology*, New Delhi: PHI Learning Private Limited, 2011.

19. Maxwell, John C., *The 21 Indispensable Qualities of a Leader*, New Delhi: The Three Ess Publications.

20. Maxwell, John C., *Developing the Leader Within You*, New Delhi: Manu Graphics.

21. Meyer, J. Paul, *Attitude is Everything*, The Leading Edge Publishing Co., 2006.

22. Paul, Guildea, *The Pepple.*

23. Peale, Garry Norman, *A Sure Way to be Successful in Life*, New Delhi: Three ESS Publications.

24. Peale, Vincent Norman, *The Power of the Plus Factor*, New Delhi: Orient Paperbacks, 2002.

25. Pausch, Randy; Jeff Zalsow, *The Last Lecture*, Hyperion Books, 2008.

26. "Records for best-selling book series". *Guiness World Records.*

27. Richards, Stephen, *Cosmic Ordering Guide.*

28. Loren Rhoads, *Morbid Curiosity.*

29. Shapiro, Marc. *JK Rowling: The Wizard Behind Harry Potter.* New York: St. Martin's Press, 2000.

30. Sharma, Robin, *The Greatness Guide 2*, Mumbai: Jaico Publishing House, 2013.

31. Schuller, Robert H., *Success is Never Ending Failure is Never Final.* Delhi: Orient Paperbacks, 1989.

32. Schuller, Robert H., *The Be-Happy Attitudes*. Delhi: Orient Paperbacks, 1989.

33. Schuller, Robert H., *Power to Grow Beyond Yourself*. Delhi: Orient Paperbacks, 1989.

34. Schuller, Robert H., *Be an Extraordinary Person in an Ordinary World*. Delhi: Orient Paperbacks, 1989.

35. Thomas Nelson, *The Holy Bible: The Newly Revised Version Catholic Edition*, Bangalore: Theological Publications in India.

36. Toler, Stan, *Minute Motivators for Teachers*, Cook Communication Ministries, USA, 2002.

37. Toler, Stan, *Minute Motivators for Graduates*, Cook Communication Ministries, USA, 2002.

38. Toler, Stan, *Minute Motivators for Teens*, Cook Communication Ministries, USA, 2002.

39. Touthang, Stephen, *Substance Abuse*, New Delhi: Maxford Books, 2011.

Magazines

1. *Indian Currents*, 25-31 October 2010, p. 29.

2. Basu, Biman (May 2012) "Book Review: Biography of Kalpana Chawla", *Science Reporter*. pp. 40-41.

3. Battelle, John, "The Birth of Google" *Wired Magazine*, August 2005.

4. Carlson, Nicholas (March 5, 2010), "At Last – The Full Story of How Facebook was Founded", *Business Insider*.

5. "Endhiran: The costliest film in India". *India Today*. August 2010.

6. Grossman, Lev (December 15, 2010), "Person of the Year 2010: Mark Zukerberg", *Time*.

7. "Facebook founder's roommate recounts creation of Internet giant", *Haaretz*, Oct. 5, 2009.

8. "Govind Jaiswal: A Rickshaw puller's son who became an IAS Officer", (Anniversary Issue, April 2012), *Career 360*.

9. "He trains India's poorest students for the IIT" *Career 360*.

10. JK Rowling. *Forbes Magazine*, 14 June 2007.

11. Loren Rhoads, "Morbid Curiosity Cures the Blues: True Stories of the Unsavory, Unwise, Unorthodox and Unusual" *Morbid Curiosity*.

12. Lyndley, Glenis (March 2005), "No Limbs, No Limits". *Signs of the Times Magazine*, Australia New Zealand edition.

13. O'Reilly, T (2011), "Steve Jobs (1955-2011)", *Nature* 479 (7371): 42.

14. Coelho, Paulo, *The Alchemist*, Harper Collins Publishers.

15. Person of the Year 2007 Runners Up: JK Rowling. *Time Magazine*, 23 December 2007.

16. smilefoundationindia.org/IAS-office.

17. "Steve Jobs' Death Certificate Reveals His Final Resting Place", *Forbes Magazine*. Archived from the original on 2012-09-16.

18. "Steve Jobs dies at 56; Apple's co-founder transformed computers and culture". *LA Times*. 6 October 2011.

19. "The World's Billionaires", *Forbes*. March 11, 2009.

20. Zaslow, Jeff (September 20, 2007), "A Beloved Professor Delivers

The Lecture of a Lifetime", *The Wall Street Journal*.

Journals and Newspapers

1. "Brin, Sergey; Rajiv Motwani, Terry Winograd (1998), "What can you do with a web in your pocket" *Data Engineering Bulletin* 21: 37-47.

2. Bush, Kent (July 30, 2008), "Bush: Pausch's dying taught others how to live", *MetroWest Daily News*.

3. Canadian Broadcasting Corporation, "JK Rowling: CBC Interview #1. *The Hogwarts Express*. 26 October 2000.

4. Chaudhary, Pranava K (14 March 2009), "Discovery to showcase Super 30 today", *The Times of India*.

5. Elgin, Ben, "Google" Whiz kids or Naughty Boys?" *Business Week*, August 19, 2004.

6. Emily Eakin, Television Review; A Girl on the Street Finds a Path to the Ivy League, *The New York Times*, April 7, 2003.

7. Facebook Founder one of the world's richest", *Metro News*. 2008-03-05.

8. Hart, Simon (September 6, 2012), "Paralympics 2012: Hannah Cockroft destroys the field as she wins T34 200 m final to claim gold for Great Britain", *The Telegraph*.

9. "I don't think anyone can compete with me: SRK", *The Times of India*.

10. "JK Rowling: Casual Vacancy tops fiction charts". *The Telegraph*.

11. Lennox, Dean (February 20, 2008), "Hollywood star is back on the big screen with latest outing for Rambo 10". *Evening Times*.

12. "Living the vilayat dream at home – Teacher who failed to study abroad coaches students to do so", *The Telegraph* 22 February, 2005.

13. Mercer, David (September 1, 2012) "Hannah Cockroft and her wheelchair 'Sally win gold", *The Independent*.

14. Mobray, Nicole (March 2, 2003), "Oprah's path to power", *The Guardian* (UK).

15. Oldenburg, Ann, "Oprah's Secret Is Out! ", *USA Today*, January 24, 2011.

16. Oxford Today, Rhodes Trust, *Huffington Post*, African Success.

17. Pearse, Damein (11 October 2010) "Harry Potter creator JK Rowling named Most Influential Woman in the UK", *Guardian* (UK).

18. Pilkington, Ed (March 10, 2011). "Forbes rich list: Facebook six stake their claims", *The Guardian* (UK).

19. "Punjab Engineering College remembers Kalpana", *The Indian Express*.

20. Roth, Mark (September 19, 2007) "CMU professor gives his last lesson on life", *Pittsburgh Post Gazette*.

21. Saner, Emine (4 August 2006), world "King of Bollywood", *The Guardian* (London).

22. Sawhney, Anubha (2002-07-13), "Anupam Kher: A retake of life's scenes", *Times of India*.

23. "Shah Rukh's big honour – Times of India", *The Times of India*, 21 November 2011.

24. "Shah Rukh Khan – journey", *The Times of India*, 11 September

2003.

25. "Steve Jobs: Master of Innovation" *SUCCESS*, May 4, 2010.

26. Sullivan, Aline (December 20, 1997), "Buffet, the Sage of Omaha, Makes Value Strategy Seem Simple: Secrets of a High Plains Investor". *International Herald Tribune*.

27. "Sunday Times Rich list – Joanne Rowling". *The Sunday Times*. 27 April 2008.

28. Tacopino, Joe (January 25, 2010), "Oprah, Glenn Beck are America's favorite TV personalities: poll" *Daily News* (New York).

29. "The Life and Times of the Legendary Steve Jobs". *Business Dictionary*, March 15, 2012.

30. "The 100 Most Influential People In The World", *Time*, April 18, 2012.

31. " *The Times of India* (15 July, 2010).

32. Turnbull, Simon (January 6, 2013), "Hurricane Hannah Cockroft builds momentum", *The Independent*.

33. Jadhav, Prashant (24 May 2011). "Launch of Harsha Bhogle and wife Anita's book on cricket", *DNA India*.

34. Rajamani, Radhika (31 March 2004). "Shots of life: Catch Harsha Bhogle unplugged over soup and salad". *The Hindu*.

35. "Sylvester Stallone, hall of famer", *Newsday*, December 7, 2010.

36. Vargas, Jose Antonio (September 20, 2010), "The Face of Facebook", *The New Yorker*.

Electronic Media Sources

1. "About Nick" Lifewithoutlimbs.org. 2013.
2. academictips.org/blogs/true-story.
3. Al Siebert, From Homeless to Harvard – Liz Murray's Story, *THRIVEnet* Story of the Month, June 2000.
4. "American Idol 2010 – American Idol Season 9" Tvguide.com
5. "American Juniors on" Tv.com 1969-12-31.
6. American Idols Reuters.
7. "Anupam Kher's life struggle" Southasiatimes.com.au.
8. "Attitude is Altitude: No Arms, No Legs, No Worries" 28 September 2009.
9. "Bai Fengli: Selfless donation to poor students". China.org
10. Bailey, Jeff; Dash, Eric (September 1, 2006), "How Does Warren Buffet Get Married? Frugally, It Turns Out". *The New York Times*.
11. Basheda, Lori (19 July 2006), "No arms, no legs – no worries", *The Orange County Register*, 28 September 2009.
12. Ben Underwood: The boy who could 'see' with his ears.
13. Bepositive.org.in/ias-officer/
14. Bhogle, Shastri, Benaud voted favourite commentators.
15. "Bollywood superstar Shah Rukh Khan is busy building his empire – Business Today", *Business Today*.intoday.in. 21 February 2010.
16. *Breaking Night: A Memoir*, Hyperion Books, 2010.
17. Brin, S.; Page, L. (1998). "The Anatomy of a Large-Scale Hypertexual Web Search Engine" *Computer Networks and ISDN Systems* 30.
18. Buffet, Warren (June 16, 2010), "My philanthropic pledge". CNN.

19. "Buffet becomes world's richest", BBC, March 20, 2008.

20. Cancerclimber.org/sean.php

21. "Cool Things – Olympic Village Letter" Cool Things, Kansas Historical Society, May 22, 2012.

22. "Corporate Information: Google Milestones" *Google,* February 23, 2007.

23. Cunningham Calls It A Career – on the University of Kansas history website

24. En.wikipedia.org/wiki/Jessica Cox.

25. En.wikipedia.org/wiki/John A Roebling.

26. en.wikipedia.rog/wiki/Lizzie Vel.

27. en.wikipedia.org/wiki/Mile-Stojkoski.

28. en.wikipedia.org/wiki/Nando-Parrado.

29. En.wikipedia.org/wiki/Sean-Swarner.

30. En.wikipwdia.org/Charles M. Scultz.

31. en.wikipedia.org/wiki/Shiv Khera.

32. Finding Oprah's Roots: Finding Your Own, by Henry Louis Gates, page 154 at Google books.

33. "Famous personalities from Himachal Pradesh" Himachal spider.com.

34. "Forbes's Youngest Billionaire: Facebook Co-Founder Dustin Moskovitz Edges Out Mark Zukerberg, Time.com"

35. Glenn Cunningham Bio and Records.

36. "Hannah Lucy Cockroft – Double World Champion", Facebook.

37. "Heroes in shooting". International Shooting Sport Federation, 2008.

38. in.linkedin.com/pub/dir/shiv/khera

39. "IPC Athletics Records", www.paralympic.org.

40. Jessica-cox.blogspot.com/

41. JK Rowling Biography. Scholastic.com

42. "Jo Rowling Interview on Oprah", The Oprah Winfrey Show. 2010-10-01.

43. Kalpana Chawla International Space University Scholarship.

44. "Kalpana Chawla Memorial Scholarship" UTEP.

45. "Kalpana Chawla Award" University of Colorado.

46. "Karoly Takacs – The official website of the Beijing 2008 Olympic Games". The Beijing Organising Committee for the Games of the XXIX Olympiad 2008.

47. "Life without Limbs: About Nick Vujicic", 28 September 2009.

48. "Limbless Motivational Speaker, Nick Vujicic Is Married! Leadership Newspaper" Leadership.ng 2012-02-16

49. Liz Murray On Movie About Her Life, Plans for Future, interview with Gabe Pressman, WNBC, April 13, 2003.

50. "London 2012 Athletes: Hannah CocKroft", Paralympics GB.

51. Lucy Ash, 'From Homeless to Harvard', *BBC World Service,* February 8, 2011 Archived from the original on 16 June 2005.

52. lizziebeautiful.tumblr.com/

53. Mark Zukerberg Forbes.com

54. Markoff, John (October 5, 2011), "Steven P. Jobs, 1955 – 2011: Apple's Visionary Redefined Digital Age". *The New York Times.* Archived

from the original on 2012-09-05.

55. Memory.loc.gov, the Library of Congress.

56. Meg Hagertymhagerty@poststar.com (2009-08-03), "Homeless to Harvard subject to speak at local benefit" Nola.

57. Nanjappa, Vicky (31 March 2009), "Swiss black money can take India to the top" *Rediff.com* 23 May 2011

58. naguvejeevana.wordpress.com/2012/

59. "On-Air with Ryan Seacrest on 102.7 KIIS FM" Ryan.kiisfm.com. 2010-06-24.

60. "Oprah Winfrey Interview", *Academy of Achievement,* January 21, 1991.

61. "Oprah Winfrey Debuts as First African-American On Business Week's Annual Ranking of 'America's Top.

62. "Paralympics 2012: Hannah Cockroft wins second sprint gold", BBC Sport. September 6, 2012.

63. peanuts.wikia.com/Charles M. Scultz.

64. "Philanthropist" (Press Release), Urban Mecca. November 19, 2004Profile from Olympic.org

65. Poststar.com

66. Randy Pausch's "*Last Lecture: Really Achieving Your Childhood Dreams",* Carnegie Mellon University.

67. Rightfooted.com

68. "Rowling, J.K." World book 2006.

69. Sweet-station.com/huang guofu/

70. "Ryan Seacrest" Buddy.com. 2006-10-13.

71. "Ryan Seacrest Biography (1974)" Filmreference.com

72. Ryan Seacrest, "Ryan Seacrest Biography" (1974) People.com

73. "Ryan Seacrest Credits on" Tv.com

74. Seanswarner.com/

75. Scultzmuseum.org/

76. SHOWBIZ "The King of Bollywood", CNN. *CNN Entertainment,* 5 February 2008.

77. "Song Request – American Top 40 With Ryan Seacrest" At40.com

78. Sports reference.com

79. "Steve Jobs: Father of the Digital Revolution". *People and Lifestyle*. October 14, 2012.

80. "Steve Jobs: Early Life", *Biography* A+E Television Networks, LLC.

81. Steve Jobs biography", Biography.com

82. Sylvester Stallone interview, Playboy, September 1978.

83. SylvesterStallone.com. August 29, 2011.

84. Taylor Redd, "Kalpana Chawla: Biogrpahy & Columbia Disaster" *Space.com*

85. "10 Best Bollywood Movies of the Decade" Rediff.com, 12 January 2011.

86. Tewary, Amarnath (21 September 2006). "Helping poor Indians crack toughest test", BBC News.

87. Timesofindia.indiatimes.com

88. "Tribute to the Crew of Columbia", NASA JPL.

89. "The Virtuous Mr Bai Fangli" Paulo Coelho's Blog.

90. "The doctor said, 'your son has no arms or legs'-Journals" CafeMom. 2013-02-27.

91. "The Walt Disney Company and Affiliated Companies – Board of Directors", The Walt Disney Company.

92. "The Traits That Made Steve Jobs Legendary", Consumer Evangelists, October 14, 2011.

93. The Biography Channel (2007), "Sylvester Stallone Biography".

94. "The Greatest Investors: Warren Buffet". Investopedia.com.

95. Thomson, Bill, "Is Google good for you?" *BBC News*, December 19,2003.

96. "University Lecture Series: Really Achieving Your Childhood Dreams", Carnegie Mellon University, 2008-06-22.

97. *"University Lecture Series: Journeys"* Carnegie Mellon University.

98. US Track and Field Hall of Fame – Glenn Cunningham.

99. www.amazers.org

100. www.iastopperstories.com/

101. www.panda.com/armless-painter

102. www.pondly.com1012 hands-free-painter

103. www.mymodernmet.com/profiles/blogs

104. www.facebook.com

105. www.huffingtonpost.com

106. www.jessicacox.com.au/

107. www.jessicacoxwing.com/

108. www.tribuneindia.com"

109. www.aboutlizzie.com/

110. www.ibtimes.com

111. www.facebook.com/aboutlizzie

112. www.rdasia.com

113. www.facebook.com/mericel.apatan

114. www.imdb.com

115. www.entrepreneur.com

116. www.milestojkoski.com/

117. www.facebook.com/Milelondon2012Marathon

118. www.paralympic.org/blog/mile-stojkoski

119. www.strengthforsuccess.com/mile-stojkoski

120. www.parrado.com

121. www.telegraph.co.uk

122. www.huffingtonpost.com/nando-parrado

123. www.facebook.com/thenandoparrado

124. www.linkedin.com/in/seanswarner

125. www.facebook.com/sean.swarner

126. www.shahrukhkhan.org/

127. www.shivkhera.com/

128. www.thehindu.com/article 4474857.ece

129. www.facebook.com/ShivKhera

130. www.slideshare/hemanthcrpatna/

131. www.goodreads.com/132676.ShivKhera

132. www.nytimes.com/1126.html